Parliament and Industry

Also by David Judge
Backbench Specialisation in the House of Commons
The Politics of Parliamentary Reform (editor)
The Politics of Industrial Closure (editor)

Parliament and Industry

David Judge

Dartmouth

Aldershot • Brookfield USA • Hong Kong • Singapore • Sydney

Published by
Dartmouth Publishing Company Limited
Gower House
Croft Road
Aldershot
Hants GU11 3HR
England

Dartmouth Publishing Company
Old Post Road
Brookfield
Vermont 05036
USA

ISBN 1 85521 085 1

Printed in Great Britain by
Billing & Sons Ltd, Worcester

Contents

Acknowledgements

This is the place where it is customary to thank everybody who has helped with the production of the book, and I will get around to that pleasant task shortly. Before then I would like to mention a few people who have not helped in this process. Pride of place goes, therefore, to Ben, my son, who gave me more sleepness nights than the book itself, and for nearly as long. The final version of the book was delayed considerably by his belief that his father should be at home occasionally to talk to, play with and be sick over. Hannah his sister came to share similar expectations but fortunately mostly spared her father the latter pleasure. My wife's, Lorraine, expectations of leading a 'normal' family life have diminished over the years; but her residual expectations restrained me from living full-time in my office and so lengthened the production process of the book.

If family life got in the way, then so too did professional life. Jeremy Richardson at Strathclyde University did not help by offering me a job half way through writing the book. Nor was the burden of production eased by those students who took my classes or those postgraduates who wanted supervision. Most academics know that one of the least conducive environments for conducting research is a British institution of higher education.

The less said the better about the installation of a new computer at Paisley College, my former place of employment, at a crucial stage in the analysis of the data. Suffice it to say that, in keeping with the subject matter of this book, my comprehensive command of 'industrial language' was exercised to the full at the time.

On the positive side, however, there is an extensive list of those to be thanked for their assistance during the five years of this project. Starting with Members of Parliament – without whom there would be no book – I gratefully acknowledge the time and effort taken by those MPs who consented to be interviewed or who responded to requests for information by letter or over the phone. Similarly I thank those officers of the House of Commons – clerks and library staff – who offered sound advice and provided invaluable information at the start of the project. My thanks are also offered to the member of the secretariat of the Industry and Parliament Trust who provided information about, and assessment of, the Trust's activities. All the aforementioned were given an assurance that their views would not be directly attributable – but they know who they are!

The computer section staff at Paisley College need to be mentioned in dispatches for their untiring efforts to meet my insatiable data processing demands. Janette Cochrane often acted as unpaid research assistant during the course of mastering the delights of the POLIS system, and Alex Hall of Scicon Ltd assisted greatly in ensuring that I got out of POLIS what I wanted. Users of POLIS will know that this is not an easy task.

Margaret Bright is here awarded a long service medal both for her efficiency and good humour in the early stages of this project and for all the other assistance she provided over the longer period of fourteen years. As a sign of the times, upon my appointment at Strathclyde, Margaret was superseded by an Apple Macintosh. So thanks Apple. Thanks also to Alison Robinson, Grace Hunter and Laura Gurevitch who helped in the initial inputting of some of the draft chapters into the Mac. Thereafter thanks to me!

Jeremy Richardson and James Mitchell read and commented on the first three chapters, Michael Rush and Malcolm Punnett did the same for chapters four through eight, and Cliff Grantham cast a discerning eye over chapters seven and eight. I thank them for expending some of their rarest commodity – time – on improving the final version. Any remaining deficiencies are not their fault.

I would have liked Stuart Walkland to have seen the final manuscript as he and I shared a common concern about the direction of the academic study of parliament. Unfortunately, he died before his incisive and irreverent critical capacities could be brought to bear on this work.

Last, and in many ways most importantly, I hereby record my deep appreciation and gratitude to the Leverhulme Trust for the award of the research grant which provided me with the funds to conduct the POLIS search and the interviews at Westminster.

Preface

This is half a book in two halves! It is half a book inasmuch as my original intention was to examine the activity of British parliamentarians upon industrial matters and their multiple linkages and connections with industry both within and outside of the Commons. In the event it has only proved feasible to consider the internal dimension of activity and, in passing, to cast the occasional glance beyond Westminster. A detailed examination of industry's connections with parliament – through companies' government relations divisions, their contacts with constituency MPs, membership of trade associations, and employment of political consultants – has had to be postponed. As it is, even this 'half' a book has taken five years to complete!

That this is a book in two halves reflects my own schizoid approach to the study of parliament. On the one side, I am convinced of the need to locate the study of parliament within the wider debates upon the nature and form of the British state. In recent decades too many British scholars in examining parliament have opted out of the grand debate about the relationship between the legislature and the state and civil society. Instead, they have remained content to focus, descriptively, upon internal procedures and behaviour within the House. The diverse analytical traditions of, for example, Redlich (1908) and Laski (1938) – both of whom made the connections between parliamentary and state development – find few echoes in most undergraduate courses or recent texts dealing with parliament. In this sense I am really concerned with parliamentarism as a system of government, rather than with parliament as an institution. It is a macro-analytical concern which links economic, social and political forces; and it is a concern of special significance in explaining the developing relationship between industry and government. If the conventional arms-length relationship between the two in Britain, and industry's own predilection for a 'hands off' relationship – reflected in the non-interventionist rhetoric of the Thatcher governments – is to be understood, then so too must the political frame and system of ideas within which this relationship developed. Chapter 1 seeks to contribute to just such an understanding. There it is argued that macro-analysis of the state-form of parliamentarism and the socio-economic form of industrialism in Britain are inextricably linked, and, in fact, account for many of the 'peculiarities' of British industrial development. The legacies of nineteenth century political and industrial development have continued to reverberate throughout the present century. Invariably, Britain's relatively poor manufacturing performance in the twentieth century is explained by reference to policies, attitudes and institutional relationships cemented in the preceding century.

The very fact that British industry has confronted periodic and repeated 'crises' throughout the present century, not to mention long-term secular decline, has placed industrial performance firmly upon the political agenda. Yet, in attempting to ameliorate industry's problems, government has come to be identified as a problem in itself. A consistent refrain, therefore, from within industry has been that governments either do not understand, or misunderstand, the issues confronting industrial companies or sectors. The 1980 statement of Sir Terence Beckett , then director-general of the CBI, to the effect that MPs 'don't understand you [industry]. They think they do, but they don't. They are even suspicious of you, and what is worse they don't take you seriously' (*Financial Times* 12 November 1980) simply echoes similar sentiments aired in most other decades this century.

Chapter 2 traces such arguments that parliamentary representation is unsuited to the needs of a complex industrial economy. In so doing it examines proposals for the conflation of parliamentary and functional representation, and analyses attempts at crisis avoidance through the incorporation of industrial representatives into tripartite bodies. In the eyes of influential commentators such as Middlemas (1979) these organisations constituted 'governing institutions' and served to subordinate parliament within the new institutional structure of the expanded state. The paradox of this new institutional structure is that it was incapable of sustaining a claim to legitimacy within the state. Thus, whilst corporatist intermediation has been deemed necessary, for a variety of reasons involving the efficacy of industrial policy, it has failed to supplant the procedural democratic norms of parliamentarism. Moreover, as chapter 2 makes clear the very undermining of corporatist structures by the Thatcher governments has been effected through recourse to the principles of parliamentary representation. The 1979 manifesto pledge to 'see that Parliament and no other body stands at the centre of the nation's life' has constituted a potent challenge to the 'corporatist bias' held by Middlemas to be at the heart of the modern British state.

But in defusing the corporatist challenge the Thatcher governments' advancement of a neo-liberal strategy for industry – essentially creating the economic conditions within which industry can look after itself – has raised other fears that an overly partisan legislature has enabled the promotion of 'doctrinal' policies against the best interests and the better judgement of industry. In a nutshell this is one strand of the adversarial politics thesis. And this thesis is outlined in chapter 3.

Chapter 3 counterposes the examination of the adversarial politics thesis with a discussion of policy communities as an alternative paradigm in the study of industrial policy. Both seek to describe 'what actually happens' in the making of policy. In so doing both residualise parliament's contribution to the policy process. Chapter 3 attempts to rescue parliament from this impasse, primarily through invoking the legitimating potency of parliamentary representation. Along with Miliband (1982:48) it is argued that the 'absolutely indispensable legitimation' of policy, and indeed of the policy process itself, derives from the elective principle of parliamentary representation. The first three chapters are thus underscored by this macro-theoretical theme.

The following chapters focus more directly upon a micro-descriptive concern with the practical involvement of parliament and its members in industrial policy matters. This leads on to the second dimension of my schizoid approach to the study of parliament. As in my earlier work (Judge 1979; 1981) I have attempted to provide data – both quantitative and qualitative – to analyse activity in the Commons. Too often British texts on parliament still rely upon anecdotal and epigrammatic 'evidence' rather than systematic data. Hence, to counteract this tendency, chapters 4 to 8 examine in some detail the occupational background of members of parliament; the levels of backbench activity upon industrial policy matters; the influences upon such activity; the extent of formal specialisation developed through the Select Committee on Trade and Industry; and the rather less formal linkages between backbenchers and industry through all-party and party groups/committees and political consultants.

These macro- and micro- concerns might appear to sit uneasily together, but what unites them is my desire to understand both what happens and why. At least the questions are right, the reader has to decide about the answers!

1 The Parliamentary State and Industry

In the literature on 'Government and Industry' parliament is notable by its absence. Recent orthodoxy in the study of industrial policy-making – with its focus upon the closed world of executive-group relationships in policy 'communities' and 'networks' – relegates parliament almost completely from the analytical frame. Rhodes, as one of the more influential analysts of these concepts, points to the restrictive membership and internal interdependence of communities and their *insulation* from parliament and the general public (see Rhodes 1988:78). Attention has come to focus therefore upon 'non-parliamentary' processes with 'policy effectively made in specialist sectors (or in the American phrase sub-governments)' (Jordan and Richardson 1987a: 28-9). Indeed, the dominant 'policy-style' in Britain has been characterised as 'bureaucratic accommodation' wherein the prominent actors are government departments and organised interests and where bargaining is the normal mode of transaction (Jordan and Richardson 1982:81). In this model, power has 'leaked' from parliament to policy communities surrounding the executive. Whilst not claiming that parliament is excluded totally from policy-making it is clear that parliament is not a major player in that process.

Offsetting this orthodoxy, however, is an increasing awareness that parliament is of major importance in the process of policy-making. This impression has come from the most unlikely of quarters – from marxists such as Ralph Miliband (1982:20):

> By far the most important institution in the British political system is the House of Commons. This might seem an odd view, since there is general agreement that its powers have declined over the years; and whether this is so or not, the House of Commons is not in any case a strong legislative body.

Reconstructed critics of parliament, such as Bernard Crick (1989:77-8), also point to the significance of parliamentary institutions in the late 1980s:

if looked at realistically as part of a complex of representative institutions in highly pluralistic societies in which effective power is not to be found at any single point of a complex system, parliamentary institutions in general are likely to become stronger, not weaker.

What this and subsequent chapters seek to assess, therefore, is the extent to which these contrasting views can be reconciled, and the reasons why. To do this requires a macro-analysis of both the development of the state form of parliamentarism and the socio-economic form of industrialism in Britain. The two are inextricably connected and help to account for some of the 'peculiarities' of British political and industrial development. If analysis of one is divorced from the other then powerful explanatory variables are lost and understanding of either British politics and/or British industry is incomplete.

Throughout the following discussion its end-point – the paradox of parliament appearing simultaneously to be both vitally important and effectively impotent at the same time – needs to be borne in mind. For, through the analysis of the development of industry, industrial society and capitalist democracy, and thus the inter-connections of the economy, society and polity, the representation and accommodation of 'interests' within the policy process will be explicated. Obviously, in such a broad ranging discussion, detail will be sacrificed to the general argument. What is important is to sketch the grand vista rather than the foothills of sectoral analysis. What is equally important, however, is that the grand vista is an acceptable guide for future detailed study.

Beginnings

Theoretical analyses of the state must be placed within the history and contemporary forms of struggle both within and between national states in the world system of capitalism. (Duncan 1989:11)

This will be the maxim for the following discussion.

The modern state in Britain can be traced back to the constitutional settlement of 1688. Thereafter a liberal state evolved wherein competitive and free market relations in the economy came to be reflected in society and ultimately in the polity. As Hall (1984:10) puts it: 'The organisational principles which enabled commerce and trade to expand .... were also the principles on which the new relations between state and individual were modelled'. What the 1688 compromise achieved, therefore, was to connect the state to the interests of the dominant commercially-minded landed upper classes through the medium of a strengthened and flexible representative assembly. The Revolution of 1688 was thus both political and economic – it both secured the predominance of parliament in the state and the interests of commerce and finance in the economy. Indeed, the specific structural and cultural characteristics of later industrial development were apparent in embryonic form in the seventeenth century.

The exact conjuncture of structural form and cultural style in Britain's industrial development is a matter of deep and heated controversy. The relationship between the landed classes, commercial bourgeoisie and manufacturing entrepreneurs and their respective contributions to the industrial revolution and subsequent relative decline have long divided historians. A particularly protracted debate has occurred amongst marxists.

However, agreement is evident that the landed aristocracy was itself commercialised by the latter seventeenth century and that British agriculture was capitalist and based directly upon exploited labour. Moreover, it is apparent that the new industrial bourgeoisie emerged out of this agrarian base and did so within the frame of the existing economic relationships. In tandem, the settlement of 1688 'also led to the creation of the Bank of England and the Stock Exchange, and therewith laid the modern foundations of the City' (Anderson 1987:30). There was both continuity, in terms of market relations of production, and discontinuity, in terms of what was produced. The paradox of continuity/discontinuity also manifested itself in the parliamentary realm.

1688 attuned state power to evolving economic power. Assuredly and consistently parliament represented the interests of the newly dominant landed classes. But it did so in such a manner as to ensure that the state was clearly separated from and subordinate to these 'private' interests. This 'redefining of the public interest to mean the safeguarding of private interests and the liberation of private energies' had as its corollary, in the opinion of Gamble (1985:75), that 'the efforts of the agencies of the British state were concentrated to a high degree on enlarging commercial opportunities for its citizens'. Even before rapid industrialisation, therefore, an essential ingredient of Britain's commercial 'culture' was its emphasis on the autonomy of individuals and of individual enterprises. Self sufficiency was the aspiration; state interferences and controls were the threats to its realisation. These commercial values and preferences found most systematic expression in the ideology of liberalism with its support for market relations, individual freedoms and its initial negative conception of the role of the state (see Macpherson 1977; Eccleshall 1986). Through the works of Locke and Adam Smith these ideas were well developed *before* the period of rapid industrialisation. Industrial development subsequently occurred within a context of ideas and social and political relations which all stressed the separation of enterprise from government. British success was thus believed to emanate from individual initiative, the self-sufficiency of the firm and resolute leadership of individual entrepreneurs. Unlike other later industrialising nations, where the state essentially 'led' the process of modernisation, Britain's initial success was believed to be dependent upon the state 'following' private enterprise and simply ameliorating the consequences of private action through limited public policies. Thus, as Dyson (1983:31) has forcefully argued, voluntarism and representation were central ideological themes in Britain's developing industrial culture. These themes found reflection in 'A preference for "arm's length" government combine[d] with a sceptism about government's competence and an unwillingness to act in advance of political pressures to do so'. Landlord and emergent industrial bourgeoisie alike shared roughly the same preferences.

As economic power shifted from land to commerce and industry so too parliament was obliged to accommodate new class forces. That it proved successful in doing so is a reflection of the fundamentalism of the 1688 settlement. That it was required to do so in the first instance is a reflection of its special importance in the liberal state system.

Just as the developing industrial bourgeoisie was able to build within the frame of pre-existing capitalist economic relations, so too its political demands were articulated in terms of integration into, not a challenge to, the pre-existing parliamentary state. Without the franchise the new industrial classes were unable to influence policy directly and remained dependent upon a concurrence of interest between themselves and legislators within parliament. The extent of this concurrence is demonstrated by Anderson (1987:36) who points out that parliaments dominated by landowners secured favourable conditions for industry – the deregulation of wages, the liberalising of foreign trade, administrative reform – well before 1832 and the first Reform Act. He concludes moreover that 'the basic design transmitted by *laissez-faire* landlords proved eminently adaptable and suitable to the needs of the first Industrial Revolution' (1987:36).

Nonetheless, the logic of parliamentarism in the post-revolutionary period was that those with an 'interest' in the market system, primarily and exclusively those with property, had the right, through their representatives, to influence public policy. Parliament could thus deliberate on state policies, resolving conflicting interests within the broad frame of capitalist-liberal values and institutions as it did so. It served, therefore, to facilitate the organisation of coalitions of interest around particular policies. Simultaneously it also excluded from the process of policy-making those sections of society whose interests were seen to be incompatible with prevailing liberal values. The franchise effectively 'filtered-out' the property-less: those with little direct stake in the dominant economic order. The absence of voting rights and their 'own' representatives conversely served as a powerful symbol of political impotence and an immediate object for political rectification by the dispossessed.

Laissez-Faire: Theory and Practice.
By 1800 Britain had ceased to be an agrarian society. Agriculture was no longer the dominant sector of the economy, occupying around a third of the population and contributing about the same proportion of the national income (Hobsbawn 1969:97). Within a further fifty years neither was it a rural society as industry became concentrated in urban areas. This remarkable transition – truly a 'revolution' – in the economy and society nonetheless left the political institutional structure largely intact. Through the parliamentary state form inherited from the constitutional settlement of 1688 the industrial revolution was fostered and its consequences ameliorated. Of necessity the massive disruptions and discontinuities in British society demanded government intervention in the industrial process despite the official rhetoric and ideology of *laissez-faire* liberalism.

There is a strong tradition of historical analysis which argues that rapid industrialisation in the nineteenth century did not substantially alter the traditional parameters of the British state. This view has recently been repeated by Anderson (1987:37) who maintains that:

> Just because industrialisation came as a spontaneous, molecular process, after a long prior build-up, there was no occasion for official intervention to promote or guide it from above: at most to buffer some of its side-effects.

In response to Anderson's unequivocal enunciation of the myth of the *laissez-faire* state Barratt Brown (1988:34-5) provides a stinging rebuttal:

> One had supposed that this myth had been finally laid to rest by Robin Murray's exhaustive listing [in *Multinational Companies and Nation States, 1971*] of the *res publica* which the capitalist state supplied in nineteenth century Britain as elsewhere.

Whereas Anderson concentrates upon a 'three-fold absence' that separated the British state from its nineteenth century European counterparts – it played no role in the development of the railway system, it ignored conscription, it deferred public education – Barratt Brown points to the permissive legislation that enabled private development of the basic social and economic infrastructure. In this sense the state, acting through private members and private bills in the House of Commons, provided an extensive framework within which industrial capital could prosper.

The significance of private legislation and of the Commons as a legislature in the late eighteenth century and early nineteenth century is well illustrated by Walkland (1968). Cumulatively great social and economic changes were effected by piecemeal legislation initiated by interests outside of parliament and incorporated in private legislation:

> Private Bill procedure gave the country enclosures of agricultural land, railways, docks and harbours, river improvements, water supplies, and many local authority services. (Walkland 1968:13)

There was no grand design to such legislation, merely incremental adjustments to existing economic relationships. The inception was certainly private but the consummation was equally public. Basic utilities such as gas, water, and railways were granted development powers by parliament (including direct infringements of private property through compulsory purchase orders); their local monopolistic position was sanctioned by parliament; and ultimately they came to be subject to regulation and public supervision through parliamentary legislation (see Grove 1962:6-8). Despite these state interventions on their behalf capitalist manufacturers in the early decades of the nineteenth century still regarded themselves as 'heroes of self-help' (Hobsbawn 1969:121). Yet, in calling upon the state to assist in the advancement of private interests, entrepreneurs were effectively involving the state in the determination of the conditions under which these interests could be pursued.

Whilst the predilections of industrialists remained grounded in *laissez-faire* theory, in practice their own actions led to increased state involvement in securing the conditions for industrial advance. As parliament was increasingly asked to adjudicate on matters of private legislation its significance was magnified for those proposing (and for that matter opposing) private bills from outside. Exclusion from the franchise was a direct impediment to the new industrial bourgeoisie's advancement of interest. Undoubtedly, the overwhelming congruence of interest between landed aristocracy and parvenu industrialists defused the revolutionary potential of the new bourgeoisie, but shared general aims and interests obscured specific matters of dispute: disagreements which in the logic of liberal parliamentarism itself should be resolved through a process of deliberation within the representative assembly. Both the logic of liberalism and the concentration of political power within the legislature in the early decades of the nineteenth century led to pressure to enfranchise the new industrial middle-classes. The details of this struggle and subsequent extensions of the franchise are sufficiently well chronicled elsewhere as to make detailed discussion redundant here (see Hobsbawn 1969; Cannon 1972; Tholfsen 1973; Judge 1983a).

What is important to note is that the franchise was conceded to those who already had internalised the values and norms of liberal society and who simply demanded their own competitive place in the established political order. The 1832 Reform Act 'did not institute a new political system because it was not intended to: it did not hand over power to the middle classes because it was not intended to' (Cannon 1972:257). Aristocratic government, in terms of the personnel of parliament and the administration, continued to preside over a developing industrial economy and society. This mismatch between the governing class and the increasingly economically powerful industrial bourgeoisie in the first half of the nineteenth century has intrigued historians – not least Marx and Engels themselves. Indeed the latter oscillate between seeing the aristocracy as in supreme control of the apparatuses of the state yet serving the political interests of the industrial bourgeoisie (see Marx 1980:53-4). In which case the aristocracy exercised delegated powers. Yet Engels (and Marx) also argued in parallel that 'the new parliament [in this instance that of 1874] represents big landed property and money capital even more exclusively' than before (cited in Anderson 1987:23). In this latter case the economic ascendancy of industrial capital is not reflected in the political system.

For over a century after the inception of the industrial revolution there was an uninterrupted succession of aristocratic cabinets and landlord parliaments (Anderson 1987:31). This preponderance of landowners was unmatched at the time in any other major western state. And it is this relationship, in all of its socio-cultural, economic and political aspects, which has been deemed to be crucial in explaining the subsequent development of the British industrial state. Given the complexity of this relationship the simplest mode of exposition is to break down the argument into its constituent parts. Thus each facet – the social, economic and political – will be examined serially and simply even though their connections in practice are simultaneous and complex.

Land, Industry and Finance
To reiterate, this section of the chapter seeks to discover the exact nature of the 'alliance' that existed between the commercialised aristocracy and the emergent industrial bourgeoisie in the period 1780 to 1880. This period is of specific importance as it is widely regarded as the 'determining' epoch for much of subsequent British history. The starting premise is the assumption of shared interests between the two economically ascendant classes. These interests – in profit, property, contract and trade – served to fuse and maintain the alliance.

Culture
The significance of this fusion of interest in a bourgeoise-aristocratic alliance for some marxists such as Nairn (1982) and Anderson (1964,1987) is that an old-style mercantilism, a limited form of capitalism, underpinned British industrialisation in the nineteenth century. The economic implications of this

old bourgeois form of capitalism will be examined shortly, the important point here is that the alliance is argued to have perpetuated values which were in essence anti-industrial. The crux of the Nairn-Anderson thesis is that traditional values, an aristocratic ethos which was anti-industrial, prevailed and subverted the establishment of a separate identity on the part of the industrial bourgeoisie. This culture simultaneously denigrated the worth of entrepreneurial endeavour and industrialism whilst emphasising the importance of financial and and commercial activity in the world market. Wiener (1981) has most emphatically argued that the pervasive culture in Britain was both non-industrial and anti-industrial. More particularly he has maintained that the prevalence of anti-entrepreneurial attitudes served as an effective block against a necessary second industrial revolution required to sustain Britain's industrial competitive position. Industrial decline in Britain can therefore be rooted in 'a cultural *cordon sanitaire* encircling the forces of economic development – technology, industry, and commerce' (Wiener 1981:1).

The thesis of unbroken aristocratic hegemony has not gone unchallenged. Paul Warwick (1985) has demonstrated the discontinuities in aristocratic cultural ascendancy. He argues that by the early nineteenth century the value of entrepreneurial endeavour and material enrichment outweighed aristocratic pretensions. He then proceeds to explain how the very success of 'bourgeois ideological production', with its liberal emphases of meritocracy, social mobility and egalitarian openness, led to its inversion into a creed of social exclusiveness by the end of the nineteenth century. In this sense the emphasis upon privilege and the status of the superior leisured 'gentleman', commonly associated with aristocratic culture, was in fact a Victorian invention. An invention which constituted a conscious strategy of exclusion. As part of this strategy an educational system was deliberately constructed to create class barriers and inhibit mobility across them' (Warwick 1985:123), a civil service was developed whose upper ranks constituted a 'sort of [bourgeois] free masonry' (Leys 1983:234), and the armed forces were led by commanding officers recruited almost exclusively from public schools. The significance of this cultural inversion for future industrial development was that: 'if the price for creating this new society was a loss of technological and industrial leadership .... it was, apparently, a price influential Victorians thought worth paying' (Warwick 1985:123).

Undoubtedly the cultural exchanges between landed aristocracy and industrial bourgeoisie are of importance in explaining the context within which state relations with manufacturing industry developed, but they are insufficient in themselves to explain later industrial performance or industrial policy-making. One consequence of the fascination with the socio-cultural aspects of the aristocratic-bourgeois 'alliance' in explanations of industrial development and decline, however, has been a distraction of attention away from economic and the 'politico-legal' dimensions (see Dyson 1983:38).

Economic Relations: Industrial and Financial Capital
It cannot be claimed however that Anderson and Nairn were so distracted, as their thesis sought to analyse the complex linkages between economic organisation and culture and state form. That this analysis resulted in a uni-dimensional and deterministic view is perhaps surprising given the initial intention of examining the complexities and anomalies of industrial society. Nonetheless, Anderson and Nairn seek to explain comparative industrial failure in terms of the pre-industrial character of basic economic relations in Britain. Thus, they argue that from the outset of industrialisation there was a disjunction between, on the one hand, the intimately connected landed aristocracy and monied interests and, on the other, industrial interests. Yet, as noted above, for most of the first century of industrialisation there was no fundamental contradiction between aristocratic/financial interests in the City and manufacturing interests. A triangular constellation of land, finance and industry; in which land permeated but did not socially fuse with the other interests, came to characterise the nineteenth century economy. In this constellation the linkages were bipartite and discrete. Financial capital was closely connected to the landed classes but not to industrial capital. The first phase of industrialisation was thus financed through reinvestment of profit by individual firms, or by short-term bank loans, or by raising finance within an entrepreneur's family. Contacts between the financial sector and industry were limited and pitched at a routinely minor level. This divergence was reinforced institutionally in the divorce between the banking system and industry. British banks, unlike their German counter-parts for example, played a passive and restrictive role: neither providing long-term finance nor actively participating in the decision-making processes of individual firms. The encouragement of technological innovation, the stimulation of industrial concentration, or the promotion of efficient production processes were beyond the common conception of British financial institutions. The safety of capital investment, defence of the free movement of capital, and the maintenance of the value of sterling on international markets were the basic preoccupations of the financial sector (see Judge and Dickson 1987).

For long periods in the nineteenth century there was a basic compatibility of interest between industrial and financial capital centred around freedom of international trade, the need for a strong currency and the availability of short -term loans. The two sectors – industry and finance – grew in parallel within a common imperial framework but with no intrinsic structural connection (Anderson 1987:34). The state was capable therefore of sustaining the conditions of growth for both sectors simultaneously. The question is whether this sustenance was conscious and continuous policy or unpremeditated pragmatism on the part of the state? A further question is whether the state served only the interests of one element of capital – either financial or industrial – or both? The answers necessarily entail an analysis of the third and political dimension of the aristocratic-bourgeois alliance.

The State and the Promotion of Economic Interests

Thus far it has been argued that the inheritance of the constitutional settlement of 1688 provided a state framework which was entirely conducive to the promotion of the interests of the industrial bourgeoisie. Moreover the centrality of parliament in this framework focused the political demands and political aspirations of the new industrial classes upon Westminster. Both the reality of political power and the logic of liberal theory led ultimately to the admission into the franchise of the foremost elements of the new industrial social strata in 1832. The Great Reform Act, although not so great in quantitative terms, with the total electorate extended to only 14 per cent of adult males, was pivotal, nevertheless, in the future development of the British state. There were various axes around which the new balance of political forces formed.

The first was the continuity of personnel in parliament identified above. Pugh (1982:20,23) notes for instance that it was only in the last quarter of the century that industrialists eventually constituted a majority in the Commons and that in this period 'despite the famous victories over reform in 1832 and the Corn Laws in 1846, government remained largely in the hands of the traditional landed men'. This was no 'mere cultural quirk or institutional anachronism. It reflected certain real and continuing disparities of material situation [between industrial bourgeoisie and landed gentry]' (Anderson 1987:31).

The second was the simple fact that the admission of the urban middle class into parliament had repercussions for the party system therein. Entering a 'one-class political system with two parties' (Anderson 1987:39), and in insufficient numbers to establish an autonomous bourgeois party, the new class was effectively channelled into the existing party system. Whilst party labels linked the pre-reform parliament with its immediate successor, the Tory and Whig parties effectively took on new identities as a result of the polarity over the issue of parliamentary reform in 1827-32 (as well as the issue of catholic emancipation). In this post-reform parliamentary context the newly enfranchised class found greater affinity with the Whigs than with the Tories (Peel's free-trade policies notwithstanding).

But not only was the 1830s a pivotal decade in terms of defining partisan allegiance in Westminster it was also crucial in clarifying the constitutional position of parties in relation to *government*. 'It was the identification of parties with *both* government and opposition, interchangeably, which marked the emergence of a modern aspect of party government in the 1830s' (Clark 1980:324). In comparison with the position before 1832 – one of party confusion and mixed party cabinets – the assumption by the mid-1830s was that each party would seek to form a government through securing an electoral majority in opposition to the other party.

As party government developed in the 1830s so 'parliament begins to *legislate* with considerable vigour, to overhaul the whole law of the country' (Maitland 1963:384). Increasingly, general acts of parliament were introduced to structure and regulate economic and social relations in a rapidly industrialising nation. Parliament's legislative output expanded in recognition of the simple fact that capital required a strong state framework within which it could then be left 'free' to act. On the negative side this framework included regulation of the worst excesses of labour exploitation through an ever widening series of general legislation dealing with working conditions, the specification of safety provisions and limitations upon the hours of work. More positively, parliament enacted, through limited liability and company legislation, the legal structuring of voluntary associations to act, for industrial purposes, as 'artificial persons'. In this proactive role it also took upon itself the provision of information in the form of the publication of official parliamentary papers and inquiries: information which profoundly influenced public opinion, legislation and administrative action in the decades after 1832 (see Florence 1957:31).

Parliament can thus be seen to be a major partner in the legislative process in the immediate decades after the Reform Act. It was through parliament and the use of the Public General Act that the statutory framework of liberal capitalism was established and the social and political ramifications of the economic system ameliorated. And as Walkland (1968:16) notes these acts 'engage[d] almost the entire attention of an increasingly representative parliament, often in the preparation of bills, always in the shaping of their detail'. But even at the time of the Common's most complete engagement in the formulation and detailed consideration and amendment of legislation, the process of incremental disengagement from a substantive legislative role had already started.

The inception of party government has been noted above, and the development of a party *system* will be examined below. But other important facets of parliamentary evolution after 1832 stemmed directly from its very legislative 'activism' (in contemporary terms). One was that within the state itself the executive accrued more regulatory responsibilities as a consequence of the legislation passed by parliament. A second was that beyond the representative institution of parliament a host of organised and sectional/functional representative bodies began to emerge, again largely as a result of parliament's own legislative engagement in the private realm of industry. The characteristics of modern British Government – the ascendancy of the executive and the system of group representation – were thus foreshadowed in the very 'golden age' of parliament itself.

i) executive agencies

The regulatory activities of the state sanctioned by parliament in the decade or so after the Reform Act required the expansion of central government to deal with these new found responsibilities. This expansion was two-fold. On the formulation side, as parliament moved towards legislating upon the general principles of legislation, the drafting of these general acts became increasingly an executive function; in addition, within the general rules adumbrated by the Commons, ministers and departments were entrusted with new delegated legislative powers (see Maitland 1963:384-5; Keir 1966:524-5; Walkland 1968:16-7). Not only did the legislative competence of the executive increase after 1832 but there was a significant increase in the scope and size of administrative discretion in the implementation of industrial policy as well; for regulatory interventions of necessity required regulators for their enactment. Thus, for example, the Factory Act of 1833 established a system of central inspection; the Home Office acquired responsibilities for the regulation of wages-in-kind after the Truck Act of 1831; the Poor Law Board was established as a result of the Poor Law Amendment Act of 1834; and the Companies Act of 1844 required joint-stock companies to register with the Board of Trade. Indeed, by mid-century the Board of Trade was a major executive agency directly concerned with many aspects of the state's relations with industry (see Grove 1962; Parris 1969). These relations were no longer characterised as arm's length but now the arm of the state was firmly embraced around important sectors of manufacturing industry.

ii) functional representation

As the strength of the state's embrace tightened it engendered a counter-response on the part of industry itself. Industry increasingly organised along functional lines to mediate between itself and government: either to defend or promote its interests in the light of encroaching state activity, and to exert pressure beyond the boundaries of party and parliamentary politics. Protective Associations such as the General Shipowner's Society (founded in 1831) and the Mining Association of Great Britain (established in 1854) formed in defence of state encroachment on their activities (see Grove 1962:13). Bodies such as the Institution of Civil Engineers and the Institution of Mechanical Engineers came into existence in the first half of the century to secure recognition of their professional status from the state. Trade Associations representing individual industrial sectors, which had their origins in the late eighteenth century amongst Staffordshire potters and Midland ironmasters, continued to develop in this period. Similarly by mid-century there were sixteen Chambers of Commerce in the major cities. These operated alongside local employers organisations in many cities, as in Sheffield for instance (see Alderman 1984:8). For the most part, however, the activity of these organisations remained regional or local. It was not until the last quarter of the century that national organisations began to characterise interest representation of industry.

What is important is that at the time of parliament's ascendancy in the British state a parallel system of functional representation was developing which was nourished by the very legislative activity of Westminster itself. The characteristics of this system are outlined by Alderman (1984:7):

> The activities of the interests were all coordinated outside parliament. And they all boasted, or came to boast, of extra-parliamentary organisations which undertook political and propaganda duties, acted as a forum of debate and for the resolution of differences, came (intentionally or otherwise) to impose upon their members a certain internal discipline, and came to be regarded, by parliament and government alike, as the authoritative bodies through which a dialogue with each particular interest might be maintained.

Changing Emphases between Parliament and Government

Three convergent factors served to engender in embryonic form the system of representation which ultimately came to be be seen as a challenge to parliamentary representation itself (see chapters 2 and 3). The first was the relative legislative activism of parliament and the changed emphasis between private and public bills. The increased usage of the latter combined with a growing propensity to allow administrative discretion on the details of such legislation, meant that at the same time as parliament acted as a *legislature* in the literal sense of the word it also abandoned 'the attempt to *govern* the country' (Maitland 1963:384). 'It beg[an] to lay down general rules .... and to entrust their working partly to officials, to secretaries of state, to boards of commissioners, who for this purpose are endowed with new statutory powers' (Maitland 1963:384). In other words a process was initiated whereby a wide variety of matters concerning industry passed from the specific purview of Westminster to executive agencies and central departments.

The second was the development of functional representation beyond Westminster. Again this tendency was related to the activities of parliament itself. Yet, whilst serving to engender interest organisations with an initial and primary political focus upon Westminster (see Beer 1969), the very nature of parliamentary legislation redirected their attention towards a symbiosis with the executive. Not only was parliament uninterested in the minutiae of technical regulation of industry (the very essence of relations between industry and administrators), it was largely unequipped, given its internal organisation and composition, to deal with such matters.

The third factor, therefore, was the nature of the House of Commons itself. The essence of parliamentary representation underwent a fundamental transformation during the course of the nineteenth century. By 1867 and the Second Reform Act the link between citizenship and property was virtually severed in the British state (Miliband 1982:25), for the first time sections of the labouring classes were admitted to the franchise. Whilst the link between property ownership and representation sustained a mortal blow by the Act, the connection between deference to property and parliamentarism was strengthened amongst the working class. Indeed, for all that the chorus of the propertyless had been a significant contributory factor to the political success of the industrial bourgeoisie in 1832 (see Judge 1983a:15), their own selective admission into the franchise was secured on the basis of relative social quiescence and a firm demonstration of proletarian 'responsibility' in their acceptance of established property relationships (McCord 1967:383). Further working class demonstrations of responsibility and integration into the economic and ideological system of capitalism were required before the universal franchise was conceded (see Therborn 1977:23; Close 1977:898; Judge 1983a:16). But this was not simply a one-way process, the 'governing classes' also sought positively to contain the demands of the industrial working classes within the bounds of parliamentary action and reformist legislation. In this respect parliament itself was crucial in 'organising' coalitions (or in marxist terminology 'power blocs'; see Poulantzas 1975:91) amongst the various forms of capital, as well as enabling the development of cross-class alliances. In fact the 1867 Reform Act has been seen as an attempt to forge just such an alliance between skilled workers and the aristocratic elements represented within the Conservative party, and so to divorce this section of working class support from industrial and commercial capital represented in the Liberal Party. In turn the Liberal party was encouraged to 'concede' the 1884 Act in order to challenge the continued political preeminence of the landed classes (see Tholfsen 1973:186).

But the importance of the the 1867 Reform Act rests not merely in its quantitative aspects, in the doubling of the electorate overnight, but more importantly in the qualitative changes wrought in British politics. The first of these, noted in the preceding paragraph, was the search for cross-class alliances. To facilitate this search, the organisation of the parties was modernised:

> For the political parties, such an enormous and sudden growth in the electorate meant that a system of centralisation became inevitable. Political leaders realised that they would have to make efforts to cater for the political aspirations of [the new electorate], and to attract their support, through constituency-based organisations and through legislation in

Parliament. This could be achieved only by the development of large-scale party organisations .... with Members united in the House of Commons to ensure the passage of promised measures. (Norton 1981:15)

The second and concomitant change was the appropriation of the term 'democracy' in the rhetoric of party politicians. 'It was in the decades following the passage of the Act of 1867 that "democracy" became part of the common coinage of political speech' (Miliband 1982:27). Yet, 'democracy' failed to impinge greatly upon the common practice of British politics. Nonetheless, the rhetoric was sufficient to wed the working classes firmly both to the institution of parliament and to the extant contours of party politics until at least the end of the century.

By the latter third of the century a place had thus been found for the working classes within the existing frame of the liberal state. Indeed, after 1884 manual male workers constituted a majority of the electorate. But they had been accommodated within the parameters of an existing state system: one in which government and its essential legitimacy derived from parliament. The supreme irony is that as the working class gained admission to what was still a sovereign legislature in theory, the slippage of 'sovereign' power to the executive was already well advanced. 'Government' was now largely the preserve of the executive.

The restructuring of the Conservative and Liberal parties after 1867, to form mass-membership organisations and to ensure adherence to party policy on the part of their elected representatives, in combination with the earlier development of party government, ensured consistency of support for executive measures. The fact that these measures were introduced within an overarching consensus, with the party in government acting 'simply [as] an agency for introducing agreed policies' (Berrington 1968:19), virtually guaranteed the mobilisation of support within the Commons. Mobilisation of opposition was to prove more problematic and it was not until the closing years of the century that party opposition became a structural feature of British parliamentary government (Judge 1983a:19). The important point is that from 1867 onwards, if not before, governments could depend upon consistent support within the House of Commons for the passage of legislation.

Equally important was the incremental extension of the executive's control over the proceedings of the House. Time as well as party support was also required to ensure the expeditious processing of legislation. In this respect the passage of the 1832 Reform Act undoubtedly marked 'a cataclysm in the internal methods of the House of Commons. It was in the 1830s that .... ministerial measures were given a frank priority' (Fraser 1960:451). Correspondingly, as noted above, the formulative role of the cabinet became routinised and standing counsel within the departments of state increasingly drafted legislation. Accelerated industrialisation and its attendant social consequences in subsequent decades simply accelerated the transition to an executive-centric state. Governments and industrial interests alike required the certainty that legislation needed to sustain the conditions for profitable private accumulation would be processed rapidly and predictably by the legislature. Predictability came with the growth of the party system. Rapidity was secured by procedural reforms effected throughout the century but most particularly in the 1840s and between 1882 and 1907 (see Judge 1983a:21).

By the end of the nineteenth century, and certainly by the end of the first decade of the twentieth, the modern British state was inimitably structured in its present institutional form: parliament was sovereign in constitutional theory but the executive was 'sovereign' in practice (see Griffith 1982). In terms of the central relationship between parliament and government the imbalance has never subsequently been redressed. This is because in Walkland's (1979:2) opinion:

> This structure has changed little in its basic assumptions concerning the role of parliament for much of the present century, and has proved equally attractive to modern governments which have felt little impulse to change a set of understandings and conventions which serve their purposes so well.

Equally, and seemingly paradoxically, the state form also served the purposes of capital and organised labour: exactly how, and how well, will be examined in the next section.

Loose Ends
The preceding discussion of procedural and political developments within parliament has led us into the twentieth century, but there still remain several 'external' loose ends in the nineteenth century to be examined.

City-Treasury-Bank Nexus
The first of these concerns the question of the dominance of financial capital over state policy (raised on page 9). It is commonly argued that state outputs in the nineteenth century reflected the 'universal' interest of financial capital in free trade and the international role of sterling. These were believed to be the preconditions of Britain's pre-eminence and prosperity in the world economy (Judge and Dickson 1987:4). Longstreth (1979:161), for example, argues that:

> On the political level the City has exercised a dominant position in the determination of economic policy, which is to say that its perceived interests have generally, although not exclusively, been the guiding thread for economic policy even when faced with opposition from the political

agents of other groups within the dominant class or from those of the subordinate class

By the latter part of the century this dominance was exerted structurally through the sheer size of the City's contribution to the British economy and more directly through the Bank of England and its relationship with the Treasury. The Bank was the state's bank and was inextricably linked with the London Stock Exchange (which had developed by the early eighteenth century on the basis of trading government stock). In practice the latter's transactions 'were completely dominated by government stock' (Ingham 1984:48). This structural connection between the state's banker and the stock exchange has persisted and has had significant ramifications for state policies ever since.

Not only were the Bank of England and the Stock Exchange symbiotically connected but in its strategic monetary role, as manager of domestic currency – and after the 1870s the *international* gold standard – the Bank operated independently of parliament (Ingham 1984:133). A monetary system thus developed in which the state's own control of the regulator of that system – the Bank of England – was consciously limited. Moreover the point at which the state had closest links to the Bank was through the Treasury with its responsibilities for fiscal management. The obverse of the Bank's monetary role was thus the fiscal role of the Treasury. The two were mutually dependent, and as Ingham (1984:132) observes, 'the Treasury's parsimony and the Bank's monetary prudence were thus complementary and mutually sustaining'. Not only that but their respective monetary and fiscal responsibilities endowed each institution with 'independent sources of power .... in their respective institutional spheres' (Ingham 1984:133). In the case of the Treasury its exertion of financial stringency over the other departments of state made it 'the real nerve-centre of the state, the dominant department of government enforcing its discipline on all others' (Anderson 1987:38). But Treasury control remained in essence negative; concerned with the curbing of profligacy rather than encouraging enterprise (Drewry and Butcher 1988:40).

With the administrative dominance of the Treasury secured by the mid-nineteenth century, and given its interactions and interdependencies with the City and the Bank of England, it then seems to be a logical step to argue that this nexus, of City-Treasury-Bank, is the most powerful variable in explaining the state's subsequent economic policies. Not surprisingly, this is precisely the step taken by Ingham, and others in amended form (see Anderson 1987).

Given the pivotal position of this nexus at the heart of the economy it is easy to see why state policy would be directly influenced by its operations. What is more difficult to explain is why its position would be hegemonic. The answer provided by Ingham and Anderson is in terms of the social composition of the nexus: in essence it remained aristocratic and reflected the pre-industrial values noted earlier. By this argument the persistence of common social backgrounds thus helped to sustain a non-industrial culture and to deny primacy in state policy to the economic interests of the industrial bourgeoisie.

Whilst this argument has a certain symmetry and simplicity, it soon unravels if the thesis of unbroken aristocratic hegemony is undermined. Ingham (1984:139) points clearly to the continued disproportionate representation of the landed classes in the British bureaucracy throughout the nineteenth century, including the post-reform period of the Northcote-Trevelyan Report. Others (Kingsley 1944; Leys 1983) make the claim, however, that the reforms of the bureaucracy undertaken in the nineteenth century were designed as a 'bourgeois protest against privilege' and a conscious attempt to open the administrative system to the new urban bourgeoisie. Similarly Barratt Brown (1988:40) suggests a major break in continuity in British administration with the movement of the new middle classes into the civil service in that century. Indeed, even Ingham (1984:139) admits that by the 1830s the Board of Trade, with its 'middle class officials, was already an instrument of the reformers'.

A second problem with Ingham's (1984: 131) thesis is the assertion that the 'Treasury view' of free trade and an international role for sterling was not only a direct reflection of City interests but was also 'largely independent of parliamentary control'. The difficulty here is that the Treasury, after the 1866 Exchequer and Audit Act and its creation of an auditing system whereby the newly created officer of Comptroller and Auditor General reported to the Public Accounts Committee, was subject to rigorous fiscal control. The purpose of the act was patently to increase parliamentary control (see Roseveare 1969:200); that it also served the interests of the City was incidental. In other words there was no overarching scheme consciously designed to promote the interests of financial capital over those of industrial capital at this juncture. Instead, one unintentional and ironic consequence, insofar as Gladstone sought the diminution of City influence over state policy, was the ultimate strengthening of the bond between the City and the Treasury. But the more important point, made by Barratt Brown (1988:36) is that industrial interests were not systematically discriminated against in the short-term by these policies; nor were industrial representatives in parliament impotent in the face of 'Treasury control' in expressing their own economic policy preferences. The simple fact is that often these preferences were coterminous with those of financial capital, or alternatively that industrial capital itself articulated no coherent view in contradistinction to that of the City-Treasury-Bank nexus.

A final problem with Ingham's thesis is the implicit assumption that the political focus of the industrial bourgeoisie upon 'parliamentary democracy' was somehow exclusive, and inimical to the promotion of their economic interests. Parliament 'proved to be a most inefficient medium for the representation and implementation of their views' (Ingham 1984:135). But it has already been noted that the bourgeoisie did not limit its political activity exclusively to Westminster, it organised rapidly and relatively early to ensure the representation of its views in Whitehall. In fact, by the 1880s, as Grove (1962:23-4) notes, officials in the Board of Trade had been instructed 'to open direct personal contacts with trade associations and Chambers of Commerce on all important matters of policy and day-to-day administration'. He sees this as an 'unprecedented step' from which grew an elaborate and systematic machinery for 'consultation with industry'. There was thus no sharp contrast between the direct and continuous links between City and state, and industry and the state, instead different departments attracted the attention of different sections of capital.

A secondary set of propositions – that the Treasury was the dominant department (and was itself dominated by aristocratic officials) and the close ally of the City – has also been challenged above. The fundamental criticism of this thesis remains, however, that the pursuit of the economic orthodoxies of the liberal economy cannot be seen simply to benefit financial capital at the *expense* of industrial capital. Their interests were not mutually exclusive. In fact for long periods of Britain's industrial history the interests of financial and industrial capital progressed along parallel, not divergent tracks. This does not mean that state policies have not proved detrimental to manufacturing industry in Britain in the long-term: manifestly they have. What it does mean is that this has been the consequence of a pattern of economic development formed out of a unique confluence of economic and structural forces. It is the very complexity of this confluence that should lead us to challenge deterministic explanations or those which depend upon class coherence and global unity of state action.

Throughout the nineteenth century the very compatibility of interest meant that industrial capital had no need to advance an alternative conception of the national economic interest other than that already being articulated (see Judge and Dickson 1987:5). Paradoxically this commitment to the principles of *laissez-faire* and market transactions inhibited and frustrated later attempts to prompt state intervention on industry's behalf long after changing international conditions required action to sustain the competitive position of British manufacturers *vis-à-vis* their main rivals in the USA and Germany. By this time, the decades at the end of the nineteenth and the beginning of the twentieth century, British supremacy was so contingent upon the internationalism of the world economy that manufacturing capital, even had it so wished, would have been (and was) unable to challenge policies in support of this internationalism. This was not because of the capture of the state machine by financial capital, but simply because the definition of the interests of the state had become so rooted in an international perspective. Certainly this was the perspective *of* the City but it was not exclusively defined *by* the

City. Rather it reflected the commonality of productive and financial interests that pre-existed the divergence of interests apparent at the end of the century.

If an explanation of the preeminence of 'City interests' in state policy is to be sustained then it has to be located within financial capital's centrality within the economy. 'In reality the City's relationship with the state is based on its economic power, and it is principally through economic levers that it acts upon the state' (Fine and Harris 1985:73). The objectives of the City have throughout reflected a commercial concern to maintain and strengthen its international trading position. This perspective helps to explain its general opposition to controls and its preference for free trade. All that has been argued above is that for long periods these objectives were shared by industrial capital as well. Thus, even at the height of the debate about Tariff Reform at the turn of the century, when Britain's comparative industrial decline was increasingly evident, significant sectors of industry opposed protection (see Hobsbawn 1969:243-4; Ingham 1984:160-2; Barratt Brown 1988:33). On this and subsequent occasions the articulation of an alternative conception of state economic policy lacked internal coherence and support amongst industrial capital. The very fragmentation of industry made it incapable of aggrandising 'its' interests into those of the 'nation'. The very unity of financial capital in Britain (see Fine and Harris 1985:74-8) and the institutional expression of its interests through the state's own bank has enabled it to appropriate the 'national interest' as its own. Industrial capital has found it extremely difficult to counter the orthodoxy of economic policies defined in these terms.

Neither should it be assumed that the interests of financial and industrial capital are discrete and unconnected. Whilst an institutional distance was maintained throughout the nineteenth century, nonetheless, there was an immediate connection of interests insofar as the trading position of the pound rested ultimately upon the overall strength of the wider British economy (see Barratt Brown 1988:34). The City's profits are linked to the profitability of the whole economy (see Oakley and Harris 1982:20-1; Fine and Harris 1985:69). Therein lies a fundamental paradox: as falling competitiveness of British industry heightens the attractiveness of overseas financial investment which in turn impacts upon industrial performance. This paradox has been at the heart of the debate on Britain's industrial decline and one which will be returned to later.

The Emergence of Labour
A second 'loose-end' from the nineteenth century, and again one that is of vital importance in explaining the subsequent development of the British state, is the emergence of a 'labour movement of a certain kind' (Coates 1983:40). There are two dimensions of this movement's character which have a particular significance for the present analysis.

The first is economic. The last quarter of the century witnessed the development not only of greater social homogeneity amongst the industrial working classes (see Pelling 1987:79-80) but also increasing collective action on their part. Trade unions had been formally legalised in the 1870s, partly in response to democratisation and to a growing working class electorate. Upon this base New Unions of unskilled workers organised alongside the older craft unions. For the most part the new unions adopted craft union practices and sought to defend past gains and acquired customs (see Clarke 1977:12). Significantly, these customs and norms predated mass production techniques. Hence, a peculiarly British dimension to the organisation of labour was propagated: one which combined a defensive orientation with decentralised and uncoordinated union structures (see Jessop 1980; Coates 1985:51; Pelling 1987:93).

This dimension of labour organisation impacted upon subsequent industrial development by engendering a propensity of manufacturers to concede outmoded work-practices in return for industrial peace. Thus, although reorganisation of the production process was a continuous feature of the nineteenth century, the strength of trade unions and their willingness to resist change on the basis of past practice frustrated technological innovation. Kilpatrick and Lawson (1980:90) go so far as to suggest that 'frequently these concessions provided the basis for further resistance so that one way or another industrial change proceeded more slowly than it would have done in the absence of resistance, and proceeded much more slowly than in other countries'. One consequence of such resistance was that British industrialists sought to avoid confrontations over the restructuring of the production process whenever possible and certainly when other alternatives existed. And free trade imperialism provided just such an alternative – in its maintenance of access to markets of the empire and its insulation of industrial capital from many of the effects of increased competition on the European stage. In this manner British entrepreneurs largely sidestepped conflict over the introduction of new techniques and working practices required to compete in the second industrial revolution. As argued elsewhere, industrial capital and labour alike thus had a vested interest in imperialism and its obscuring of the symptoms of relative industrial decline (Judge and Dickson 1987:7). Concern with the defensive power of trade unions has remained a constant feature of Britain's poor industrial performance.

The second dimension of the organisation of the labour movement in the late nineteenth century, and one which was to be of immense importance throughout the twentieth century, was political. An essential part of the liberal inheritance of the labour movement in Britain was its parliamentarism. Apart from a brief flirtation with syndicalist ideas in the 1830s (see Thompson 1968:912-3), and marxist ideas at the periphery in the latter decades of the century, organised labour consistently identified parliament and the vote as the key to political power. The very logic of liberalism, at least as accepted by the disfranchised, entailed the responsibility of parliament for processing the political demands of the electorate into law (see Poggi 1978:123,139). The enactment of amelioratory social and industrial legislation throughout the century also appeared to sustain the theory in the eyes of labour. Access to state power thus appeared synonymous with access to parliament. In this labour was not disabused by the existing parties and their desire to accommodate working class demands into their electoral programmes after the second and third Reform Acts. Thus in the words of Ralph Miliband (1982:23):

> Nothing weighed more heavily upon labour politics in Britain than the existence of a strong framework of representation however inadequate and undemocratic it might be, there did exist, it was believed, a solid, proven structure that could be made more adequate and democratic, that had already undergone reform, and that could in due course be used to serve whatever purpose a majority might desire.

When, at the end of the century, the existing party system eventually proved unsuited to the defence of the interests of organised labour, and when labour sought to organise its own political voice, there were few doubts that that voice should be articulated within parliament. Independent and direct representation of labour within the House of Commons thus came to be the pinnacle of working class political ambition: an ambition ultimately fulfilled upon the initiative taken by the TUC Congress in 1899 to establish the Labour Representation Committee in 1900 as the forebear of the Labour party itself in 1906. Thereafter the orthodoxy of the party was labourist and parliamentarian (see Miliband 1972, 1982; Coates 1975, 1979; Hinton 1983; Gamble 1985). As will be seen in the next chapter the orientation of labour to the state was to have profound consequences both for the industrial development of Britain and for the state form itself.

Tight Knots

The loose ends of analysis dealt with in the preceding section came in practice to be 'tight knots' binding the development of the British economy and state throughout the twentieth century. The legacies of the nineteenth century have reverberated throughout the present century: the preeminence of the City and its internationalism; the continuance of an imperialist mentality expressed through successive governments' obsession with international status and a 'world role'; the subordination of the requirements of domestic industry to this 'universal' policy perspective; the absence of the adoption of coherent and long-term industrial policies by the state in the face of a general belief in the virtues of self-reliance within industry; and the persistence of voluntarism and defensiveness on the part of the organised labour. None of these have been immutable, there have indeed been changes. But the general characteristics of state-industry relations distilled in the last decades of the last century remain visible in the last decades of this century. What is important is that changes and continuities have all been accommodated within the form of the parliamentary state.

2 Functional Representation: Governing Institutions and Corporatism

The problem at the heart of the British state and politics throughout the course of the twentieth century is that it has been built upon a theory of representative and responsible government, a view of legitimate political power enunciated by liberal theorists, which has never corresponded to political reality throughout that period. The ascendant paradigm of Dicey (1885) which specified that power flows serially from the electorate to parliament and thence to the government, with no counter-currents or intermediate institutions, was from the time of its inception an 'idealised view' of the constitution (see Birch 1964). The political developments chronicled in the last chapter – the mutually reinforcing tendencies of legislative activism, bureaucratic expansion, party organisation and mobilisation, executive control of the Commons, the organisation of extra-parliamentary functional interests – reflected the wider requirements and imperatives of the national economy. What the twentieth century witnessed therefore was a growing divergence between the idealised liberal version of legitimate government and British political practice itself.

In this analytical disjunction parliamentarism was supplanted by other 'isms', most influentially pluralism and corporatism, as empirically more precise descriptions of British politics. New 'idealised' views of the constitution thus came to replace the liberal fallacy of Dicey. Where Dicey over-emphasised parliamentary sovereignty the new paradigms consciously de-emphasised the contribution of parliament to the decision-making process. Political analyses identified the development of a 'post-parliamentary' state to parallel those analyses positing a progression towards a post-industrial, indeed a deindustrial, economy and society. Economic crises gave rise to representational crises. In turn, strategies to stem industrial decline were seen increasingly to marginalise parliamentary modes of representation; displacing parliament from the centre of the state system and refocusing representation upon the executive and the major 'corporations' of the state. Moreover, not only was representation refocused, in pluralist theory, it was also reformulated, in corporatist theory, into intermediation. In both instances 'theory' lagged behind the practice of British politics.

The first objective of this chapter, therefore, is to chronicle the expansion of functional representation throughout the course of the twentieth century, and in so doing to assess its interconnections with, and consequences for, parliamentary representation. The subsequent argument revolves around the premise that far from displacing parliamentary democracy, functional representation has operated only within its aegis and been contingent upon the balance of class and social forces represented and organised therein. What modern pluralist and corporatist analyses have recorded is not the relegation of parliament itself in the state system, but the dismembering of an idealised view of the parliamentary system which was already outmoded by the late nineteenth century at the very zenith of its academic ascendancy.

A second and equally important objective is to reveal the complex interconnections between industrial and economic performance and political strategies for their management (inevitably expressed in the language of 'crisis management'). In this context, much recent academic attention has concentrated upon the incorporation of major industrial interests into the decision-making process as an *endemic* feature of late capitalist development. This tendency is seen to be both long-term and pervasive: organised groups have crossed the threshold into government itself and in so doing have displaced elected representatives in parliament. What this chapter seeks to demonstrate, however, is the fragility and contingency of the processes of corporatist intermediation. By this argument parliament is still located at the centre of the state system but, to paraphrase Ghita Ionescu (1975), it is no longer *the* centre of decision-making. The history of the past century has been dominated by the constellation of interests revolving around this fulcrum. When centrifugal political forces have threatened to destabilise decision-making, the powerful imagery of parliamentarism has been evoked to reconstitute a balance around a 'national' project. But this is to jump ahead in the discussion. What is required first of all is a brief review of the development of the representation of functional industrial interests this century.

Governing Institutions and Corporatist Bias

In 1979 Keith Middlemas, concerned that the practical experience of British government had made accepted liberal versions of the constitution at best inadequate and at worst erroneous, sought to discover a 'hidden code' which would more realistically explain political institutional behaviour. The 'code' deciphered by Middlemas (1979:20) was one of 'corporate bias'. By this he meant a process whereby a 'triangular pattern of cooperation between government and the two sides of industry .... led to the elevation of trade unions and employers' associations to a new sort of status: from interest groups they became "governing institutions"'. These institutions were differentiated from 'pressure groups' as they became 'partners' of governments with permanent rights of access and accorded devolved powers by the state (1979:381).

The origins of this system were traced back to the first decades of the twentieth century when British governments encouraged the development of the new tripartite institutional structure in order to maintain public consent (Middlemas 1979:371). 'Thus at an earlier date than in any other industrial country, British governments made crisis avoidance top priority and called into being a tripartite political structure, designed *inter alia*, to contain working class power' (Booth 1982:202). Thereafter, trade unions and employers' representative organisations existed as 'estates of the realm' bound into a system of cooperation with the state despite continued specific opposition to particular party governments. State power was thus extended, through recognition by government of the special importance of producer groups, but the state itself was not corporatist. Middlemas is adamant that the British political system reflects a corporate *bias* but that the system itself was not corporatism. Too many fluctuations in the central relationship amongst the tripartite partners existed to ensure a stable system. In which case Middlemas (1979:380) concludes: 'like the bias of a wood at bowls [corporate bias] is in itself no more than a tendency always to run to one side' and that this description must suffice given the tentative, even fragile nature of its development.

Nonetheless, this bias had ramifications for the representation of interests both through parliament and through established interest groups. The pervasiveness of corporate bias at all levels of political activity was such that it reduced, on the one hand, the power of interests and organisations beyond the 'threshold' of tripartism, whilst, on the other, simultaneously it replaced 'for all practical purposes, classical democratic theory' as it had been understood for most of the twentieth century (Middlemas 1979:374). By 1945, therefore, Middlemas (1979:376) is in no doubt that tripartite collaboration had resulted not only in a 'uniquely low level of class conflict' but also the subordination of parliament in the new institutional structure of the expanded state. The next twenty years after 1945, according to Middlemas (1979:428-9), witnessed:

> the apogee of political stability, industrial equilibrium and economic prosperity, fortified by prolonged absence of ideological or class cleavages in society or the political parties. .... Britain seemed a model of the harmonious relations of governing institutions; and the corporate bias a necessary component of a political system in which intelligent economic

management ensured that there was no need to defer gratification, and where social change could be achieved without undue stress to any group.

Thereafter, however, Middlemas' account of the continuing trend of 'corporate bias' becomes more circumspect. By the late-1950s he identifies its continued operation as a precondition of triangular harmony, even though the communication between the three parties became indistinct and distorted (1979:429). Indeed, the period 1966-74 is then characterised as one in which the system of corporate bias was apparently deliberately destabilised by the major parties, and Middlemas (1979:450) is left to speculate whether the system could be 'restored'. A few pages later, however, he is insistent that the British state still (in 1979) was composed of governing institutions alongside the formal state apparatus and that crisis avoidance and the maintenance of political harmony could only be achieved through their incorporation (1979:460). Revealingly he argues that governments in the 1960s and 1970s had 'no other model' (1979:429) upon which to base their actions.

Whether there was an alternative model available to governments will be returned to later, a more immediate concern is whether Middlemas' historical review sustains his thesis of an unbroken, if fragile, development of 'corporate bias'. One particularly convincing challenge to Middlemas' thesis is provided by Alan Booth (1982) who queries the strength of the linkages between government and industry in the first half of the century and more especially the continuity of corporate bias within the state.

Both Booth and Middlemas are in agreement that the origins of corporatist experience in Britain are to be found in the immediate period after the first world war and arose out of efforts to avert social and economic instability through tripartite intermediation (a term explained below). Tripartism was continued subsequently as an invaluable method of economic management. Where Middlemas and Booth part company, however, is over the extent of continuity of corporatist tendencies within twentieth century Britain. As noted above Middlemas sees corporatist bias as a pervasive feature of political development throughout the first two-thirds of this century. Booth (1982:219), however, identifies three major breaks in the development of corporatist structures when they have been 'painlessly and easily terminated to allow industrial and financial capital to respond rapidly to more intensive competitive pressures'. The three periods identified are 1919-22, 1930-3 and post-1976. In each of these periods Booth (1982:200) argues the corporatist form was rejected by key groups in British society enabling 'anti-corporatist policies' to be pursued by government. Thus, far from being a consistent political strategy designed to integrate labour into the capitalist state (as argued for example by Panitch 1980), corporatism comes to be seen as 'little more than a technique of economic management .... developed during periods of *national* economic difficulty' (Booth 1982:200). When international economic crises overwhelmed the British national economy then the tripartite system came to be identified by key groups – most particularly financial capital, internationally-oriented industrial capital, sections of organised labour itself and significant elements within the mass electorate – as an impediment to necessary economic restructuring. In these circumstances the consensual pattern of tripartite cooperation and mutual accommodation is no longer merely 'fragile' (as described by Middlemas) but is actually fractured. Indeed, the experience of political and economic development since 1979 is perhaps in itself the most convincing refutation of the belief in the 'tenacious durability' (Panitch 1981:40) of corporatist structures in Britain. This period will be examined shortly; but for now what is required is a brief résumé of what corporatism has entailed in twentieth century Britain. Paradoxically the simplest method of discovering the essence of corporatism is to identify what corporatism is *not*.

What Corporatism Is Not

One accomplishment of the Thatcher governments has been to confirm, through their deeds, earlier academic scepticism of some of the initial 1970s' conceptualisations of corporatism. One particularly influential formulation at the time was provided by Jack Winkler, singly and in combination with Ray Pahl (Pahl and Winkler 1974; Winkler 1976, 1977). At the forefront of the wave of corporatist analysis Winkler argued that a new political economy was emerging which was distinct from both capitalism and socialism. Moreover, he predicted that the new economic system would be instituted in Britain within a decade. Yet, well before that time had elapsed, both the analysis and the prediction were swamped by successive waves of academic criticism (see for example Westergaard 1977, Panitch 1980, Cox 1980, Cawson 1978, 1982) and policy disjunction alike. On a practical plane, economic and industrial policy increasingly diverged from Winkler's conception of a 'directive' role for the state. Whilst on an analytical plane no alternative endemic rationale of a corporatist economy was articulated; distinct that is from private accumulation, the extraction of surplus value, and profit. In other words the necessary prerequisites of a new political economy were never established. Nor were the indirect mechanisms of state influence over its corporate partners elaborated. Not surprisingly given these deficiencies 'the Pahl/ Winkler version of corporatism had by the end of the 1970s virtually sunk without trace' (Williamson 1989:13).

Other academic analyses of corporatism have been more robust, though still with their own analytical flaws. Of most relevance here are those analyses which identify corporatism in Britain variously as a system of industrial relations (Crouch 1977, Panitch 1979, 1980, Strinati 1979, 1982); a new state form (Jessop 1979); or as a *system* of interest intermediation (Schmitter 1979, 1982; Cawson 1982, 1989).

Industrial Relations

Those who argue that 'corporatism is a particular form of state control of industrial relations' (Strinati 1979, 1982; Crouch 1979, 1985) do so generally within the wider discussion of class relations in late capitalist society. Strinati in an opaque discussion of corporatism and industrial relations repeats the suggestion that state policies since the mid-1960s have been informed by corporatism. He takes corporatism to mean 'the external mode of control of industrial relations associated with state interventionism together with the regulation of the role of unions as the internal mode of controlling industrial relations' (Strinati 1979:207-8). Panitch (1980:174), somewhat more lucidly, identifies corporatist structures as:

> the form of economic planning and incomes policy bodies, involv[ing] the integration of trade unions in economic policy-making in exchange for their incorporation of capitalist growth criteria in union wage policy and their administration of wage restraint to their members.

Both Panitch and Strinati thus see corporatism as a particular, contingent and contradictory strategy for the incorporation of the working class more closely into the interstices of the capitalist state. Moreover, it is a state-induced form of collaboration (Panitch 1980:175). In this descriptive approach, corporatism is identified as both specific and partial: pertaining to specific tripartite structures and to a partial mode of interest representation – one that neither encompasses all forms of interests nor displaces parliamentary representation itself. Nonetheless, despite these qualifications, the clear assumption is that corporatism is both a valid analytical category and an adequate description of industrial relations in the decades preceding the first Thatcher government.

Hyman (1986:99) denies that either is the case. As an analytical construct he sees corporatism 'congeal[ing] conceptually an essentially fluid and many-layered social relation'. As an empirical description of state-labour relations it is based on 'ahistorical obfuscation'. In Hyman's view the history of industrial relations in Britain has been marked by a sharp divergence from a corporatist model. Thus, for example, the system of labour law established in the last quarter of the nineteenth century was negative rather than positive in character; prescribing immunities rather than rights for trade unions. Significantly, this pattern was to characterise British industrial relations for much of the following century; building as its corollary the belief on both sides of industry that the common affairs of trade unions and employers were best conducted away from legislative or government interference. Thus, not only does Hyman (1986:81) point to a historical detachment between 'politics' and industrial relations he also argues that in the absence of statutory support for union representation 'there has been no reciprocal requirement for "responsible" behaviour"' on the part of organised labour. Trade union responsibility cannot therefore be seen as part of a corporatist 'trade-off'. Nor have British trade unions displayed a strong capacity to control their members. There have been major restraints on bureaucratic and hierarchical control within unions thus diminishing their leaderships' capacity to collaborate in corporatist agreements (see also Metcalfe and McQuillan 1979).

When examining the two decades immediately preceding the election of the first Thatcher government Hyman (1986:84) points to the fact that institutional symbolism obscured the uneven and asymmetrical growth of corporatism in that period. What is significant about the 1960s, therefore, is just how little success was achieved in incorporating organised labour into the state system.

Similarly, what is apparent in the 1970s is the internal corrosiveness of corporatist structures. For Hyman (1986:99) corporatist bargaining approximates to a zero-sum game wherein the objectives of any individual partner in tripartite structures can only be achieved in general by frustrating those of others. In other words, the very dynamic of the interrelationship between state-capital-organised labour is unstable and disruptive of the necessary consensus essential for corporatist development (see MacInnes 1987: 158-9).

Hyman's analysis is of particular significance in assessing the trajectory of industrial relations after 1979. Given the paradigmatic shift in academic fashion in the 1970s towards an acceptance of liberal-corporatism or neo-corporatism, the abruptness of the changed relationships between trade unions and the state after the election of the first Thatcher government 'surprised and confounded nearly all observers and analysts of British industrial relations' (Longstreth 1988:413). Industrial relations policies post-1979 have been characterised by the use of deflationary macro-economic policies to undercut the bargaining strength of unions, and by a series of measures designed to deinstitutionalise industrial relations and to deregulate labour markets. Whilst the details of these policy changes would divert the focus of the argument here, they are outlined in chapter 5 and well chronicled elsewhere (see Rubery 1986; Coates and Topham 1986; MacInnes 1987; Longstreth 1988). In parallel the Thatcher government has also sought the 'delegitimisation' of trade unions as political institutions. In this respect the range of action covered 'the reduction of contacts between union leaders and government ministers, limiting union participation in government bodies to the area of industrial relations strictly defined and a more general if diffuse attack on union recognition as a normal industrial relations practice' (Longstreth 1988:417). The ability of the Thatcher government so to marginalise trade union participation in state decision-making reflects not only upon the over-exaggerated claims of organised labour's contribution to that process in the preceding decades, but equally importantly points towards the inherent contradiction in the theorisation of neo-corporatism as a mode of political representation. In turn, this contradiction opens up the second and related aspect of corporatism: namely the state form.

State Form

From the perspective of the literature on industrial relations corporatism as a system of representation is contrasted with, and is seen to be 'clearly inimical' to, parliamentarism (see Strinati 1979:202; 1982:23-4; MacInnes 1987:45). The representative institutions of liberal democracy are seen to be displaced by the progressive expansion of a tripartite process of decision-making. Extra-parliamentary bodies of functional representatives come to constitute the major institutions for the articulation and resolution of economic demands. Parliament is thus further marginalised in the process of representation. Corporatism in its macro-form of tripartism – of the incorporation of organised labour and industrial capital into the process of executive decision-making – is presented therefore as an extension of the tendency towards functional representation endemic within British industrialism. As such it has been claimed that there is little need for the development of a theory of corporatism:

> In Britain the tradition of secret 'efficient' government developing through *ad hoc* pragmatic adjustments and legitimated by a 'dignified' parliamentarism reduces the need for participants in the process to have any sort of theory of corporatism. (Harden 1988:43)

Yet, as will be seen later, 'participants' at Westminster were well aware of the 'challenge' posed by corporatist representation and anxious to accommodate such developments within the orbit of parliament itself. The specific paradoxes of such schemes will be examined below. Here, however, the general contradictions posed by corporatist representation within a system of parliamentarism need to be examined.

One method to resolve these contradictions, at the level of theory at least, is to maintain that corporatism represents a discrete 'state form' distinct from parliamentarism. The early formulation of corporatism in Jessop's (1978) work provides one example of this approach. In trying to link the contemporary discussion of corporatism to marxist political economy Jessop arrives at the position that:

> corporatist institutions are *displacing* parliamentary institutions as the dominant state apparatus in Britain and that these constitute a *contradictory unity*. Both corporatist and parliamentary representation are necessary to the reproduction of capital in the present situation.

Corporatism is seen to be the highest form of social democracy, particularly appropriate to the interventionist state in the 'post-Keynesian period' of the mixed economy and welfare state. In such periods it is necessary to ensure the active and continuous involvement of labour and capital in the state's economic interventions. In Jessop's opinion this is the significant contribution of corporatism because it realigns the system of political representation to the new forms of state intervention.

> Corporatism thus entitles the political organs of capital and labour to participate in the formulation and implementation of policies concerned with accumulation so that responsibility for such intervention is placed on those immediately affected rather than mediated through parliamentary representation ....(Jessop 1979:200)

Yet the problem is that corporatism does not constitute a complete system of representation. At best it takes a hybrid form. Whilst corporatism merges representation and intervention in functionally based institutions, it also necessarily institutionalises at the centre of the state conflicts based upon the economic division between labour and capital. This interaction of the functional representatives of labour and capital at the level of the state is the central contradiction pointed to by marxists (see Jessop 1978,1979; Panitch 1980). Corporatism with its emphasis upon consensual and cooperative modes of decision-making is based upon the representation of socio-economic and divergent (class) interests. What is distinctive about corporatism, therefore, is that the functional groups at the heart of the system are 'constituted in terms of a contradictory relation to one another' (Panitch 1980:176), and that this relationship is focused upon the very economic interests that divide them in the first instance.

The deficiencies of early marxist analyses of corporatist developments in Britain, with their emphases upon the functionality of corporatist decision-making to capital accumulation and monocausal consideration of the incorporation of labour into the state, without fully examining the complexity of labour's response (or, equally importantly, capital's response) to these developments, have been well documented (see Cox 1980; Cawson 1982, 1989; Birnbaum 1982; Williamson 1989). However, what is not denied is the value of marxist accounts in pointing to the contingency of corporatist development. Thus Jessop (1978:49; 1980:51) repeatedly states that the transition from parliamentarism is not automatic but is dependent upon the specific conjunction of political forces at any period. Whether this means in practice that corporatist development will proceed in Britain remains unresolved in Jessop's work. In 1978 he concluded that the 'exact nature and significance of corporatism and the extent of its democratisation are open issues' (1978:49). A year later he identified the 'dominant tendency in the modern state is towards social democratic tripartism [with a secondary tendency towards the development of a strong state]' (1979:211). One year on again he located the rise of the 'strong state' in Britain in part to the failure of the 'incipient corporatist system' to function effectively (1980:54). And by 1986 he was contemplating the 'monetarisation of corporatism' and the 'crisis of corporatism' (Jessop 1986:115, 123). Within a further two years the Thatcher governments' systematic demotion of functional representation is acknowledged and the crisis of corporatism confirmed (Jessop et al 1988:83). Yet, Jessop then proceeds to argue that 'corporatism should not be unequivocally rejected by the left' as a future alternative to Thatcherism, and that the ideas of 'democratic corporatism must be introduced as major elements into economic management' (1988:123). Fortunately, the detours in Jessop's analytical odyssey do not need to detain us here, what is important is the consistency of his argument pertaining to the relationship between corporatism and parliamentarism as systems of representation.

Throughout, Jessop recognises that corporatism in itself is incapable of providing the necessary legitimation for policies derived from tripartite bargaining without the existence of a 'determinate (although pluralist and non-unitary) sovereign authority' (1979:195). Although not linked analytically, he refers elsewhere to the legitimation and flexibility afforded by 'electoral politics' (1978:43). What is vitally important is the very strength of the 'parliamentary tradition in Britain' (1978:43). Consequently, 'the most that can be expected is the displacement of the dominant position within the hierarchy of state apparatuses of representation from parliament to tripartite institutions' (1978:43). In this manner Jessop reaches the position noted above that there is a contradictory unity where a fusion of corporatist and parliamentary representation is required but is unsustainable. An inherent conflict is identified between the social bases of representation in the two systems (see Jessop 1978:44-5; 1979:205): between organised labour and capital and their preference for centralisation and concentration of state power; and the unorganised, the jobless, small capital, petit bourgeois interests, wider social movements, and what Jessop calls 'popular-democratic forces' for whom parliament still remains a favourable political terrain for the mobilisation and articulation of interest. By this point, however, it is apparent that corporatism is no longer seen to be a discrete state form distinct from parliamentarism: at its most developed it is at best a hybrid form (which is the essence of Jessop's argument), at its least developed stage it is simply a variant of functional representation within parliamentarism.

Having reached this stage in the discussion it is perhaps advisable to postpone the consideration of the paradoxes identified by Jessop – the inherent conflicts in the social bases of representation and the legitimising role of parliament in the state system – until after the examination of the third variant of what corporatism is not.

System of Interest Intermediation

What is clear thus far from the examination of the concept of corporatism is that it is in essence a form of functional representation within the frame of a liberal democratic state. What is less than clear, however, is how this system of representation is constituted, the extent of its development, its inclusiveness, its internal coherence, or the degree to which it has displaced other modes of representation. To further complicate matters a strong academic stream of neo-corporatist analysis, following the lead of Phillippe Schmitter (1974,1979,1982,1985), has conceived of corporatism in terms of interest *intermediation* rather than interest representation.

'Intermediation' came to prominence in neo-corporatist thought from the humblest of origins. Schmitter, in the light of criticism of an earlier draft of his 1979 essay, substituted the concept of 'intermediation' for that of 'representation', and outlined in a footnote his reason for so doing. In using the term he sought to emphasise that:

> [formal interest] associations not only may express interests of their own, fail to articulate or even to know the preferences of their members, and/or play an important role in teaching their members what their interests 'should be', but also often assume or are forced to acquire private government functions of resource allocation and social control. Representation (or misrepresentation), hence, may be only one of the activities of these associations, occasionally not even the most important one.

The social control and private government functions of organised interests became essential defining characteristics of neo-corporatism thereafter. As Crouch puts it: 'Many political arrangements exhibit inter-group cooperation; what is distinctive about corporatism is that leaders are prepared to enforce on their members compliance with the terms of agreements they have reached with their *contraparti*' (Crouch 1983:455; see also Cawson 1978:184; Schmitter 1982:263; Williamson 1989:101-16).

Again, as with most things pertaining to corporatism, the very concept of intermediation is ambiguous and contested. In part the ambiguity is inherent within the initial formulation provided by Schmitter (1979:65) as he included alongside corporatism, pluralism and syndicalism as 'generic modes of interest intermediation'. Successive use of the term has been less ambiguous and commentators have been willing to argue not only that intermediation is an 'essential element of the corporatist model' (Williamson 1989:117), but also that it is doubtful whether 'pluralism can be described as a theory of interest intermediation' (Grant 1985:21). Intermediation has come, therefore, to distinguish corporatism from pluralism.

Indeed, a primary purpose of Schmitter (1974) in constructing an elaborate general model of corporatism in the first place was to develop an alternative paradigm of interest politics to that of pluralism. Unlike some later contributors to the debate, Schmitter was keenly aware of the shared assumptions of pluralism and corporatism (1974:96), but he maintained that their prescriptions and their images of the institutional form of interest representation diverged. Moreover, he was convinced that corporatism described political reality more accurately than pluralism did. Battle has been joined ever since between the respective supporters of these 'divergent' paradigms.

In many respects the battle between corporatists and pluralists has been a shadow-boxing contest, with the protagonists defining and redefining their opponents' case out of existence, or blurring the distinctive features of their own paradigm (and frequently achieving both simultaneously). Ultimately both concepts, given the theoretical heterodoxy within both camps, have been heavily reliant upon description. Yet, in descriptive mode the differences between the two perspectives are prone to evaporate, leaving the contestants to call for more rigorous conceptualisation to reassert the initial points of divergence (see for example Martin 1983a, 1983b; Crouch 1983; Jordan 1984, Jordan and Richardson 1987b; Cox 1988; Williamson 1989). Whilst the intricacies of this heated debate are not of direct relevance here, there are two related elements of the debate of importance for establishing what corporatism is not.

The first is that corporatism is not a distinctive method of public policy formulation and implementation. Schmitter (1982:259) in acknowledging that the discussion on corporatism had moved away from his earlier preoccupation with interest intermediation to a 'collateral emphasis on the process of policy-making and implementation' suggests that the former concern should be labelled corporatism$_1$ and the latter corporatism$_2$. Corporatism$_1$ is theoretically driven as an ideal-typical model of the state form; corporatism$_2$ is a description of public policy-making and implementation. As corporatism$_2$ comes to be concerned with particular policies and examined at meso- and micro- levels so too in the eyes of its critics does it lose its distinctiveness from pluralism (see Jordan and Richardson 1987b:104-6; Cox 1988:298-303). But in redirecting the focus of analysis towards policy-making and away from macro-level tripartite state structures in an attempt to sustain their claims for empirical accuracy, neo-corporatists encounter the danger that the very concept becomes redundant. If the revised version now rests upon 'insights into policy-making that pluralist theory did not and could not achieve' (Cox 1988:299), then the concept loses credibility if similar insights are discernable within pluralism itself. The work of Jordan (1984; Jordan and Richardson 1987b) has been particularly acerbic and effective in dismembering neo-corporatist claims to novelty in this respect. For him (Jordan and Richardson 1987b:104) neo-corporatists are in danger of 'reinventing the wheel' of pluralism. Indeed, the general verdict on corporatism$_2$ is that it constitutes little more than 'corporatist pluralism': a variant of pluralism with a history pre-dating parvenu neo-corporatist analysis (see the various formulations of Martin 1983a; Jordan 1984, Jordan and Richardson 1987b; Cox 1988). It is perhaps also significant that Schmitter (1982:263) prefers to conserve the term 'corporatism' for interest intermediation (i.e. corporatism$_1$), and to use the label 'concertation' for corporatism$_2$.

The second element points to the dilution in corporatist thought occasioned by a conceptual refocusing away from tripartite structures to bipartite bargaining. Thus, recent neo-corporatist analyses have emphasised that 'in assessing the role of corporatist processes in Britain in the late 1980s it is important not to equate corporatism with *tripartism*' (Harden 1988:38). The author of this quotation then proceeds to identify the bipartite relations between government and companies and quangos as corporatist forms. Yet there is no adequate explanation of why they should be seen in this way. Similarly, other enthusiasts of the corporatist cause appear willing to identify corporatism in most bargaining relationships between government and single special interests where an element of membership control is exercised (see Crouch 1983; Grant 1985; Cawson 1985, 1986, 1988). Thus, Cawson (1988:312) for example, defends the applicability of the corporatist label to state-firm relationships as an 'indication that in such cases where monopoly interest associations are absent state actors seek to intervene directly at the level of the firm to harmonise corporate strategies with political objectives'.

In examining state-firm relationships not only does the focus of corporatist analysis move from tripartite to bipartite bargaining, but it also moves from the macro- to the micro-level. In between, meso-level studies have emerged which have been concerned with sectoral interests rather than the peak national associations associated with macro-level corporatism (see Cawson 1985; 1986; Grant and Streeck 1985). Even within the ranks of corporatist theorists doubts have been expressed about the operationalisation of the concept at this intermediate level (see Williamson 1989:163). Doubts at the meso-level become certainties at the micro-level; with even those sympathetic to corporatist theory having to concede that 'it is not really legitimate to talk of "micro-corporatism", certainly as presented .... as bilateral negotiations between the individual firm and the state. It just does not appear to accord with the broader conceptualisation of corporatism' (Williamson 1989:165). Similarly, Grant (1987:16) makes the general point that the interventionist relations between government and micro-interests are perhaps best described as instances of private interest government rather than corporatism. In the hands of critics of corporatism the dismissal of micro-corporatism is scathing:

The idea of bipartite deals between government and interest groups is interesting but it would appear we are a long way from the corporatist state which Schmitter and Winkler were talking about in 1974. Indeed for Cawson corporatism exists if the government gives a firm a special contract and lets it implement it! One can be excused for throwing one's hands up in horror on reading this. When a colleague is forced to redefine large firms as interest groups in order to accommodate their bipartite deals with government within the corporatist schema, then one knows there is something radically wrong with that concept. (Cox 1988:302)

What is denied here is not the importance of the research into the policy role of business associations and firms, but the applicability of corporatist theory to such analysis. Once corporatist analysis is applied below the macro-level of the state, beyond tripartite structures and the process of intermediation, then its analytical utility is severely, indeed fatally, flawed. In these circumstances other concepts – 'concertation' (Schmitter 1982) or 'private interest government' (Streeck and Schmitter 1985) – appear of more value. Pluralists have been making a similar case for a long time!

What Corporatism Is

If we know what corporatism is not and the reasons why not, then we are now in a position to establish what it is and why it is. From this position it is necessary to return to those issues – the challenges posed to parliamentary representation by corporatist intermediation, and the conflicts arising from the divergent social bases of representation – postponed for consideration from above. In addition the distinctiveness of corporatist representation from pluralist representation, deferred from consideration in the last paragraph, will have to be addressed. And the question will then have to be posed of whether in disposing of the challenge of corporatism we have merely strengthened the pluralist case and its own claims of 'post-parliamentary' democracy?

Given the diversity and heterogeneity of corporatist writings there appear to be as many versions of corporatism as there are theorists. Indeed, Williamson (1989:5) has described the cumulative picture as one 'of an elastic concept with a somewhat uncertain core'. What has made the definitional problem more complicated still is the existence of parallel theoretical and empirical modes of analysis and a propensity on the part of many commentators to switch from one to the other with seemingly reckless abandon. To require an unambiguous definition in this context is perhaps unrealistic. Instead, the most that can be offered are components of a corporatist model. These should be coherent and explicatory and so capable of differentiating corporatism from any other form of representation. Already the elements of corporatism are being assembled even in these introductory assertions – model and representation – are in themselves key words.

Hereafter, corporatism is taken to mean a model of political representation. One which entails tripartite structures at the level of the state (i.e. the macro-level) and one which involves the exchange of statuses between state and organised associations. In other words, the state confers 'public' status upon producer associations in return for some control or regulation of the associations activities themselves; often in the form of expected implementation of the outputs of the tripartite bargaining process. 'Intermediation' encapsulates this relationship insofar as associations act as *intermediaries* between public and private realms. Inbuilt into this concept is the notion of representational distortion – internally whereby the interests and demands of members' are reinterpreted within the associations own hierarchy; and externally whereby other associations beyond producer groups are denied the same privileged access to the state.

This is a model based upon historical experience within one country, Britain, and is not therefore ideal-typical in the sense of being a purified abstraction. Moreover it has no pretensions of universalism, of applicability to all other variants of corporatism. Instead it seeks to conceptualise the linkage between state and interests in order to comprehend the circumstances under which corporatist forms emerged (in that sense it is not even a predictive model) and how they relate to other forms of representation. From this last statement it is apparent that corporatism is also taken to be contingent and partial rather than systemic and universal. Posited in the negative it is not a state form nor a complete system of representation. It coexists, often uneasily, with pluralist forms of interest representation within the overarching frame of parliamentarism. It is, therefore, a liberal (societal or neo-) variant of the generic form of corporatism.

If that is what it is, then how distinctive is corporatism, so defined, from pluralism and what are the paradoxes of its liberal form?

Paradoxes of Representation Within Liberal/Neo-Corporatism
A common element of all of the variants of liberal/neo-corporatism considered above is the progressive displacement of traditional parliamentary modes of representation by tripartite (or bipartite) interest intermediation. Functional representation, required for efficacious economic management (whether at times of national economic crisis or more permanently is a matter of dispute) nevertheless challenges territorial and individualistic notions of representation. In many corporatist analyses there appears to be an inbuilt logic within late capitalism towards a representative process based upon 'mutually supportive and exclusive relationships between the state and organised *producer* interests' (Cawson 1989:241). This is so because increased state activity and interventions in the economy and industry require a 'purposive-rational' decision-making process, where decisions are justified in terms of effective

results rather than legitimate procedures, rather than simple legal-rational modes of decision-making within parliament (see Cawson 1983:179). This is the contradiction pointed to by Jessop (1979:202-3) who notes that corporatism and parliamentarism as systems of representation:

> have different decisional rules (unanimity vs. majority), different principles of legitimacy (functional vs. electoral), and different political bases (corporations vs. parties). This at least suggests that the preferred policy outcomes in one system might be incompatible with those favoured in the other system and that conflicts and immobilism could result.

The major contradiction here is that of legitimacy. Neo-corporatism, given its development *within* a liberal democratic frame, and given also the very strength of that frame in Britain (Jessop 1978:43; Miliband 1982), has proved incapable of asserting its 'principles of legitimacy' above those of parliamentarism. In fact, as Schmitter (1982:266) observes, neo-corporatism has consistently been 'very weakly legitimated by the political cultures in which it is embedded'. It lacks, again in the words of Schmitter (1982:267), 'the socialised normative support and explicit ideological justification' necessary to sustain its claims to legitimacy. Thus, although corporatist intermediation might be necessary – variously because of 'the long term requirements of policy-making and policy-implementation' (Cawson 1989:241); or 'the imperatives of capital accumulation' (Jessop 1978:41); or for the 'contain[ment] of the political and economic strength of the working class' (Panitch 1980:174) – it is neither a complete system of representation nor one capable of exerting hegemony in relation to the procedural democratic norms of parliamentarism.

Recognition of the conflict between the representational bases of corporatism and parliamentarism, the specificity of the former and the universality of the latter, and the dependency relationship between the effective policy-making and implementation afforded by the one and the wider legitimation of the policy-process by the other, has led to many attempts to resolve this dilemma over the years. Practical schemes to incorporate functional representation within the parliamentary system itself, or analytical models proposing the existence of a 'dual polity', have both been proposed out of a recognition of the essential duality of the modern industrial state.

Functional Representation and Parliament: A House of Industry?
There appears to be a roughly asymmetrical pattern between the advocacy of schemes for the institutional inclusion of functional representation within parliament and disjunctions within the development of corporatist structures themselves. The three periods identified by Booth (1982), when the corporate

form has been explicitly rejected in the practice of British politics, paradoxically have also produced powerful advocacy of the institutional extension of functional representation. The first period (1919-22) corresponded with the publication of G.D.H. Cole's (1920a, 1920b) schema of Guild Socialism, the Webb's prescriptions in their *Constitution for a Socialist Commonwealth of Great Britain* (1920) and Herman Finer's drafting of *Representative Government and A Parliament of Industry* (1923). The second (1930-33) witnessed Churchill's famous call for an economic sub-parliament made in his 1930 Romane's lecture; Macmillan's (1933) less publicised but equally significant *Reconstruction*; along with the publication of Hobson's *The House of Industry* (1931). In turn, the third period has also seen a revival of interest in some form of advisory 'Council of Industry' especially on the part of some industrialists (Parker 1977; Chandler 1984; see also Gilmour 1977; Smith 1979; Coombes 1982).

What these periods appear to have in common is a heightened awareness of economic and political malaise. Economically these periods are marked by widespread recognition of Britain's relative industrial decline and economic weakness reflected in high unemployment (see Booth 1982; Pollard 1983, 1984; Gamble 1985); politically they constitute periods of 'representational crisis' (see Jessop 1978) when the legitimacy of electoral politics is questioned by extra-parliamentary activity – massive industrial unrest in 1919-22; the genesis of the British Union of Fascists via Mosley's New Party in the early 1930s; symptoms of 'pluralist stagnation', 'overload' and 'ungovernability' and the anti-democratic remedies proposed in the period after 1976. The general normative prescriptions of liberal democracy remained sufficiently strong in these periods to restrain the wilder excesses of anti-parliamentarism, yet could not contain detailed and specific disillusion with the operation of the institution of parliament and the parliamentary parties. Within parliamentarism therefore there was a fundamental contradiction between the overriding legitimacy derived from the *system* of parliamentary government and the pronounced concern about the institution and effectiveness of parliament itself. In these circumstances one political strategy recurred: the conflation of parliamentary and functional representation to combine the perceived effectiveness of the latter with the equally necessary legitimation of policy derived from the electoral process in the former. Yet, simultaneously, in the very same circumstances, an economic strategy recurred: the disengagement from existing corporatist arrangements and a return to economic liberalism and orthodox financial policy. A further paradox (a paradox within a paradox!) is that the political method of effecting this economic strategy invariably entailed the reassertion of the principles of parliamentary sovereignty if not the practice.This was particularly so in the last of the three periods (see below).

Before examining this period it is worthwhile outlining some of the proposals designed to fuse corporatist and parliamentary representation. This will reveal both the contemporary concern with the inadequacies of parliament in the process of industrial policy-making and also the inherent contradictions within such schemes.

Unsuitability of Parliamentary Representation
The common feature of the schemes considered in this section is that they all start from the premise that a parliament based upon individualistic principles of representation is unsuited to the needs of a complex industrial economy and society. From this initial premise there is a wide divergence in the character of the schemes subsequently proposed.

Early formulations of functional representation, for instance, often contrasted economic democracy with existing political democracy of representative government. In this contrast parliamentary representation was invariably dismissed as 'misrepresentation'. For Guild Socialists in particular: 'True representation .... like true association, is always specific and functional, and never general and inclusive' (Cole 1920a:106). The problem with parliament therefore is its territorial basis and its omnicompetence:

> Parliament professes to represent all the citizens on all things, and therefore as a rule represents none of them in anything .... Members of Parliament muddle because they are set the impossible task of being good at everything, and representing everybody in relation to every purpose. (Cole 1920a:108)

'Real democracy' for Cole would only be found in a future decentralised socialist state. In contrast to the early twentieth century British liberal democratic state, a future socialist state would be based upon syndicalist and pluralist principles. Parliament would be replaced by a system of 'coordinated functional representative bodies' (Cole 1920a:108) with the basic building block of the new system being the internally self-governing workplace (for details see Cole 1920b; Birch 1964:109-12; Smith 1979: 10-13; Judge 1981 31-2). If Cole's proposed remedies were drastic and riven with inconsistencies there was nonetheless 'a compelling logical consistency to his analysis of the problems facing representatives in a complex industrial society' (Judge 1981:31). Thus, although later schemes of functional representation ignored Cole's radical prescriptions they did share common diagnoses of the malaise of parliamentary democracy.

The Webbs shared the concern that unless the parliamentary system was reformed it would become increasingly incapable of providing effective economic management. The appearance of 'big government' in the last decades of the nineteenth century had also led to the appearance of 'big business and big unionism' (Beer 1975:xvi) in politically organised form. By the 1920s, therefore, the position now taken as axiomatic by modern pluralist analysts was already apparent:

> In short, the real government of Great Britain is nowadays carried on, not in the House of Commons at all, nor even in the Cabinet, but in private conferences between Ministers, with their principal officials, and the representatives of the persons affected by any proposed legislation or by any action on the part of the administration. (Webb and Webb 1920:69)

For the Webbs the solution in a socialist society would be to enhance the position of parliament. They maintained that the legimating and socialising capacity of representative institutions could not be surpassed by any other mode of representation. Thus, despite its manifest faults, parliamentarism provided for the participation of citizens in decision-making and the attendant legitimisation of the decision-making process itself. Hence, one of the key sentences in the *Constitution* is:

> The very fact that all the people affected by the institution of the community in which they live can alter these institutions if a majority of them concur has, in itself, a great psychological influence in obtaining general acquiescence. (Webb and Webb 1920:92)

What was needed, therefore, was 'more democracy', further channels of representation to supplement existing parliamentary representation. In repudiation of Guild Socialist ideas, however, the Webbs both rejected the demise of parliament as an institution and the principle of functional representation. Instead, they advocated two co-equal and independent representative assemblies: a 'political' and a 'social' parliament. The latter was to acquire, in the absence of the market mechanism in a socialist commonwealth, the economic task of allocating resources as well as the social task of determining their distribution.

Although rejecting the principle of functional representation the Webbs nonetheless conceived of the internal organisation of the Social Parliament along functional lines (Webb and Webb 1920:117-121). Operating through standing committees, following the model of local government, members of the Social Parliament were to be assisted by national boards whose own memberships would be constituted along vocational lines and whose responsibilities would cover specific functional departments. In this way it was assumed that the Boards would promote the highest efficiency in each functional policy area, and to prompt them in this direction each standing committee was to employ specialist staff to monitor their activities.

Two main considerations thus influenced the Webbs' proposals for reform: the pursuit of efficient policy-making and the sustenance of parliamentarism. 'They attempted to show', as Smith (1979:9) observes, 'that efficiency and democracy were not incompatible goals'. Significantly in the Webbs dyarchy the representational bases of the 'efficient' and the 'democratic' elements of the state reflected the fundamental divide between functional and territorial representation. The main executive agencies of the state – the boards – were to be based upon functional organisation; whereas both of the coequal parliaments were to be based upon 'general' principles of territorial/individualistic representation. The inherent problem here, as with all subsequent and more explicit schemes of functional representation, is whether the 'efficient' element within the state would ultimately challenge the legitimating element.

In a sense this problem could be sidestepped by the Webbs as their scheme was a design for a future socialist commonwealth: a system based upon a basic communion of interest with no class divide at the heart of the production process and no fundamental antagonism within the state system itself. Other schemes, not based upon the premise that the 'capitalist system .... has demonstrably broken down' (Webb an Webb 1920:xxxvii), have been more sensitive to the representational relationship between parliament and functional organisations.

Reconciling Parliamentarism with Functional Representation?
Early 1920s
Writing in 1923 Herman Finer published, through the Fabian Society, *Representative Government and a Parliament of Industry*. The main part of the book examined the work of the German Federal Economic Council in order 'to help towards a better perception of our own problems and towards their solution' (Finer 1923:34). Following Cole and the Webbs, Finer located the problem of parliamentarism within the context of the increased scope and technical complexity of policy-making in the twentieth century industrial state. The consequences for parliament were two-fold: first, parliamentary representation, based upon territorial principles, had failed to ensure that decision-makers had 'due acquaintance with the interests of the nation' (1923:7); and, second, the rise of organised interests and their gradual incorporation into the administrative system had undermined the authority of parliament as a representative institution:

> we have seen in this and other countries the gradual rise of institutions and ideas commendable perhaps from the standpoint of good government, but not so commendable upon the old and pure assumptions of representative democracy. (Finer 1923:12)

If the diagnosis is much the same as that of Cole and the Webbs, i.e. the incapacity of a miscellaneous representative assembly to discharge the modern interventions required in the late capitalist state, the prescription is significantly different. It is also more attuned to later calls for the institutionalisation of a functional element within the parliamentary system.

Problems within the British state were clearly visible and held 'all the portents of dissensions and violence in the state' (Finer 1923:230). What was needed was 'good sense'. And 'good sense' and 'communal sense' could be promoted through the creation of an English (sic) Economic Council based on the German model. Indeed, Finer pointed to an institutional model indigenous to Britain, the National Industrial Conference (NIC), which had been convened at the height of industrial unrest in 1919. Although established as a mechanism for averting crisis, Finer (1923:32) maintained that the stark realities of the industrial system in Britain called for a similar, permanent body, 'something in the nature of an Industrial Parliament'. Hence, he proposed an Economic Council composed of employers and employees, in parity, with minority representation for consumer and local authority interests. In addition he advocated the inclusion of a limited number of technocrats used 'to the handling and the objective analysis of sociological and economic argument' (Finer 1923:216).

The contradiction at the heart of the relationship between functional and parliamentary modes of representation is subsumed away by Finer. There 'would be no division of authority' within the state as parliament would remain the locus of sovereign power. The Economic Council would 'advise', 'scrutinise' and 'carefully comment' on policy, drawing upon its 'representative and expert character' (1923:217); *but*, and it is a vitally important qualification,

> In all of these activities it resolves what the nation *ought* to do, but to the political parliament is reserved the power to say what the nation *shall* do. (Finer 1923:219)

Advice of the Economic Council would thus not detract from the 'sole and indivisible responsibility' of the House of Commons. This might be the case in theory but it asserts away the whole contradiction in practice between the bases of 'authority' and 'legitimation' of functional and parliamentary representation. The initial problematic is simply defined out of existence in the stipulation of a *fusion* of functional and parliamentary modes; and thus their essentially *contradictory* nature is denied (see Judge 1981:31-2).

Early 1930s
Economic decline became a palpable fact of British economic life in the early 1930s. Hobsbawn (1969:207) graphically summarises the impact of the depression:

The sun, which, as every schoolboy knew, never set on British territory and British trade, went down below the horizon.

In the resultant economic gloom, politicians and industrial interests alike searched the horizon for shafts of inspiration. Whilst inspiration eventually came in divergent forms, the analysis of the problem often started from convergent premises. Significantly, economic failure was invariably ascribed to political causes. Ironically, the proposed remedies separated many politicians, the 'practitioners' referred to above, from industrial and financial interests. Amongst the former there was strong advocacy of the case for greater institutionalisation of corporatist representation within the parliamentary system. Many representatives of industry, however, argued the reverse – the abandonment of those corporatist forms which had been tentatively reestablished in the late 1920s.

Amongst the politicians, Winston Churchill, given his status within the Conservative party, attracted most attention for his call for the creation of an Economic Sub-Parliament. Initially his schema was proposed during the course of his Romanes lecture at Oxford University in 1930 (Churchill 1930), and then elaborated in his evidence to the Procedure Committee in 1931 (HC 161 1931). His underpinning premise was that parliament had 'shown itself incapable of dealing with .... fundamental and imperative economic need' (Churchill 1930:15) and there was thus 'grave doubt .... whether institutions based on adult suffrage could possibly arrive at the right decisions upon the intricate propositions of modern business and finance' (1930:9). Churchill based his argument upon a fundamental separation of the economic and political dimensions of the liberal democratic state and in so doing drew upon the constitutional orthodoxy derived from the seventeenth century settlement noted in chapter 1. Yet he exaggerated this separation arguing that the major issues confronting the British state since 1918 had been economic and not political, and that 'the nation is not interested in politics, it is interested in economics' (Churchill 1930:7). However, when the nation 'turn[ed] to parliament asking for guidance', although voluble in so many matters, parliament was 'on this one paramount topic dumb' (1930:7).

If the House of Commons, and the executive therein, was thus unsuited to the effective management of the economy then the solution for Churchill was to 'build another storey upon them [traditional representative institutions] equally well-proportioned, symmetrical and unified' (1930:12). This was to take the form of an Economic Sub-Parliament, to consist of some 120 members: 40 MPs with experience of economic matters, and 80 representatives drawn from both sides of industry or who were themselves 'economic authorities'. The envisaged remit of this body was essentially advisory and deliberative, with all bills dealing with trade and industry referred to it after they had been given a second reading in the Commons (Butt

1969:139). This certainly would be an innovation, with the Economic Sub-Parliament 'debating day after day with fearless detachment from public opinion all the most disputed questions of finance and trade, and reaching conclusions by voting' but in Churchill's (1930:16) view it would be 'an innovation easily to be embraced by our flexible constitutional system'.

Whilst Churchill (1930:12) saw no reason why 'the new system should be at variance with the old', given his assertion that parliament's sovereignty would not be questioned in the new arrangement, there are manifest problems as to how functional representation could be reconciled with individualistic bases of representation. In fact, several contradictions are inherent within Churchill's schema, not the least of which is the ability of a 'political' parliament – based upon territorial/individualistic principles of representation with representatives pledged to reflect the diversity of public opinion on the miscellany of public policy – controlling or reversing the 'advice' of a functionally constituted sub-parliament based upon expertise and reflecting the industrial power of its own representatives (for others see Butt 1969:139; Smith 1979:19-21; Judge 1979:103-4).

Exactly the same contradiction is to be found in other contemporary proposals made by Percy (1931) and Macmillan (1933). Indeed, the latter provided, in the opinion of Carpenter (1976:11), 'one of the most comprehensive corporatist models produced in [Britain]'. If anything, given the emphases upon *executive* government, the 'sovereign' position of parliament would have been even harder to sustain in these schemes. Yet, in proposing respectively the creation of a Ministry of Economic Development alongside a new functionally-based 'deliberative body' (Percy 1931:61), or a Central Economic Council dominated by industrial interests (Macmillan 1933), these bodies move beyond being merely advisory and become endowed with 'executive authority' (Carpenter 1976:11). In which case the existing bases of parliamentary representation would be undermined still further.

Ultimately more damning than the internal logical inconsistencies of these functional schemes was the simple fact that the very industrial interests to be incorporated in the new institutional order either saw no need for institutional innovation (see Birch 1964:113), or were opposed to 'the pursuit of consensus policy at national level through [existing] corporatist structures' (Booth 1982:213).

Late 1970s through the 1980s.
What links the earlier periods with the Thatcher years for Booth (1982) is that corporatism has been rejected as a technique of economic management at times of international economic downturn and domestic unemployment crises. Booth's analysis is important because it helps to explain *why* the corporatist

structures developed in the post-war period were marginalised or abandoned by the Thatcher governments. Where it is less informative, however, is in *how* the anti-corporatist campaign was waged.

The residualisation of corporatist structures in fact predated the election of the Thatcher government. Despite its public support of tripartite structures the Labour government after 1976 reluctantly pursued economic policies incompatible with a corporatist consensus (see Coates 1980). That it did so was a reflection of the gap that had opened up between the perceived interests of major sections of British capital (and for that matter of organised labour and significant sections of the electorate) and state policy. Financial capital, represented through the City, was openly supportive by the mid-1970s of monetarist policies deemed incompatible with the corporatist design (see Booth 1982:213-4; Hyman 1986:95-6). Similarly, significant sections of industrial capital voiced opposition to corporatist intermediation and began to demonstrate an 'abrasive .... anti-corporatist bias' (Hyman 1986:90). Undoubtedly, one factor prompting this repudiation was an 'anxiety about where corporatism and tripartism could lead as the pressures of Britain's poor economic performance grew' (MacInnes 1987:94). Indeed, by the end of 1980 the CBI, which as late as 1978 supported the idea of a tripartite Economic Forum, had been forced by 'grass roots' pressure to move decisively away from tripartism. For those industrial sectors under severe competitive pressure 'the impact of depression is felt inevitably and unfolds too rapidly to make tripartite negotiation at all useful' (Booth 1982:215). Moreover, organised labour's ambivalent attitude to corporatist developments manifested in its traditional predilection for voluntarism (see Hyman 1986; MacInnes 1987), in combination with its own structural weakness at the end of the 1970s, ensured only tokenistic defence of the tripartite structures of the preceding social-democratic era.

If it is apparent why corporatist developments were put into reverse after 1979, simply because they were no longer needed for the purposes of economic management, it remains to be seen how this retreat was conducted.

In essence the retreat was effected through restructuring the state, reasserting the traditional principles of the liberal polity, and undermining corporatist institutional structures. As Jessop et al (1988:175) comment, 'Thatcherism has been exceptionally adroit in circumventing, riding out and and abolishing the social democratic apparatuses of intervention and representation'. Few remnants of tripartite structures remain at the core of the central state in Britain. Indeed, the ease with which corporatist representational structures were undermined brings into question the conceptual bases of the 'dual crisis of the state' thesis and the notion of the contradictory unity of corporatist and parliamentary modes of representation. Indeed, so profound has the challenge to corporatism been that even the strongest proponent of the 'dual crisis' thesis has been led to conclude that the 'dual crisis' of the state is 'now perhaps over' (Jessop et al 1988:177). The significant point for the present discussion is that the 'contradictory unity' identified in Jessop's earlier works has been resolved through the reassertion by the Thatcher governments of the primacy of parliamentarism over that corporatism.

The revival of liberal political economy within the Conservative party under the leadership of Mrs Thatcher brought into question not only the nature of the economy but also its relationship with the state itself. In New Right philosophy (see King 1987; Gamble 1988) the very politicisation of the economy in the post-war era was at the root of Britain's economic and industrial malaise. Infringements of the market order were viewed as endemic to the social democratic state and as such the solution rested in the creation of a new political order to break the old Keynesian economic framework. One constant theme throughout the Thatcher years has thus been a strategic attack upon the institutional form of the social democratic state.

The liberal critique of the social democratic state, and particularly the role accorded to organised labour, was apparent in the earliest statement of aims set out by Mrs Thatcher upon assuming control of the Conservative party. *The Right Approach* (1986) whilst acknowledging the legitimate role of trade unions in the process of policy consultation trenchantly maintained that:

> But the trade unions are *not* the government of the country. .... It is Parliament, and no other body, which is elected to run the affairs of the country in the best interests of all the people.

This argument found reflection in the party's 1979 manifesto. Under the heading *The Supremacy of Parliament* it was noted that parliament had been weakened in two ways:

> First, outside groups have been allowed to usurp some of its democratic functions. .... Second, the traditional role of our legislature has suffered badly from the growth of government over the last quarter of a century.(1979:23)

Following from this diagnosis came the pledge that 'We will see that Parliament and no other body stands at the centre of the nation's life and decisions'. This pledge was echoed four years later in the party's 1983 election manifesto. Using the same heading as in 1979 the manifesto announced:

> The British Constitution has outlasted most of the alternatives which have been offered as replacements. It is because we stand firm for the supremacy of Parliament that we are determined to keep its rules and procedures in good repair. (1983:34)

Once more, one of the major tasks confronting the next Conservative government was identified as upholding parliamentary democracy and strengthening the rule of law. The specific enactments designed to secure this objective are outlined in chapter 5 and more fully elsewhere (see Judge and Dickson 1987:24-6, Grant 1989a:34-5). The point of importance here, however, is that the reassertion of the political principle of parliamentary sovereignty was clearly designed to rectify economic disjunctions. The 'illegitimacy' of corporatist representation and its malignant economic consequences was consciously counterposed by the legitimacy of parliamentary representation and its benign effects upon the liberal economy. In the government's view:

> The ability of the economy to change and adapt was hampered by the combination of corporatism and powerful unions. Corporatism limited competition and the birth of new firms whilst, at the same time, encouraging protectionism and restrictions designed to help existing firms. (Cm 278 1988:1).

A break with corporatist forms of decision-making was thus required and, in the opinion of Lord Young, the former Trade and Industry Secretary, the break has been completed successfully: 'We have rejected the TUC; we have rejected the CBI. .... We gave up the corporate state' (*Financial Times*, 9 November 1988).

Whilst both the extent to which the corporate state developed in Britain before 1979 and the extent to which 'corporatist' forms (if bipartism is included in these forms) have actually been supplanted since 1979 are matters of contention, there is no doubt that the fundamental challenge to these arrangements came in the Thatcher governments' commitment to the symbols of representative democracy. The political success of Mrs Thatcher has been to evoke the powerful legitimatory symbolism of parliamentarism to defuse the potency of other modes of representation in the national policy making process. Despite the continuous involvement of organised interests in policy making, and the active encouragement of business involvement in both the formulation and implementation of policy, through such initiatives as TA, UDCs and the latest example of Scottish Enterprise, the government has been successful in obfuscating the importance of such functional representation through emphasising its diffused, 'decentralised' – in its market orientation – and accountable nature.

In practice, however, a neo-liberal state form has not been constructed, organised interests remain inextricably intermeshed in policy communities and consultative arrangements. But these representational forms are encapsulated within the over-arching frame of parliamentary representation. Conservative governments since 1979 have disengaged the state from national corporatist structures, whilst pragmatically retaining myriad functionally-based pluralistic structures. In this 'decoupling' David Held (1989:140) identifies the reinvigoration of the idea of the state as 'a powerful, prestigious and enduring representative of the people or nation' as a major achievement of the Thatcher administrations. The authority of the state has been asserted, or reasserted, in accordance with the liberal democratic tradition of parliamentary sovereignty. In this sense Jessop (1989:175) is probably correct to point to the creation of a general political climate in which a corporatist, interventionist strategy is electorally unpopular and unsustainable. As noted earlier, he has already conceded that 'the dual crisis of the state is now perhaps over'. Under Mrs Thatcher's governments parliamentarism has 'seen off' corporatism. But the other stated objective of the incoming government in 1979, to make parliament 'effective in its job of controlling the executive (*Conservative Manifesto* 1979:23) and to 'increase the authority of Parliament and its power over the executive' (*Right Approach* 1976:43) has been quietly jettisoned. The paradox of the Thatcherite strategy is that it has evolved a 'strong', some would say 'authoritarian' state form, on the basis of the reassertion of the principles of parliamentary government. Only if parliamentary government is taken to entail parliamentary sovereignty in the Diceyean sense, rather than the reality of executive sovereignty (see Griffith 1982) does a paradox unfold. It is the powerful symbolism of representational *form* that the Thatcher governments have evoked, rather than the *substance* of 'parliamentary' government itself.

3 Policy Communities or Adversarial Politics ?

The analysis of modern British government is replete with paradoxes; most of which revolve around the distinction between the *form* and the *substance* of parliamentary government. The *form* of parliamentarism still specifies parliament as the quintessential institution of legitimation within the policy process. The *substance* still describes a process which is executive-centric and enmeshed in 'policy communities' based upon the representation of organised interests. In this process parliament has a residual role at best. Invariably the two are counterposed and, importantly, form and substance have been associated respectively with discrete levels of academic analysis. On the one side micro-analyses tend to reveal a view of the democratic process which is 'to an extensive degree non-partisan and non-parliamentary' (Jordan and Richardson 1987a:28). Whereas, at least one important strand of macro-analysis displays a concern for an overly partisan and adversarial parliamentary system (see Finer 1975, Walkland 1983). In examining the contrasting perspectives of industrial policy-making provided at these distinct levels of analysis, this chapter seeks to place 'disaggregated' sectoral studies within the context of the systemic analysis developed thus far in chapters 1 and 2. Only if form and substance, and micro- and macro-levels of analysis, are considered together can parliament's contribution to policy-making on industrial matters be appreciated fully.

Policy Communities

The very time at which the concept 'policy community' has become the new descriptive orthodoxy of the policy-making process in Britain has also witnessed the semantic wrangling once so characteristic of the academic debate over the meaning of corporatism. If there is agreement that 'policy community' is an essential component of analysis, there is disagreement as to the exact nature and definition of the term. Without becoming too embroiled in these linguistic convolutions it can be stated that there is a basic division about both the intellectual origins and the actual definition of the concepts of networks and communities.

Intellectual Antecedents

Grant Jordan (1990) in reviewing the wider literature on policy networks, subgovernments and communities locates the analytical roots of the concept in America in the writings of Griffiths (1939), Freeman (1955), and Ripley and Franklin (1976) amongst others. In stark contrast with constitutionalist approaches, and their preoccupation with formal institutions, the subsystems/subgovernment approaches focused attention upon the interactions of organised groups, governmental agencies and congressional committees. The descriptive heart of these accounts was policy sectorisation or segmentation and a disaggregated process of policy-making. In the words of Truman (1971:xix) this provided a more accurate account of 'how the system actually operated'. Similarly, when the British political science tradition moved beyond a formalistic concern with institutions, proponents of a pluralist approach came to describe the British policy process in terms of disaggregation and subgovernments. As Jordan (1990) notes, description came first and recognition of the American intellectual roots followed later. With hindsight he acknowledges the conceptual 'lack of novelty' of the British literature on policy communities.

In contrast Rhodes, as one of the leading British proponents of network analysis, bases his work not on American political science sources but upon European sociology and its contribution to interorganisational analysis. This allows his, and other British contributions to be located within neo-pluralist theory and a distinctively non-American tradition (see Rhodes 1988:94; Dunleavy and O'Leary 1987:306-9).

Contested Meanings

Fortunately, conceptual genealogy is not the primary focus of concern here, and so the debate about antecedents can be short-circuited by stating simply that there is a distinct British tradition in the analysis of policy communities. Even Jordan concedes that the recognition of American intellectual antecedents was post-dated, and came after the initial analytical studies had been completed in Britain. In which case the substantive issue revolves around the meanings of 'policy community' and 'policy network' found in the British literature. On this issue there is a fundamental divide between those who see policy community as one type of policy network and those who believe that community does not necessarily mean network. Essentially this divide distills into a debate between Wilks and Wright (1987; Wright 1988), who subscribe to the latter view, and other British commentators such as Jordan and Richardson (1982; Jordan 1990) and Rhodes (1988) who subscribe to the former view.

For Wilks and Wright (1987:296) 'community is not the same as network'. Members of a community share a common interest or identity. The common interest derives from the 'public policy issues and problems which arise or may arise for their community' (Wright 1988:606). Members 'transact' in an attempt 'to balance and optimise their mutual relationships'. A policy network, on the other hand, is the linking process by which 'some members of one or more policy communities interact in a structure of dependent relationships' (Wright 1988:606). Not all communities generate policy networks, and some networks may draw together discrete policy communities within the same, or even different, policy areas. The value of this distinction in the analysis of industrial policy is that it affords for Wright (1988:611) description, classification and comparison between industrial sectors and between countries. The variety of policy systems at sectoral and sub-sectoral levels of industry can thus be revealed and explanations provided 'of what actually happens' (Wright 1988:611).

If nothing else, other British analysts of policy communities and networks share a common concern with Wilks and Wright to describe 'what actually happens'. The difference arises in the latter's 'reconstruction' (Wilks and Wright 1987:295) of these concepts. In 'unpacking' the concepts to foster micro-level analysis Wilks and Wright have been criticised for *redefining* them and so confusing and obfuscating 'a "traditional" language [with] its own rationale' (Jordan 1990). In this 'traditional' language a policy community is 'a special type of *stable* network which has advantages in encouraging bargaining in policy resolution' (Jordan 1990). The effective sharing of attitudes on a policy problem engenders a policy community, and a policy network is constituted through 'a statement of shared interests in a policy problem' (Jordan 1990). What differentiates community from network in this formulation is 'stability'. A stable policy community has a regularity and permanence to its interactions which has important ramifications for the style of policy-making. This differentiation is implicit within Rhodes (1988:78) statement that:

> policy communities are networks characterised by stability of relationships, continuity of a highly restrictive membership, vertical interdependence based upon shared delivery responsibilities and insulation from other networks and invariably from the general public (including Parliament).

The very stability of relationships influences the process of policy-making itself. Bargaining; consensus, based upon shared understandings of the nature of a problem; dependency, in the form of the exchange of information and professional expertise; and compromise are the internal characteristics of the process. In turn these characteristics stem from the 'Balkanisation' (Self 1976:293) of the policy process. 'Sectorisation' (Jordan and Richardson 1982:82) becomes an essential ingredient in the development of policy communities, with communities organised around individual government departments and their client groups. In this compartmentalisation consensus within communities is facilitated through the exclusion of groups and political institutions 'outside' of its own specialist professional or ideological norms. Ultimately, therefore, the process of policy-making comes to be conceived of as 'a series of vertical compartments or segments – each segment inhabited by a different set of organised groups and generally impenetrable by "unrecognised groups" or by the general public' (Richardson and Jordan 1979:174). The term 'bureaucratic accommodation' has come to typify the 'normal' policy style in Britain. This term defines a system in which the 'prominent actors are groups and government departments and the mode is bargaining rather than imposition' (Jordan and Richardson 1982:81).

Parliamentary Democracy and Policy Communities

As an analytical proposition, the idea of policy communities clearly provides a good fit with the available empirical evidence on how decisions are made in British government. The existence of such policy communities does, however, raise some worrying problems for normative democratic theory. (Grant 1989a:31)

Indeed, it has already been noted above that Jordan and Richardson (1987a:28) and Rhodes (1988:78) identify a process of decision making which is essentially 'non parliamentary'. Jordan and Richardson repeatedly point out that there is 'little opportunity for participation by Parliament', that the agenda of the group-government world is not that of Parliament' (1987b:7), and 'an important factor in the decline of the House of Commons .... is the "leakage" of power to the myriad of policy communities surrounding the executive' (1982:102). Their description of the segmentation of policy-making and the development of policy communities residualises the involvement of the legislature and leads them to conclude that 'the traditional model of cabinet and party government is a travesty of reality' (Richardson and Jordan 1979:191). In successive studies they found it increasingly difficult to reconcile the 'empirical world of government-group relations' (Jordan and Richardson 1987b:287-8) with the prescriptions of the British liberal democratic constitution. Indeed, so profound was their scepticism of accepted notions of parliamentary representation that they found it hard to answer the question 'of whether the House contributes more to the policy process or to the tourist trade' (Jordan and Richardson 1987a:57).

Throughout their work, therefore, Jordan and Richardson contrast the 'clear-cut and traditional principles of parliamentary and party government' (Richardson and Jordan 1979:74), 'traditional notions of democracy, accountability and parliamentary sovereignty' (Jordan and Richardson 1987b:288), and 'traditional notions of parliamentary and electoral democracy' (Jordan and Richardson 1987b:289) with the reality and practice of group politics in Britain. In making this contrast a recurring theme in their writings has been the 'devalued status' of the British House of Commons (Richardson and Jordan 1979:133; Jordan and Richardson 1982:102; 1987a:57). Despite acknowledging that the 'gap between constitutional principles and political practice is long established' (1987a:56), nonetheless, they do not attempt to formulate a view of representative democracy beyond 'the story-book' version (1987a:58). In setting the practice of groups against the theory of parliamentary democracy Richardson and Jordan characterise the British system of government as 'post-parliamentary'. Indeed, for over a decade this characterisation has been largely unchallenged and has found reflection in other important commentaries (see for example Marquand 1988:182-6).

Recently, however, a critique of the notion of 'post-parliamentary' democracy has begun to be constructed (see Judge 1990) and is in the process of elaboration (see Judge 1992). This critique is multi-stranded entailing analysis of both the theory and the practice of parliamentary representation alongside the theory and practice of group representation.

At the level of 'theory' Richardson and Jordan focus upon an idealised and uni-dimensional version of parliamentary representation and perhaps inevitably, and certainly not surprisingly, find that reality does not correspond to the ideal liberal vision of the constitution. Yet, in essence, this paradox is an artificial contrivance and one that arises out of the conflation of liberal theories of representation with a Diceyean view of liberal government (see Judge 1990:19-25). Of more significance to present concerns, however, is the theoretical connections between parliamentary and group representation.

Whereas Richardson and Jordan and others involved in the micro-analysis of policy communities conceive of a policy process which is private, specialised, incremental and invariably 'closed' to parliamentary participation, and hence 'non-parliamentary', this vision minimises the symbolic and legitimating functions of parliamentary representation. And it does so by deemphasising a prerequisite of pluralist 'theory': namely the very existence of electoral/ representative institutions themselves. Certainly, Richardson and Jordan are aware of the legitimating functions of parliament, but in their painstaking analyses of the practice of pressure groups they accord little emphasis to these functions. In so doing, the macro-theory within which their micro-studies are grounded is not fully explicated, with the consequence that the tenets of representative and pluralist democracy appear to be counterposed. But, as argued elsewhere (Judge 1990:28-31), the pluralist process in itself is incapable of legitimising the policies stemming from policy communities. To understand the operation of these communities also needs a recognition of the wider system of political ideas within which they operate. Stated at its simplest: the existence of representative institutions is a prerequisite of the group system. Thus, as Dunleavy and O'Leary (1987:25) observe: 'If representative institutions are not a *sufficient* condition for the existence of genuine liberal democracy, they are none the less recognised as *necessary* conditions'. Robert Dahl (1956:136) as one of the leading pluralist 'theorists' (though he would deny the title of 'theorist' himself) acknowledges the need within a pluralist system for 'a more or less representative body to legitimize basic decisions by some form of assent – however ritualized'. Another major pluralist theorist, David Truman (1951:515-6), argues that:

> To assert that the organization and activity of powerful interest groups constitutes a threat to representative government without measuring their reaction to and effects upon the widespread potential groups ['rules of the game'] is to generalize from insufficient data and from an incomplete conception of the political process.

An adequate conception of policy-making thus requires the activities of policy communities to be located within the broader framework of representative government. To conclude that the legislature's substantive contribution to law-making is limited, even peripheral in the case of detailed formulation and implementation, does not mean that parliament is peripheral to the process of policy-making itself. To use the language of systems theory, it is insufficient merely to consider policy outputs in the light of initial demands – to decide which groups successfully advanced their preferred policy proposals – what also needs to be considered are the 'supports' which enable demands to be processed and outputs to be implemented. Of particular importance is the concept of 'diffuse support', that is support constituted by 'generalized attachment to political objects .... not conditioned upon specific returns at any moment' (Easton 1966:272-3). The difficulty in substantiating this statement is that 'diffuse support' is a nebulous and under-researched concept in the study of legislatures (see Judge 1992). Nonetheless, even advocates of the concept of a 'post-parliamentary system' concede that this system has been legitimised in the language of parliamentary representation itself (Marquand 1988:185); though this in turn gives rise to the concern, noted above, about the discrepancies between liberal language and the character of late twentieth century British government. All that is being suggested here, however, is that the discrepancies arise because functional representation – in this case through a pluralist process – is incapable of legitimising its own outputs. Only the enshrinement of the elective principle in the House of Commons 'provides the absolutely indispensable legitimation for the government of the country' (Miliband 1982:48). If this is the case then the very process of 'bureaucratic accommodation' is predicated upon a pregiven 'political accommodation'. This is not to deny that in practice group representation is *the* potent force in policy-making, but simply to point out that the legitimacy of this system derives from the wider 'authorisation' of elected representatives. At a conceptual level, therefore, policy-making in policy communities cannot be disaggregated from parliamentary representation. In this way the 'normal' style of policy-making identified by Richardson and Jordan is *structurally constrained* by the parliamentary system.

General and Specific Constraints upon Communities

To argue that 'bureaucratic accommodation' is dependent ultimately upon the 'authorisation' of elected representatives is not to state that parliament is routinely or actively involved in detailed policy discussions. Instead, it simply means that parliament impinges upon policy communities in the general sense of delimiting the independence of any single community, and in injecting into the closed world of Whitehall a general requirement to consider broader partisan/parliamentary/public concerns – even if only in the limited sense of seeking to anticipate or to forestall possible future public criticism in parliament.

The independence of any policy community, and hence the general centrifugal tendencies of sectorisation, is constrained by the formal requirement of the political executive to answer collectively to parliament. The coordination of policies invoked in the principle of ministerial responsibility and in the practice of interdepartmental and cabinet committees is a formal expectation in British government. Even though this expectation is frequently disappointed it remains true to state that:

> sub-governments .... in Britain, lack the cohesion and authority of the American. We can attribute their lack of authority to the fact that, despite the diffusion of power that has occurred in recent years, the cabinet-parliamentary system still creates a focal point for power in the cabinet. Because the cabinet-parliamentary system still accords an important coordinative role to cabinet, the independence of sub-governments in .... Britain is less certain and more variable than it is in the United States. (Pross 1986:241)

In addition to the expectation that the cabinet should preside over a coordinated process of policy-making, there is also a requirement that intra-departmental decision-making should be coordinated and responsible to political direction. Individual civil servants are constrained in their negotiations with interest representatives by the knowledge that the result of those deliberations must be compatible with other departmental policies and also capable of defence if necessary by a minister before parliament. In this sense, British higher civil servants are trained to act as 'quasi-politicians', to work within the policy confines of the 'minister's mind' (Sissons 1966:13). They have to be aware of the parliamentary/ political ramifications of those decisions made in the name of the minister. Whilst the boundaries of ministerial thinking might be transgressed in practice, the scope for transgression is limited by the fear that significant divergence from ministerial wishes would leave the civil servant exposed to direct parliamentary criticism without the conventional support of a minister. Thus, although it is conventional to dismiss the convention of ministerial responsibility as part of the mythology of British government, it still acts as part of the 'critical morality' (see Marshall 1984) of the constitution, a morality imbued in the psyche of politicians and bureaucrats alike, and one which provides criteria of assessment of political behaviour at any given time. More particularly, it prescribes that parliament should be the judge of that behaviour.

So if the core of policy-making is policy communities comprised of government departments and institutionalised interest groups it is surrounded, encompassed and ultimately delimited by the legitimating frame of the parliamentary system itself. To use Pross' (1986:103) instructive phrase, 'hovering on the edge of .... sub-government is parliament'. From this position parliament can interject wider concerns into and, when called upon to do so, articulate 'communitaire' concerns beyond the closed world of sub-government. How and why parliament is capable of becoming involved in community matters will be examined shortly. For the moment, however, what needs to be examined is the extent of the development of policy communities within the field of industrial policy-making in Britain and the degree to which they characterise the 'normal' style of policy-making.

The Dynamics of Policy Communities

Jordan and Richardson (1982:81) identified a set of '*standard* operating procedures' based upon bargaining, rather than imposition, between the 'prominent actors' of government departments and groups. These procedures were held to constitute the 'normal' policy style. And so compelling was this style that they concluded that the 'logic of negotiation is difficult to escape' (1982:108). Yet, in reaching this conclusion they also noted three important modifications to the 'normal' policy style and a further three types of issues 'not suited to the standard operating procedures' (1982:100). Moreover, there was a general recognition that the growing complexity of policy-making led sometimes to the deemphasis of 'the image of order and compromise implied in the term "policy community"' (1982:100).

What has become clear in subsequent studies of industrial policy-making is the absence of a 'standard' policy style. The composition, interactions and very stability of 'policy communities' varies not only amongst industrial sectors but also within industrial sectors over time. This picture of fluidity and uncertainty in government-industry relations becomes more apparent as more empirical evidence is accumulated.

Sponsorship Divisions
'Bureaucratic accommodation', as noted above, entails competitive sectorisation within central government, with departments locked into regular consultative and exchange relationships of a clientelistic character with organised groups. Indeed, Jordan and Richardson (1982:83-4) conceive of a process whereby departments and their 'client' groups coordinate their activities in order to 'sell' consensual community policy to other departments. For much of the post-war period, as Grant (1987:42; 1989a:58: 1989b:88) describes, just such a clientelistic relationship was apparent in various government departments, most especially successive industry departments, with their sponsorship divisions representing the interests of particular industries within central government. The sponsorship divisions acted as a conduit between government and industry providing a two-way flow of information into and out of Whitehall. This dual role was neatly summarised by the Department of Industry itself:

> The basic aim of sponsorship is to help the industries to be successful, and to this end to ensure that in the formulation of policies by government .... the particular interests of the industries sponsored are identified in consultation with them; and that these policies so far as possible support and promote those interests. Conversely Industry Divisions seek to ensure that their industries understand the reasons for and the implications of Government policy. (HC 367 1980:55)

Indeed, in the 1970s the 'guiding bureaucratic philosophy' of the Department of Trade and Industry (DTI) in its various forms 'held as a core value that the department should do its best, for its industrial clients' (Grant 1989b:89). Throughout that decade sponsorship divisions developed a 'proactive' relationship with their respective industries, with divisions acting in many instances as internal lobbyists for the industry concerned (see Grant et al 1988:77). Hence, the linkage of industry to central departments through sponsorship divisions apparently conformed in that period to the picture of 'bureaucratic accommodation' sketched by Jordan and Richardson in the early 1980s.

At the time, though, there were doubts about the significance of the sponsorship function. The very duality of the role of sponsorship divisions, facing inwards and outwards at the same time, raised fears within Whitehall that they were simply the mouthpieces of industry, and within industry that they were simply the apologists of government (see Englefield 1984:127). One academic assessment of the sponsorship of the motor industry in the 1970s found that the concept at best 'proves an elusive idea' and at worst is 'to some extent a pretence' (Wilks 1984:193-4). Even in a period of government commitment to intervention, sponsorship was seen to be just a 'passive, best-endeavour sort of relationship, ...involv[ing] no planning and little policy-implementation capability' (Wilks 1984:193-4).

Sponsorship and the Thatcher Governments
If there were doubts about the practical utility of sponsorship divisions before 1979, the return of a Conservative government, one which denied the need for an 'industrial strategy' and sought the disengagement of government from industry, raised fundamental questions about the theoretical justification of sponsorship divisions. Sponsorship divisions were clearly part of the interventionist inheritance and fitted uneasily with the rhetoric of successive Conservative industry ministers about the free market and entrepreneurial endeavour. Yet it was not until 1988 that these vestiges of the interventionist tradition were finally abolished (see Grant 1989b:90-3). In between time the sponsorship divisions responded to the new political context by adopting a more reactive role than in the 1970s.

This change was indicative in itself of a broader redirection of industrial policy (see chapter 5). Companies were expected to look after themselves, to make their own decisions and to be less dependent upon government direction. This message was apparent to manufacturing industry long before the sponsorship divisions were disbanded within the DTI in 1988 (see chapter 6). The routine circuits developed for the purposes of information transmission between divisions and their 'client' companies and trade associations were now more subject to political 'noise' and disruption. The value of sponsorship divisions, their role within the DTI and within government generally, was clearly seen by industrialists to have been undermined by the Thatcher government. This perception was highlighted in Grant et al's (1988) interviews with those involved in the chemical industry. One industrialist observed that: 'The sponsoring department concept has been substantially weakened in recent years .... there is no specialisation now, they are trying to keep a relationship with many industries and failing' (Grant et al 1988:78-9).

In 1988, in recasting the image of the DTI as the 'Department of Enterprise' the Secretary of State, Lord Young, emphasised that: 'It is in nobody's interests for the DTI to be an uncritical spokesman in Whitehall for business interests' (Cm 278 1988:39). The message that 'industry is responsible for its own destiny' had as its corollary that sponsorship 'can give the impression of "responsibility" for particular sectors of industry' (Cm 278 1988:38). On these grounds sponsorship divisions were replaced by market divisions within the DTI. Market divisions were designed to deal with broad policy issues in a particular market rather than dealing with particular industries (Cm 278 1988:39). The linkage between the DTI and industry was now to be at the level of individual companies rather than trade associations. And Lord Young (*Financial Times* 16 January 1988) made no attempt to hide his distaste of trade associations which 'produc[ed] mutual dependency between sectors and sponsoring civil servants'. Significantly, this criticism struck at the very stability and clientelistic form held by Jordan and Richardson to be the characteristic style of British policy-making. Thus, in the case of the DTI the organisational embodiment of 'bureaucratic accommodation' was subject to question throughout the 1980s, and ultimately rejected in 1988 with the abolition of sponsorship divisions.

Instability in Industrial Policy Communities and the Thatcher Governments
The change of direction in industrial policy after 1979 not only impacted upon the organisational structure of the DTI but also destablised many existing group-government relations. This process is revealed in several of the studies carried out under the auspices of the ESRC government-industry initiative (see Wilks and Wright 1987). In the chemical industry, for instance, Grant et al (1988:78-82) record, in addition to the comments noted above, the general perception of a distancing in the relationship between government and industrial groups. Indeed, even more illuminating is that Grant et al (1988:58) in describing the core chemical policy community place the emphasis upon 'inter-firm relations *within* the industry, rather than in partnership with government'. They also note that in comparison with the German core chemical community the British one is less well defined and less tightly knit (1988:70). Indeed, several of their respondents commented upon the fluidity of the 'rules of the game' pertaining to government-industry relations in the chemical sector. One interviewee concluded that 'many people would deny that they even exist', another was unsure whether they were meaningful as 'different individuals have different rules' (Grant et al 1988:63). The significance of these comments for the discussion of policy communities is that Rhodes (1988:92-2) specifies 'conventional' (though certainly not immutable) rules of the game which limit discretionary behaviour in policy communities.

The foundry sector in Britain is found by Appleby and Bessant to have a fragmented policy community. In this sector 'the behaviour of the industry is essentially the sum of many individualistic actors, lacking coordination, and the ability to speak with one voice' (Appleby and Bessant 1987:186). This does not prevent close links being established between industry and government, with DTI officials developing a deep appreciation of the industry's problems (Appleby and Bessant 1987:200). But, significantly, there is no 'standard' policy style across the foundry industry as a whole. In effect, therefore, implementation and the impact of interventionist policies cannot be assessed on an industry-wide basis. Instead, Appleby and Bessant (1987:207) point to the necessity of adopting a 'more fine-grained level of analysis' which in turn reveals that the links between government and the industry 'tend to be particularized and that the effects of policy intervention will be inconsistent between sectors'. Importantly, these inconsistencies are located within the context of the non-interventionist predilections of the Thatcher governments as the policy towards the foundry industry in the 1980s moved 'from self-help to no help from government in restructuring the industry' (Appleby and Bessant 1987:201).

In the pharmaceutical sector a more clearly defined policy community was apparent and one which 'adhere[d] closely to the characteristic pattern of government-interest group relations described by Richardson and Jordan' (Macmillan and Turner 1987:121). Nonetheless, relations between the pharmaceutical industry and government were subject to considerable stress after 1983 and the announcement in that year of a limited list of prescription medicines within the National Health Service. Unlike the period before 1983, when such a policy had been excluded 'out of deference to the combined political influence of the pharmaceutical industry and the BMA' (Macmillan and Turner 1987:127), the announcement was made without prior consultation with these influential groups and precipitated a refusal on the part of the Association of the British Pharmaceutical Industry (ABPI) and the BMA to consult with the DHSS. Far from exhibiting the consensual, consultative and exchange relationships characteristic of a policy community the announcement of the limited list created such antagonism that Macmillan and Turner (1987:128) concluded that to describe the reaction as 'a political furore would be an understatement'. What is important to note here is that this furore was engendered from the unilateral pursuit of government objectives – in this instance the control of expenditure in the health service. Relations in the pharmaceutical policy community were thus dislocated by government policy deemed by the industry itself to be 'hostile'.

Other established policy communities have also witnessed the propensity of the Thatcher government to act unilaterally. Notable disturbances within settled sectoral communities have been occasioned by the pursuit of the privatisation programme since 1979. Whilst, as a general rule, the process of privatisation revealed extensive bargaining between affected groups and departments (see Richardson 1990:26-7), nevertheless, certain issues 'escaped' the closed world of bureaucratic accommodation and placed themselves firmly on the public and parliamentary agenda. Two of the clearest examples involved resistance within nationalised industries to piecemeal privatisation. British Gas, for instance, maintained fierce opposition in the first Thatcher parliament to the sale of the corporation's oilfield at Wytch Farm in Dorset and to its offshore oifields, as well as opposing the privatisation of its showrooms. Far from reflecting a consensual and negotiated process the government ultimately was forced to issue a directive instructing the chairman of British Gas, Sir Denis Rooke, to sell the corporation's holdings in its various oilfields. 'The tenaciousness of his rearguard action .... the Corporation's propaganda campaign, and threats of strike action by the unions, scared the government's backbenchers to such effect that plans for forced disposal were pigeonholed [until after the 1983 election]' (Bruce-Gardyne 1984:82). It is significant for the present argument that Bruce-Gardyne, as a Treasury minister at the time, should record parliamentary reaction to the fissures within the policy community occasioned by the unilateral action of the Energy department. Moreover, when the announcement of the privatisation of the corporation was made in May 1985:

> It came as most leaks do, as a somewhat unpleasant surprise to the gasmen. Senior British Gas officials had no hint of anything in the air, before they read last weekend of the plans for privatising their industry .... 'We honestly thought [plans for the sell-off] were dead and buried' one senior gas official admitted. (*Sunday Times* 5 May 1985)

Similarly, John Lister as Chairman of British Shipbuiders revealed the lack of consultation between his company and the DTI over the issue of the piecemeal sale of BS's yards. *The Times* (15 June 1988) recorded his 'bitter attack on the government's privatisation strategy for BS and its approach to domestic shipbuilding'. It is of some significance that this attack was advanced within Westminster whilst Lister presented evidence to the Select Committee on Trade and Industry. The issue 'escaped' from the closed world of Whitehall into the parliamentary domain.

Bringing Parliament Back In
Conflict, imposed policy, and ideological conviction; rather than bargaining, consensus, and compromise, have thus come to characterise government-industry relations in some sectors in recent years. This reflects a more general turbulence in the group-government world. Indeed, Richardson (1990a:22) now acknowledges the conscious challenge of Conservative governments over the past decade to the 'power of existing policy communities, and especially the power of groups within those communities'. Conflict within communities has been 'self-induced' as 'basically, the Government had decided that policy change was necessary and realised that change would challenge existing fiefdoms' (Richardson 1990:26). In adopting a confrontational style on certain policy issues the government has effectively breached the established 'rules of the game' – particularly with regard to

mutual advantage (see Wilks and Wright 1987:305). Likewise, groups within these policy areas have responded by broadening the breach – particularly with regard to confidentiality. Increasingly, they have sought to air their policy grievances in public and actively to involve parliament and parliamentarians in the dispute. Significantly, two of the most influential groups identified by Jordan and Richardson (1987a:173) in their respective communities – teachers and doctors – that is groups which 'really mattered' and possessed the 'ability to exercise some kind of veto', have found themselves in the central lobby of the House of Commons and in its committee rooms precisely because of their failure to veto policies (see Judge 1990:34-5). In these circumstances parliament became the focus of group attention. Groups attempted to influence parliamentary opinion through letter writing campaigns, petitions and mass lobbies to parliament. Traditionally these have been the tactics of the politically 'dispossessed'!

None of this should be taken to mean that the process of consultation/ negotiation within policy communities has been displaced into more public forums. 'Bureaucratic accommodation' still perhaps best typifies the process of policy-making, but in a myriad of differing styles within different sectors and communities. All that is being suggested here is that there has been a greater propensity for issues to 'exit' closed communities and to be 'voiced' in the parliamentary arena in the last decade, and that this is a consequence of 'elements of the "strong state" hav[ing] crept into government-group relations in Britain, alongside more traditional group politics' (Richardson 1990:26).

A good example of this phenomenon, taken from the literature on policy communities, is the imposition of the limited list of medicines introduced into the NHS. Macmillan and Turner's (1987) study of this episode reveals that once the decision had been taken unilaterally by ministers then the ABPI and the DHSS 'conducted a tug-of-war .... for the hearts and minds of MPs':

> Receptions were held, briefing papers distributed, refutations and counter-refutations issued and backbenchers implored lobby ministers [*sic*] to withdraw the plan. .... Affected companies typically contacted MPs whose constituencies were likely to be affected or who were known to be sympathetic ....[there were] trade union delegations to parliament on behalf of the work forces of beleaguered companies ....Letters to GPs enjoined doctors to write to MPs and to encourage patients to do the same. (Macmillan and Turner 1987:128-9)

Ultimately, the department successfully defused Conservative backbencher's opposition by a series of tactical concessions (Macmillan and Turner 1987:128). And, if anything, the ABPI's campaign, alongside that of individual companies, was counterproductive in many respects; succeeding in alienating many Conservative MPs and in 'adversely affecting the working relations between ABPI and DHSS at official level' (Macmillan and Turner 1987:131).

Even in those established consensual policy communities which have not been subject to the turbulence of ideological impositions, groups will often operate a 'dual strategy' of simultaneously working with departments and maintaining channels of communication with parliament. As one leading political consultant, Charles Miller (1987), notes, successful groups will operate 'globally' out of an awareness that decisions are rarely single-faceted, or the result of departmental-group consultation alone.

Routinely, groups are active when legislation affects their interests. For example, the Parliamentary Adviser of the Chemical Industries Association held considerable numbers of briefing sessions and attended every debate and committee meeting on the Animals (Scientific Procedures) Bill 1986 – a bill of considerable significance for the development and testing of chemicals (see Grant et al 1988:82-3). But, not only is parliament of value in retrieving details lost at the formulation stage of legislation, it is also of significance in assessing the implementation of existing policy and so of raising issues onto the agenda for future consideration within 'closed' communities. This point is made convincingly by Pross (1986:259) in his statement that 'policy implementation [and parliament's overseeing of that process] .... is often part of the "next round" of policy development'. This argument is of particular relevance to the consideration of the role of select committees in the House of Commons and will be returned to in detail in chapter 7.

More generally, however, parliament may be targeted in an attempt to generate or maintain a climate of opinion sympathetic to a group's aims. Indeed, such 'climate setting' activities have become increasingly apparent in recent parliaments (see chapter 8; Jordan 1989; Grantham 1989). The importance of such activity is that parliament serves to articulate dissonent concerns beyond the immediate consensual priorities of those encapsulated within a policy community. In so doing parliament remains 'marginal' to the community itself, as Grant et al (1988:83) point out with regard to the chemicals community, but nonetheless remains capable of injecting into the community broader issues for consideration. In the case of the chemical industry for instance environmental issues have become of increased salience to the industry in recent years. In the new era of 'green' politics Grant et al (1988:99) are led to concede that, although they had identified a peripheral role for parliament in relation to the chemical industry, 'this is likely to change in the future .... as environmental questions occupy a more central place on the political agenda and require more frequent legislative action'.

Back In? Never Out?
This chapter started by outlining the fundamental paradox of modern British

government: the tension between the *form* and *substance* of parliamentary government. In terms of industrial policy-making this paradox is apparent insofar as parliament is both of paramount importance for the legitimisation of the outputs of policy communities but is often, simultaneously, peripheral to much of the daily business of those communities. In the first case, parliament is an essential ingredient of what Wright (1988:599) terms the 'behaviourial norms' of the political system, and what Hayward (1986:19) calls 'enduring norms' or 'prescriptive values'. These norms and values are essential to the authentication of conduct (Hayward 1986:19), and provide the 'general contours of policy' (Wright 1988:599), but they neither equate with day-to-day behaviour nor provide the detail of policy. Such systemic behavioural norms encompass in Britain 'ideals or aspirations such as government by consent, sovereignty of parliament, parliamentary privilege .... ministerial responsibility and a non-political, independent and permanent bureaucracy' (Wright 1988:600). That these norms are essentially prescriptive does not lessen their capacity to overwhelm competing paradigms (as seen in relation to corporatism in the preceding chapter), nor to challenge existing styles of policy-making which governments may deem to obstruct the advance of their own policy objectives. The Thatcher governments have legitimised their attack upon 'vested interests' – whether these be trade unions, professional interests or sub-national governmental institutions – through the invocation of 'parliamentary sovereignty' (see Conservative Manifesto 1979:23-4; 1983:34; Bogdanor 1989:134).

The legitimatory potency of the values incorporated within the concept of 'parliamentary sovereignty' has been obvious over the past decade. In this sense there has never been a need to bring parliament 'back into' the study of policy communities. It has always been an integral part of the general normative system required to sustain the particular outputs of policy communities. The argument here, however, is that in addition to this general normative significance parliament has become involved in the consideration of some industrial issues, which before 1979 might normally have been resolved within the closed world of policy communities. In other words there has been increased 'leakage' of manufacturing issues into the chamber and corridors of Westminster.

As later chapters will reveal the Thatcherite commitment to break the post-war legacy of interventionist industrial policies, irrespective of its actual success in this endeavour, has had a profoundly destablising effect in many manufacturing sectors and in the traditional styles of policy-making within those sectors. In these circumstances Richardson (1990:21), as one of the key proponents of the concept of 'post-parliamentary democracy', has come to acknowledge that 'parliament may have been somewhat underrated in pressure group studies' as more issues have suddenly exited the bureaucratic arena and 'achieved greater political salience and, hence, parliamentary involvement'.

Out of the Policy Community Frying Pan into the Adversarial Politics Fire?

Whilst the concept 'policy community' has gained widespread acceptance in the analysis of industrial policy-making in Britain in the 1980s still its descriptive accuracy has not gone unchallenged. Certainly in the first half of the 1980s much attention was focused upon the adversarial politics thesis and the potential of an adversary system to produce marked discontinuities in policy-making. In stark contrast to the incremental process characteristic of policy communities, the adversarial politics thesis saw only 'notorious policy switches between and within every Parliament which makes the British political environment so much a curse to the business community' (Brittan 1983:262). Indeed, Sir Geoffrey Chandler (1984:3), a former director of the NEDC, whilst ruminating upon Britain's manufacturing decline, maintained that: 'the adversarial nature of politics has damagingly infected the .... institutions of industry and the whole national debate, so preventing what should be an attainable consensus at least within industry itself'. Similarly, a committee established by the Hansard Society to investigate government-industry relations concluded in 1979 that 'the practice of adversary politics is deeply embedded in British constitutional convention .... this practice is now producing increasingly pernicious effects so far as industry is concerned' (Hansard Society 1979:56). Some eight years later the chairman of Rolls Royce, Sir Francis Tombs, reiterated this point:

> The principal difficulty which the country has experienced post-war, and which may lie in the future, is the governmental system we enjoy, which has great advantages but is also adversarial. The two principal parties tend to contradict whatever has happened in the previous administration, to go back, almost as a matter of principle, on many changes made. That imposes tremendous uncertainty on industry. It makes it very difficult to plan, very difficult to have confidence. The most crying need is for common agreement between the parties on the need for wealth creation before wealth spending. (Quoted in Heller 1987:127)

Such simple observations upon the effects of adversarial competition conceal, however, complex issues of causality and responsibility for industrial malaise. In order to disentangle these complex linkages it is advisable to outline briefly the essence of the adversarial politics thesis – or more accurately theses. There are in fact a variety of strands which, although interconnected in practice, can be separated for analytical purposes.

The first strand concerns itself with the political effects of an adversarial system: with the process of party competition in an essentially duopolistic legislature; the polarisation of political discourse; and its impact upon the group system and the policy expectations of the electorate. The second, related, strand deals with the policy effects of this system: with the problems of policy discontinuity stemming from the fragmentation of policy consensus and the apparently exponential capacity for policy 'overload'. There are of course several variations upon these policy themes. Andrew Gamble (in Gamble and Walkland 1984:27) provides a particularly novel one in his argument that it is not only the discontinuities of policy which are harmful but equally the continuities themselves: 'An adversary style of politics concentrates debate and party competition around a few issues, while policy in many other areas is relatively neglected'. This point will be examined below and is of particular significance in that it makes the linkage with the policy community model. In the meantime, as background to the consideration of the implications for industrial policy, it is advisable to sketch the political dimensions of the adversary politics thesis.

One malignant feature of adversary politics in the eyes of its critics has been the emphasis placed upon short-term vote maximisation by British political parties. Governments, on the one side, are accused of operating 'political-business cycles', whereby votes are 'bought' by engineering pre-election booms in the economy (see Alt and Chrystal 1983:103-25; Dunleavy and O'Leary 1987:100-2; King 1987:92-3). On the other side, opposition parties are forced to bid for votes by promising policies which are qualitatively and quantitatively in excess of those on offer by the government. In this process of competitive bidding 'the logic is to promise anything which you think will bring you votes without regard for the mutual compatibility of your promises or their long-run consequences for the country' (Beer 1982:16). One significant vote-maximising strategy appears to be to detach group support from an opposing political party by offering specific and advantageous policy inducements to members of organised interests (see Brittan 1977,1983; Beer 1982; Hoover and Plant 1989:64-6). The growth of government, the rise of interest group politics, the increase in popular expectations of government, and the development of a political-business cycle thus appear inextricably linked in the adversary politics thesis. Importantly, for New Right theorists this development is inherently malignant.

Most empirical analyses of the political consequences of the adversary politics thesis have tended to refute the bases of the model (see below). However, this has not prevented the Thatcher governments from invoking the spectre of elements of the model, most notably public choice and political business cycle arguments, to challenge the style of politics inherited from its predecessors. Even though the Thatcher governments have targeted the political malignancy of the adversarial system the actual extent to which the bases of electoral competition has been changed is open to question. What 'evidence' there is appears to be contradictory. Dearlove and Saunders (1984:53-4) maintain for instance that:

the Conservatives won the election of 1979 with a specific commitment *not* to manage the economy on the basis of short-run considerations alone, and they won again in 1983 *without* creating a mini boom and with over 3 million unemployed which surely confounds a thesis which suggests that economic good times are the major route to electoral success.

In contrast, Sanders et al (1987:281), writing about the same period, argue that 'by our account the renewed popularity enjoyed by the Thatcher Government from the spring of 1982 onwards was the result largely of intelligent (or, perhaps, cynical or even fortuitous) macro-economic management'. Similarly, cynical interpretations of the 1986 autumn financial statement are not hard to find. David Smith (1987:128) states for example: 'In November 1986, with eyes firmly on the forthcoming general election .... Nigel Lawson became convinced of the virtues of public spending .... It was electioneering, and of a more blatant kind than Sir Geoffrey Howe had embarked upon in 1983'.

Equally the extent to which the process of party competition has been insulated from group pressure in the last decade remains an open question. Hoover and Plant (1989:66), for example, identify the 1983 Labour party's manifesto as the zenith of the process of party bidding for group support. It consisted, in the eyes of its critics at least, of 'little more than a list of promises to a coalition of interest groups without any great thought about how the range of promises hung together and the overall coherence of the programme'. The Conservative party itself has been ambivalent in bidding for group support. As seen above, it has prided itself in its resolute promotion of policies in the face of 'lobby-led demand for more resources' (Kenneth Clarke, *The Independent* 28 July 1989). The application of free market principles has been promoted despite the potential loss of support from many producer interests. Mrs Thatcher has been a keen publicist of her government's attacks on 'vested interests' (see Grant 1989a:154). In practice, however, the Thatcher governments have not been averse to courting consumer groups for electoral gain. The most blatant example is the continued financial benefits provided by the state to owner-occupiers (see Gamble 1989:358). But concessions have also been offered by the government to environmental groups, partly as a result of party competition for the 'green vote' (see Murie 1989:222).

Policy Consequences of Adversary Politics
Industry does not like political uncertainty. Investment decisions and production schedules within industry extend far beyond the immediate time horizons of politicians looking to the next election. Sir Austin Pearce, then chairman of British Aerospace, made this point forcibly in a radio interview:

> When you recognise that the life of a government is, say, four or five years and you recognise that it takes about eight years to develop an aircraft and actually get it flying, and then you expect it to have a twenty-five year life, there's a total inconsistency of time here. (Quoted in Heller 1987:28)

In one sense, therefore, there is a structural mismatch between the time-scales of decision-makers within manufacturing industry and those in government. Yet at the heart of the adversarial politics thesis is the belief that this inherent mismatch is exacerbated by the uncertainty generated by frequent policy reversals effected by successive, and ideologically opposed, governments. The essence of Finer's (1975:3) argument, an argument which reawakened debate about the adversarial system in the mid-1970s, was that the 'stand-up fight between two adversaries for the favour of the lookers-on' was detrimental to effective policy-making. At its simplest, therefore, the adversarial system exaggerates discontinuities in policy over time according to the extent of polarisation between the two contestants (Finer 1975:14; 1980:208). If the ideological distance between the major parties is slight, as in the period commonly caricatured as the post-war consensus, then the effects of adversarial competition upon policy-making are not necessarily harmful. What worried Finer and other proponents of this thesis (Johnson 1977; Walkland 1983) was that from the mid-1960s the major parties had been captured by their respective extremists and that the resultant polarisation was 'inimical to the good conduct of the nation's affairs' (Finer 1975:12).

In addition to the detrimental political consequences of this polarisation proponents of the adversarial thesis pointed to the policy consequences of 'repeated extreme alterations in government policy' and the 'premature abandonment of measures that call for a non-partisan, long-term approach' (Coombes 1982:116). From Coombes' statement it is clear that there is an underpinning belief that a 'correct' – i.e. long-term and consensual – approach exists and that this approach is frustrated by the 'ideological' and hence 'unsound' policies of the major parties (see Gamble and Walkland 1984:25). It is this conflation of the continuity of policy with ideologically driven policy which complicates the adversary politics thesis.

If the thesis was solely concerned with discontinuity then the problem would be reduced, and possibly removed, by a lengthy period of single party government stemming from a dominant party system. In such circumstances there would be no drastic change in policy from one parliament to the next, and, correspondingly, no period of 'manifesto madness' as an incoming government sought to dismantle the policies of its predecessor. Certainly, the very longevity of the Conservative government has challenged the central tenet of rapidly alternating 'extremist' parties; for, even if it is argued that 'extremist monopoly' has come to characterise the post-1979 period, the consequences are not the same as under a system of 'extremist duopoly'. But this begs the question of whether such rapid reversals and rereversals necessarily accompanied a change in the partisan composition of government in the first place. Clearly, advocates of the adversarial politics thesis maintained that it did (Finer 1975:16-7; Walkland 1983:51; Coombes 1982:116-7), but a host of subsequent studies have demonstrated that in most policy areas the process of policy-making did not reveal consistent patterns of policy discontinuity. Rose (1984:xxix) has found that in economic policy: 'the direction of the British economy is primarily influenced by the long-term secular trends independent of party and not by the movement of parties in and out of office'. Gamble (Gamble and Walkland 1984:35) echoes this assessment in his observation that in foreign economic policy it is the continuity of policy that is striking. In stabilisation policy he finds that 'the evidence for continuity is rather more plain than the evidence for discontinuity'. Nor does Cox's (1984:85) historical survey of land-use planning reveal an unambiguous picture of adversarial politics. Similarly, Moran's study (1984:39) of banking competition and credit control concludes that adversary politics cannot make sense of the important policy changes in this sector.

There is one policy area, however, which constitutes a major exception to this general lack of substantiation of the thesis, and this is *industrial policy*. As Gamble (Gamble and Walkland 1984:36) puts it: 'It is in the field of industrial policy that the adversary politics thesis comes into its own'. But even here he notes that the pattern of policy development is more complex than a crude version of the adversarial politics thesis would indicate. Nonetheless, an adversarial process is identified in the crucial issue areas of industrial relations law, nationalisation/privatisation, and industrial planning. This finding is reinforced by Coombes (1982:117) in his observation that an examination of industry/government relations highlights the range of aborted policies and the number of 'short-lived experiments with institutions and powers'.

Industrial policy in the 1970s certainly appeared to epitomise an adversarial process. In the course of this decade industrial relations legislation was enacted and abolished, industrial 'strategies' came and went, and preliminary skirmishes were conducted over the size of the state's holdings in industry as Conservative and Labour governments alternated in office. The 1980s manifestly were different. The continuous electoral success of the Conservative party refocused the initial analytical concern of the adversary politics thesis – the detrimental effects of policy discontinuities occasioned by a change of party in government – upon the pursuit of 'doctrinal' policies by a dominant party. What had started as a theory concerned with party competition became a theory concerned with the effects of party monopoly.

Thus, Ingle (1987:202), in making the statement that 'from the perspective of the late 1980s, the balance of argument may be judged to weigh in favour of the adversarians', bases his conclusion upon the fact that 'parties do make a difference' both to the nature of legislation and to the expectations of other actors in the policy process. But his primary focus in reaching this conclusion is upon the 'ideologically based, manifesto-led' policies of the Conservative party. The concern of political analysts in the 1970s, with policy reversal, features only marginally in Ingle's subsequent discussion. By the early 1990s a new party consensus, stemming from a decade of Thatcherite government, had been identified by some commentators (see Hughes and Wintour 1990; Crewe 1990). The extent of possible policy reversal by an incoming government is now more of an an open question than a decade before. One strand of this debate holds that in this period there has been a 'rapid, massive and continuing shift to the right taken by the opposition parties' (Crewe 1990:5). Another strand takes the specific case of the Labour party and maintains that: '[it] has now revised its policies to fit the new mood and the new approach to issues which the Conservative government has initiated' (Peele 1990:144).

Linked to the perceived deradicalisation of Labour party policy and its causes is the changed relationship between industrial producer groups and the main political parties. Here again the adversarial politics thesis has to be reformulated to make sense in the 1990s. In 1983 Walkland made the case for a 'new and permanent political context' (in contrast to the instability associated with the adversarial process) 'to which the powerful economic interests would have to adjust'. In particular he pointed to the failure of the two-party system in 'relating the unions to public purposes' and argued that as realists the unions, and for that matter the CBI, would have to 'accommodate to a political framework in which the abandonment of policy for electoral gain would no longer feature so prominently'. The same logic is apparent in Chandler's (1984:9) observation:

> The policy swings from government to government have been increased rather than diminished by industry's chief institutions, the CBI and TUC. Each has lent weight to party political views rather than slowing the pendulum by using its unrivalled experience of industry as a counterweight to dogma. Under Labour Governments the trade union movement has sought legislation to strengthen its own position regardless of the impact on industrial success and regardless of management response. Under Conservatives the CBI has done likewise.

According to Chandler (1984:8), this problem could be averted if industrial groups 'recognised that their common interests are greater than their differences' and that conflicts can be resolved without recourse to the respective political parties. The belief that the solution is to be found in consensus is shared by Walkland (1983:50) who argues that 'public purposes' rather than sectional or partisan purposes will only be pursued by industrial groups when the 'ideological indulgences of Labour and Tory' are moderated.

Yet the pursuit of 'public purposes' by organised industrial groups in the 1980s was conditioned, and indeed the very notion of 'public purpose' was defined, by the 'ideological indulgences' of a single party – the Conservative party (or more accurately neo-liberal elements within the party). In these changed circumstances certainly there has been greater acknowledgement of the issues which unite both sides of industry, but largely in the defensive and negative sense of trying to sustain remnants of social democratic interventionist policies and institutions (such as regional policy and the NEDC) from attack from government (see Judge and Dickson 1987:23-4). Equally producer groups from both sides of industry have had to accommodate themselves to the government's definition of the 'public purpose' rather than defining this purpose for their own advantage. Thus the trade union movement has been led to reconsider its political and social roles. The 'new realism' of the post-1983 era has led 'individual unions .... to modify both their political and industrial strategies and to negotiate new forms of collective agreements which fitted the requirements of the "Thatcher Revolution"' (Taylor 1989:155). In tandem the CBI has had to accommodate its own policy preferences to those of the government. Although Gamble (1988:217) argues that the government received the full support of the CBI for its reshaping of the policy agenda, in practice this 'support' has often only been tokenistic and grudgingly given. In particular, the CBI has been persistent in its public criticism of the high exchange and interest rate policies pursued since 1979. Indeed, in 1980 the CBI's chairman advocated a 'bare knuckle fight' with the government over this issue. Even though receiving an early and severe bruising in this fight, and subsequently moderating its tone, the CBI, nevertheless, continued to record its opposition to key elements of macro-economic policy at its annual conferences. One thing is clear, however, and that is that the past decade has perceptibly weakened the political linkages between respective industrial producer groups and parties and the policy influence of the former over the latter.

'Doctrinal Policy' and Elective Dictatorship

If the experience of the Thatcher governments has undermined several of the central tenets of the adversarial politics thesis, particularly policy discontinuity resulting from the changed party complexion of government and the partisan 'infection' of producer groups, then can the thesis be sustained in the early 1990s? The answer, in short, is: only with significant amendment.

To sustain the adversarial thesis requires a reformulation of the analysis away from duopolistic party competition towards party monopoly of office. In which case the problem is not the two-party system as such but the pursuit of 'ideological' programmes by the respective parties in office. According to Wilks (1984:36) in these circumstances 'it might, therefore be more appropriate to refer to "doctrinal policy" rather than "adversarial politics"'. Yet what links the two is the institutional structure which sustains and perpetuates the form of party competition or the substance of policy outputs. The connection is made through a Diceyean view of the constitution – of unfettered parliamentary sovereignty – with the majority party in government empowered to make or unmake any policy it so desires. That this view rapidly degenerates into the practice of elective dictatorship has been noted repeatedly in the era of ideological polarisation in Britain (see Hailsham 1978; Bogdanor 1989). The simultaneous election of a parliament and a government enables the latter to exercise sovereign power in the name of the former. Parliament in this political formulation is both all important and at the same time equally and routinely peripheral to the adversarial process. It is all important as the source of legitimation for governmental actions. As noted above, successive Conservative manifestoes have supported the constitutional orthodoxy of parliamentary sovereignty and ministers have frequently invoked the principle in defence of their policies. Thus, as Bogdanor (1989:137) comments: 'To criticisms that the government's actions strain the limits of the constitution, ministers reply that Britain is a unitary state in which Parliament enjoys the power to alter political relationships as and when it pleases'.

But just as parliamentary representation is used to justify a monopolistic process of governmental decision-making, and so to sustain that very process; equally the institutionalisation of adversary procedure within the House of Commons itself negates constructive opposition. Ironically, therefore, the paradox identified in the examination of policy communities – of the paramountcy of the parliamentary system and the apparent impotence of parliament in the policy process – reemerges in the adversarial politics thesis.

Thus, on the one side, the parliamentary system, and specifically the nature of the British electoral process, is blamed for what Walkland (Gamble and Walkland 1984:92) calls 'dysfunctional politics'. This argument holds that the parliamentary system has 'frustrated the development and implementation of positive industrial strategies over the time-scale necessary to produce substantial results' (Gamble and Walkland 1984:92). If the system of elections generates uncertainty then the logic of the adversarial theory is to change the electoral system. A system of proportional representation would by this logic make the present defects disappear, or become less obnoxious (Finer 1980:208). Needless to say, this view has been fiercely contested (see Judge 1981, 1983b; Norton 1982).

On the other side, however, the contribution of parliament as an institution (as opposed to parliamentarism as a *system* of government) to the process of policy-making is largely discounted. For Johnson (1977:75) 'the adversary mode erodes and weakens the instruments for the control of government'. This is because unless parliament as an institution can perceive itself as distinct from the government and opposition then 'there is the certainty that much of the activity of Parliament will be reduced to the level of an elaborate charade' (Johnson 1977:75). Similarly, Walkland (Gamble and Walkland 1984:168) criticises the adversarial procedures of the Commons, particularly debate on the floor of the House, which have become 'infantile' in character and serve to reduce parliamentary discourse merely to 'charge and countercharge, accusation and rebuttal'. The cumulative impact of ideologically polarised party competition and adversarial procedures upon parliament is that they are 'inexorably destroying the political vitality of Parliament itself' (Johnson 1977:61). In sum, the characteristic features of adversarial politics in the House – 'constant petty squabbles; the mindless negation of government through excessive (and purely partisan and irresponsible) opposition; the oversimplification of complex issues into two (and only two) contrasting alternatives; and the grand clash and confrontation of the cult of debate' (Dearlove and Saunders 1984:48-9) – diminish the potential positive contribution of the Commons to the making and scrutiny of policy. Whilst the House is conducting open warfare over the ideological principles of policy, industrialists and organised industrial interests have to look elsewhere for the satisfaction of their pragmatic and consensual policy requests. 'Elsewhere' in Britain has increasingly come to mean Whitehall. In these circumstances policy is the result of 'compromises which .... ministers hammer out in private .... with outside interests in their Whitehall offices' (Finer 1975:14). And these private negotiations have as their corollary the reduction of the House's role to that of 'a pianola playing out jaded tunes that have been recorded elsewhere' (Finer 1975:14). This conclusion takes the present discussion full-circle – back to the consideration of policy communities!

Policy Communities and Adversarial Politics

For all that the writings on policy communities and adversarial politics are largely discrete with few cross-references there are, nonetheless, certain commonalities. Both seek to describe what actually happens in the making of policy. And, although the respective starting points of analysis, the underpinning assumptions, and the emphasis placed upon individual elements within the process all differ, eventually a 'mixed' partisan/group process is identified. Importantly for present purposes, each analytical perspective residualises the practical contribution of parliament to the policy process.

What ultimately separates the two perspectives is the legitimacy and efficacy of policy made within closed 'communities'. For neo-pluralists, policy communities are essentially benign and beneficial to the political system and its policy outputs. But from the perspective of the adversarial politics thesis one of the malign consequences of adversarial politics is the 'leakage' of decision-making into these closed policy communities. Walkland (Gamble and Walkland 1984:169), in his usual trenchant style, makes the connection between the operation of electoral politics and group politics:

> The operation of [the British] electoral system .... guarantees unrepresentative government, grossly magnifies swings in electoral opinion, exaggerates class and regional divisions, [and] facilitates access to political power of favoured but unrepresentative groups ....

Even critics of the thesis acknowledge that one consequence of adversarial politics has been the concentration of policy-making in the hands of a small number of ministerial, departmental and group participants. In those issue areas beyond the superficial clash of party ideologies there has been a fundamental continuity of policy. Long-term policies in these areas are never properly subjected to parliamentary or public scrutiny and debate. Hence, the adversarial process, whilst generating instability in a few policy areas, provides for an unchallenged and unreflective policy consensus in many other areas. Either case – continuity or discontinuity – is problematic!

Where Are We Now? And Where To From Here?

The answer to the question 'where has this chapter led us?' is, first, to a position which points out the complexity of the policy-making process in Britain. Analyses which attempt to generalise across the range of institutions and breadth of policy fields will invariably provide a balance of inaccurate and accurate conclusions. Analyses of 'policy communities' with their micro-level concerns have been prone to discount the political/'high politics' dimension of policy-making. In contrast the adversarial politics thesis has placed too much emphasis upon an ideological dynamic within the policy process. In practice the relative importance of consensual/ideological factors undoubtedly varies over time and from policy area to policy area, and even within sub-fields within these areas. This is not to argue that generalisations cannot be made about the British policy process, but merely to state the obvious that in doing so the analytical target is, on occasion, as likely to be missed as hit.

Second, this position is not too distant from that presently held by Richardson (1990:30) who, having earlier pronounced the existence of a 'normal' policy style (Jordan and Richardson 1982), now recognises a more 'mixed' policy style:

It is, therefore, increasingly difficult to sustain the relatively simple image of pressure group politics in Britain. Though no doubt accurate for most of the post-war period, the characterisation is now more complex. .... the breakdown of the post-war consensus, ... the particular desires of the post-1979 Conservative governments to introduce significant, and indeed radical, policy change in some hitherto stable policy areas; .... all suggest that we may be witnessing a paradigm shift in the rules of the game for group involvement.

Similarly, the adversarial politics thesis whilst over-stating the role of parties, eventually acknowledges, even if disapprovingly, the contribution of policy communities to policy-making. Once again a 'mixed' policy style is conceded.

But to point to a 'mixed' style of policy-making – entailing both party and group participation – still does not reinstate parliament as a major contributor to the policy process. One thing 'policy community' analysts and adversarial politics theorists are agreed upon is the marginal involvement of the legislature in the detailed process of policy formation and implementation. This general conclusion is not denied here, but, as with all generalisations, it obscures differentials in both involvement and influence across different policy areas and across time. What needs to be examined is the activity of parliament in specific policy areas. Hard data on activity in specific policy areas within parliament is still sparse. The chapters that follow, therefore, seek to provide data on the activity of parliament in the field of industrial policy.

The guiding premise of subsequent chapters is that parliament is neither an irrelevance nor a distraction in the study of the industrial policy. The first three chapters of this book have sought to demonstrate that parliament is of importance in a dual sense. First, at a macro-level, it plays a vital legitimating role (even if unprovable other than through counter factuals). Second, at a micro-level, it has become of more policy salience for industrial groups, partly because of procedural and attitudinal changes internal to the House over the past decade; but largely because of the disruption of the interventionist policy consensus by the Thatcher government itself. This is the hypothesis at least. What now needs to be established is how, to what extent, and for what reasons is parliament as an institution and its individual members concerned with matters of industrial policy.

4 Theories of Representation and the Representation of Industry in the Commons

In the development of representative government in Britain only a limited range of representative theories have been influential; and, of these, the most widely accepted appear simple in outline and are often deceptively simply outlined in basic texts on parliament. Such apparent simplicity, however, obscures the inherent ambiguities, contradictions and empirical implausibility of many of these theories. Yet, there is a tendency merely to describe the theories without entering into a critical analysis of their conceptual bases. In this approach, which is tantamount to an orthodoxy amongst British commentators, the important issues of representation in a late 20th century, industrially declining and socially divided state are obscured. Too often the descriptions of Whig and Liberal theories, of the dichotomies of mandate-independence and interest-opinion, relegate to the sidelines of discussion the contemporary issues of 'legitimacy' and 'regime support' through representation. Hence for example, one of the standard texts on the British parliament dismisses the notion of functional representation as 'alien' and claims: 'in both British political thought and practice, the argument for a socially typical House has never taken root' (Norton 1981:55). The first aim of this chapter, therefore, is to re-examine British theories of representation and in so doing to reinstate the importance of those theories so often summarily dismissed in British texts. The second aim is then to examine the composition of the House of Commons in the light of the theoretical discussion.

Representation as Legitimate Decision-making

If British authors have eschewed the intricacies of representative theories, the same cannot be said of American political scientists. Hanna Pitkin (1967) spends some 300 pages trying to discover the 'real nature' of the concept of representation, admittedly with only limited success. Eulau and Wahlke (1959, 1978) have developed a new orthodoxy on 'representational roles' and spawned an academic industry devoted to the empirical testing of these roles. Furthermore, 'demand-input' models have been derived from systems theory in an attempt to predict the linkage between citizen and representative. In all of these studies representative government is essentially conceived as the process of the transmission of the citizen's opinions and interests to the agencies of decision-making, and the accommodation of these opinions and interests into the outputs of government. In this process, the views of the electorate, however constituted and conceived, are 'made present' without the electorate actively being present in the agencies of decision-making. This accords with Pitkin's (1967:89) definition that 'representation, taken generally, means the making present *in some sense* of something which is nevertheless *not* present literally or in fact' (original emphasis).

The emphasis upon decision-making and normative theory of how decisions ought to be made in representative government has, however, conflicted with empirical data on how decisions are made in practice (see Eulau and Wahlke 1978:75). Yet, empirical dismantling of the linkages between elector and representative does not in itself mark a 'crisis' of representative government or the movement towards 'post-parliamentary politics'. Instead, as Wahlke (1971:19) has argued, such findings should redirect our attention to the role of representation in maintaining what functionalists and systems theorists call 'support'. Such public support for the representative system within the demand-input model has been seen to derive from 'specific satisfactions obtained from the system with respect to a demand that [is made]' (Easton 1966:268); or more broadly may constitute a 'generalised attachment to political objectives .... not conditioned upon specific returns at any moment' (Easton 1966:272-3). S. H. Beer (1971:310), in his examination of the British political system conducted some twenty years ago, maintained that parliament's main task was 'certainly not the representative function by which in greater or lesser degree the legislature brings the grievances and wishes of the people to bear upon policy-making'; instead it was that of 'mobilising consent'.

In following the direction set by Wahlke and Beer, what needs to be analysed here are those elements of representative theory which serve to 'support' the political system and which identify the outputs of that system not only as 'public' – and hence the domain of public policy – but also as legitimate and authoritative policies. This analysis is perhaps made easier if the component parts of the following discussion are abstracted and examined separately and sequentially. These elements are: authority; citizenship; 'specific' interest; and 'national' interest.

The nature of political authority in representative theory is limited. The very fact that power is conditional, that elections are periodic and that the tenure of the representative is dependent upon his responsiveness to his electors (even if only in the limited sense of being told when to go), reinforces a belief in the fragmentation of authority and also that no single person or institution is in perpetuity all powerful. Representation, therefore, highlights the partial nature of political authority; in the sense that a part of the polity – whether an individual, a party, or an institution – temporarily exercises power (Kateb 1981: 360). It also acknowledges a societal division of labour whereby the mass of the population is excluded from directly contributing to decision-making; and where differentiation within society on class, ethnic, racial, gender or other lines is reflected in the representative institutions, whether institutionalised into parties or not. In this sense, a part of society, whether simply in terms of the number of representatives, or more specifically in terms of partisan control of the legislature, claims to act for the wider society. In the party sense, the existence of ideological alternatives amongst competitive parties means that struggles against those 'in authority' and in control of the legislature can be defined as challenges to the present incumbents of elected office. Hence, opposition to an elected government can be accepted as a challenge to one possible right answer (advanced by the particular set of office holders at any specific time) and not as a challenge to an absolute right answer nor to the system itself (Kateb 1981:360-1). Indeed, several recent analyses of British political culture support this contention. Thus Dennis Kavanagh (1986:48), whilst acknowledging the existence of 'many indicators of public dissatisfaction with politicians, institutions, and policies', finds no indication of 'out-and-out rejection of the political system' in Britain. A similar verdict is reached by Richard Rose (1989:144):

> When the public is asked to evaluate government by elected representatives, 94 per cent support it as very good or fairly good .... The idea of a revolution overthrowing representative parliamentary institutions is inconceivable to the great bulk of English people.

And, as noted earlier, Ralph Miliband (1982:20), from a different perspective, maintains that a representative House of Commons 'provides the absolutely indispensable legitimation for the government of the country'.

A second element of representation of importance in securing allegiance for the political system is the notion of 'citizenship'. As Pitkin (1967:217) states: 'one of the most important features of representative government is its capacity for resolving the conflicting claims of the parts, on the basis of their common interest in the welfare of the whole'. Representative government, therefore, necessarily posits as a minimum requirement that a member of the state has the legal status of citizenship and the legal entitlement to vote. Moreover, there is implicit, here, the idea that a citizen is a member of an association (the state) whose interests are capable of being promoted within the context of that association. A harmony is thus adduced between the individual with specific interests and the state with a collective interest.

The reconciliation of specific and general interests is central to all representative theories, but the mode of reconciliation varies from one theory to the next. Burke, for example, maintained that each sectional interest in each locality had a stake in the national interest merely by being part of the whole. Through deliberation in parliament sectional interests could be articulated; and, armed with this information about all affected interests, representatives could discover, collectively, the national interest. Pitkin (1967:187) summarises this position: 'True interest must be discovered by deliberation, and the discovery of the national interest and of other fixed and permanent interests of the kingdom are simultaneous processes'. Starting from different premises about 'what' is to be represented, J. S. Mill and the earlier utilitarians nonetheless agreed with Burke about the primacy of parliamentary deliberation in ascertaining the national interest. Only through such deliberation will the 'opinion which prevails in the nation make itself manifest as prevailing' (Mill 1861:240). Parliament therefore could no more 'usefully employ itself than in talk, when the subject of talk is the great public interests of the country, and every sentence of it represents the opinion either of some important body of persons in the nation, or of an individual in whom some such body have reposed their confidence' (Mill 1861:240). So, from the fragmentation of objective economic interests (in Burke) and from the diversity of individual opinions (in Mill and Utilitarianism) stems the reconciliation of those parts to the whole through the medium of representative government.

Jeremy Bentham in addressing this issue saw no real problem as the 'national interest [was] nothing more than an aggregate of the several particular interests' (Bentham vol. 9 1843:161). If this was the case then the corollary was that all interests should be represented in the House of Commons. The legislature 'will be the better .... in proportion as its interest is similar to that of the community' (Bentham vol. 2 1843:301). Clearly this was a microcosmic conception of representation. As Birch (1971:55) notes, representatives were thus 'to constitute, in themselves, a microcosm of the nation, so that if (leaving aside their temporary and peculiar interests as politicians) they pursue their personal interests, they will reach decisions which will maximise the happiness of the whole community'. With such extensive representation within the legislature the 'gratification of any sinister desire at the expense of the universal interest' would be frustrated as such sinister interests 'cannot hope to find cooperation and support from any considerable number of his fellow citizens' (Bentham vol.9 1843:100).

At the time Bentham's arguments were a critique of the contemporary representative arrangements, and their significance remains that they provide a critical standard against which any system of representation can be assessed (without necessarily subscribing to utilitarian concepts of the state and individual). The radical implications of Bentham's arguments remain; for, although legislatures are manifestly not microcosms of the nation, the force of his case is that they should be. Thus, for all that Norton is dismissive of the impact of these arguments upon British political thought and practice, Bentham's views continue to have currency.

In reviewing the impact of Benthamite theory on political debate in Britain A. H. Birch (1971:59) is led to conclude, in contradiction of Norton, that 'Benthamite argument contains a kernel of truth that makes it likely to find sympathisers in any society while social divisions are thought to have political significance'. In Britain 'divisions of class and occupation predominate in people's consciousness' (Birch 1971:59), therefore, it is not surprising to find that demands for a more representative legislature have traditionally, though not exclusively, focused upon aligning the composition of the House more closely to the economic forces within the electorate. Underpinning all debate on representation in Britain therefore has been an implicit acceptance that the Commons should 'be the repository of all interests within the state' (Thomas 1939:160). The exact nature of the electorate or of the interests for which the Commons was to be a microcosm has varied. Whether these interests encompassed merely property – as in Burkean theory; or all interests with a respect for property – as in Liberal theory; or class interests – as in collectivist theory; clearly differentiates one theory from the next. But the common assumption is that the House should, for different reasons admittedly, 'make present' economic interests of individuals or of social groups organised around these interests.

Manifestly economic assumptions guided political assumptions over representation (see Macpherson 1973:173). This point has already been made forcefully in chapter 1, but it is worth reiteration in slightly different form here: the theory and practice of representation in Britain has had a significant 'functional' element within it. Far from being 'alien', functional representation (in modified form) guided Burke's view of virtual representation; liberal theory was based upon a view of interest which was essentially economic (see Pitkin 1967:190-203; Macpherson 1977:25-6; Mill 1861:255-6 acknowledges 'class' interests); and the collectivist theory of the Labour party initially was based openly upon securing the direct representation of organised labour in the House of Commons. In a specific sense, therefore, the theory and practice of representation in Britain has implicitly and consistently internalised 'functional' elements within it (see Thomas 1939:31). Indeed, if parliamentary representation is to legitimise the political system based upon the competitive economy, then the various economic elements within the state should be represented. This is the essence of all the theories examined above. How these elements are to be represented, how they are conceived – whether in terms of individuals, groups, classes or geographical constituencies as aggregates of economic interests – clearly differs. But the House of Commons should clearly 'make present' these interests in the formulation of the 'national interest'. In so doing, the legislature will necessarily weight and reorder the priorities of these interests. The process of assessment and restructuring of interests into an aggregate 'national interest', in turn, involves the legislature in representing this new and qualitatively different interest to the electorate and the diverse interests constituted therein. In this way the representative process is a two-way directional flow: representatives in the Commons represent the electorate in the process of government and simultaneously represent the state and its outputs to the electorate. Thus, as Sartori (1968:467) observes: 'Present-day parliaments are Janus-faced: they represent the citizens to the state and the state to the citizen'. It is vital, in these circumstances, that the Commons should be portrayed as the 'repository of all interests within the state'.

Indeed, there is a continuity in the history of the analysis of the socio-economic composition of the House of Commons which implicitly accepts that the legislature should be a microcosm of the wider electorate. Writing in 1955 J. F. S. Ross (1955:199) criticised the composition of the Commons for being 'in many respects extraordinarily lopsided' and stated that 'we want a better balanced House, one more truly representative of the community it exists to serve'. Some years later Colin Mellors (1978:126) identified the 'uncharacteristic' nature of the Commons as a continuing problem and by implication one in need of rectification. More agnostically, Michael Rush (1981:57) states that:

> there is no evidence that parliament or the nation would necessarily be better served by a House of Commons which was a microcosm of the electorate, but it is at least arguable that a House which contained .... a greater variety of occupations, would have the advantage of drawing on a broader and deeper pool of knowledge and experience and would add to rather than detract from parliament's ability to scrutinise the executive.

When the argument is made for a 'more representative' House it is important because 'people believe that the degree to which the Commons is socio-economically representative of the electorate is important' (Rush 1981:53). Whilst it is easy to demonstrate that this belief confuses 'representativeness' with 'representation', for most people this is merely an academic distinction. What is significant is the belief that the legislature would be more responsive to the electorate if the House were representative in a microcosmic sense.

The Representation of Industry in the House of Commons

The job an MP did before entering the House [is] crucial to his parliamentary work. (Labour MP in interview)

This MP clearly believed that the pre-parliamentary occupation of members was vital in ensuring effective decision-making on industrial matters within the House. Effectiveness in this instance is measured by two criteria: the process of decision-making, and the outputs of that process.

The process of decision-making within the Commons has been widely criticised. In the specific context of industrial policy, the Hansard Society (1979:44) found that 'decisions were often taken without the technical know-how required'. The CBI (1987:9) has noted that its members complain 'that too few politicians understand the problems .... They lack experience'. The *Chief Executive* magazine (1986:16) has lamented the information deficiency within the House and its consequences for the process of decision-making: 'Far too few members can .... from practical experience [of industry] point out the dangers of proposed policies'. In all these observations there is the manifest belief, outside of the Commons at least, that the occupational composition of the legislature is of some significance in determining both how industrial policy questions are addressed and, in some indirect sense, how the questions are resolved. Whether this belief is well-founded will be examined in later chapters. For the moment, however, our task is to analyse the extent to which MPs bring into the House industrial experience from their the pre-parliamentary occupations.

Pre-Parliamentary Occupation
The first thing to establish in any analysis of the socio-economic composition of the House of Commons is what constitutes pre-parliamentary occupation. Many diverse strategies have been adopted to deal with this definitional problem (see Thomas 1939,1958; Ross 1948,1955; Mellors 1978; Rush 1981). Most recent surveys, however, utilise a definition of occupation based upon the Registrar General's classification, and one which has been condensed in successive Nuffield Election Studies to produce a four-fold categorisation of professional, business, miscellaneous and manual occupations. On this basis, professional and business occupations have been seen to be predominate the House in the post-war period (see Mellors 1978:58-79). The 1983 House was no exception to this post-war pattern (see Table 4.1). However, such broad classifications of occupation do not discriminate by industrial sector. 'Industry' is merely subsumed within each of the occupational groups. The Industry and Parliament Trust, for example, encountered this problem when it attempted to ascertain the industrial experience of MPs. The Trust resolved the problem by commissioning its own survey of members' occupational backgrounds. The results revealed that, in January 1983, 16 per cent of members had some direct experience of industry, 32 per cent had some indirect experience, and 52 per cent had no experience whatsoever of industry (Industry and Parliament Trust 1986:4). Unfortunately, the survey reveals neither how 'industry' was defined, nor the

depth of members' industrial experience (recording, as it did, simply all MPs who had been employed in industry 'at some time' before they entered the House). It is not mere pedantry, therefore, that requires the specification of how 'industry' is to be defined for the purpose of the following analysis.

Industry

'Industry' is frequently used as a synonym for 'economic activity'. So much so that any form of the provision of goods and services can make a legitimate claim to the title industry (see SIC 1980:2). It is not uncommon, for example, to find references to the 'leisure industry', to the 'retail industry', or, increasingly, to the 'agriculture industry'. The extensiveness of the term 'industry', when treated as a synonym for economic activity, can be gauged from the Standard Industrial Classification with its 10 divisions, 60 classes, 222 groups and 334 activity headings (see SIC 1980). Such a broad classification, however, appears to include everything and exclude nothing.

Hence, a more closely delimited meaning of 'industry' is stipulated here. 'Industry' is defined in terms of the productive and extractive industries (SIC Divisions 1, 2, 3, 4, 5, 7). In this definition the common distinction (see HL 238 1985; ABCC 1985) is made between manufacturing industry (SIC Divisions 2-4) and the service sector (SIC 6, 8, 9). Indeed, the inclusion of the extractive, construction, transport, and telecommunication industries (SIC Divisions 1, 5, 7) along with manufacturing industry, reflects both the interconnection of these industrial sectors and also their importance in terms of economic output and employment. A clear, if necessarily arbitrary, differentiation, thus, is made in the following discussion between 'industry' and the agricultural and service sectors of the economy.

Industrial Experience

Any study of the occupational backgrounds of MPs is confronted by the fact that many members have been employed in several occupations before entering the House. Invariably, analyses of occupation have resolved this problem by recording 'principal occupation' (Rush 1981: 49), 'appropriate occupation' (Ross 1948: 60), or 'formative background' (Mellors 1978: 8). In other words, for the purposes of analysis, each Member is deemed to have been engaged in a single primary occupation. In turn, it is usually acknowledged that such allocations are a 'matter of judgement' (Mellors 1978: 8) and that 'complications arise' (Ross 1948: 60). Nonetheless, the reader is normally assured that significant problems of classification occur only in a minority of cases. Whilst, this might be the case in broadly structured categories of occupation, for a *detailed* analysis of industrial background and experience it would be unproductive to restrict, arbitrarily, the range of each member's prior industrial employment simply to one industrial sector. This is not to deny that many MPs have worked exclusively in one industry – miners provide an obvious example – but, equally, there are many members with experience of several diverse industries. Thus, for example, Terence Davis (Labour, Hodge Hill) worked at various times in the motor, oil and footwear industries. Similarly, Robert Haywood (Conservative, Kingswood) gained industrial experience with Esso, Coca Cola, and GEC before entering the House.

Using standard biographical sources (Roth 1984; Dod 1985; Times Guide 1983; Labour Party 1983; Conservative Party 1983), the length of each member's involvement in each industrial sector before entering the House was recorded. Industrial sector was coded in accordance with SIC divisions, and length of employment was coded in number of years. Where the number of years was not specified for any particular period of employment a missing value was coded. In the following discussion it should be remembered, therefore, that pre-entry experience is a *minimum* level of recorded industrial experience; and one that is subject to the vagaries of the unofficial chronicling of biographical details of British MPs.

Industrial Experience of MPs

It was noted above that there is a general impression in industry that the number of MPs with industrial experience is too low. Interestingly, an assessment of what constitutes an adequate number of experienced members seldom accompanies that belief. However, one obvious criterion of assessment is provided by microcosmic theories of representation – namely a proportionate representation of the employment profile of the electorate in the House. Even here though an exact correspondence of 'both sides' of industry – in the distribution of employees and employers amongst the industrially active populace – would not necessarily be welcomed by the proponents of greater industrial representation within the House of Commons (see Ross 1948:196; CBI 1987:9). There is a tendency, still, to equate 'industrial representation' with managers and industrialists.

One writer who utilised microcosmic criteria in the assessment of the 'representativeness' of the House of Commons was J. F. S. Ross (1948, 1955). Ross found it 'astonishing' that so little academic attention had been paid to the personnel of parliament: 'We discuss theories of representation and methods of voting .... anything and everything about members except the members themselves' (1948:8). He believed that one of the root causes of parliamentary malaise was to be found in 'this neglected question of the personnel of representation'. In particular, the rise of the 'professional politician' had undermined the capacity of the House to contribute effectively to the policy process. What was required, therefore, was a 'better balance of occupational experience amongst members' (Ross 1948:196) because the composition of the House was 'utterly unlike' the occupational profile of the electorate.

In detail, Ross discovered that in the inter-war period there was a proportionate 'under-representation' of all industrial sectors in the House, with the exceptions of the mining, printing, and food and drink industries. In comparison with the number of adults employed in the textile industry, for example, the textile and clothing industries had 'less than one-fourth of its proportion of members. Even this scanty representation is untypical; three-fourths of it consists of employers and managers .... So the great bulk of the group's quarter-million men and half-million women are, occupationally, unrepresented' (Ross 1948:68). Indeed, only in the mining industry was there; first, an 'over-representation' in the House; and, second, a predominance of workers, rather than owners and managers, amongst MPs. The reason for this was simple: 'there are many constituencies in which miners dominate the elections to an extent that has no parallel in any other occupation; they can practically choose their own members of parliament' (Ross 1948:72). In fact, miners constituted the largest group of Labour MPs throughout the inter-war period; much larger than the second largest group, the metal workers, and the third and fourth groups, teachers/lecturers and journalists.

Yet the immediate post-war elections, 1945, 1950 and 1951, significantly skewed Labour representation away from industrial and manual occupations in favour of professional and non-manual jobs. The miners became the second largest group of Labour MPs, behind teachers/lecturers; and journalists, clerks/secretaries, and barristers came close behind the miners. The metal workers, as the second ranked industrial grouping of MPs after the miners, were outnumbered approximately two to one by journalists, clerks and barristers alike (Ross 1955:438). This lack of proportionality with the electorate could not, in Ross' opinion be 'at all healthy or desirable' (1955:445); for the danger in his eyes was that we were 'giving them [the "talking classes"] too big a share in controlling our destinies, by comparison with the people who *do* things instead of holding forth about them' (Ross 1948:77, original emphasis).

J. F. S. Ross' concern over the 'unhealthy' tendencies of representation would only have been heightened by an analysis of the composition of the House of Commons returned at the general election in 1983. If, for the moment, we utilise Ross' methodology – by assigning each MP a single, 'primary' occupation, and by comparing the occupational profile of the House with that of the working population – then it can be seen that the 'productive' sector of the economy alone remains 'under-represented' in the Commons (see Table 4.1).

Table 4.1   MPs' Primary Occupation and Working Population 1983

	MPs		Working Population	
	n	%	n/000	%
Agriculture	23	3.5	595	2.5
'Productive'	*163	25.1	9252	38.7
'Business Services'	222	34.2	7610	31.8
'Other Services'	<u>242</u>	<u>37.2</u>	<u>6454</u>	<u>27.0</u>
Total	650	100.0	23911	100.0

Working population = *employees and self employed*
'Productive' = *manufacturing, production, construction, transport*
'Business Services' = *banking, finance, legal, retail*
'Other Services' = *education, military, police, media*
Primary Occupation = *longest stated period in single occupation.*

* 217 MPs in total had *some* experience of industry before entering parliament.

(Source: Working Population = Social Trends 1986: 65-6).

The 'talking classes' continued to dominate the House of Commons. 16 per cent (n 104) of members in 1983 were recruited from the legal profession alone, and a further 13 per cent (n 84) were drawn from the world of education. In total, over two-thirds of the House (71 per cent) had been employed in the service sectors of the economy, whereas 59 per cent of the working population were employed in these sectors in 1983.

However, in assigning a 'primary' occupation to each member (in accordance with the longest stated period of employment in any occupation) the number of members with some industrial experience is reduced. In addition to the 163 MPs whose longest period of employment was in the 'productive' sector, a further 54 members had also worked in this sector. A total of 217 MPs had thus been active in industry at some stage of their careers before entering parliament. This larger number (i.e. 33 per cent of all MPs) was still below a proportionate representation of the working population (at 38.7 per cent); but was perhaps not as small as many industrialists outside of Westminster appeared to believe it to be. In fact, the number of members with prior industrial experience, as measured by 'primary' occupation, in the 1983 House was above the 20th century mean (at 23.4 per cent) and ranks fifth in terms of the industrial composition of modern Houses for which comparable data is available (see Table 4.2).

Table 4.2   MPs' Primary Occupation: 'Productive' Industries

Year	MPs with ind. exper	Total n. of MPs	% MPs with ind. exper
1918	166	707	23.5
1922	176	615	28.6
1923	186	615	30.2
1924	163	615	26.5
1929	168	615	27.3
1931	95	615	15.5
1935	130	615	21.1
1945	146	640	22.8
1950	121	625	19.4
1951	112	625	17.9
1983	163	650	25.1
Total	1626	6937	23.4(Average)

* Figures for 1906, 1910J, 1910D Houses are excluded as data from J.A. Thomas does not allow for recording by 'primary' occupation.

(Source: Figures for 1918-51: J. F. S. Ross 1948, 1955).

Representation of Industrial Sectors
Not surprisingly 'primary' occupation provides only a basic guide to the experience of industry brought to the House by MPs. What also needs to be considered is the distribution of experience amongst the various industrial sectors and how the industrial composition of the House reflects the changing composition of industry outside. The continuities and changes of industrial representation in the 20th century House of Commons are revealed in Table 4.3. Inspite of incomplete data it can be seen that in the early parliaments of this century, the dominant industrial sectors were the railway, shipping, mining, metal extraction, metal manufacturing, engineering, and textile industries. Together these sectors accounted for 69 per cent of industrially experienced members. Although the traditional heavy industrial sectors predominated, the new 'second wave' industries – chemicals, motor manufacturing, and rubber – secured representation in the House. As J.A.Thomas (1958:16) remarked of the composition of the 1906 and 1910 parliaments: 'It did not take a new industry [motor manufacturing] very long to stake a claim to have its voice in the affairs of the nation'. Indeed, one of the characteristics of the Commons has been its ability to reflect, no matter how slowly or unintentionally, the changing composition of British industry.

Table 4.3 Representation of Industrial Sectors

Sector	1906		1910		1911		1918		1922		1923		1924		1929		1931		1935		1945		1950		1951		1983	
	n	%	n	%	n	%	n	%	n	%	n	%	n	%	n	%	n	%	n	%	n	%	n	%	n	%	n	%
Coal	38	8.0	43	9.7	43	10.2	34	20.5	52	29.5	52	28.0	46	28.2	50	29.8	25	26.3	40	30.8	45	30.8	38	31.4	36	32.1	25	8.2
Coke	-	-	-	-	-	-	-	-	-	-	-	-	-	-	-	-	-	-	-	-	-	-	-	-	-	-	1	0.3
Oil Extr	-	-	-	-	-	-	-	-	-	-	-	-	-	-	-	-	-	-	-	-	-	-	-	-	-	-	3	1.0
Petrol	18	3.8	21	4.7	19	4.5	-	-	-	-	-	-	-	-	-	-	-	-	-	-	-	-	-	-	-	-	8	2.6
Elect/Gas	15	3.2	20	4.5	18	4.3	-	-	-	-	-	-	-	-	-	-	-	-	-	-	-	-	-	-	-	-	10	3.3
Water	4	0.8	2	0.5	2	0.5	-	-	-	-	-	-	-	-	-	-	-	-	-	-	-	-	-	-	-	-	2	0.6
Met Extr	33	6.9	29	6.5	31	7.3	-	-	-	-	-	-	-	-	-	-	-	-	-	-	-	-	-	-	-	-	2	0.6
Met Man	22	6.3	27	6.1	29	6.9	19	11.4	22	12.5	23	12.4	24	14.7	23	13.7	13	13.7	18	13.8	18	12.3	16	13.2	12	10.7	15	4.9
Min Prod	5	1.1	2	0.5	2	0.5	-	-	1	0.6	1	0.5	2	1.2	2	1.2	1	1.1	1	0.8	-	-	-	-	-	-	3	1.0
Chem	17	3.6	17	3.8	12	2.8	8	4.8	5	2.8	3	1.6	2	1.2	1	0.6	1	1.1	-	-	-	-	-	-	-	-	18	5.9
Met Gds	-	-	-	-	-	-	-	-	-	-	-	-	-	-	-	-	-	-	-	-	-	-	-	-	-	-	3	1.0
Mech Eng	39	8.2	35	7.9	31	7.3	-	-	-	-	-	-	-	-	-	-	-	-	-	-	11	7.5	10	8.3	9	8.0	35	11.4
Data	-	-	-	-	-	-	-	-	-	-	-	-	-	-	-	-	-	-	-	-	-	-	-	-	-	-	9	3.0
Elect Eng	-	-	-	-	-	-	-	-	-	-	-	-	1	0.6	-	-	-	-	-	-	-	-	-	-	-	-	15	4.9
Motor	-	-	-	-	-	-	-	-	-	-	-	-	-	-	-	-	-	-	-	-	-	-	-	-	-	-	17	5.6
Trns Eq	2	0.4	1	0.2	1	0.2	-	-	-	-	-	-	-	-	-	-	-	-	-	-	-	-	-	-	-	-	20	6.5
Instr Eng	-	-	1	0.2	1	0.2	1	0.6	1	0.6	1	0.5	1	0.6	1	0.6	1	1.1	1	0.8	-	-	-	-	-	-	2	0.6
Food/Drink	26	5.5	26	5.9	28	6.6	17	10.2	12	6.8	12	6.5	13	8.0	9	5.4	8	8.4	7	5.4	-	-	-	-	-	-	19	6.2
Textiles	37	7.8	27	6.1	28	6.6	22	13.3	19	10.8	24	12.9	17	10.4	24	14.3	9	9.5	11	8.5	5	3.4	3	2.5	2	1.8	16	5.2
Leather	-	-	1	0.2	1	0.2	-	-	-	-	-	-	-	-	1	0.6	2	2.1	2	1.5	-	-	1	0.8	1	0.9	-	-
Foot	5	1.1	3	0.7	3	0.7	4	2.4	6	3.4	9	4.8	7	4.3	11	6.5	5	5.3	8	6.2	4	2.7	5	4.1	4	3.6	2	0.6
Furn/Tmb	6	1.3	6	1.4	6	1.4	16	9.6	19	10.8	20	10.8	17	10.4	10	6.0	9	9.5	12	9.2	9	6.2	5	4.1	2	1.8	5	1.6
Paper	40	8.4	41	9.3	31	7.3	-	-	-	-	-	-	-	-	-	-	-	-	-	-	6	4.1	1	0.8	-	-	21	6.9
Rubber	20	4.2	17	3.8	16	3.8	-	-	-	-	-	-	-	-	-	-	-	-	-	-	-	-	-	-	-	-	6	2.0
Misc	9	1.9	8	1.8	10	2.4	-	-	-	-	-	-	-	-	-	-	-	-	-	-	29	19.9	23	19.0	23	20.5	5	1.6
Construct	5	1.1	7	1.6	9	2.1	10	6.0	10	5.7	11	5.9	8	4.9	11	6.5	8	8.4	8	6.2	5	3.4	5	4.1	5	4.5	18	5.9
Rail Trans	70	14.7	64	14.4	60	14.2	-	-	-	-	-	-	-	-	-	-	-	-	-	-	14	9.6	11	9.1	11	9.8	7	2.3
Sea Trans	13	2.7	12	2.7	15	3.6	35	21.1	29	16.5	30	16.1	25	15.3	25	14.9	13	13.7	22	16.9	-	-	-	-	-	-	3	1.0
Road Trans	41	8.6	33	7.4	26	6.2	-	-	-	-	-	-	-	-	-	-	-	-	-	-	-	-	8	6.6	7	6.3	6	2.0
Air Trans	-	-	-	-	-	-	-	-	-	-	-	-	-	-	-	-	-	-	-	-	-	-	-	-	-	-	3	1.0
Telecom	2	0.4	-	-	-	-	-	-	-	-	-	-	-	-	-	-	-	-	-	-	-	-	-	-	-	-	7	2.3
Man Gen	-	-	-	-	-	-	-	-	-	-	-	-	-	-	-	-	-	-	-	-	-	-	-	-	-	-	-	-
Total	475	100.0	443	100.0	422	100.0	166	100.0	176	100.0	186	100.0	163	100.0	168	100.0	95	100.0	130	100.0	146	100.0	121	100.0	112	100.0	306	100.0

(Total for 1983 includes multiple counts for MPs who have previously been employed in more than one manufacturing occupation)

By 1983, as Table 4.3 shows, the decline of the shipping, railway and metal extraction industries was reflected in their diminished representation in the Commons. The engineering, construction, paper and chemical industries replaced them at the top of the industrial representation league. The mining industry, though much reduced in terms of employment and output, nonetheless continued to retain substantial representation in the House. By 1983, however, the number of members with experience of the textile industry had declined from its early 20th century level. There were more members from the motor industry and from food and drink manufacturing than textiles, and the latter's representation was challenged in number by the electrical engineering sector. Indeed, the capacity of the Commons to respond to industrial change, and to do so in an unstructured and partial manner, is perhaps best reflected in the representation of the 'data' industry. Some 3 per cent of MPs brought experience of this new technology industry into the House. Although the number remained small, nonetheless, it was a greater proportionate representation of the data industry in the House than the proportion of the 'productive' industry workforce engaged in the data industry itself (3 per cent compared with 1.1 per cent of the actual workforce). In this limited respect the House was 'representative' of the stage of development of the data industry in the 1980s – despite suspicions outside to the contrary.

Extent of Industrial 'Experience' in the House

In itself, a simple listing of the number of members with some prior industrial employment does not inform us of the extent and the depth of experience brought to the House in any specific industrial sector. To remedy this defect, Table 4.4a outlines for each sector the aggregate pre-parliamentary experience of members. (Aggregate experience is simply the sum of individual members' length of prior involvement in each industrial sector).

Perhaps the simplest means of understanding the significance of Table 4.4a is to note that the mean age of MPs at the start of their parliamentary career in the post-war period is just under 42 (Mellors 1978:34), and the commonest age range of new entrants is between 30 and 49 (Rush 1981:43). If we take the post-war mean, then, on average, members have spent *at least* 20 years in other occupations before entering the House. Collectively, therefore, members bring to the House *at least* 13,000 years occupational experience. Hence, if pre-parliamentary experience was evenly distributed amongst the ten SIC classes, each would have a cumulative total of 1,300 years experience. In turn, if the six SIC classes constituting the productive and extractive industries were grouped together, the House would have a *minimum* of 7,800 years aggregate experience of industry. And, assuming that prior occupational experience was evenly distributed amongst these sectors, each of the 31 sectors in Table 4.4a would have a total of at least 251 years. Manifestly, however, this is an unrealistic assumption in the light of Table 4.1.

Nonetheless, the aggregate figures of 7,800 years total experience for 'productive' industry generally, and 251 years for each industrial sector specifically, provide hypothetical minimum criteria for the assessment of the actual extent and depth of industrial experience in the House.

Table 4.4a shows, for each industrial sector, the aggregate length of prior activity by MPs in that sector. Clearly the total industrial experience of MPs, at 2,797 years, is only just above one-third of that which might have been expected if the House's cumulative occupational experience had been spread evenly across the SIC classes. Moreover, only the mechanical engineering and mining sectors, with respectively 416 and 406 years, exceed the 'expected' minimum figure of 251 years.

In the mechanical engineering sector, 35 members collectively brought 416 years pre-parliamentary experience to the House: 16 Conservatives contributed 152 years service (mean 9.5, maximum 25, minimum 2, no responses 3); and 16 Labour members contributed a further 234 years (mean 14.6, maximum 29, minimum 3). Of the Labour MPs, Bernard Conlan, Robert Hughes, Stan Orme, Ernest Roberts and Harold Walker all had worked for over 20 years in the engineering industry. Correspondingly, two Conservatives, Lewis Stevens and Peter Thurnham, had each been active in this industry for over 20 years.

A close second, in terms of aggregate experience, was the coal industry. 25 MPs, all but two of whom were Labour members, had accumulated 406 years employment in the industry before entering the Commons. Six Labour members had each notched up over 30 years, with Bill O'Brian, Mick Welsh and Alec Woodall having respectively worked 38, 39 and 41 years in the mines. Indeed, no other industrial sector could match the average industrial experience of the miners.

Beyond the mechanical engineering and mining industries, however, the collective experience of the other industrial sectors within the House was notably limited. The construction industry, with 230 years was the third-ranked sector. Just twelve Conservative members contributed nearly three-quarters of this total (168 years). Albert McQuarrie had served for 37 years as chairman and managing director of his family building firm; John Spence was for 30 years chairman of the Nicolson Construction Company and a director of numerous property companies; John Ward had spent 28 years as a chartered civil and structural engineer and had latterly been a director with Taylor Woodrow and its subsidiaries. On the opposition benches, Eric Heffer had been employed as a building site joiner, and shop steward, for 26 years; and James Hamilton had been a construction engineer for some 18 years.

The fourth ranked industry was the chemical industry. Nineteen MPs, two-thirds of whom were Conservative members, brought 168 years experience of this industry to the House. The range of Conservative experience varied from that of executive (Alan Haselhurst and David Crouch at ICI), through management (Andrew Bowden at Unilever and a paint manufacturers),

Table 4.4a Length of Prior Industrial Experience of MPs ('Productive' Industries)

SIC Sector	Conservatives n		sum years	Labour n		sum years	Total (inc Others) n		sum years
Coal	2		6	23	(4)	400	25	(4)	406
Coke	0		0	1		7	1		7
Oil	3		14	0		0	3		14
Petrol	7		20	1		2	8		22
Elect. &Gas	2		14	8	(1)	102	10	(1)	116
Water	1		4	1		5	2		9
Met. Extract	2		18	0		0	2		18
Met. Manuf	5		25	10	(2)	102	15	(2)	127
Min. Extract	3		8	0		0	3		8
Chemicals	12		131	6	(1)	37	18	(1)	168
Met. Goods	2		2	1		8	3		10
Mech. Eng.	16	(3)	152	16		234	35	(3)	416
Data	7	(1)	76	2		14	9	(1)	90
Elect.Eng.	7		42	7	(1)	44	15	(1)	89
Motor	5		35	11	(1)	90	17	(1)	128
Trans Equip	8	(2)	39	11	(3)	111	20	(5)	152
Instrument	0		0	2	(1)	7	2	(1)	7
Food	11		70	2		16	14		90
Drink	4		45	1		7	5		52
Textile	12	(1)	91	3		13	16	(1)	144
Footwear	0		0	1		3	2		6
Furniture	5		27	0		0	5		27
Paper	14	(2)	70	5	(3)	16	21	(5)	122
Rubber	4		41	1		10	6		57
Miscell.	4		38	1		3	5		41
Construct.	12		168	5	(2)	54	18	(3)	230
Rail Trans.	0		0	7	(2)	57	7	(2)	57
Road Trans.	1	(1)	-	2		17	3	(1)	17
Sea Trans.	4		34	2		37	6		71
Air Trans.	3		29	0		0	3		29
Telecom.	3		29	3	(1)	31	7	(1)	67
Total	159	(10)	1216	133	(22)	1427	306	(33)	2797

(Figures in brackets are the n. of missing values recorded within the total n, i.e. e.g. coal total = 25 of which 4 score 0.01)

through industrial chemist (Michael Clark at ICI and Smiths Industries), to that of statistician (Linda Chalker at Unilever). On the Labour benches, Ted Garrett was by far the most experienced former employee of the chemical industry, with 21 years service with ICI as an engineer and AEU shop steward. Jeremy Bray, with 7 years as an automation control executive with ICI; and Gregor MacKenzie with 6 years as a sales executive with International Paints brought more varied, and more tangential knowledge of the industry to the Labour side of the House.

Table 4.4b Ten Leading Industrial Sectors: Aggregate Experience By Party Within the Commons

| *Conservatives* | | *Labour* | | *Total* | |
SIC	*sum/years*	SIC	*sum/years*	SIC	*sum/years*
Construction	168	Coal	400	Mech. Eng.	416
Mech. Eng.	152	Mech. Eng.	234	Coal	406
Chemicals	131	Trans. Equip.	111	Construction	230
Textiles	91	Elect & Gas	102	Chemicals	168
Data	76	Metal Man.	102	Trans. Equip.	152
Food	70	Motor	90	Textiles	144
Paper	70	Rail Trans.	57	Motor	128
Drink	45	Construction	54	Metal Man.	127
Elect. Eng.	42	Elect. Eng.	44	Paper	122
Rubber	41	Chemicals	37	Elect. & Gas	116

Of the other industrial sectors identified in Table 4.4b Conservative members dominated the textile and paper sectors in both numbers and length of prior experience. Labour MPs, on the other hand, collectively had greater experience of the transport equipment manufacturing sector, as well as the motor, metal manufacturing, and 'energy' industries. Indeed, the party differences apparent in Table 4.4b represent a basic divide between the old heavy industries (coal, power, shipbuilding, metal manufacturing, and railways) as the mainstay of Labour representation, and the 'newer' industrial sectors (chemicals, data, electronics and rubber) with greater Conservative representation. The 'data' industry provides a good example of this inter-party difference. This sector was ranked fifth in the Conservative party but was ranked only sixteenth in the Labour party. In fact, well over half of the House's aggregate experience of the data industry was provided by just three Conservative members: John Butcher had 12 years involvement in the computer industry; Tim Wood had worked for 23 years, 20 with ICL, in this sector; and Eric Forth had 17 years sales and management experience with Rank Xerox and Burroughs. Thus, for all Labour's claims to be the party of industry, in this specific instance it was the Conservative party that had its finger, no matter how tentatively, on the new pulse of industry.

Other Occupational Experience

To place the data contained in Tables 4.4a and 4.4b into perspective it is instructive to analyse the wider pre-entry occupational experiences of those 217 members who had been employed in industry at one time or another before entering the Commons. The basic point is that even amongst these 217 MPs their collective experience of many other 'non-industrial' occupations outstrips that in most industrial sectors. This is best illustrated in column 1 of Table 4.5 where experience of SIC sector 96 ('other services provided to the general public' – including trade unions, social welfare services, etc.) outranks all but five industrial sectors; and, individually, the public administration and education categories outrank all but six industrial sectors.

If the second column in Table 4.5 is examined, then the comparative weakness of industrial experience in the House becomes even more apparent. Included there are 279 MPs who had either pre-entry and/or post-entry involvement with industry (post-entry experience entailed, in the main, directorships, consultancy, sponsorship). Amongst this group of members there is more collective experience of the business services than there is in all but two industrial sectors. The exceptions are mechanical engineering and coal. Similarly, the non-industrial sectors of public administration, education, 'other public services', and the media outstripped all but the three top-ranked industrial sectors. Whilst the banking sector outranked all but the top four industries listed in Table 4.4b

Just how restricted is the industrial experience of the House is perhaps best revealed in the third column of Table 4.5. Listed there is the profile of pre-parliamentary experience of 579 MPs who had either some occupational experience of industry (pre-entry and/or post-entry), or who had participated in industrial debates or tabled questions in the House in either session 1983/4 or 1984/5. Hence, any MP with *any* observable interest in industry, no matter how remote, is included in this third column. With this extensive coverage, incorporating nearly 90 per cent of all members, it becomes apparent that the pre-parliamentary experience of MPs is massively skewed towards the service sector of the economy. The collective experience of the business services, education, public administration, 'other public services' and the media outstrip the House's aggregate experience of any industrial sector. In fact, the experience of the business services sector, measured in total number of years, is three times greater than that of the mechanical engineering industry. Moreover, only three industrial sectors outrank the cumulative experience of agriculture and the retail trade within the Commons.

Table 4.5   **Non-Industrial Pre-Parliamentary Experience of MPs Active on Industrial Matters.**

	Industrially 'Active' MPs					
	Pre-entry		Pre/post entry		Pre/post/in House	
SIC	*n*	*sum/years*	*n*	*sum/years*	*n*	*sum/years*
Agriculture	7 (1)	14	13 (8)	57	37 (17)	216
Retail	5	74	6	92	20	213
Hotel	3 (1)	18	4 (2)	31	5 (2)	47
Banking	13 (1)	84	23 (2)	161	62 (4)	399
Busin. serv.	12 (1)	98	32 (2)	343	138 (10)	1318
Pub. Admin	30 (5)	142	39 (5)	241	70 (6)	540
Education	22 (2)	139	34 (2)	221	117 (4)	1018
R&D	1	8	1	8	1	8
Medical	0	0	2 (1)	6	9 (2)	127
Other public.	39 (3)	148	46 (3)	178	107 (5)	610
Media	11 (1)	67	24 (2)	170	64 (3)	544
Pers.Service	1	11	2	21	3 (1)	21
Domestic	0	0	2 (2)	na	2 (2)	na

n. in brackets = n. of members with recorded missing values

Industrial Experience and Entry Cohorts

Byron Criddle (1984:230-9), in his analysis of the socio-economic composition of the new House of Commons in 1983, notes the over-riding continuity with the 1979 parliament. Generally, the occupational profile of the House strengthened the patterns developed in preceding parliaments. Yet, in terms of industrial representation, there was a more complex pattern than Criddle's broad analysis would suggest.

Table 4.6   **Entry Cohorts and Pre-Parliamentary Industrial Experience**

	Entry							
	Pre-1970		1970-8		1979		1983	
Ind. Experience	*n*	*%*	*n*	*%*	*n*	*%*	*n*	*%*
Industrially Active	53	28.8	80	40.8	38	33.6	46	29.3
Industrially Inactive	131	71.2	116	59.2	75	66.4	111	70.7
Total	184	100.0	196	100.0	113	100.0	157	100.0

Overall, there was a marginal decrease in the proportion of newly elected MPs with prior industrial experience (see Table 4.6). This general statement, however, obscures notable inter-party differences (see Table 4.7). Newly elected Labour MPs accounted for 18.6 per cent of the PLP but only 13.6 per cent of Labour members with industrial experience. There was thus a decrease in the number of new Labour members with pre-entry involvement in industry. In contrast, on the Conservative benches, there was a slight proportionate increase in the number of newly elected members with prior industrial experience. The 1983 cohort constituted 26.7 per cent of industrially 'experienced' Conservative members as against 25.4 per cent of the parliamentary party overall. In part, this might account for the aggressive business mindedness of the 1983 entry noted by David Thomas (1984:160). But more specifically it represents the simple fact that several new Conservatives were swept into the House on the tide of the party's electoral success. These new members were often in the middle of an industrial career, and when selected were not expected, even by themselves, to be elected.

Table 4.7 Entry Cohorts, Party and Industrial Experience

	Cons		*Labour.*		*Total (inc. others)*	
Entry	*n*	*%*	*n*	*%*	*n*	*%*
Pre-1970	22	19.6	30	31.6	53	24.4
1970-78	44	39.3	30	31.6	80	36.9
1979-82	16	14.3	22	23.1	38	17.5
1983	30	26.8	13	13.7	46	21.2
Total	112	100.0	95	100.0	217	100.0

Industrially Experienced MPs by Party

When the entry cohorts are crosstabulated with aggregate industrial experience in each sector (Table 4.8) it is apparent that the 1983 cohort has a narrower focus of experience than the other entry cohorts. Indeed, the 1983 intake has no experience of 12 of the 31 industrial sectors listed in Table 4.8. Moreover, whilst there is a continuity of experience across cohorts in the mechanical engineering and coal industries – reflecting in large part the sponsorship policies of the AEU and the NUM (see chapter 6) – the 1983 intake has greater experience of the new industries (data, telecommunications, and electronics) than do the 'older' parliamentary generations. Indeed, the 1983 cohort accounts for over one-half of the aggregate experience of the data industry, over 40 per cent of that of the telecommunications sector, and over one-quarter of that in the electronics industry.

Table 4.8   Entry and Industrial Experience by Industrial Sector

SIC Sector	| Entry							
	pre-1970		1970-8		1979-82		1983	
	n	%	n	%	n	%	n	%
Coal	7	8.7	7	6.3	4	8.3	7	10.6
Coke	1	1.2	-	-	-	-	-	-
Oil	-	-	1	0.9	-	-	2	3.0
Petrol	2	2.5	4	3.6	-	-	2	3.0
Elect. &Gas	4	4.9	3	2.7	2	4.2	1	1.5
Water	1	1.2	-	-	1	2.1	-	-
Metal Extract.	1	1.2	1	0.9	-	-	-	-
Metal Manuf.	5	6.2	4	3.6	-	-	6	9.1
Mineral Extr.	-	-	2	1.8	1	2.1	-	-
Chemicals	10	12.4	4	3.6	2	4.2	2	3.0
Metal Goods	1	1.2	2	1.8	-	-	-	-
Mech. Engin	10	12.4	13	11.7	4	8.3	8	12.1
Data	-	-	3	2.7	2	4.2	4	6.1
Elect. Engin	3	3.7	3	2.7	3	6.2	6	9.1
Motor	5	6.2	7	6.3	1	2.1	4	6.1
Trans. Equip.	6	7.5	5	4.5	5	10.4	4	6.1
Instrument.	-	-	-	-	2	4.2	-	-
Food	1	1.2	7	6.3	2	4.2	4	6.1
Drink	2	2.5	2	1.8	1	2.1	-	-
Textile	5	6.2	6	5.4	2	4.2	3	4.5
Footwear	-	-	1	0.9	-	-	1	1.5
Furniture	1	1.2	2	1.8	-	-	2	3.0
Paper	4	4.9	13	11.7	4	8.3	-	-
Rubber	1	1.2	2	1.8	3	6.2	-	-
Miscell.	1	1.2	3	2.7	1	2.1	-	-
Construction	4	4.9	5	4.5	4	8.3	5	7.6
Rail Trans.	2	2.5	3	2.7	2	4.2	-	-
Road Trans.	-	-	-	-	1	2.1	2	3.0
Sea Trans.	3	3.7	2	1.8	-	-	1	1.5
Air Trans.	-	-	3	2.7	-	-	-	-
Telecom.	1	1.2	3	2.7	1	2.1	2	3.0
Total	81	100.0	111	100.0	48	100.0	66	100.0

Total includes multiple counts for MPs with experience in more than one sector.

On the other hand, there is an 'aging' profile of representation of several of the traditional industries. This is particularly pronounced in the chemical industry with MPs first elected before the 1970 general election contributing over 60 per cent of the House's experience of that industry; and over 93 per cent amassed by MPs elected before 1979. Similarly, members elected before 1970 contributed over 60 per cent of the House's experience of the railway industry. In addition, members elected before the 1979 general election accounted for 78.4 per cent of experience in the electricity and gas industries; 66.4 per cent in the motor industry; 67.8 per cent in transport equipment; 88.9 per cent in textiles, 85.3 per cent in paper; and 76 per cent in shipping. It should be remembered that MPs first elected before 1979 accounted for only 58.5 per cent of the total number of MPs.

Conclusion
Clearly the House of Commons is not a microcosm of the composition of British industrial society. The proportion of MPs with direct pre-entry experience in the productive industries is less than the corresponding proportion within the working population as a whole – though not as low as many industrialists outside of the House appear to believe. Of more significance for the performance of parliamentary roles, however, is the House's limited collective experience of major sectors of industry. Only the mining and mechanical engineering industries were represented beyond the minimum aggregate experience threshold in the 1983 parliament. And the sponsorship policies of the major unions concerned with those industries largely accounts for these levels.

Generally, the Labour party remained the party most representative of the workforce of heavy industry. The Conservative party in contrast reflected the newer industrial sectors of the data and electronics industries. Moreover, newly elected Conservative members in 1983 proportionately had more pre-entry experience of working in industry than had newly elected Labour MPs. In practice, the occupational linkage of Labour MP's with industry became even more tenuous in 1983 and chapter 6 will examine this issue in greater detail. Before then, however, it is necessary to establish the nature, level and sectoral focus of backbench activity upon industrial matters. Chapter 5, therefore, seeks to construct a profile of such activity in two parliamentary sessions in the 1983 parliament.

5 The House of Commons and Industrial Policy: Sessions 1983/4 and 1984/5

There is no such thing as a 'typical' parliamentary session. Whilst there is a residuum of routine business, of processing the Consolidated Fund, the Finance Act and the Estimates, along with administrative regulations relating to the House, the majority of the parliamentary agenda is determined, nevertheless, by non-routine events. The efforts of the governing party to translate its manifesto commitments into substantive outputs, whilst defining the overall direction of parliamentary business, are invariably disrupted by the vagaries of international affairs, the uncertainties of economic competition and their reverberations throughout the social and political structure of Britain. In this sense, no two parliamentary sessions are alike. The two sessions under consideration in this chapter are no exception. Hence, although generalisations can be made about behaviour in the House of Commons, they need to be made conditional upon the context within which the observed behaviour takes place in the first instance. It is necessary, therefore, to sketch the main industrial issues in Britain in 1983/4 and 1984/5, and their relative importance, before considering activity in the House in some detail.

For a government which denied the need for an 'industrial strategy' the second Thatcher administration was far from inactive on industrial affairs after the general election of May 1983. The irony of the Thatcherite position was that the disengagement of government from industry, the belief in the reinforcement of entrepreneurial endeavour and the operation of the free market, required a protracted legislative programme to establish facilitative 'policies for industry' in place of orthodox 'industrial policy' developed in the preceding era of Keynesian social democratic consensus. Thus the House of Commons was confronted after 1983 with a series of policy decisions which emanated both directly and indirectly from the ideological predilections of the Thatcher government. Most of the features of the government's policies for industry had in fact emerged in the first parliament, but after the second election victory their centrality to the government's project, their fundamentalism and their irreversibility, became increasingly manifest. Moreover, the interconnections between the broader macro-economic strategy and the micro-economic policies relating to industry were reinforced.

General Indices: Manufacturing Output and Employment

Industrial output and employment in Britain were both in decline before 1979 (see Judge and Dickson 1987:28) but the recession after 1979 certainly steepened the trajectory of decline. In the first year of the Thatcher government high interest rates and exchange rates contributed to a fall in manufacturing output of 15 per cent (this compares with a fall of 6.9 per cent in 1930-31, and 5.5 per cent in the worst year of the great depression in 1878-79). Although manufacturing output had begun to recover in 1983 and continued to improve throughout the next two years, nonetheless, by the end of 1985 output had still only returned to the levels of 1970/1 (See Table 5.1).

Table 5.1 Index of Output in British Manufacturing Industries (1980=100)

	Total manufacturing industries						
Quarter	*1979*	*1980*	*1981*	*1982*	*1983*	*1984*	*1985*
1	107.4	106.9	92.7	94.7	95.9	99.7	103.4
2	112.3	102.3	93.1	94.9	95.4	100.4	104.6
3	108.3	97.5	95.0	94.1	97.6	101.6	103.7
4	110.0	93.3	95.3	93.1	98.9	101.6	103.2
Average	109.5	100.0	94.0	94.3	96.9	100.8	103.7

Source: CSO, Economic Trends, Annual Supplement, 1988 edn., HMSO

Moreover, the effects of the Thatcher-induced recession were more keenly felt by employees in manufacturing industry than those in other sectors of the economy (see Table 5.2). The flotsam of this industrial wreckage was increasingly washed into the House of Commons, either bodily in the delegations of trade unionists and the mass lobbies of threatened workers; or spiritually in the chamber by constituency MPs raising the spectre of plant closures and redundancies. Indeed, throughout 1983/4 and 1984/5 unemployment continued to reach new post-war record levels, eventually reaching 3.1 million in the fourth quarter of 1985.

It was against this general background, and the opportunity provided by manufacturing decline, high unemployment, declining trade union membership and the depoliticisation of plant closure, that the Thatcher government pursued its policies of dismantling the industrial policies of the social democratic consensus.

Table 5.2   Employment by Activity 1979-85

SIC Sector	1979 %	1980 %	1981 %	1982 %	1983 %	1984 %	1985 %
Agriculture	2.7	2.6	2.7	2.7	2.7	2.7	2.6
Mining, quarrying	1.4	1.4	1.5	1.4	1.4	1.3	1.2
Manufacturing	29.5	28.3	26.5	25.6	24.7	24.1	23.8
Elect, gas,water	1.4	1.4	1.5	1.4	1.4	1.4	1.3
Construction	6.4	6.5	6.4	6.2	6.1	6.2	6.0
Trade: wholesale, catering, retail	18.9	19.3	19.6	20.0	20.3	21.0	21.2
Transport,communic	6.2	6.3	6.3	6.2	6.1	6.0	5.8
Finance, Insurance, business services	7.0	7.3	7.9	8.3	8.6	8.8	9.1
Community, social and personal services	26.5	26.7	27.6	28.1	28.7	28.7	28.9
Total	100.0	100.0	100.0	100.0	100.0	100.0	100.0

Source: OECD, Labour Force Statistics 1964-1985, 1987, p. 451.

Privatisation

In its first period in office privatisation was deemed 'peripheral' to the government's overall industrial policies (see Holmes 1984:171) and its theoretical justification was never adequately stated (see Heald and Steel 1984:337). The Conservative manifesto of 1983 clearly aimed to redress this situation in its announcement that 'we shall transfer more state-owned businesses to independent ownership' (Manifesto 1983:15) in order to reduce the burden of financing state industries and the need to finance this burden through increased taxation and government borrowing. The importance of the wider economic implications of the privatisation programme was perhaps most tangibly demonstrated by the fact that John Moore, as Financial Secretary to the Treasury, was appointed as the minister responsible for the programme. Moore was a proselytiser for the faith of privatisation. The objectives of the programme was not merely 'to raise money. The benefits .... are planned to be much more far-reaching and longer-lasting' (quoted in Wilks 1986:9). Indeed, by 1983 privatisation had become in Heald and Thomas's graphic phrase (1986:52) a 'matter of theology'. This was so in four specific senses:

> as a central vision of a different society; in the way that its propositions have become a matter of belief, so that the testing of claims against the

apparent reality is not regarded as conclusive; by the sweeping rejection of notions of accountability which do not operate through market mechanisms; and by the unwillingness to consider existing constraints upon the operation of public sector organisations other than as a further reason for privatisation.

The policy consequences of this theology were apparent in both the style in which privatisation policies were implemented, and the manner in which the achievements of the remaining nationalised industries were dismissed and their managements were undermined.

Effectively there were three interrelated strands in the Thatcher government's privatisation policy after 1983 (see Heald 1983:299-317; 1984:38-45; Beasley and Littlechild 1986:2-5; Young 1986:236-51). These were: denationalisation, the selling off of public enterprises; deregulation, the liberalisation of the trading and competitive position of state enterprises to allow for private sector competition; and the tendering/contracting out of public services for private sector provision. On all three counts the sessions 1983/4 and 1984/5 were pivotal in the promotion of the privatisation programme. Yet each advance was fiercely and doggedly exposed to the criticisms of the opposition parties. Disquiet with the various aspects of privatisation policy, on the part of both management and trade unions in the public sector, found amplification in the Commons, as the opposition parties worked assiduously in the House to reveal the inconsistencies within the denationalisation programme, and its irrelevance to Britain's fundamental economic difficulties. In this sense Abromeit's judgement that 'the opposition did astonishingly little to hinder the government from implementing its privatisation programme' (1987:6) is mistaken. The protracted nature of questioning, the private delegations to ministers, the number of mass lobbies, and the extensive consideration of privatisation measures on the floor of the House and in committee all point to significant attempts to hinder the government. That such opposition failed is another matter!

The first privatisation measure to be introduced was the Telecommunications Bill in June 1983. This bill had been introduced originally in session 1982/3, but had fallen upon the calling of the general election in May 1983. The bill was designed to convert British Telecom (BT) into a public limited company (PLC) operating under the Companies Act; to abolish BT's monopoly; and to establish a regulatory agency – the Office of Telecommunications – under the supervision of a Director General of Communications. Despite the vote of all opposition parties against the bill at its second reading, the government easily maintained its majority (356 to 219), and the bill progressed remorselessly through committee in October and December, before receiving its royal assent in April 1984 after the House of Lords had secured a number of minor amendments. Subsequently, BT became a PLC in August 1984 and in November provided the then largest ever share offer in the world.

The second major denationalisation measure of the first session was the Ordnance Factories and Military Services Bill which provided, in the first instance, for Royal Ordnance factories to become part of a PLC owned wholly by the state, but able to own its own capital and ultimately capable of being privately owned. Indeed, the factories were eventually sold to British Aerospace in April 1987.

In addition to these public bills the privatisation programme was also advanced by executive orders. In July 1983 the sale of a further 7 per cent of BP's equity was announced, following on from the sale of 5.6 per cent in June 1981; similarly a further 22 per cent of Cable and Wireless shares were sold in December 1983 bringing the total sale of the company's equity to 71 per cent. In March 1984, against the background of the loss of a Britoil contract for a North Sea oil rig, the lower-Clyde shipyard of Scott Lithgow was sold to Trafalgar House. A month later the remaining shares in Associated British Ports were floated, followed in June by the marketing of British Enterprise Oil (which had taken control of the oil assets of British Gas). The latter flotation, however, was undersubscribed, with RTZ, against the objections of the government, buying up 30 per cent of equity. In the following month, this time in the face of fierce opposition from Labour MPs and against the advice of the Select Committee on Trade and Industry, the announcement was made of the privatisation of Jaguar Cars – the profitable subsidiary of British Leyland. On this occasion the share issue was massively oversubscribed.

Indeed, July 1984 was a hectic month in the advancement of the privatisation programme; British Shipbuilders was ordered to sell off its profitable warship yards; Sea Link, the ferry subsidiary of British Rail, was sold to Sea Containers Ltd; and it was announced that the state was to shed its shareholding in the electronics innovatory company, INMOS. This latter sale was completed with Thorn-EMI in August 1984, and in the same month the computer firm ICL was sold to Standard Telephones.

The momentum of the first session of the new parliament was continued into the second: in May 1985 the remaining 59 per cent of British Aerospace shares were sold; in August the second, and final, flotation of Britoil shares was completed; and plans were announced to privatise as 'speedily as possible' British Gas and the British Airports Authority as well as to hand the Royal Naval Dockyards over to private management. Preliminary statements of the government's intent to denationalise BL, Rolls Royce, and British Airways also featured in this session.

In terms of legislation, however, the main privatisation bill in 1984/5 was the Transport Bill. In essence the bill was both a denationalisation and a liberalisation measure. The National Bus Company was to be broken up and then sold (eventually after August 1986) and restrictions on local competition were to be removed. At its second reading, on 12th January 1985, the bill was opposed by the main opposition parties, and faced a Conservative backbencher's amendment (defeated 290 to 210) that the second reading should be postponed until after the investigation of the Select Committee on Transport had been published. In fact, the committee stage of the bill was delayed until the select committee had reported, but in the following 94 hours of debate the reasoned conclusions of the committee found inadequate reflection in the partisan debate, and one which left whole sections of the bill unconsidered.

A further privatisation measure was the Oil and Pipelines Bill introduced in May 1985 and which received the Royal Assent in October of that year. This bill was not an unambiguous move towards liberalisation, for, whilst abolishing the British National Oil Corporation, it established, nonetheless, a small oil and pipelines agency to perform essential and continuing functions previously performed by BNOC. Thus, whilst ministers continued to argue that the abolition of BNOC was justified, given that its price stabilisation role had been undermined by the significant downturn in world oil prices and changes in oil markets, they maintained that a government agency still had a role in managing the oil and pipeline system in disposing of royalty in kind and in acting as custodian of participating agreements (see HC Debates 1985 vol 79:cols 189-96). Not surprisingly the Labour party criticised the bill for the doctrinaire dismantling of a highly successful and profitable corporation. Equally without surprise was the support of the government backbenchers for a bill which was 'philosophically based' and the only course open to 'a Conservative government committed to free enterprise, to ensuring that the ingenuity, skill and market response which can only come when the private sector can operate' (Michael Brown, HC Debates 1985 vol 79:col 242).

Nationalised Industries

The obverse of the government's privatisation strategy was the application of private sector techniques and philosophy to the management of the remaining public enterprises. The buzzwords of private sector management – 'financial targets', 'efficiency', 'strategic objectives', 'performance measurement' – became essential ingredients in the vocabulary of managers in the public sector. That these words were only loosely defined and their application generally limited was less important than their symbolic value for the government (see Woodward 1986; Davies 1988).

The main form of control over the nationalised industries was exercised through External Financing Limits (EFL) which specified the amount of government grants and loans each industry was to receive in any year. These limits were fixed in accordance with the government's desire to limit the Public Sector Borrowing Requirement (PSBR) rather than with the actual investment needs of the public corporation (Parris et al 1987:132-3). By 1984, however, the cumulative impact of decreased investment in the nationalised industries resulted in an easing of EFLs and concessions in investment funding for British Rail and British Aerospace. In July 1984 British Rail was granted £306 million for capital investment. This followed the earlier announcement in March of launch aid of up to £250 million for British Aerospace to participate in the A320 European airbus programme.

In the older traditional, and declining, industries – particularly coal, steel and shipbuilding – the government was forced to relax its financial limits on several occasions during the course of 1983/4 and 1984/5. In November 1984 the Minister of State for Trade and Industry (Norman Lamont) pointed out to the House that British Shipbuilders had received £1,170 million since 1979. In 1984 alone £217 million in support had been granted, of which £100 million was designated for long-term investment. Mr Lamont also noted the government's desire for the European Community to sanction increased intervention fund support (see below).

Similarly, the coal and steel industries continued to receive substantial government assistance. In particular, the coal industry's external financing limits and accumulated borrowing limits had to be raised on several occasions through draft orders (see HC Debates 1983 vol 45:cols 729-46; 1984 vol 68:cols 717-54) and two Coal Industry Bills. A significant element in these increases was money to fund redundancy payments in order to quicken the pace of pit closures. In return for increased loans, therefore, the government required greater productivity to be brought about through restructuring within the industry. Indeed, the government's commitment to this policy was reaffirmed in August 1983 with the appointment of Sir Ian Macgregor as chairman of the National Coal Board. Macgregor's reputation, gained through his handling of the restructuring of BSC, preceded him. In turn, Robert Haslam was appointed as Chairman of BSC to maintain his predecessor's efficiency drive. In their combination, these appointments simply underlined the government's intention of exerting political control over the nationalised industries. But, Macgregor's appointment to the NCB – with his aggressive managerial style and his commitment, from the outset, to eliminate what he described as 'uneconomic output' – signalled an inevitable confrontation with the National Union of Mineworkers (NUM).

The Miners' Strike: March 1984 to March 1985
The miners' strike dominated the industrial agenda for much of its twelve months duration. At heart the dispute was political. Its issues were 'basic, fundamental, ideological and apparently unbridgeable' (John Lloyd, *Financial Times* 29 July 1984). Popularly, it was perceived as the clash of two extremisms, of rival abstractions: 'profitability' versus 'community';

closure on economic grounds versus continued production on social grounds. In retrospect, as Huw Beynon (1985:20) notes, 'the strike represented not so much the front line as the last ditch'. As such it stands alongside other heroic but ultimately futile gestures of defiance.

The precipitating event for the strike was the announcement of the closure of the Cortonwood pit in Yorkshire on 1st March 1984. Five days later the NCB stated its intention to reduce coal capacity still further. In one sense the NCB's announcements simply quickened its rationalisation programme which had been proceeding, with only isolated resistance, in Scotland, South Wales and other peripheral areas for some twelve months. However, the closure of Cortonwood in the heartland of the coal mining industry, and with guaranteed working for a further five years, was clearly a provocative act by the NCB. It has to be seen as a calculated act to force a strike at the least propitious time for the NUM – in the spring, with massive coal stocks and reducing consumer demand for electricity in the coming summer months. The government also guessed, correctly, that the NUM President's obduracy, particularly his inflexibility on the issue of 'uneconomic closures', would serve to alienate public support; more so as the NUM had accepted and co-operated in the closure of collieries in the past. Thus, 'the stark, bitter fact', as Saville (1986:307-8) notes, was that throughout the strike 'large sections of public opinion did not believe that the miners had a viable case against closures'. More damning ultimately than public agnosticism, however, was the failure of significant sections of the NUM's own membership and the wider trade union movement to accept Mr Scargill's posturing.

On 8th March 1984 the NUM's national executive sanctioned regional strikes against closures. The strategy was designed to generate a 'domino effect' whereby strike action would be spread from area to area eventually culminating in a national stoppage, but without formally calling for a national strike, and so avoiding the NUM's constitutional requirement for a ballot to be conducted before national action could take place. Ironically, the refusal of the national executive to ballot its members simply served to reinforce the regional divisions within the NUM; with those areas least threatened by 'Macgregor's butchery', Nottinghamshire in particular, choosing not to support the campaign against pit closures. More dramatically, these regional divisions were deepened, irreconcilably as it turned out, by the use of flying and mass picketing in areas which refused to join the strike. In this context, Mr Scargill's class rhetoric of a universal fight on behalf of all workers, and not simply miners, was counterposed by the violent disunity of his own membership.

But the 'universalism' of Mr Scargill's case was eroded further by the failure of other, significant, unions to support the miners' cause. The steelworkers (ISTC) and the EEPTU in the power stations persistently ignored the pleas and the pickets of the NUM. The ISTC, in particular, faced by the threat of the closure of one or more major steel plants, was adamant in its refusal to join the NUM. In Scotland, ISTC members at Ravenscraig, rejected the miners' demands for sympathetic strike action as 'completely unacceptable'. In order to maintain coal supplies to Ravenscraig, steel workers were willing to unload coal at the docks, in the face of dockers' refusal to do so; to allow coal to be transported by non-union haulage contractors, in the face of the NUR's refusal to do so; and to cross NUM picket lines. Correspondingly, power workers made apparent their opposition to any blockading of coal and oil supplies to power stations. In the light of this opposition the decisions of the TUC General Council, in August, and of Congress, in September, to offer 'total support' to the NUM were little more than token gestures.

One consequence of the NUM's internal and external conflicts was the escalating levels of violence during the course of the dispute. The initial coercion of worker by striker rapidly became a subsidiary theme to the coercion of the striker by the state. The militaristic tactics of police 'support units', the national recording centre's co-ordinating role of an effective national riot squad, the intimidation and the prevention, not merely the regulation of, all picketing have been recorded elsewhere (see McIlory 1985; Fine and Millar 1985). But the sheer scale of policing was unprecedented, costing over £200 million by the end of 1984 alone, with 9,000 arrests and over 7,000 people charged with criminal offences. In addition, the use of police road blocks, the general harassment of striking miners' communities, and the enforcement of a night-time curfew as part of the bail conditions imposed upon three Doncaster miners, all raised fundamental questions of civil liberties.

In parallel with the criminal law, the civil law was also used to undermine the resolve of the NUM. Although the NCB, BSC and other major employers affected by the dispute hesitated to use the provisions of the 1980 and 1982 Employment Acts, some working miners did not. Thus, in the summer months of 1984 a series of court actions were instigated against the NUM. The culmination of this process was a High Court ruling, in September, that the strike was unofficial and unlawful. The refusal of Mr Scargill to accept this ruling, in turn, led to a personal fine of £1,000 and a corporate fine for the NUM of £200,000. The NUM's refusal to pay this fine resulted in the sequestration of the union's funds. The spiral of court actions continued as the NUM successfully foiled the sequestrators, Price Waterhouse, and a group of working miners returned to the courts to seek the removal of control of the NUM's assets from the union's trustees and to place them in the hands of the receiver. Thus, as Coates and Topham (1986:111) wryly observe: 'In total, the recourse to law by a variety of individuals and agencies occasioned by the miners' strike broke all records'.

The response of the leadership of the Labour party to the strike, however, was less than 'record breaking'. The PLP leadership systematically distanced itself from the NUM leadership. In doing so, Neil Kinnock placed particular emphasis upon the union executive's failure to call a national ballot. This emphasis reflected the Labour leader's belief that a successful national ballot would have removed the 'unlawful' character of the strike, and so enabled more vociferous support from within the shadow cabinet; or, alternatively, a defeat for the NUM leadership in a ballot would have defused the issue altogether. Indeed, the desire to act, and be seen to act, within the bounds of 'legality', encapsulated in the ballot issue and magnified in Mr Kinnock's consistent condemnation of violence on the picket lines, simply reinforced the party leadership in its reluctance to raise the miners' strike in the House of Commons. Thus, John Saville (1986:321-2), in his reflections upon the performance of the Parliamentary Labour Party during the strike, notes the unwillingness of the Labour frontbench to meet the government head-on, and quotes the *Guardian*'s remark that 'the historian of the future will not go to the pages of Hansard for a detailed commentary on the strike because it was not in fact a matter of serious concern for the House of Commons: measuring concern by the number of columns relating to the strike in Hansard'.

Yet, this conveys only an impressionistic account of the activities of the official opposition frontbench. For example, on 7th June 1984, Stan Orme from the frontbench, initiated an opposition day debate on the dispute; and on the 31st July the 19th opposition day debate on the government's economic, industrial and employment policies provided the springboard for Labour backbenchers to plunge into the dispute (even though Mr Kinnock merely dipped a toenail in these muddy waters in his opening speech). Similarly, in the 1984/5 session, the 3rd opposition day was used to attack the deductions made to the welfare benefits of the dependents of striking miners. In this sense it is inaccurate to state that the opposition leadership did nothing to raise the strike issue in the House. That the leadership was ambivalent in its attitude to the strike is another matter.

No such reservations inhibited the left of the PLP and those backbenchers from militant mining areas. As Eric Heffer (1986:63) notes they 'asked questions wherever they could, and took every opportunity to speak on behalf of the miners in debates on the economy and other matters'. Thus a sustained campaign of written questions was launched, and motions under Standing Order 10 for emergency debates were a regular feature of parliamentary sittings. Peter Hardy and Dave Nellist both used adjournment debates to propagandise the cause of the miners (see HC Debates 1984 vol 61:cols 783-84; vol 64:cols 283-90; vol 68:cols 123-130); collective disorder (see HC Debates 1984 vol 68:cols 385-6; 1985 vol 71:col 524); and the suspension, on separate occasions, of backbenchers Denis Skinner and Martin Flannery for gross misconduct, also brought the attention of the House back to the strike.

Trade Union Legislation and Industrial Relations

The Queen's Speech in 1983 made it clear that the government intended to pursue its policy of 'making markets work better' by removing the capacity of trade unions to frustrate the free working of the market. A start had been made in the 1980 and 1982 Employment Acts which had removed trade union immunities for secondary and other 'unlawful' industrial action; made secondary picketing unlawful; and restricted the closed shop by requiring periodic ballots and permitting non-membership on 'conscience' grounds. The Trade Union Bill introduced in November 1983 was a further step in the government's 'step by step' reform of trade union rights.

The prime purpose of the Trade Union Bill was to curb the independence of trade union leaders by 'democratising' the internal workings of the unions. To this end it required the election of the membership of unions' principal executive committees at least once every five years; secret ballots before industrial action, if immunity from civil action for damages was to be maintained; and special resolutions by ballot if unions wished to operate a political fund (see Coates and Topham 1986:64-112; Fatchett 1987).

The bill had its second reading on 8th November 1983 with the Alliance parties supporting the bill, with reservations, and with a government majority at the end of the debate of 362 to 189. During the course of the 37 sittings of the standing committee on the bill, the government tabled an amendment withdrawing legal immunities from any union which called a strike without a secret ballot. This was clearly in response to the NUM dispute. The amended bill returned to the floor of the House in March 1984, and eventually completed its parliamentary passage in July before receiving the Royal Assent in October 1984.

Throughout most of the period that the Trade Union Bill was under consideration by parliament, the issue of trade union rights was spotlighted by the government's decision to proscribe trade unions at GCHQ in Cheltenham. The imperious attitude of the government served further to sour relations between itself and the labour movement and simultaneously to unite the PLP in its attacks upon the government in the House. Outside of the Commons, the GCHQ decision prompted civil service unions to organise a national half-day stoppage and to challenge the decision, unsuccessfully, in the High Court and the House of Lords. In addition, the TUC registered its dismay by withdrawing from the NEDC for six months from March 1984, until that decision was overturned at the TUC Congress in September. In the debate at Congress, Ken Gill, general secretary of TASS, pointed out the futility of the boycott given that trade union membership of the NEDC merely constituted 'loitering without intent in the corridors of power'.

This general sense of impotence in the face of government policy and legislation was reinforced in a series of other industrial disputes. In the last months of 1983 the NGA became embroiled in a violent dispute with the Stockport Messenger Group of newspapers over the cancellation of a closed shop agreement. Apart from the sheer ferocity of the violence outside the Warrington plant, the dispute was of importance for the series of injunctions granted against the NGA under the 1982 Employment Act. The lesson of the dispute was clear: 'Had the (Act) not existed, the outcome of the dispute might have been different' (Gennard 1984:13). Equally, the Post Office Engineering Union's (POEU) action against Mercury, a private communications company, as part of its opposition to the privatisation of BT, was effectively defused by the company's recourse to legal action.

One other strike of significance, in demonstrating the increased importance of law as a tool of industrial relations strategy, was that at Austin Rover in November 1984. As noted above, the 1984 Trade Union Act requires unions to hold a secret ballot before industrial action. At Austin Rover the joint negotiating committee called a strike on the basis of a vote at a mass meeting of workers. The company immediately sought injunctions requiring the six unions involved to postpone the strike until a ballot had been held. Of the six unions, only the TGWU refused to disown the strike action, with the other five complying with the law. In these circumstances the strike crumbled and there was a rapid return to work. Hence, by the end of 1984 'most unions .... accepted that defiance would not succeed' (Hyman 1987:99).

Regional Policy

The basic sediment of industrial policy in Britain has formed around regional policy (see Judge and Dickson 1987:14). For most of the post-war period regional policy served as a form of 'spatial Keynesianism' to reduce unemployment in depressed areas. Not surprisingly, therefore, in view of the Thatcher government's wider rejection of Keynesianism, regional policy was an obvious target for reduction in the DTI's spending programme. In 1979 and 1982 the government had launched preliminary attacks but a sustained assault was launched in December 1983 when Norman Tebbit, as Secretary of State at the DTI, initiated a twelve month period of consultation and discussion on the future of regional policy. In the White Paper on Regional Industrial Development (Cmnd 9111 1984), which heralded the start of the review, the case for regional policy was advanced as 'principally a social one' rather than an industrial or economic one. In which case, the White Paper argued, regional aid should be more selective with the emphasis placed upon job-creation rather than job maintenance. Under existing schemes manufacturing industries in special development areas had been eligible for significant grants for capital investment (22 per cent) irrespective of the number of jobs created. After November 1984, and the announcement concluding the consultation period, (in which the government 'appeared to have ignored almost everyone it consulted' [*Guardian* 30 November 1984]), the special development areas were abolished. In their place a two-tier system of development areas (covering 15 per cent of the working population) and larger intermediate areas (covering a further 20 per cent) was retained. In this new system the emphasis was to be firmly on 'value for money' and cost-effectiveness, and for the first time was extended to include the service industries.

Whilst the £300 million reduction in regional aid stemming from these changes led the opposition spokesman on Trade and Industry, John Smith, to question the sanity of ministers (see HC Debates vol 71:col 537), and for his colleague, Geoffrey Robinson, to comment that 'for this government, regional policy is a euphemism for cuts – in pits, factories and regional responsibility' (*Guardian* 29 November 1984), the dilution of regional industrial aid was not as severe as might have been expected. Indeed, the intense inter-departmental conflicts between the DTI and the Scottish and Welsh Offices, the extensive lobbying of the CBI and TUC alike, the expectations of multinational corporations of financial packages to induce them to invest in peripheral areas, and the simple fact that the EC regional fund allocated assistance on the basis of defined areas of regional need, all served to constrain the selectivity of the new policy. All of which kept the issue of regional industrial aid alive throughout the first two sessions of the 1983 Parliament.

European Legislation

If regional policy, with its 'sub-national' focus was of consistent concern, so too was the 'supra-national' focus of European Community (EC) legislation in this period. By 1983 it was apparent that the reach of EC directives extended into most aspects of British industrial life. In 1983/4 some 42 EC instruments considered by the Select Committee on European Legislation (ELC) dealt directly with industrial matters, and in 1984/5 the corresponding figure was 30. These instruments ranged from the technical competitiveness of EC industry; aid to the coal and steel industries; through telecommunications; air transport policy; weights of heavy goods vehicles; to the environmental issues of the noise emissions of motor cycles, lawn-mowers; lead in petrol; and industrial air pollution (see Judge 1987). In turn, many of these issues found their way onto the floor of the House in the form of debates on the reports of the ELC, or in questions, or in general debate. In particular, EC policy on reducing capacity and curbing subsidies to the steel and shipbuilding industries, was used, on the one hand, by the British government to justify its own ideological predilections in industrial policy, and, on the other, by the Labour opposition to condemn the government for presiding over the most savage reduction of jobs in traditional industries of all EC countries, and for not supporting British industry in the face of EC competition (see HC Debates 1983 vol 49:cols 126-42).

Whilst specific directives gave rise to sporadic activity throughout 1983/4 and 1984/5, the general consequences of EC membership for British industry increasingly began to impinge upon the consciousness of politicians and industrialists alike. In May 1984 the Select Committee on Trade and Industry published a report on the trade in manufactures with the EC. It revealed that not only was 1983 the year when Britain recorded its first-ever overall trade deficit in manufactured goods, but that the same year also witnessed a £8 billion deficit in UK trade in manufactures to the EC alone. The committee considered this to be 'a problem which urgently needs examination' (HC 461 1984:ix), and specific aspects of this imbalance were considered by the House throughout the following months.

Although the focus of EC directives considered by the House was skewed towards the traditional manufacturing industries, the European Commission itself sought to redress the problems of declining industries through the positive promotion of new technologies and industrial processes. On 28th February 1984 the EC adopted a programme for research into information technology (ESPIRIT); in December of that year an agreement was reached on further R & D programmes, including basic research in industrial technologies (BRITE), a biotechnology programme, and in June 1985 a new R & D programme in advanced communication technologies (RACE) was announced.

Backbench Activity on Industrial Matters 1983/4 and 1984/5

It has been seen above that the two sessions under scrutiny marked a period of significant change in industrial policies: privatisation, trade union reform and the restructuring of regional policy all reflected the ideological drive of the government towards the restitution of a 'free enterprise economy'. But industrial policy was not alone in being subject to the ideological dynamic of change. Other significant policy areas were also subject to upheaval. Major legislative changes were introduced in the fields of law and order, law reform, local government, housing, social security, national health service, and financial and company regulation. The Queen's speeches of 1983 and 1984 clearly revealed the legislative activism of the Thatcher government; fifteen bills were announced in the first speech and a further eighteen were introduced in the second. Thus, there was plenty of competition for the attention of backbenchers in the House. What the rest of this chapter seeks to examine, therefore, is, first, the extent to which industrial matters were raised on the floor of the House in the light of other pressing policy changes; second, the sectoral focus of industrial policy issues; and, third, the number of backbenchers active upon these matters in the chamber.

Unfortunately, as with so many aspects of parliamentary study in Britain, there is little hard data upon which to develop research hypotheses. All too often, assumptions and assertions are offered in place of empirical evidence in the discussion of activity in the House of Commons. The problem which subsequently arises is that contradictory statements are made about activity in the House. Hence, it is possible to find within the existing literature two contrasting assessments of the level of activity on industrial affairs. On the one side, in common with the assumptions examined in chapter 4, it is asserted that the collective attention of the House is neither focused consistently nor adequately on industrial matters (see Hansard Society 1979:43-44). In contrast, however, statements to the effect that there is significant parliamentary interest in industrial affairs can also be found (see Coombes and Walkland 1980:55; Grant 1982:38). The problem with either assessment is that they are based essentially upon assertion rather than fact. In which case, the question of the extent of backbench activity on industrial matters is not only basic but also important in itself. It is important to replace speculation with empirical data.

However, one novel empirical analysis, a wider examination of backbench specialisation in the Commons in the early 1970s (see Judge 1981), does indicate, admittedly tangentially, the extent of backbench interest in industrial policy. Fortuitously, the period examined – sessions 1970/1 and 1972/3 – was itself characterised by significant industrial policy changes. Yet the sample of backbenchers revealed the limited attention paid to industrial matters in the House. Such matters attracted on average no more than 7 per cent of backbenchers' questions in each session, and no more than 11 per cent of speeches. Whilst attention to industrial policy matters was thus limited in absolute terms, nonetheless, in relative terms, in comparison with other policy issues, industry ranked as one of the two major policy considerations in both sessions (see Judge 1979:224-9).

Table 5.3 Total Industrial Activity: All MPs (Including Ministers)

	Oral PQs			*Written PQs*			*Debate*		
	Ind	*Total*	*Ind*	*Ind*	*Total*	*Ind*	*Ind*	*Total*	*Ind*
	n	*n*	*%*	*n*	*n*	*%*	*n*	*n*	*%*
1983/4	637	9435	6.8	1659	46798	3.6	4523	31690	14.3
1984/5	408	7326	5.6	1267	35052	3.6	3491	27952	12.5
83/4 + 84/5	1045	16761	6.2	2926	81850	3.6	8014	59642	13.4

From the findings of this earlier study it is at least possible to hypothesise that there will be fairly restricted activity in the House on industrial policy in absolute terms, but that such activity will be of significance in relative terms.

This indeed appears to have been the case in sessions 1983/4 and 1984/5. In the first session 6.8 per cent of oral questions and 3.6 per cent of written questions were directly concerned with industrial matters as defined in chapter 4 (see also Appendix A1). In the second session the corresponding percentages were 5.6 and 3.6 (see Table 5.3). In relative terms, however, industrial questions ranked amongst the most important subject areas. In comparison questions on 'defence', for instance, accounted for 1.8 per cent of oral, and 1.3 per cent of written questions over the two sessions; and the corresponding figures for 'employment' were 1.7 per cent and 2.1 per cent.

When the contribution of backbenchers to debate is considered, then the proportion of total activity expended on industrial matters rises to approximately 13 per cent across both sessions. Again there appears to be some consistency over time with the level of activity observed in the 1970s, though given the methodological difficulties in arriving at these figures too much weight should not be accorded to this finding. But, as maximum levels of participation, these figures reveal the limited opportunities for the discussion of industrial policy on the floor of the House, and, hence, the necessity for backbench contributions to be both informed and 'professional' on these occasions. Whether the quality of debate overcomes the limitations of quantity will be explored in the next chapter. Of more immediate concern here is the identification of the number of backbenchers actively engaged in the consideration of industrial policy matters.

Backbenchers: Industrial Activity and Party

In total 456 backbenchers (86 per cent of all backbenchers) participated in the consideration of industrial matters on the floor of the House at some stage in the period June 1983 to October 1985. In other words, eight out of ten backbench MPs showed some interest, by asking at least one question or intervening at some stage in debate, in industrial policy. 86 per cent (n 261) of all Conservative backbenchers, and 91 per cent (n 166) of all Labour backbenchers displayed some interest in such matters.

Table 5.4 reveals the breakdown of activity on industrial matters in each of three procedures, oral and written questions and debate, when crosstabulated by party. With the exception of oral questions, Labour backbenchers are collectively more active on industrial matters than Conservative MPs. Moreover, as Table 5.5 shows, Labour MPs generally display higher levels of individual activity than their Conservative counterparts. Certainly, in each procedure there are more Labour than Conservative members at the highest levels of activity (significantly so in debate). Whether this is a function of different policy priorities and interests between backbenchers in the major parties is open to question. Undoubtedly, one factor in explaining this difference may be the restraints felt by Conservative backbenchers, as supporters of the government, in pressing their own frontbenchers too vigorously for action, or of being too critical of policy.

Table 5.4   Total Industrial Activity: Backbenchers By Party

	Oral PQs				Written PQs				Debate			
	1983/4		1984/5		1983/4		1984/5		1983/4		1984/5	
Party	*n*	*%*	*n*	*%*	*n*	*%*	*n*	*%*	*n*	*%*	*n*	*%*
Cons	272	50.5	181	50.2	609	39.4	485	41.5	1283	40.4	1110	46.4
Lab	243	45.2	160	44.3	862	55.7	612	52.4	1754	55.2	1158	48.4
Other	23	4.3	20	5.5	76	4.9	72	6.1	139	4.4	123	5.2
Total	538	100.0	361	100.0	1547	100.0	1169	100.0	3176	100.0	2391	100.0

However, to state that Labour MPs are generally more active on industrial matters does not necessarily mean that they are any more specialised in these matters than their Conservative counterparts. Indeed, as Table 5.6 reveals, there are no significant differences between Labour and Conservative backbenchers in terms of the percentages of members ranked at the various levels of specialisation. (Specialisation is measured here in terms of the percentage of a member's total activity devoted to industrial matters). Each procedure does, however, reflect a different profile of specialisation, with debate being most specialised, followed in turn by oral questions and then written questions. These differences reflect the distinct 'costs of participation' exacted by each procedure (see Judge 1981:69-76) and account for the differing interval widths for each procedure in Table 5.6 (see Appendix A2). It is noteworthy, however, that there is a significant positive correlation between the level of activity and the degree of specialisation. Taking Conservative and Labour backbenchers together the correlation coefficients are 0.32 for oral questions (n 272, $p < 0.000$); 0.27 for written questions (n 382; $p < 0.000$); and 0.58 for debate (n 400; $p < 0.000$) In other words, the more active MPs are on industrial matters, the more likely they are to devote more of their overall attention to such matters. This is the case in both parties, and is particularly the case in the Labour party. The respective coefficients for the procedures of oral questions, written questions and debate for the Conservatives are 0.24 (n 147, $p < 0.001$); 0.18 (n 209, $p < 0.004$); and 0.52 (n 221, $p < 0.000$); and for Labour 0.44 (n 108, $p < 0.000$); 0.34 (n 145, $p < 0.000$); and 0.62 (n 155, $p < 0.000$).

Table 5.5   Industrial Activity by Party by Procedure

Oral Questions

N Ind	Conservative				Labour				Other			
	83/4		84/5		83/4		84/5		83/4		84/5	
OPQ	n	%	n	%	n	%	n	%	n	%	n	%
1	49	43.8	52	54.2	33	36.7	29	43.3	3	33.3	5	45. 5
2-3	40	35.7	34	35.4	35	38.9	25	37.3	4	44.4	5	45. 5
4+	23	20.5	10	10.4	22	24.4	13	19.4	2	22.3	1	9. 0
Total	112	100.0	96	100.0	90	100.0	67	100.0	9	100.0	11	100. 0

Lab v Cons	83/4	x^2	1.09	df 2	$p< 0.6$
	84/5	x^2	3.24	df 2	$p< 0.2$

Written Questions

N Ind	Conservative				Labour				Other			
	83/4		84/5		83/4		84/5		83/4		84/5	
WPQ	n	%	n	%	n	%	n	%	n	%	n	%
1	55	33.1	64	43.0	36	28.1	31	25.6	9	37.5	5	25.0
2-3	62	37.3	42	28.2	37	28.9	38	31.4	6	25.0	7	35.0
4-5	21	12.7	20	13.4	22	17.2	21	17.4	5	20.8	2	10.0
6+	28	16.9	23	15.4	33	25.8	31	25.6	4	16.7	6	30.0
Total	166	100.0	149	100.0	128	100.0	121	100.0	24	100.0	20	100.0

Lab v Cons	83/4	x^2	5.09	df 3	$p< 0.15$
	84/5	x^2	10.08	df 3	$p< 0.02$

Debates

N Ind	Conservative				Labour				Other			
	83/4		84/5		83/4		84/5		83/4		84/5	
Cols	n	%	n	%	n	%	n	%	n	%	n	%
1- 5	106	56.7	104	57.5	61	42.1	58	46.0	10	62.5	9	56.3
6-10	46	24.6	46	25.4	29	20.0	28	22.2	1	6.2	4	25.0
11-15	16	8.5	21	11.6	19	13.1	12	9.6	2	12.5	1	6.2
16+	19	10.2	10	5.5	36	24.8	28	22.2	3	18.8	2	12.5
Total	187	100.0	181	100.0	145	100.0	126	100.0	16	100.0	16	100.0

Lab v Cons	83/4	x^2	16.44	df 3	$p< 0.001$
	84/5	x^2	19.18	df 3	$p< 0.000$

Table 5.6   Level of Industrial 'Specialisation' by Party by Procedure

Oral Questions

Level Indust 'Spec'	Conservative 83/4 n	%	84/5 n	%	Labour 83/4 n	%	84/5 n	%	Other 83/4 n	%	84/5 n	%
Low	30	26.8	32	33.3	31	34.4	18	26.9	5	55.6	5	45.4
Medium	43	38.4	25	26.1	31	34.4	26	38.8	2	22.2	4	36.4
High	39	34.8	39	40.6	28	31.2	23	34.3	2	22.2	2	18.2
Total	112	100.0	96	100.0	90	100.0	67	100.0	9	100.0	11	100.0

Lab v Cons	83/4	x^2	1.30	df 2	$p < 0.5$
	84/5	x^2	3.00	df 2	$p < 0.2$

Written Questions

Level Indust 'Spec'	Conservative 83/4 n	%	84/5 n	%	Labour 83/4 n	%	84/5 n	%	Other 83/4 n	%	84/5 n	%
Low	56	33.7	44	29.5	52	40.6	34	28.1	10	41.7	14	70.0
Medium	46	27.7	34	22.8	34	26.6	32	26.4	10	41.7	4	20.0
High	64	38.6	71	47.7	42	32.8	55	45.5	4	16.6	2	10.0
Total	166	100.0	149	100.0	128	100.0	121	100.0	24	100.0	20	100.0

Lab v Cons	83/4	x^2	1.6	df 2	$p < 0.4$
	84/5	x^2	0.5	df 2	$p < 0.8$

Debates

Level Indust 'Spec'	Conservative 83/4 n	%	84/5 n	%	Labour 83/4 n	%	84/5 n	%	Other 83/4 n	%	84/5 n	%
Low	66	35.3	64	35.4	46	31.7	32	25.4	9	56.2	8	50.0
Medium	64	34.2	72	39.8	41	28.3	48	38.1	5	31.3	4	25.0
High	57	30.5	45	24.8	58	40.0	46	35.5	2	12.5	4	25.0
Total	187	100.0	181	100.0	145	100.0	126	100.0	16	100.0`	16	100.0

Lab v Cons	83/4	x^2	3.4	df 2	$p < 0.2$
	84/5	x^2	5.8	df 2	$p < 0.06$

Sectoral Focus of Industrial Activity
The impact of the miners' strike is clearly seen in Table 5.7. In sectoral terms
the coal industry attracted the single largest proportion of backbench activity in
each procedure. In oral questions, for example, well over one-quarter of all
'industrial' questions focused upon the problems of the coal industry (see
Appendix B1). Indeed, this may be taken as further evidence that the general
issues raised by the miners' strike were aired in the Commons. However, the
extent to which the coal dispute skewed the sectoral focus of backbenchers in
sessions 1983/4 and 1984/5 is revealed by examining the figures in
parentheses in Table 5.7. These represent the proportion of activity in each
industrial sector once contributions dealing specifically with the miners' strike
have been excluded. In this respect these figures are probably indicative of a
more 'normal' distribution of activity amongst sectors. Even so, the problems
associated with the contraction of the coal industry clearly remained of major
concern to backbenchers in the sessions under study. This was particularly so
for Labour backbenchers. In each procedure the majority of contributions,
two-thirds in fact for written questions and debate, came from Labour
backbenchers (see Appendices B1 and B2).

Not surprisingly, the sectoral focus of backbench activity is heavily
influenced by the legislative programme in any specific session; manifestly so
in debates. Hence, the sectors affected by privatisation (telecommunications,
oil extraction, road transport, shipbuilding) engaged a considerable proportion
of MPs' attention throughout the period 1983-85. However, interspersed
amongst such 'legislative-driven' activity was also discussion of the problems
of the declining traditional industries – especially steel and textiles. Moreover,
the role of new technology and its impact upon British industry was the
subject of a private member's debate initiated by Don Dixon in February
1984, and was chosen again as the subject of the 11th opposition day debate
in May 1985. In addition to Labour MPs intent on criticising government
failure to assist adequately the new industries, there were also more positive
contributions from Conservative backbenchers with information technology
industries in their constituencies: these included Ian Lloyd (Havant) with IBM;
Philip Oppenheim (Amber Valley) with Micro-Image Technology, a
subsidiary of Laporte concerned with the manufacture of micro-chips; and
Tim Wood (Stevenage) with ICL, and Standard Telephone and Cable.

In parallel with activity in debate, backbenchers also used questions to
pursue their interest in specific sectors. Indeed, as a cost-efficient mode of
backbench activity (see Judge 1981:72), questions enable MPs to advance an
argument by repeatedly asking ministers for more information from
departments, and, in the process, so to expose and publicise the details of
policy. The introduction of the limited list of prescription drugs, already
outlined in chapter 3, provides just such an example. The decision prompted a
series of questions designed to elicit further information from the Health

Table 5.7   Activity on the Ten Major Industrial Sectors : Controlling for the Effects of the Miners' Strike (1983/4 and 1984/5)

	Oral Questions		*Procedure* *Written Questions*			*Debate*		
Sector	*total* *%*	*(% – miners)*	*Sector*	*total* *%*	*(% – miners)*	*Sector*	*total* *%*	*(% – miners)*
Coal	28.0	(16.0)	Coal	8.7	(4.1)	Coal	17.7	(9.8)
Metal Man.	5.3	(6.2)	Construct	7.5	(7.9)	Trans. Equip.	9.7	(10.6)
Construct	5.2	(6.1)	Chemical	4.1	(4.3)	Telecom.	6.1	(6.7)
Elect/Gas	5.1	(6.0)	Textiles	3.7	(3.9)	Road Trans.	4.3	(4.8)
Motor Man.	3.3	(3.9)	Trans. Equip.	3.0	(3.2)	Data	4.2	(4.6)
Trans. Equip.	3.2	(3.8)	Food	2.9	(3.1)	Motor Man.	3.8	(4.2)
Textiles	2.1	(2.5)	Elect/Gas	2.7	(2.9)	Oil Extract.	3.4	(3.8)
Data	1.6	(1.8)	Metal. Man.	1.7	(1.8)	Metal Man.	2.7	(2.9)
Paper	1.2	(1.4)	Motor Man.	1.6	(1.7)	Construct	2.4	(2.6)
Leather	1.2	(1.4)	Data	1.6	(1.7)	Textiles	2.2	(2.4)

minister about his department's dealings with the pharmaceutical industry. For instance, Michael Morris (Conservative, Northampton South), with experience of the industry as a former director and parliamentary consultant for Reckitt and Colman and other pharmaceutical companies, tabled several questions asking why there had been no prior consultation with the pharmaceutical industry on the list (HC Debates 1984 vol 69:cols 166-9). In contrast, Richard Hickmet (Conservative, Glanford and Scunthorpe) repeatedly questioned whether the expenditure of the ABPI in its advertising campaign against the introduction of the limited list would constitute an allowable expense under the pharmaceutical price regulation scheme (HC Debates 1985 vol 75:cols 386-7; vol 76:cols 95-6).

One particularly striking use of questions to highlight backbench interest in a specific industrial sector was Labour MP Robert Parry's concern with employment practices in the construction industry. As an ex-building trade worker, former full-time NUPE organiser, and a sponsored member of the TWGU, Parry tabled a total of 43 written questions upon the construction industry – largely on health and safety matters and the employment consequences of government policy. The campaigning nature of Parry's questions can be gauged from the fact that some 32 were tabled on just four days (see HC Debates vol 49 1983:cols 446-8; vol 50 1983 cols 325-451; vol 71 1985:cols 362-89). On the Conservative side, some 85 written questions focused upon the construction industry, with John Heddle and Michael Latham being more active than most of their other colleagues. Heddle's occupational background was that of consultant surveyor; he also acted as vice-chairman of the Building Societies Association and chairman of the Conservative backbench Environment Committee. Similarly, Michael Latham had close connections with the building industry as director of Lovell Homes, vice-president of the Building Societies Association and former chief executive of the House Builders Federation. Detailed examination of the linkages between activity in the House on industrial matters and members' occupational backgrounds and interests is, however, the preserve of the next chapter. Before then it is worthwhile analysing the substantive focus of backbench activity on industrial policy.

Substantive Policy Focus of Industrial Activity

This last section of the chapter examines the substantive policy focus of backbenchers' activity on industrial policy matters in the House. Once more it is evident that the miners' strike and the ideological predispositions of the Thatcher government largely set the policy agenda for the period under study. The miners' strike certainly concentrated backbench attention upon industrial relations throughout the period under study. Some 17 per cent of oral questions, and over 10 per cent of the policy content of speeches, had industrial relations as the primary policy concern. (Indeed, if activity specifically dealing with the miners' strike is excluded, the respective proportions of activity dealing with industrial relations in oral questions and debate respectively fall to 3.5 per cent and 2.3 per cent).

Equally, the impact of the government's economic policies upon the competitiveness and trading position of British industry was of major interest for backbenchers in the mid-1980s (see Appendices B4, B5 and B6). In turn, this concern was linked to others about the levels of assistance provided by government, and the amount of government regulation still prevailing in industry.

All four policy concerns – industrial relations, economic policy, government assistance and regulation – along with the issue of privatisation, tended to be approached in a partisan manner and, invariably, reinforced the divide between backbenchers on different sides of the House. In combination these five policy issues dominated activity on the floor of the House, accounting for 42.6 per cent of oral questions and featuring in 50.5 per cent of backbench contributions in industrial debates. It is significant perhaps that in the less adversarial context of written questions these issues accounted for only 22.8 per cent of substantive policy concerns.

Also of significance, however, is the spatial dimension of backbench activity on industrial policy. A pronounced constituency orientation is evident, particularly in Labour backbenchers' activity. Indeed, the territorial dimension is often placed ahead of functional considerations. In the strictest definition of geographical area – parliamentary constituency – the spatial focus of backbenchers' activity is apparent in 6.0 per cent of oral questions, 5.9 per cent of written questions and 12.4 per cent of contributions to debate. However, if the definition is widened to include both primary reference to constituency and to region then the respective percentages rise to 13.9, 11.2 and 20.6. Moreover, it is also important to observe here that EC industrial policies added a further 'spatial' dimension to the substantive policy foci of many members. As a consequence, 'territorial' foci thus outranked most other individual policy concerns. The reasons for this, and the wider significance of constituency, will be examined in the next chapter.

6 Backbenchers and Industry: Influences on Activity in the Commons

The force of generalisations about the behaviour of backbenchers in the House of Commons is limited by the multiplicity of influences guiding their activity on any particular issue. Many MPs are themselves sceptical of academic attempts to analyse their actions in the House. The belief that their behaviour is unique, and that the influences upon that behaviour are exceptional can still be found in many members' responses to academic enquiries. In these circumstances many British studies of backbenchers have never left the safety of the description of the functions and roles of the parliamentary institution and its members. Certainly, the last decade has witnessed an increased willingness of British students to use, what Norton (1978:13-18) calls the 'scientific method'; but there are still relatively few detailed studies of the influences upon activity in the House: of constituency, electoral vulnerability, ideology, party, or pre-parliamentary experience. Whilst there have been analyses of these independent variables in isolation, analyses invariably conducted by American political scientists, there remains a dearth of comprehensive analyses of the influences on backbench activity. The aim of this chapter, therefore, is to provide both a quantitative and qualitative assessment of the activity of backbenchers upon industrial policy issues and the independent variables associated with that activity.

Constituency
At the end of chapter 5, it was noted that spatial considerations – constituency and regional foci of activity – are of some significance in the consideration of industrial policy issues by backbenchers. Overall, it was apparent that spatial foci, where backbenchers had as their primary concern the geographical area of constituency or region, proportionally outweighed most other individual 'functional' concerns. The significance of this finding is that it challenges one of the established views of the relationship between the 'functional' and 'territorial' dimensions of MPs' contributions to the policy process. Richard

Rose (1982:88-90), for example, has argued that MPs are more functionally than territorially oriented, and that constituency interests, as such, are of secondary importance in their considerations of policy issues. This of course raises the question of how 'functional' and 'constituency' foci can be distinguished? One answer is provided in a recent and highly relevant article by David Wood (1987). Wood suggests that area-specific interests involve three material values which affect people in different parts of the country in different ways. These values are shared by: i) all or many of the inhabitants in a geographical area; ii) by members of different socio-economic groups; and iii) are not necessarily shared by inhabitants of other areas. In turn these material values cross-cut ideological groupings, both inter- and intra-party, to the extent that these values serve to differentiate MPs from regional areas with shared industrial experiences from other members who do not share the same combination of spatial and sectoral interests (see Wood 1987:397; also Richardson and Jordan 1979:124-7).

Wood thus provides a perspective on industrial policy which enables an examination of the impact of area upon industrial sectoral policies through the analysis of their different effects upon inhabitants in various parts of the country. But, in turn, the identification of 'localised industrial policies, proceeding from purely territorial, as opposed to functional concerns' (Wood 1987:398) raises the question of the *extent* to which backbenchers engage in such activity. On the basis of conventional views, there would be little expectation that MPs would devote much of their parliamentary activity to territorial as distinct from sectoral industrial concerns. Indeed, Wood's original research hypothesis, based upon the earlier findings of Searing (1985) was precisely that the pursuit of 'localised industrial policies' would not be a major concern of backbenchers. Yet, in the course of interviews with 70 Conservative MPs in 1983/4, Wood was led to the conclusion that many of his sample included as part of their role definition the task of constituency lobbyist on behalf of local economic and industrial interests. Not only was the importance of territory manifest in interview but Wood argues 'the evidence that local industries are a pre-occupation of numerous MPs, especially those representing areas where jobs are in jeopardy, is readily available from an examination of debates and of oral and written questions (Wood 1987:409). Unfortunately, no substantive quantitative evidence is provided. To rectify this deficiency, therefore, the following section provides a detailed analysis of the territorial focus of backbenchers in their consideration of industrial policy issues in sessions 1983/4 and 1984/5.

Spatial Focus of Backbench Activity

The importance of 'territory' is illustrated in Table 6.1 where 15.4 per cent of backbenchers had at least one of their oral questions focused specifically upon a constituency industrial concern; 21.7 per cent displayed a similar concern in written questions; and 36 per cent directly related part of their contribution in debate to the territorial impact of industrial policies. When the definition of 'territory' is widened beyond electoral constituency to include region, then approximately one-third of backbenchers displayed a direct concern with territorial issues in their questioning activity, and well over one-half of all MPs speaking in debates on industry felt obliged at some stage to relate their contributions to their local geographical area. Not surprisingly, those

Table 6.1 Constituency Focus of Backbenchers' Industrial Activity

Oral Questions

	Ind active MPs n	Constit Focus n	Constit Focus %	Region Focus n	Region Focus %
Conservative	147	15	10.2	36	24.5
Labour	108	25	23.2	41	38.0
Other	17	2	11.8	6	35.3
Total	272	42	15.4	83	30.5

Written Questions

	Ind active MPs n	Constit Focus n	Constit Focus %	Region Focus n	Region Focus %
Conservative	209	26	12.4	51	24.4
Labour	145	49	33.8	72	49.7
Other	28	8	28.6	15	53.6
Total	382	83	21.7	138	36.1

Debate

	Ind active MPs n	Constit Focus n	Constit Focus %	Region Focus n	Region Focus %
Conservative	221	60	27.2	108	48.9
Labour	155	77	49.7	99	63.9
Other	24	7	29.2	7	29.2
Total	400	144	36.0	214	53.5

members from regions with area-specific industries, such as coalmining or shipbuilding, were particularly prone to add a territorial dimension to the deliberation of sectoral policies. This tendency has already been identified in an earlier study of MPs' consideration of European Communities' industrial policy instruments (see Judge 1987:12-3).The emphasis upon constituency concerns was particularly pronounced in the deliberation of these instruments with, on average, 55 per cent of backbench participants specifically referring to their geographical constituency.

Similarly, analysis of debates on coalmining or shipbuilding for instance reveals the territorial pre-occupation of many participants. To take but one example, the opposition day debate on the shipbuilding industry on 27 November 1984 (HC Debates 1984 vol 68:cols 832-78) attracted seventeen substantial backbench contributions, and with only one exception, all the speakers came from shipbuilding areas. The major shipbuilding areas of Tyneside, Merseyside and Wearside, along with the more peripheral areas of Aberdeen, Dundee and Southampton, found their interests reflected in the speeches of seven Conservative, eight Labour and two Alliance members. All but four of these members focused their attention upon the effect of governmental policy upon their constituency. Labour backbenchers paid particular attention to the insensitivity of the government to the needs of shipbuilding areas and to the detrimental consequences of industrial policy for shipbuilding communities. Frank Field (Birkenhead) sought, in his words, 'to give the Government three messages. They come not from me, but from my constituents; the second of which was that 'if Cammell-Laird is allowed to fold, that could be the end of a community in our area' (HC Debates 1984 vol 68:cols 854-5). Don Dixon (Jarrow), in turn, ruefully observed:

> This is the first time in living memory that no ships are being built on the south side of the Tyne. This Government have done what Hitler's bombers could not do during the last world war. The Government have no feeling for the shipbuilding communities. (HC Debates 1984 vol 68:col 865)

On the Conservative backbenches the contributions of Michael Fallon (Darlington) and Cecil Franks (Barrow and Furness) both made direct and primary reference to their constituencies, yet both also revealed their Thatcherite proclivities by demonstrating how entrepreneurial endeavour would enhance the prospects of the shipbuilding industry. Thus, Franks ended his speech with the resounding call:

> Barrow and Furness welcomes privatisation and looks forward to its prosperity continuing to grow. We welcome privatisation – managers and labour – and the Government will give us our opportunity. (HC Debates 1984 vol 68:col 854)

In microcosm, this debate illuminates the general finding of Wood that ideology is not a good predictor of the adoption of the constituency 'lobbying' role. A 'constituency lobbyist' is defined by Wood (1987:396) as a member who sees 'the constituency as an economic whole to be defended and promoted' and who engages in a range of promotional activities on behalf of local industries at Westminster and beyond. Clearly, by the mid-1980s the role of constituency lobbyist was an integral part of many backbenchers' jobs. Indeed, a survey conducted by the House of Commons All Party Reform Group (1985) revealed that whilst 72 per cent of MPs regarded the constituency welfare-officer role as important or very important, this was surpassed by the 88 per cent who saw their role as spokesman for local interests to be important or very important. Moreover, as noted above, over half of Wood's interviewees (n 36) indicated that they identified themselves as promoters of constituency, industrial and economic interests.

In an attempt to explain the discrepancy between his findings and those of Searing's (1985) study, which identified only 4 per cent of backbenchers as 'local promoters' in the early 1970s, Wood advances the argument that the intervening decade between the two sets of interviews witnessed an increased sense of economic vulnerability in British politics. In these changed circumstances, MPs engaged more in industrial promotion because of the insecurity of the industrial base in many constituencies. This economic 'insecurity' is a generalised phenomenon affecting most MPs to the extent that 'it may be deemed useful to "be seen" to be active in attempting to forestall or redress local economic misfortunes' (Wood 1987:400). This may help to explain why over half of the Conservative 'dry' MPs in Wood's sample were classified as 'lobbyists', and why 'at the level of basic principle, the relationship, wet = lobbyist, dry = non-lobbyist, is not supported' (Wood 1987:402).

Evidence to support Wood's conclusion can also be found from the interviews conducted for the present study. Of fifteen Conservative backbenchers interviewed, eight were overtly 'Thatcherites', four were 'centre right'; and three were 'wet' or 'dampish'. (This categorisation was based upon biographical material and a study of the voting record on key issues of the MPs concerned. The accuracy of this initial categorisation has been verified subsequently in Norton's categorisation of Conservative MPs [1990]). Yet, with only two exceptions, all recognised the importance of promoting constituency industrial interests. Significantly, only one 'dry' member was openly protectionist insofar as he sought government action against the dumping of mineral products from other European Community states. In defending the industrial interests of his Midlands constituency he arranged private meetings with the Minister of State at the DTI, took delegations of trade unionists to see the same minister, and had a private meeting with Mrs. Thatcher. The Prime Minister was, in this backbencher's own pithy words, 'sympathetic. In fact, she was generally as pissed off about dumping as I was'.

Another Conservative, again on the 'dry' side of the party, and who represented an industrial constituency in the North of England, was more reflective on the impact of his constituency upon his parliamentary role:

> If you compare the size of British constituencies to that in the United States and in Europe, you find that ours are much smaller. As a result, consumer interests are subjugated to industrial and production interests. This means that the system is protectionist, MPs are led to protect their own constituency industrial interests, particularly when they are mass employers in that area. Take my constituency, industry is to a massive extent dependent on government. The major [chemical] firm is almost totally dependent on government grants and subsidies. Most private firms similarly are dependent on government subsidies, and local authority spending has a significant influence on the private sector.
>
> Yet, industrially, my constituency is changing. There has been a significant reduction in the manufacturing workforce. My job is to bring about the recognition of that change and to promote new developments revolving around new technologies .... I also try to bring consumer interests to bear, so as to offset the direct and immediate industrial interest with that of the 'general' consumer interest.
>
> All of this means that I get involved with closures and with firms applying for government assistance (for example I do a lot of work in help with exports, for export credits), but all of the time I am attempting to make industrialists and trade unionists aware of those wider consumer interests. This is often difficult. Whereas in United States districts, functional organisations regulate themselves with industrial, agricultural, and consumer interests forming countervailing blocs, in Britain, I come back to the point, that organised industrial interests are not offset by general/consumer interests.

The most 'resolute' line, however, was taken by another Thatcherite loyalist from an essentially rural/service constituency which had a declining bulk chemical plant alongside a prosperous pharmaceutical industry. He maintained that there should be no protection for industry: 'I wouldn't support protection even if there was a constituency interest. I'm all in favour of an intransigent line on this issue'. Shortly afterwards he did recognise, nonetheless, that 'there might be a case for trimming some of these views if my constituency had industries which were particularly suffering. Even then, though, if you calculated it, local industry wouldn't represent all that many votes'.

These statements lend support to Wood's criticism of Searing's hypothesis that Conservative 'wets' would be more likely to be constituency lobbyists than right-wingers (Searing 1982:249; Wood 1987:204). Moreover, the data from sessions 1983/4 and 1984/5 also bring into question Searing's finding that Conservative MPs were more likely to identify themselves as 'local promoters' than Labour MPs. In his interviews in 1972/3 Searing discovered that more Labour backbenchers than Conservative saw themselves as constituency members, yet a greater proportion of Conservative constituency members (24 per cent) than Labour members (9 per cent) depicted themselves as 'local promoters'. What Table 6.1 reveals, however, is that Labour backbenchers were consistently more likely to 'promote' their constituency in the formal proceedings of the House by specifically mentioning the territorial area of their constituency. Nearly one-half of Labour backbenchers active in industrial debates made clear their constituency focus, in contrast to just over one-quarter of Conservative backbenchers. When the territorial definition is widened to include 'region', then 64 per cent of Labour participants in debate and 49 per cent of Conservatives sought to advance or defend regional industrial interests.

Table 6.2   Industrial Debates: Activity as Regional Lobbyist by Major Party by Constituency Type.

| *Type of Constituency* | *Conservative* | | | | *Labour* | | | |
| | 'region lobbyist' | | *Ind. Active Bbs* | | 'region lobbyist' | | *Ind. Active Bbs* | |
	n	%	n	%	n	%	n	%
Resident/Agric	27	25.0	80	30.7	3	3.0	12	7.2
Mixed	40	37.0	96	36.8	31	31.3	45	27.1
Manufacturing	41	38.0	85	32.6	65	65.7	109	65.7
Total	108	100.0	261	100.0	99	100.0	166	100.0

Table 6.2 demonstrates, however, that in 'promoting' the interests of a geographical area in industrial policy debates one-quarter of Conservative backbenchers did so from a 'non-industrial' base – using Wood's classification of constituencies (1987:403). In part their involvement in industrial policy issues was negative in the sense of attempting to redirect the attention of the government away from declining manufacturing sectors towards the service and tourist sectors. Regional policy itself was one issue area where the constituency 'lobbyist' role is both pronounced and involves representatives from 'non-industrial' areas in the consideration of industrial policy. Thus in the debate on the substantive motion of 17 January 1985 Conservative constituency lobbyists from 'non-industrial' areas were active for a variety of reasons. Roger Gale (Thanet, North), for example, approved the government's reallocation of regional aid money (HC Debates 1985 vol

71:cols 571-3). In contrast, Norman Miscampbell (Blackpool, North) deplored the loss of assisted area status for his own region (HC Debate 1985 vol 71:cols 544-5).

Overall in debate Conservative promoters of territorial industrial interests tended to be drawn more from 'mixed' and 'manufacturing' constituencies. This was even more the case on the opposition benches where nearly two-thirds of those backbenchers advancing the cause of their constituency and wider region represented industrial constituencies. Indeed, the distribution of territorial lobbyists in both major parties in debating activity roughly parallels the overall distribution of seats according to industrial 'type' of constituency.

In addition to formal activity in the chamber, it is normal for backbenchers to promote local industrial interests through representations to ministers and their departments. These informal meetings are frequently acknowledged in debate. Thus, for instance, Patrick Nicholls (Conservative, Teignbridge) prefaced his speech during the course of the discussion of regional policy by stating:

> My hon. Friend the Under-Secretary of State is well aware from correspondence that I had had with him, from debates in the House and from a delegation which I led to see him before the decision was made how I feel about the withdrawal of aid from my constituency. (HC Debates 1985 vol 71:col 525)

But, as Wood (1987:399) observes, constituency economic lobbying is not restricted to government ministers: 'MPs lobby and are lobbied by the head offices of firms with plants or offices in their constituencies, as well as firms that might be enticed to make a move into the area. Local authorities, local business groups, trade unions and individual firms often turn to the MP for help in convincing a central government official to make a favourable ruling on a matter of concern to them'. These local pressures were also clearly acknowledged in the interviews conducted for the present study. Of the eighteen Labour backbenchers interviewed, fourteen could be identified as constituency lobbyists and all fourteen easily listed various constituency interests – individual firms, trade unionists, local authorities, trade councils – with whom they maintained regular contacts and by whom they were briefed about developments within their constituencies. Eleven of the Labour lobbyists claimed to make regular visits to the major industrial firms within their constituencies. One north-west MP pointed to the fact that:

> factories like you to visit because they know you will end up talking about their problems. Management allows you to talk to the shop stewards and workforce and you end up with a broad look at what is happening.

Not surprisingly, most Labour interviewees emphasised their contacts with trade unions and other labour organisations. As one Nottinghamshire representative commented:

> I've certainly made connections with the [textile] industry. Textiles is a significant industry in my constituency, and I'll visit firms any time. But my real connections are with the trade union movement. I'm able to get the lay of the land, to know what's likely to happen in the future.

A West of Scotland member went out of his way to point to his ability to keep in contact with 'both management and trade unions, though I have friendlier relations with the latter. Having said that, I do have a good working relationship with managements in some local firms. I get on well with [manager of shipyard] who is tough but he's also fair. But equally the yards are blessed with first class trade union representatives'.

The necessity of performing the constituency lobbyist role was particularly apparent for those MPs reacting to industrial closure. Nearly all of the Labour interviewees gave examples of how they had been called upon to defend local industry threatened by closure. The general problem encountered in these circumstances was clearly identified by a left-wing Merseyside member:

> With closure, MPs are reactive. They're often not called in until the situation is well developed. There's little opportunity for MPs to identify a problem. It becomes an issue for them only when it reaches a critical period. In fact, workers are often given preference over MPs by being taken into management's confidence. All this means is that they are shown the books, which make closure seem inevitable.

Nevertheless, four of the fourteen Labour 'lobbyists' claimed to have had some success in fighting closures in their constituencies. One Northern backbencher pointed to his success in securing government assistance for an ailing carpet firm:

> [Name] carpets went through a rough patch. It looked as though the company would fold. Well, morale dropped through the floor. Management couldn't cope. Fortunately though in this context the shop stewards were able to promote views and eventually there was a buy-over by a foreign firm though the name of the company remained the same. Anyway, the new managing director is marvellous, he quickly understood the problems. He put on a pair of overalls and went to see what was happening on the shop floor. He got the trust of the trade union, even though he forced through 200-300 redundancies. Then he sought a government grant to sustain the firm in the short-term.

My input was that I helped to get the grant. I wrote to the minister who wrote back saying that there was a need to spend some time considering the application. I wrote back to the silly bugger saying that by that time there would be no need for a grant as the firm would be bust. I'm pleased to say the firm got the grant and now there's a bouyant share-owning workforce.

Another member, this time from the Midlands noted:

This week I've had a letter from a company in my constituency saying that the firm will have to close unless something is done about their high energy costs. So I'll arrange a question at energy questions, then ask the Secretary of State to meet the engineer of the firm (this is better than the manager, as he'll speak with real knowledge). Ministers are generally receptive to the personal approach. Sometimes it's better to walk up the corridor and knock on the Minister's door, rather than make a big fuss in the chamber. You can put ideas into ministers' minds and then they start asking awkward questions to their civil servants.

An interesting variation on the theme of fighting closure was provided by a backbencher from a Scottish constituency:

I had rough exchanges with [an electronics firm] when they announced notices. I was asked to organise a sit-in, which was a nonsense. What I did instead was to obtain a promise from the firm that where and when it was possible in the future to re-recruit people they would do so. Seven months later I was assured that most of those who had been made redundant had been offered re-employment. That was a success. It is a good example, I believe, of a member working closely with a non-unionised firm and extracting promises to assist the employees. In other words I was acting as a surrogate trade union convenor. This is an area of study not written up!

Offsetting these successes, however, Labour backbenchers provided numerous examples of 'tea and sympathy' but no action from ministers. The prime minister herself was mentioned by three interviewees for her emollient approach. One North-East backbencher commented:

When [an electronics] factory closed in my constituency, I met Mrs. Thatcher. I got a cup of tea and bugger all else. She'll meet a constituency member but won't go near a delegation.

The Midlands member, noted above for his action on high energy costs, also recalled:

I went to see Thatcher, who was having difficulty answering questions on unemployment at the time. She'd made a statement that any MP having difficulty with local closure was always free to knock on her door. So I did. To give her her due, we had a full discussion of the problem of this knitwear company. And she did ask the Minister of State at the DTI to convene a meeting with the firm. But in the end nothing came of it, and the firm closed.

In addition to dealing with declining industries, all of the Labour 'lobbyists' identified the need to promote new industry in their constituencies. A representative from a large northern city constituency noted:

I'm highly involved with the local authority and its major initiatives to attract industry. This spills over into my work in the House. I get myself involved in all sorts of committees, often apparently unlikely ones, to put the case of [my city] and the region.

A colleague from a neighbouring Yorkshire constituency openly acknowledged:

There's a need to attract industry, to put energy and resources into doing this. Basically, I serve as an ambassador for my constituency. I work with the local authority to attract grants and bring in industry. At the moment I'm asking the government to make my constituency a development area. Industry needs to know that there is a stable grant. It needs to know what is happening before they come into the area. I think we're on the threshold of a breakthrough.

Yet the role of 'lobbyist', as is apparent from Table 6.2, is not the exclusive preserve of Labour backbenchers. Of the fifteen Conservatives interviewed, eight could be identified as 'lobbyists'. One of these 'lobbyists' from a semi-rural constituency pointed out that:

Industrial developments move very fast. For all that there is a variable interface between industry and my constituency it's going to grow. In recognition of this, I have organised a constituency group of businessmen who keep me, and themselves, in touch. This is reinforced by my contacts with chambers of commerce, trade associations, and very usefully, rotary clubs. Plus, I visit four or five small businesses every quarter and get involved on the training side through enterprise agency work, job training projects etc. One particularly useful facet of my work is that I help industry on the export side, on trade matters and in pushing on export promotion.

Less structured relationships with constituency interests were noted by a Midlands Conservative, who stated that he didn't have formalised meetings on a regular basis with management or workers:

> It's not my business to be involved in industrial relations matters or to tell managers how to operate on a day-to-day basis. But I do have very close contacts with both sides in the largest plant in my constituency. It just so happens, however, that in the last 24 hours I've spoken with both sides – from the managing director down to the shop-steward of one section on the shop floor.

The most professional approach to maintaining contacts with local industrial interests was displayed by a new Conservative recruit to the backbenches who represented a marginal North-Eastern constituency. He undertook regular visits to those major companies which employed more than one thousand workers; and, in addition, was in frequent contact with smaller firms and trade associations. Moreover, he sought to establish closer contacts with the AEU district secretary and at the time of the interview (December 1986) was deeply embroiled in discussions over redundancies at a major engineering works. But, what was noteworthy about his approach to the 'lobbyist' role was his usage of informal networks within the Conservative party:

> What I've found is that ex-ministers are an invaluable source of advice. I've just contacted Leon Brittan about how to handle this [engineering] closure in my constituency. The other day I had a chat with Cecil Parkinson about his visit to Japan. His information on Japanese investment intentions in the North East of England was particularly useful. Not forgetting that it is relatively easy to see ministers. In fact, I talk to [Minister of State] at the DTI at least twice a week about some regional assistance policy matter.

Generally, however, the assessment of the impact of such 'lobbying' by Conservative backbenchers was sanguine. One 'dry' Conservative did observe that there had been some success in his 'ideological' lobbying of government:

> Government shouldn't act as a bran tub for industry, whereby the latter can simply dip in and help itself. What has been important under our government is that the balance has been redressed away from the Heath/Wilson consensus. I admit that the impact of government has been less dramatic on industry than is popularly imagined – but expenditure as a proportion of GDP is, nonetheless, going down.

Spatial Focus and Electoral Vulnerability

Wood's (1987) study found that there was some support for the proposition that MPs from economically and politically vulnerable constituencies are more inclined than other MPs to engage in lobbying for constituency industrial interests. However, the correlation coefficient was sufficiently low (at -0.22) to indicate that significant numbers of MPs from 'safe' constituencies also engaged in constituency lobbying. Indeed, Wood initially appeared to be at a loss in explaining why some MPs act as lobbyists and others do not, but eventually argued that in safe constituencies a high level of activity is prompted by the MP seeking 'more to develop the local area economically than it is to protect his or her base politically, since that is relatively secure' (Wood 1987:408).

Again the general findings of the present study tend to support Wood's specific observations. In terms of overall levels of activity on industrial matters, for instance, the size of the percentage margin of the MP's vote over that of his nearest opponent appears to have little impact upon his formal behaviour in the House. The profile of activity for members from marginal constituencies displays relatively minor differences from that of their safer colleagues (see Table 6.3). Equally, electoral vulnerability appears to have little effect upon the proportion of an MP's overall activity devoted to industrial matters. Whilst the percentage of 'vulnerable' members grouped at the highest level of industrial specialisation in Table 6.4a is greater than for less vulnerable backbenchers, even so it is only marginally greater than for members from 'intermediate' and 'safe' constituencies.

There are, nonetheless, some interesting intra-party, as well as inter-party differences in the proportions of activity devoted to industrial matters. In the Conservative party, backbenchers from electorally vulnerable seats were more likely to concentrate their formal activity on the consideration of industrial policy than were other Conservative members. By far the greatest percentage of electorally vulnerable Conservatives were ranked at the highest level of industrial specialisation. Indeed, the attention of vulnerable Tories appeared to be focused more upon industrial policy on the floor of the House than was the case for most vulnerable Labour backbenchers. Undoubtedly, this is a reflection of the nature of electorally vulnerable constituencies in the two parties, with marginal Conservative constituencies to be found predominantly in the north of England and Scotland, Labour's traditional industrial heartland; whilst Labour's marginals tending to be found in the more economically diverse suburban seats (see Butler and Kavanagh 1984; Crewe 1983). At the other end of the scale Labour MPs from solid traditional areas are more inclined to focus their activity upon industrial matters in the House than are their 'safe' Conservative counterparts. Once more this reflects the different 'core' areas of support of the two major parties.

Table 6.3 **Industrial Activity by Procedure By Electoral Vulnerability (Backbenchers 1983/4 and 1984/5)**

Oral Questions

Industrial Questions		Electoral Vulnerability				
	0-5%		*6-10%*		*11+%*	
n	*n*	*%*	*n*	*%*	*n*	*%*
1	18	36.8	10	26.3	63	34.1
2-3	15	30.6	16	42.1	59	31.8
4+	16	32.6	12	31.6	63	34.1
Total	49	100.0	38	100.0	185	100.0

Written Questions

Industrial Questions		Electoral Vulnerability				
	0-5%		*6-10%*		*11+%*	
n	*n*	*%*	*n*	*%*	*n*	*%*
1	12	20.0	10	19.2	59	21.9
2-3	14	23.3	13	25.0	79	29.2
4-5	12	20.0	9	17.3	43	15.9
6+	22	36.7	20	38.5	89	33.0
Total	60	100.0	52	100.0	270	100.0

Debate

Columns		Electoral Vulnerability				
	0-5%		*6-10%*		*11+%*	
n	*n*	*%*	*n*	*%*	*n*	*%*
1-5	18	30.0	13	25.0	95	33.0
6-10	16	26.7	11	21.2	69	23.9
11-15	9	15.0	8	15.4	43	14.9
16+	17	28.3	20	38.4	81	28.2
Total	60	100.0	52	100.0	288	100.0

Table 6.4a Level of Industrial Specialisation by Electoral Vulnerability (1983/4 and 1984/5)

Level of	Electoral Vulnerability					
	0-5%		6-10%		11+%	
Specialisation	n	%	n	%	n	%
Low	23	32.9	17	29.3	109	33.9
Medium	21	30.0	20	34.5	112	34.7
High	26	37.1	21	36.2	101	31.4
Total	70	100.0	58	100.0	322	100.0

x^2 1.51   df 4   p< 0.8

Table 6.4b Level of Industrial Specialisation by Electoral Vulnerability by Major Party (1983/4 and 1984/5)

Level of	Electoral Vulnerability											
	0-5%				6-10%				11+%			
	Cons		Labour		Cons		Labour		Cons		Labour	
Special.	n	%	n	%	n	%	n	%	n	%	n	%
Low	11	26.8	8	38.1	7	25.9	7	26.9	75	38.9	26	21.9
Medium	10	24.4	8	38.1	11	40.7	8	30.8	70	36.2	38	31.9
High	20	48.8	5	23.8	9	33.4	11	42.3	48	24.9	55	46.2
Total	41	100.0	21	100.0	27	100.0	26	100.0	193	100.0	119	100.0

This pattern is also broadly repeated when the propensity of backbenchers to mention their constituency is examined (Table 6.5). In oral activity in the chamber – oral questions and debate – Conservative backbenchers from marginal constituencies are more inclined to relate functional industrial policy directly to their geographical constituency than are their Labour counterparts. Equally, these Conservatives are over-represented amongst those Conservative backbenchers who have an identifiable territorial industrial focus. In oral questions 40 per cent, and in debate 30 per cent of Conservative members making direct reference to their constituency, came from electorally vulnerable constituencies (compared with 16 per cent of vunerable backbenchers in the party as a whole). But, Table 6.5 also reinforces the point that even backbenchers from objectively safe constituencies see some advantage in linking functional issues with the areal concerns of their constituencies. This applies across both major parties, but is particularly the case for Labour members.

Table 6.5 Constituency Focus By Procedure by Electoral Vulnerability (1983/4 and 1984/5)

Elect					Constituency Focus							
Elect		Oral	Questions			Written	Questions				Debate	
Vul.		Cons		Labour		Cons		Labour		Cons		Labour
%	n	%	n	%	n	%	n	%	n	%	n	%
0-5	6	40.0	2	8.0	4	15.4	9	18.4	18	30.0	11	14.3
6-11	2	13.3	4	16.0	3	11.5	9	18.4	11	18.3	12	15.6
11+	7	46.7	19	76.0	19	73.1	31	63.3	31	51.7	54	64.3
Total	15	100.0	25	100.0	26	100.0	49	100.0	60	100.0	77	100.0

Spatial Focus and Entry Cohorts

In chapter 4 it was noted that there are 'generational' differences in the experience of industry brought into the House by backbench MPs. In the Labour party for instance it is easy to characterise the most industrially experienced members as older, more proletarian and trade unionists. In turn it is expected that they would be the very members who would devote much of their parliamentary activity to the consideration of industrial policy matters, and who would bring expertise into the House. This expectation was held by many of the older generation of Labour backbenchers themselves. Hence, one Labour MP, with 24 years service in the House, commented:

> You have a look at these new [Labour] blokes. Many of them are academics. Some of the arrogant blighters think they know everything on everything. But when it comes to industry they know sod all. What you need is people with practical experience of the shopfloor, people with a solid trade union background. I'm almost tempted to say 'people like me'.

Another Labour member stated:

> I've been here over 20 years now. When I first came here, South Wales was represented by old miners who had a feel for their community and that community had a sheer loyalty to them and to the Labour party. Mind, some of them were idle, but they had this all embracing, overriding sense

of community and experience of working class life. Now, the Labour party is divorcing itself from these communities, with GMC's determined to select new candidates who are middle class, and who, I believe, are detrimental to Labour.

If industrial experience is increasingly concentrated in the hands of older generations of Labour members, in the Conservative party the reverse appears to be the case. In part, this is a reflection of the 'new breed' of commercially oriented recruits (see chapter 4) but, also in part, and occasionally reinforcing personal experience, it reflects the fact that several of the 1983 generation of Conservatives were elected for electorally marginal seats in the industrial North-East and West Midlands. This generational divide was aired by 'new' Conservatives in interview:

I've got four businesses of my own and I continue to be concerned with their running. In my constituency I have various industries connected with energy, so I pay close attention to energy matters in the House. In all, I'm an industrialist with an industrial life. I seek to utilise my knowledge of the *processes* of industrial life in the House, in energy or whatever.

The present parliament does have a collection of knowledgeable people in here. More so on our side than on the opposition side. There is a new kind of Tory member who came into the House by surprise and brought a terrific amount of knowledge of the business and industrial worlds with them. These guys are helping to put the traditional lawyers in the party in the shade.

The element of surprise was referred to by another new recruit:

I have to say in all honesty that I was selected, I suspect, because the Association thought there wasn't too much of a chance of winning the seat. My commercial experience probably helped, but only because the high fliers, the lawyers, barristers, weren't out in force. Well I'm here now. I'm working hard, I'm 'putting myself about a bit' as they say. Business knows me in my constituency, I've built up good contacts and they know they can approach me if they want to.

The impressions and expectations of backbenchers, noted above, mirror fairly closely the linkages in the House between functional and territorial foci of the various entry cohorts. Hence, eleven of the fifteen Conservatives (73 per cent) who directly mentioned their constituency in oral questions are drawn from the 1983 cohort. In the Labour party, on the other hand, thirteen of the twenty-five backbenchers (52 per cent) with a specific constituency focus to their oral questions on industry came from the pre-1979 generation of MPs. A similar pattern is repeated in industrial policy debates with over half of Labour constituency 'advocates' (45 out of 77 backbenchers) drawn from the pre-1979 cohort, whilst 60 per cent of Conservative 'advocates' were 'new' recruits (36 out of 60 backbenchers). If the geographical focus is extended to encompass 'region' then the same tendency for 'new' Conservatives, and 'old' Labour MPs to emphasise the territorial focus is apparent. Taking activity in oral questions, for example, the 1983 cohort accounted for twenty of the thirty-six Conservative backbenchers (56 per cent) who directly mentioned their constituency. In the Labour party, MPs first elected before 1979 constituted the majority (56 per cent, n 23) of those with a specific constituency focus to their oral questions.

In part these findings are suggestive of the reinforcing impact of geography and generation, with a dichotomy of 'new' Conservatives from more 'vulnerable' constituencies and 'old' Labour backbenchers from 'safe' constituencies sharing the propensity to emphasise the territorial dimension of industrial policy. The exact nature of this relationship and the perceptions of members of the areal role in industrial policy provide fertile ground for future research. Here, however, the next independent variable in explaining backbench activity on industrial issues – that of trade union sponsorship – will now be examined.

Trade Union Sponsored MPs

The complex interlinkage of areal and functional foci of representation, and of trustee and delegate styles, is revealed in the parliamentary activity of trade union sponsored members. It is generally assumed that sponsored MPs will speak for the functional interests of their unions, and that sponsoring unions will seek safe constituencies for 'their' representatives. On both counts areal and functional considerations are intermixed. On the one side, although sponsored MPs clearly advance the functional interests of their unions, they are required by the rules of privilege to represent their 'constituents and .... the country as a whole, rather than .... any particular section thereof' (HC Debates 1947 vol 440:col 365); yet, given the nature of many safe Labour seats, functional and areal concerns coalesce to reinforce each other. This is most clearly the case with area-specific industries such as coalmining and shipbuilding. Here the conjunction of relatively homogeneous sectoral and territorial interests tacitly serve to restrict the scope of the representative's 'independence'. In which case, the sponsored MP may well act as a 'delegate' of the functional interests of his union without being formally mandated or 'controlled' by that union. However, expectations as to 'typical' behaviour by sponsored MPs have been confused in recent years by some industrial trade unions extending sponsorship to sitting MPs from safe and industrially 'mixed' constituencies and who have no prior functional link with the union concerned. In these circumstances the potential for conflict between areal and functional roles increases, as does the expectation that the scope of the representative's parliamentary activity and subject interests would be widened.

At the 1983 general election 119 sponsored MPs were returned to the Labour benches, 97 of whom were sponsored by 'industrial' unions (those organised around the manufacturing, extractive and productive industries), and 83 of whom were backbenchers at the time of our study. In general, whilst the trend identified by Muller (1977) and Mellors (1978), of a changing social profile of sponsored MPs – towards younger, more educated, and more 'careerist' members – continued in 1983 (see Park et al 1986); nonetheless, the trade union group of MPs remained less 'embourgeoisified' than the rest of the PLP. The heart of the trade union group remained working class, with 'industrial' trade unions ensuring that workers with direct experience of industry continued to be elected to the House. In this sense there is still a commitment on the part of many 'blue collar' unions to, what Ellis and Johnson (1974:2) call, 'actual representation'; that is representation of industrial and working class interests by MPs with direct experience of those interests.

One consequence of 'actual representation' is that sponsored members are frequently older than their other PLP colleagues when first elected. Certainly, in the past, the rules and procedures of several of the major industrial unions effectively ensured that nomination to the union's panel was delayed until considerable practical industrial experience had been amassed by prospective candidates. Under the rules of the National Union of Mineworkers (NUM) operating in 1983 (later amended in 1985) the union required a panel member to have been a working miner and a union member for at least five years. In practice, the 'political apprenticeship' was invariably much more protracted (see Taylor 1984:119-23). Even more protracted, and exacting, is the practice of the Amalgamated Engineering Union (AEU) which expects its panel members to have been time-served engineers and union members for at least seven years. In addition, AEU nominees have to submit themselves to a rigorous selection procedure including interviews, discussion and formal speech-making sessions, and written examinations before becoming AEU parliamentary panel members. The AEU is rightly proud of its selection procedure, believing that it brings dedicated and able members into the House. Members who are capable of understanding the complexities of industrial policy and also of articulating and promoting the interests of the AEU in the House. The benefits to be derived from this selection procedure were repeatedly emphasised by AEU MPs in interview. As one AEU sponsored backbencher put it:

We've got members who know what they are talking about in the House, who are listened to, who are respected for their knowledge, who have something of substantive importance to say. We don't go in for imported big names, we don't have a huge panel. But what we've got is quality – quality of industrial experience, a quality of contribution to the scrutiny of economic and industrial policy.

Equally, interviewed AEU members believed that the examination of industrial policy would be greatly improved in the Commons if other unions followed the AEU's procedures. 'The problem', as one AEU MP remarked, 'is that we think our practice is best, but then so do all the other unions!'

Increasingly, the 'best' selection procedure identified by several other major unions has come to emphasise 'parliamentarist' ambitions – the achievement of frontbench status by their sponsored members – rather than 'actual representation' of industrial experience and skills in the House. Effectively, therefore, these unions seek to recruit candidates with the potential to be successful in a parliamentary 'career' and who possess the general attributes of education, oratorical skills and a dynamic image. In 'backing winners', in blatantly choosing 'careerists', and in selecting candidates in accordance with 'market criteria', such unions willingly break the direct connection between first-hand industrial experience and parliamentary activity. Not only, therefore, are their sponsored members unrepresentative of the socio-economic profile of ordinary union members, but they are also untutored in the practical skills and working experiences of the union rank and file.

Of the industrial unions, the largest, the TGWU (with 21 MPs in 1983), has pursued a consistent strategy in recent years of picking parliamentary winners – to the extent that in 1983 nine frontbench spokesmen, including the leader of the party were drawn from this union alone. In effect, the TGWU has virtually separated its industrial and political wings by discouraging its own officials from combining trade union and parliamentary careers (Ellis and Johnson 1974:12). This policy has not been endorsed wholeheartedly by its own sponsored MPs with practical experience of industry. In the words of one such TGWU sponsored member:

> The TGWU is tying itself to ministers and potential ministers. Something like one-third of the TGWU Group are shadow spokesmen. Now that isn't a coincidence. If you look at the majority of our group they weren't even in the TGWU when they were working. They joined the union since coming here. I've made the argument to the executive that we should seek more shopfloor men and women, and that the balance has tilted too far to the 'talking classes'. Practical experience is the bedrock of how this place should be influenced. Full regard should be given to shopfloor workers. Nothing can replace the real intellectual and practical experience of those on the shop floor. They *know* things from experience, their views are respected.

This opinion also echoed in the comments of several non-TGWU sponsored members, and was perhaps best summarised in the words of one NUM member:

> There has been a shift in the balance of the PLP in terms of industrial intake. What's happened is that the party's selection system has brought in more people from legal and professional jobs. Some trade unions have aided and abetted this process – like the TGWU and Boilermakers – where people who haven't been near a factory, who don't even know what one looks like, miraculously become workers' representatives. I don't accept the argument that PLP members have to be horny-handed sons of toil, but most of them, now, don't have the feel for industrial struggle .... it's not part of a lawyer's or a lecturer's life to be on a picket line, they have no experience of it, so they can't feel part of it.

Yet, the pressure to select candidates beyond the immediate membership of the union is felt increasingly by all sponsoring unions. In 1976, for example, the National Union of Railwaymen (NUR) extended its selection procedures to include non-railwaymen. Thus enabling former lecturers, lawyers, and others such as Donald Dewar, Robin Cook, Tam Dalyell and John Marek to become NUR sponsored members. Even the NUM, the most cohesive grouping of 'workers' in the PLP, discussed the possibility, after the miners' strike of 1984-85, of widening the pool of recruits beyond working miners. This opened up the way for what one NUM MP described as 'quasi-sponsorship', by dropping the requirement that the union's sponsored members had to be drawn from NUM members with direct experience of colliery work. The compelling logic of this move was to counter the decline in the NUM's membership, and the union's subsequent diminution of influence within constituency Labour parties in mining areas.

Given the changing composition of the trade union group in parliament, with its diversity of social and sectoral characteristics, and the increased importance of 'general' and 'white-collar' unions, then the traditional assumptions about sponsored MPs' behaviour, outlined above, may well be outdated in the 1980s. The diversity of the trade union group has certainly led to changed patterns of activity in the House. Over a decade ago, Muller (1977) found sponsored MPs to be generally less active in formal participation in the Commons, more loyal to the party leadership and more specialised in their attention to industrial and social welfare issues than other Labour backbenchers. By the mid-1980s, however, Muller (1986:43) indicates that trade union MPs were 'no more of a bulwark of PLP leaders than non-sponsored MPs and maybe less so' and that whilst not deserting industrial and social welfare issues 'their interests have broadened to include most aspects of public policy'.

Table 6.6   Levels of Activity by PLP TU (Industrial) Sponsored MPs

Oral Questions

	1983/4				1984/5			
Level of	other PLP		ind spons		other PLP		ind spons	
Activity	n	%	n	%	n	%	n	%
1-15	22	26.5	20	24.1	23	27.7	28	33.7
16-22	19	22.9	28	33.7	33	39.8	24	28.9
23+	42	50.6	35	42.2	27	32.5	31	37.4
Total	83	100.0	83	100.0	83	100.0	83	100.0

1983/4	x^2 2.46	df 2	$p < 0.29$
1984/5	x^2 2.18	df 2	$p < 0.34$

Written Questions

	1983/4				1984/5			
Level of	other PLP		ind spons		other PLP		ind spons	
Activity	n	%	n	%	n	%	n	%
1-54	24	28.9	25	30.1	31	37.3	41	49.4
55-164	11	13.3	22	26.5	13	15.7	15	18.1
165+	48	57.8	36	43.4	39	47.0	27	32.5
Total	83	100.0	83	100.0	83	100.0	83	100.0

1983/4	x^2 5.4	df 2	$p < 0.67$
1984/5	x^2 3.7	df 2	$p < 0.16$

Debate

	1983/4				1984/5			
Level of	other PLP		ind spons		other PLP		ind spons	
Activity (cols)	n	%	n	%	n	%	n	%
1-59	16	19.3	33	39.8	17	20.5	32	38.6
60-107	26	31.3	21	25.3	26	31.3	23	27.7
108+	41	49.4	29	34.9	40	48.2	28	33.7
Total	83	100.0	83	100.0	83	100.0	83	100.0

1983/4	x^2 8.49	df 2	$p < 0.01$
1984/5	x^2 6.89	df 2	$p < 0.04$

Table 6.7 **PLP Backbenchers: Total Industrial Activity by TU (Industrial) Sponsorship (1983/4 and 1984/5)**

Oral Questions

| Industrial Activity | Sponsorship | | | |
| | other PLP | | ind spons | |
	n	%	n	%
1	16	31.4	17	29.8
2-3	15	29.4	18	31.6
4+	20	39.2	22	38.6
Total	51	100.0	57	100.0

x^2 0.65 df 2 p< 0.97

Written Questions

| Industrial Activity | Sponsorship | | | |
| | other PLP | | ind spons | |
	n	%	n	%
1	12	16.7	9	12.3
2-3	18	25.0	15	20.5
4-5	8	11.1	20	27.4
6+	34	47.2	29	39.8
Total	72	100.0	73	100.0

x^2 6.23 df 3 p< 0.1

Debate

| Industrial Activity (cols) | Sponsorship | | | |
| | other PLP | | ind spons | |
	n	%	n	%
1-5	18	24.0	16	20.0
6-10	22	29.3	16	20.0
11-15	9	12.0	12	15.0
16+	26	34.7	36	45.0
Total	75	100.0	80	100.0

x^2 2.95 df 3 p< 0.40

Indeed, an examination of the parliamentary activity of sponsored MPs in sessions 1983/4 and 1984/5 reveals that, with the exception of debates, there is very little difference between their overall profile of activity and that of their other PLP colleagues. Trade union members were not markedly less active in the total of oral and written questions tabled, though they were more inclined to be less active in general debates than other PLP members (see Table 6.6). When attention is directed away from aggregate levels of activity to activity specifically on industrial matters, it is also apparent that sponsored members from industrial unions are not pronouncedly more active on industrial matters, as measured by the number of questions and contributions to debate on these matters, than their backbench colleagues (see Table 6.7). Where sponsored MPs do differ, however, is in their propensity to focus more of their attention on industrial matters.

Table 6.8 shows that over half of sponsored MPs from industrial unions are clustered in the highest range of industrial specialisation as measured by the proportion of total activity devoted to the consideration of industrial policy issues. Other PLP members, however, are almost equally distributed amongst the other levels of specialisation.

Table 6.8   Industrial Specialisation by TU Sponsorship

Level of Specialisation	*Sponsorship*			
	other PLP		*ind spons*	
	n	%	n	%
Low	28	33.7	13	15.7
Medium	28	33.7	26	31.3
High	27	32.6	44	53.0
Total	83	100.0	83	100.0

x^2 9.6 df 2 $p < 0.008$
$r = 0.24$ $p < 0.001$

In addition to differences between sponsored MPs and other PLP members the existing literature also generates the expectation that there would be different patterns of activity within the trade union group itself. 'Blue collar' sponsored MPs would be expected to be less active and less vocal in their formal activity in the chamber than those sponsored MPs who had been recruited by industrial unions but who had previously been employed in the professions or the service sectors. Indeed, in the sessions under study, sponsored MPs from non-industrial backgrounds were generally more active in questions and markedly more so in debates. Whereas 53 per cent of 'blue collar' sponsored members recorded fewer than 60 columns in Hansard, some 43 per cent of 'white collar' members sponsored by industrial trade unions contributed 110 columns or more to debates. Offsetting the generally higher levels of overall activity in the House, however, is the finding that those sponsored members without previous industrial experience were less specialised in industrial matters than their blue collar colleagues. Whereas, nearly two-thirds (64.2 per cent) of the latter rank as high specialists, only one-third of their 'white-collar' counterparts are ranked at this level of specialisation (x^2 7.36, df 2, p < 0.03; r = 0.28; p < 0.005). There is, therefore, a significant correlation between industrial experience gained before entering the Commons and the level of specialisation upon industrial matters within the House even amongst the sponsored members of industrial unions themselves.

Although sponsored MPs were differentiated from other Labour backbenchers in terms of specialised activity on industrial matters, when the sectoral focus of their activity is examined it is found that it did not differ greatly from that of non-sponsored members. Trade union MPs were marginally more concerned with the problems affecting the declining industrial sectors – steel, shipbuilding, heavy engineering – whereas other Labour backbenchers tended to have a less specific sectoral focus insofar as a greater proportion of their questions and contributions to debate was of a 'general' nature (see Table 6.9). This concern with industry in general, rather than with specific sectors, is also noticeable in the substantive focus of non-sponsored members. It can be seen in Table 6.10, for instance, that non-sponsored Labour MPs are more likely to involve themselves with the wider connections between industrial policy and economic and trading policies, whereas sponsored members from industrial unions concern themselves more with specific aspects of government assistance for particular industrial sectors, industrial safety and health matters, and, not surprisingly, trade union matters. In all other areas there is little to differentiate the activity of sponsored and non-sponsored Labour MPs. It is perhaps noteworthy, in the light of the discussion above, that sponsored MPs are just as likely to relate the consideration of industrial policy directly to the geographical area of their constituency as are other Labour backbenchers.

The special concern of sponsored MPs with trade union matters was particularly in evidence throughout the passage of the 1984 Trade Union Bill (see HC Debates 1983 vol 48:cols 157-244; 1984 vol 58:cols 829-55). All fourteen Labour backbench contributors to the debates on this bill on the floor of the House were sponsored MPs, and nine of whom represented 'industrial' trade unions. Furthermore, of the sixteen Labour backbenchers who intervened in these debates (that is without making a substantial speech) only four were not sponsored by a trade union. At the committee stage of the bill, which lasted for over 100 hours and involved 37 sittings, all but three of the sixteen Labour backbench members were sponsored members, and nine of the latter represented 'industrial' unions.

Table 6.9 Subject by PLP Sponsored MP by Procedure (1983/4 and1984/5)

	Oral Questions						Written Questions						Debate					
	Spon		Other		Tot PLP		Spon		Other		Tot PLP		Spon		Other		Tot PLP	
	n	%	n	%	n	%	n	%	n	%	n	%	n	%	n	%	n	%
Coal	70	33.0	67	35.1	137	34.0	115	17.0	43	5.4	158	10.7	370	21.6	282	23.5	652	22.4
Coke	0	0.0	0	0.0	0	0.0	0	0.0	0	0.0	0	0.0	3	0.2	2	0.2	5	0.2
Oil Extr	1	0.5	0	0.0	1	0.2	2	0.3	1	0.1	3	0.2	32	1.9	30	2.5	62	2.1
Petrol	1	0.5	1	0.5	2	0.5	2	0.3	8	1.0	10	0.7	2	0.1	4	0.3	6	0.2
Nuclear	1	0.5	0	0.0	1	0.2	10	1.5	3	0.4	13	0.9	11	0.6	18	1.5	29	1.0
Elect/Gas	6	2.8	10	5.2	16	4.0	7	1.0	16	2.0	23	1.6	29	1.7	40	3.3	69	2.4
Water	0	0.0	0	0.0	0	0.0	2	0.3	5	0.6	7	0.5	10	0.6	14	1.2	24	0.8
Met Extr	1	0.5	0	0.0	1	0.2	0	0.0	1	0.1	1	0.1	0	0.0	0	0.0	0	0.0
Met Man	15	7.1	4	2.1	19	4.7	16	2.4	11	1.4	27	1.8	66	3.9	41	3.4	107	3.7
Min Extr	0	0.0	2	1.0	2	0.5	1	0.1	4	0.5	5	0.3	0	0.0	0	0.0	0	0.0
Min Prod	0	0.0	0	0.0	0	0.0	2	0.3	2	0.3	4	0.3	1	0.1	0	0.0	1	0.1
Chemical	3	1.4	4	2.1	7	1.7	21	3.1	18	2.3	39	2.6	9	0.5	10	0.8	19	0.7
Man Fibre	0	0.0	0	0.0	0	0.0	0	0.0	0	0.0	0	0.0	0	0.0	0	0.0	0	0.0
Met Good	1	0.5	1	0.5	2	0.5	10	1.5	21	2.6	31	2.1	0	0.0	0	0.0	0	0.0
Mech Eng	2	0.9	2	1.0	4	1.0	11	1.6	9	1.1	20	1.4	22	1.3	10	0.8	32	1.1
Data	3	1.4	1	0.5	4	1.0	16	2.4	6	0.8	22	1.5	56	3.3	30	2.5	86	3.0
Elect Eng	1	0.5	3	1.6	4	1.0	7	1.0	18	2.3	25	1.7	0	0.0	0	0.0	0	0.0
Motor Man	8	3.8	6	3.1	14	3.5	27	4.0	21	2.6	48	3.3	42	2.5	40	3.3	82	2.8
Trans Eq	12	5.7	2	1.0	14	3.5	2	0.3	0	0.0	2	0.1	221	12.9	117	9.7	338	11.6
Inst Eng	0	0.0	0	0.0	0	0.0	29	4.3	21	2.6	50	3.4	0	0.0	0	0.0	0	0.0
Food	1	0.5	0	0.0	1	0.2	22	3.3	22	2.8	44	3.0	11	0.7	10	0.8	21	0.7
Textiles	2	0.9	7	3.7	9	2.2	2	0.3	0	0.0	2	0.1	21	1.2	13	1.1	34	1.2
Leather	0	0.0	4	2.1	4	1.0	1	0.1	2	0.3	3	0.2	0	0.0	0	0.0	0	0.0
Furniture	0	0.0	1	0.5	1	0.2	5	0.7	6	0.8	11	0.7	0	0.0	0	0.0	0	0.0
Paper	2	0.9	1	0.5	3	0.7	2	0.3	0	0.0	2	0.1	26	1.5	11	0.9	37	1.3
Rubber	0	0.0	0	0.0	0	0.0	3	0.4	6	0.8	9	0.6	6	0.4	0	0.0	6	0.2
Miscel	0	0.0	0	0.0	0	0.0	71	10.5	39	4.9	110	7.5	4	0.2	40	3.3	44	1.5
Construct	14	6.6	10	5.2	24	6.0	3	0.4	3	0.4	6	0.4	32	1.9	51	4.2	83	2.9
Rail Trans	1	0.5	1	0.5	2	0.5	5	0.7	3	0.4	8	0.5	15	0.9	9	0.7	24	0.8
Road Trans	0	0.0	1	0.5	1	0.2	6	0.9	6	0.8	12	0.8	98	5.7	30	2.5	128	4.4
Sea Trans	0	0.0	0	0.0	0	0.0	3	0.4	3	0.4	6	0.4	40	2.3	2	0.2	42	1.4
Air Trans	1	0.5	0	0.0	1	0.2	2	0.3	1	0.1	3	0.2	4	0.2	0	0.0	4	0.1
Telecom	0	0.0	0	0.0	0	0.0	0	0.0	0	0.0	0	0.0	118	6.9	51	4.2	169	5.8
General	66	31.2	63	33.3	129	32.0	270	40.0	500	62.6	770	52.2	461	22.0	347	28.9	808	27.7
Total	212	100.0	191	100.0	403	100.0	675	100.0	799	100.0	1474	100.0	1710	100.0	1202	100.0	2912	100.0

Table 6.10 Specfic Focus of Industrial Attention PLP Sponsored MPs By Procedure 1983/4 and 1984/5

| | Oral Questions | | | | | | Written Questions | | | | | | Debate | | | | | |
| | Spon | | Other | | Tot PLP | | Spon | | Other | | Tot PLP | | Spon | | Other | | Tot PLP | |
	n	%	n	%	n	%	n	%	n	%	n	%	n	%	n	%	n	%
Constit	18	8.5	17	8.9	35	8.7	55	8.1	58	7.3	113	7.7	237	13.9	182	15.1	419	14.4
EEC	12	5.7	11	5.8	23	5.7	16	2.4	72	9.0	88	6.0	18	1.1	36	3.0	54	1.9
Econ. Pol	9	4.2	16	8.4	25	6.2	23	3.4	62	7.8	85	5.8	133	7.8	142	11.8	275	9.4
Employ.	13	6.1	8	4.2	21	5.2	101	15.0	68	8.5	169	11.5	38	2.2	31	2.6	69	2.4
Gvt Asst	16	7.5	11	5.8	27	6.7	28	4.1	25	3.1	53	3.6	294	17.2	128	10.6	422	14.5
Gvt Regu	3	1.4	8	4.2	11	2.7	22	3.3	22	2.8	44	3.0	6	0.4	10	0.8	16	0.5
Ind Envir	1	0.5	0	0.0	1	0.2	4	0.6	7	0.9	11	0.7	0	0.0	11	0.9	11	0.4
Ind Injury	2	0.9	0	0.0	2	0.5	36	5.3	21	2.6	57	3.9	1	0.1	10	0.8	11	0.4
Ind Invest	7	3.3	10	5.2	17	4.2	18	2.7	16	2.0	34	2.3	3	0.1	0	0.0	3	0.1
Ind Output	7	3.3	2	1.0	9	2.2	31	4.6	45	5.6	76	5.2	12	0.7	15	1.2	27	0.9
Ind Regul	1	0.5	1	0.5	2	0.5	20	3.0	24	3.0	44	3.0	14	0.8	32	2.7	46	1.6
Ind Rels	46	21.7	38	19.9	84	20.8	68	10.1	34	4.3	102	6.9	184	10.8	185	15.4	369	12.7
Ind Safety	0	0.0	0	0.0	0	0.0	21	3.1	17	2.1	38	2.6	56	3.3	23	1.9	79	2.7
Ind Train	6	2.8	3	1.6	9	2.2	61	9.0	37	4.6	98	6.6	29	1.7	24	2.0	53	1.8
Local As	5	2.4	4	2.1	9	2.2	20	3.0	13	1.6	33	2.2	2	0.1	0	0.0	2	0.1
MNCs	1	0.5	2	1.0	3	0.7	0	0.0	2	0.3	2	0.1	0	0.0	0	0.0	0	0.0
Nat Inds	4	1.9	6	3.1	10	2.5	12	1.8	12	1.5	24	1.6	3	0.2	2	0.2	5	0.2
New Tech	0	0.0	0	0.0	0	0.0	3	0.4	1	0.1	4	0.3	3	0.2	9	0.7	12	0.4
Privatisat	6	2.8	7	3.7	13	3.2	15	2.2	12	1.5	27	1.9	296	17.3	141	11.7	437	15.0
Prod Gen	1	0.5	0	0.0	1	0.2	2	0.3	0	0.0	2	0.1	0	0.0	0	0.0	0	0.0
R&D	1	0.5	0	0.0	1	0.2	7	1.0	1	0.1	8	0.5	15	0.9	4	0.3	19	0.7
Reg Aid	3	1.4	1	0.5	4	1.0	13	1.9	29	3.6	42	2.8	88	5.1	85	7.1	173	5.9
Regional	14	6.6	11	5.8	25	6.2	11	1.6	29	3.6	40	2.7	39	2.3	10	0.8	49	1.7
TUs	17	8.0	7	3.7	24	6.0	23	3.4	12	1.5	35	2.4	214	12.5	84	7.0	298	10.2
Trade Agr	13	6.1	13	6.8	26	6.5	54	8.0	94	11.8	148	10.0	25	1.5	37	3.1	62	2.1
Trade Vol	6	2.8	15	7.9	21	5.2	11	1.6	86	10.7	97	6.6	0	0.0	1	0.1	1	0.1
Total	212	100.0	191	100.0	403	100.0	675	100.0	799	100.0	1474	100.0	1710	100.0	1202	100.0	2912	100.0

Perhaps the supreme irony of the 1984 Act, however, was that legislation which was clearly designed to challenge the link between the political and industrial wings of the trade union movement actually cemented this link more firmly together. Indeed, through the actions of sponsored members in contesting the bill in the House, and through the nationwide campaign waged by unions over the question of ballots, the positive representational advantages in having sponsored MPs was brought home to ordinary trade union members (see Coates and Topham 1986:147-69; Fatchett 1987:61-81; Taylor 1987:217-34). The enhancement of the status of sponsored MPs was a notable feature of the union's campaign outside of parliament. Co-ordinated by the Trade Union Co-ordinating Committee (TUCC), the campaign to retain political funds had as its central theme the necessity of direct labour representation in the House of Commons. The TUCC in its background brief to all affiliated trade unions argued that sponsored members had as their first duty a responsibility to their constituents:

> But they also put the point of view of our members directly in Parliament. As MPs, they have been able to reflect the unions' industrial and occupational interests at all the important decision making levels in Parliament: union MPs can also help individual union members, not least where the local MP is unsympathetic to trade unionists.

This belief echoed throughout the individual campaigns of affiliated unions. Hence, the TGWU in its document *Why and How We Should Keep the Fund* made the point that:

> A balanced parliamentary democracy must represent the widest possible range of interests in the community. When trade unions first began to sponsor MPs they did so to redress the balance in a Parliament dominated by landed and manufacturing interests. This need is still present since big business influence in Parliament is now stronger than ever.

Every effort, therefore, was made throughout the campaign to ensure that trade unionists were made aware of their voice in parliament. In fact, several union journals followed the lead of the AEU and introduced regular parliamentary reports and columns written by sponsored MPs. The success of this strategy is perhaps best demonstrated in a private poll of GMBATU members, conducted after the campaign, which indicated a substantially increased interest on the part of the rank and file membership in securing more information about the activities of their sponsored members in the Commons.

But the ultimate paradox of the campaign was that, although all of the activity and argument was about the role and position of sponsored MPs, the union MPs themselves played little part in the campaign outside parliament.

Pre-Entry Industrial Experience
The belief that the composition of the House of Commons was somehow deficient in the representation of industrial interests was noted in chapter 4. There, a pervasive feeling that industry was inadequately represented both in quantitative and qualitative terms was noted, and that this under-representation led in turn to a lack of understanding within Westminster of the practical requirements of productive industry. Implicit within these beliefs are the assumptions that MPs with direct experience of industry would possess just such an understanding; that they would willingly act as the 'spokesmen' for the relevant industrial sector, or for 'industry' generally; that they would make informed contributions to the deliberation of industrial policy; and that they would be highly active on such policy issues in the House. Conversely, MPs without prior industrial experience would be assumed to be less active, less specialised, less informed and less able to comprehend the complexities and technicalities of industrial policy. However, as the preceding section on trade union members illustrated, the connection between prior industrial experience and activity in the Commons is more complex than general assumptions suggest.

In 1983, 79 Conservative backbenchers (26 per cent of all Tory backbenchers) and 80 Labour backbenchers (44 per cent of the Labour total) had been employed in industry at some stage in their careers before entering Parliament. Only seven backbenchers (24 per cent) from the other parties had such experience. Moreover, over 40 per cent of industrially experienced backbenchers also represented industrial constituencies, with a further one-third (36 per cent) representing mixed manufacturing/service constituencies. The corresponding percentages for backbenchers without such experience were 31 and 35.

From Table 6.11 it can be seen that in terms of aggregate levels of activity in tabling questions and speaking in debates on industrial matters, then there is little to distinguish members with prior industrial experience and those without. There is no significant difference between the two groups of MPs in the frequency distributions for oral and written questions, and even though there is a statistically significant difference for activity in debate, the magnitude of this difference is relatively limited. The main difference to be found between industrially 'experienced' and 'inexperienced' backbenchers appears in their respective degree of specialisation on industrial issues in their formal parliamentary activity. In both 1983/4 and 1984/5, and in all procedures, industrially experienced MPs display a significantly higher profile of specialisation than do other backbenchers (see Table 6.12). This difference

Table 6.11 Industrial Activity Levels by Pre-Parliamentary Experience (1983/4 and 1984/5)

Oral Questions

| N Industrial Questions | Pre-Parliamentary Experience | | | |
| | Active | | Inactive | |
	n	%	n	%
1	33	32.0	59	34.9
2-3	33	32.0	57	33.7
4+	37	36.0	53	31.4
Total	103	100.0	169	100.0

x^2 0.61 df 2 p< 0.7

Written Questions

| N Industrial Questions | Pre-Parliamentary Experience | | | |
| | Active | | Inactive | |
	n	%	n	%
1	22	15.5	59	24.6
2-3	42	29.6	64	26.7
4-5	28	19.7	36	15.0
6+	50	35.2	81	33.7
Total	142	100.0	240	100.0

x^2 4.9 df 3 p< 0.2

Debate

| N Industrial Columns | Pre-Parliamentary Experience | | | |
| | Active | | Inactive | |
	n	%	n	%
1-5	41	27.7	85	33.7
6-10	29	19.6	67	26.6
11-15	21	14.2	39	15.5
16+	57	38.5	61	24.2
Total	148	100.0	252	100.0

x^2 9.6 df 3 p< 0.02

Table 6.12 Level of Industrial 'Specialisation' by Pre-Parliamentary Experience by Procedure

Oral Questions

Level of Ind. 'Spec'	1983/4				1984/5			
	Active		Inactive		Active		Inactive	
	n	*%*	*n*	*%*	*n*	*%*	*n*	*%*
Low	20	23.0	46	37.4	14	21.2	41	38.0
Medium	31	35.6	44	35.8	19	28.8	36	33.3
High	<u>36</u>	<u>41.4</u>	<u>33</u>	<u>26.8</u>	<u>33</u>	<u>50.0</u>	<u>31</u>	<u>28.7</u>
Total	87	100.0	123	100.0	66	100.0	108	100.0

1983/4 x^2 6.65   df 2 $p < 0.04$

1984/5 x^2 8.96   df 2 $p < 0.01$

Written Questions

Level of Ind. 'Spec'	1983/4				1984/5			
	Active		Inactive		Active		Inactive	
	n	*%*	*n*	*%*	*n*	*%*	*n*	*%*
Low	32	26.7	86	43.4	23	20.7	69	38.8
Medium	33	27.5	57	28.8	28	25.2	42	23.6
High	<u>55</u>	<u>45.8</u>	<u>55</u>	<u>27.8</u>	<u>60</u>	<u>54.1</u>	<u>67</u>	<u>37.6</u>
Total	120	100.0	198	100.0	111	100.0	178	100.0

1983/4 x^2 13.5   df 2 $p < 0.001$

1984/5 x^2 11.3   df 2 $p < 0.004$

Debate

Level of Ind. 'Spec'	1983/4				1984/5			
	Active		Inactive		Active		Inactive	
	n	*%*	*n*	*%*	*n*	*%*	*n*	*%*
Low	36	26.9	85	39.7	33	25.4	71	36.8
Medium	40	29.9	70	32.7	39	30.0	85	44.0
High	<u>58</u>	<u>43.3</u>	<u>59</u>	<u>27.6</u>	<u>58</u>	<u>44.6</u>	<u>37</u>	<u>19.2</u>
Total	134	100.0	214	100.0	130	100.0	193	100.0

1983/4 x^2 10.2   df 2 $p < 0.006$

1984/5 x^2 24.2   df 2 $p < 0.000$

is most marked in the aggregate specialisation (index scores for both sessions combined) with over half of experienced backbenchers ranked as high specialists, whilst only 21.7 per cent of 'inexperienced' members reached this level. Indeed the correlation coefficient between pre-entry occupation ('inexperienced' coded 0, 'experienced' coded 1) and the aggregate index score is 0.29 and significant at 0.0000 level.

In quantitative terms, therefore, industrially 'experienced' backbenchers are not significantly more active on industrial matters in questions and debates, but they are more prone to concentrate their attention upon those matters than their other colleagues. In qualitative terms, however, it is difficult to assess the respective value of the two groups' interventions on industrial issues in the House. 'Experienced' MPs clearly believe that their previous industrial employment adds authority to their pronouncements in the chamber. Indeed, debates on industry are replete with backbenchers drawing upon first-hand knowledge to support their arguments. In this context, trade union sponsored members are particularly prone to refer to their occupation before entering the House. Thus, for example, John McWilliam prefaced his speech on the report stage of the Telecommunications Bill by stating:

> I should like to declare an interest. I am sponsored by the Post Office Engineering Union. In fact, I am on leave from BT without pay .... This is an important subject for those who still work for BT, who could be in the position I was before I became a Member of the House. (HC Debates 1983 vol 50:cols 1044-7)

Similarly, Frank Haynes in the second reading of the Coal Industry Bill, made direct reference to his own industrial background, and the lack of such experience on the Tory benches:

> I have served for 35 years in mining and other Opposition backbench Members have served for donkey's years in mining. The problem is that Conservative Members have had their connections with the management in industry. Many of them have been directors of this, that and the other company, and have been associated with firms that have failed. Yet, the Government suggest they know how to deal with the future of coal mining. (HC Debates 1983 vol 48:col 748)

Equally, on the government backbenches, Conservative members with pre-entry industrial experience sought to bring that experience to bear upon the deliberations of the House. Timothy Wood, for example, pointed out during the second reading of the Data Protection Bill that, 'until June last year I was involved with International Computers Ltd on systems of the type that we might wish to control and regulate via the Bill' (HC Debates 1984 vol 53:col 88). Even more senior Conservative backbenchers still harked back to their own industrial experience. Thus, Sir David Price, stated in the eleventh opposition day debate on 'Industry and the New Technologies' that:

> I have a personal reason for intervening in the debate. I am fundamentally an industrial animal. I came to the House 30 years ago from industry. I still retain a modest working connection with industry. Indeed, I find this helps me to keep closer to economic reality. I still feel more at home on the shop floor than on the Floor of the House. (HC Debates 1985 vol 79:col. 375)

Repeatedly, industrially experienced members emphasised the importance of their experience. Of the eighteen Labour members interviewed, sixteen had worked in industry at some stage in their previous career. One of them, regarded by himself and some of his PLP colleagues as a political 'maverick', had, in fact, owned his own company. In this respect he maintained that:

> I am not representative of Labour MPs. My perception is different to most other Labour members. I have what you might call a 'capitalist background'. Generally, Labour has little business experience, it doesn't really know what happens on the management side. Some PLP members pick up company directorships, but this isn't real experience. It doesn't tell you what it's like to have employees dependent upon you for a wage packet at the end of the week.

One other interviewee had, however, been a managing director of a large engineering manufacturer and believed both that the PLP was lacking in management experience and that his own experience was therefore an invaluable asset for the party in the House.

Of the other Labour interviewees, all but two were sponsored members. In turn, these trade union members all had considerable first-hand experience of industry and, without exception, all of them pointed to the influence that their previous occupation had had upon their parliamentary activity. In the opinion of one TGWU member:

> Practical experience is the bedrock of how this place should be organised. Full regard should be given to shopfloor workers, nothing can replace that knowledge. They *know* things. Their opinions are based upon this knowledge and their views are respected.

The same backbencher then proceeded to illustrate how practical knowledge can be used in the House, and how, all too often, it is absent in the detailed consideration of industrial policy in the Commons. After criticising many of his backbench PLP colleagues who were 'still influenced by student politics rather than by practical understanding' he then outlined his own experience on a standing committee examining a major industrial bill:

> I served on this committee, right, no one else had been employed in the industry. So my views carried some weight because the other members knew that I knew what I was talking about. In fact, it was ridiculous sometimes. I'd invent names for parts of machinery just to see how much ministers knew. They never caught me out! Talk about lack of experience. In fact, the whole government side were clueless.

The belief that the status of backbenchers in industrial debates was enhanced through the possession of practical knowledge was voiced by an unsponsored Yorkshire member:

> I was told recently by a Tory member, of all people, that when I speak on the industry 'people listen' .... because of my experience spanning over 30 years. Having said that though, very few members ever approach me informally to ask my opinion. This place is very much like a monastery in that respect.

Of the Conservative backbenchers interviewed, seven had previously worked in one or more production industries at some stage of their career. Unlike Labour members, who invariably placed industry at the head of their parliamentary interests, Conservative members tended to rank industrial policy alongside other interests without according it a priority. This view was summarised by a 'new' Conservative MP:

> MPs are involved in thousands of issues in the House. One often has to adopt a leading role on an issue simply because of force of circumstances. I've recently been highly active on medical research and child welfare, for example. Whilst I have a background in engineering, and that background is invaluable because I can pick up on engineering matters and run with them when necessary, but I can't say that my main interest is consistently there.

One highly experienced Conservative, both in industrial and parliamentary terms, noted:

> My interest in industry and my other interests go in tandem. The problem you encounter, if you look at what happens in the chamber, is that people like me don't waste our time being reported in Hansard. The House of Commons is simply a media exercise. I'm much more active outside of the

House promoting industry nationwide and on an international level. What I can say is that my work in the House has had reality injected into it because of my work in industry outside. It's this reality which is sadly lacking in the work of many other MPs. Too many fellows are 'jet set' professional politicians who go around either igniting or putting out fires!

Other government backbenchers, while sharing this belief in the vital importance of practical experience of industry were less willing to write off the Commons as a mere 'media exercise'. As a member from a mixed residential/industrial constituency argued forcefully:

Britain lives by its earnings, lives by its industry. Industry is fundamental to our collective future. It is absolutely essential. It generates billions of pounds. It should be the prime concern of our democracy. What you have to remember, however, is that parliaments and executives are entirely different. Executives want to starve MPs of information. Thus, to wrest control from the executive you need knowledge in the House. This is absolutely crucial. You can mess about with select committees – but they've been swallowed by departments. What it comes down to is MPs themselves. And given that research facilities in this place are a laugh, members need their own information resources. So that is why 'hands on' experience – first-hand information – is so very valuable, because it provides specialist knowledge. And only specialists have influence.

Post-Entry Industrial Experience

One method of sustaining and enhancing MPs' 'specialist' knowledge of industry was identified by several Conservatives in interview: this was to be involved with industrial firms and associates whilst serving as a Member of Parliament. Conservative backbenchers on the whole acknowledged the advantages to be derived for the House in having members with outside occupations. Indeed, this view reflects those to be found in all recent reports and debates on the question of MPs' outside interests (see HC 57 1969; HC 102 1974; Cmnd 8881 1983; HC Debates 1985 vol 89:cols 218, 232, 243). The standard argument is that work outside of the House keeps MPs in touch with the world of commerce and industry and so counteracts the tendency of full-time representatives to 'revolve around their own axis' (Wyatt, letter to *The Times* 6 July 1983). Experience, expertise and judgement are claimed to be brought into the House by members with outside occupational interests .

On the Labour benches, however, there is a general suspicion of 'outside interests' and an equation of paid additional employment with J. S. Mill's (1861) 'sinister interests'. This criticism is twofold: first, it is contended that these other interests become the primary focus of representation for such members. The classic statement of this argument was provided by James Callaghan (see HC 269 1965) in his rebuke to Tory members who were opposing his Finance Bill:

> I do not think of them as the Members for x, y, or z; I look at them and say "investment trusts", "capital speculation" or "that is the fellow who is the stock exchange man who makes a profit on gilt edge". I have almost forgotten their constituencies, but I shall never forget their interests. I wonder sometimes who they represent, the constituency or their friends' particular interests?

A second criticism is that outside employment detracts from the 'real work' of the MP inside the House (see Judge 1984a:60). The interconnection of these two strands of argument was apparent in Dave Nellist's intervention in the 1985 debate on the Register of Members' Interests when he castigated Tory MPs for 'moonlighting by working here when their real interests lie outside the House' (HC Debates 1985 vol 89:col 226).

In the arguments of both the proponents and opponents of parallel parliamentary and industrial/commercial occupations there is an acceptance that outside employment has consequences for the work of an MP inside the House. These consequences are seen to be beneficial or detrimental largely in accordance with the political party a member belongs to. But the actual relationship is rarely examined and hard to establish. Certainly, there is plenty of evidence to suggest that members employed as directors, advisers or consultants for commercial firms and organisations seek to keep the House 'informed as to current developments with these outside bodies'. Indeed, the wider role of political consultants will be examined in chapter 8. However, here, it is sufficient to note the impact that outside involvement with industry has on activity upon industrial matters in the House.

One indicator of the connection between extra-parliamentary activity and work in the chamber is the declaration of pecuniary interest required of members when speaking and voting in the House. Thus, for instance, in accordance with the procedures of the House, Sir Dudley Smith prefaced his contribution to the adjournment debate on the imposition of Value Added Tax on construction work by declaring:

> My hon. friend the minister knows of my interest as a consultant with the newly named Building Employers' Federation, formerly well-known as the National Federation of Building Trades Employers. I do not believe in special pleading, and rarely indulge in it, particularly when I have a professional interest. However, I believe that this is something of an exception. (HC Debates 1984 vol 55:col 367)

The ability of outside organisations to feed information into the House through MPs acting as their consultants was well illustrated when Sir David Price used data from a survey conducted by his 'own professional institution, the Institution of Industrial Managers' (HC Debates 1985 vol 79:col 376) to reveal the extent of import penetration of machine tools into British industry.

Yet, the formal declaration of interest in the chamber does not reveal the extent of members' continued involvement with industry, nor does it adequately measure the impact of this extra-parliamentary activity upon work in the House. The detailed analysis of behaviour in the sessions 1983/4 and 1984/5 does establish, however, that 103 backbenchers (82 Conservative, 18 Labour and 3 'other' members) were actively associated with industry – normally as directors, executives, shareholders, advisers or consultants – and that 60 per cent of these members simply continued or developed pre-entry contacts with industry. This still left 40 per cent (n 41) of members who were involved with industry but who had not been employed or associated with industrial interests before entering the Commons. Moreover, only one-quarter of the 'industrially active' members represented industrial constituencies, with the largest number (n 41) actually sitting for rural/suburban areas. Indeed, 21 backbenchers from this latter group also had not been employed in industry before election. Labour MPs, perhaps rightly, question the extent of the substantive interest of such MPs in the practical issues confronting industry.

When the profile of activity on industrial policy issues in the Commons is examined, it is apparent that the 82 Conservatives with a continuing outside involvement with industry were not significantly more active on such issues than other Conservative backbenchers. In fact, 48 per cent of the former did not table oral questions on industrial matters throughout 1983-85; nearly one-quarter did not table any written questions, and eleven made no contribution to industrial debates in this period. Similarly, when aggregate specialisation scores are examined, MPs with a post-entry involvement with industry were not markedly more specialised than their other backbench colleagues ($r = 0.10$ $p < 0.01$). Overall, therefore, there is little to distinguish the extent of industrial policy activity within the House on the part of those MPs with or without outside interests in industry. Indeed, as Robert Adley concluded in the debate on members interests: 'The assumption .... that hon. Members have outside interests only to pursue parliamentary campaigns .... is rubbish'. (HC Debates 1985 vol 89:col 242).

Conclusion

The influences prompting members' activity upon industrial matters in the House are numerous and varied. This chapter has isolated six independent variables: spatial focus, electoral vulnerability, parliamentary generation, trade union sponsorship, pre-entry industrial experience, and post-entry involvement; and these have been analysed discretely here in order to examine each fully. Obviously, though, their interlinkage and interdependence has to recognised and provides an area for future multi-variate analysis. But even at a simple level of analysis some of the complexity of describing the influences upon backbench activity is apparent.

Certainly, 'territorial' considerations are of some importance for many MPs active upon industrial matters in the Commons. Backbenchers from regions with spatially determined industries, most notably coalmining and shipbuilding, are especially likely to make reference to locality in their deliberations in the House, and Labour backbenchers are particularly prone to do so. Electoral vulnerability, on the other hand, appears to have only a limited impact upon the general level of members' activity and the degree of specialisation on industrial matters. Nevertheless, there is an intricate linkage between electoral vulnerability, party membership, spatial focus and parliamentary generation insofar as the highest concentrations of industrial activity are to be found amongst newly elected Conservative backbenchers from marginal constituencies and established Labour members from 'safe' seats. Both groups share a propensity to link the consideration of functional policy with territorial concerns.

In examining the activity of sponsored MPs from industrial unions the initial hypothesis was that they are to be expected to be particularly active on industrial matters in the House. However, in terms of the number of questions and contributions to debate they are not notably more active on such matters than their other backbench colleagues; only in their concentration upon industrial issues does their profile of activity differ from other Labour MPs. Indeed, a similar pattern is observable for MPs with pre-entry occupational experience of industry – whereby they are not markedly more active on industrial matters in the formal procedures of the House but they do display a more specialised profile of activity upon industrial policy issues. In both instances – trade union sponsorship and pre-parliamentary experience – initial expectations have to be qualified significantly. Similarly, major qualifications have to be made to any expectations that backbenchers' post-entry connections with industry necessarily impact upon their activity on the floor of the House, as, indeed, Robert Adley's comment above makes clear.

Thus, the present chapter has revealed the profile of backbench activity on the floor of the House and the 'informal' dimension of specialisation upon industrial matters (for a discussion of informal specialisation see Judge 1981). What needs to be considered now, however, is activity away from the floor of the chamber and the degree of formal specialisation in the area of industrial matters developed through the Select Committee on Trade and Industry. This, indeed, is the purpose of the next chapter.

7 Trade and Industry Select Committee

In March 1979 the report of a Hansard Society investigation into government-industry relations recommended that 'consideration should be given to ways of developing the committee system in the House of Commons in such a manner as to enhance the use of practical expertise in industrial affairs' (Hansard Society 1979:58-9). This recommendation was aimed at overcoming the continuing problems of recruiting MPs with direct experience of industry into the Commons. Its underpinning logic was clearly that if MPs did not have primary knowledge of industry then it was essential to provide secondary knowledge through regular contacts and discussions with those involved in industry and in the formation of industrial policy.

The Hansard Society's investigation into government-industry relations was undertaken at the same time as the House of Commons Select Committee on Procedure was coming to the conclusion that a system of new departmental committees should be established to serve as the 'eyes and ears' of the Commons in relation to government departments and their subject responsibilities. A key role of these new committees was to provide 'advice and informed comment which can nourish the work of the House in scrutinising and criticising the activities and proposals of the executive' (HC 588 1978:lxiii). Guiding the Procedure Committee's recommendation was the belief that the 'power to obtain information is a prime requirement for the exercise by the House of its functions' (HC 588:lxxxviii). Indeed, the belief in the power of information *per se*, of information as power, not only ran through the committee's report, but had provided more generally the main inspiration in the development of select committees in the post-war period, as well as the foundations of most reformist arguments in that period (see Judge 1981).

The problem as perceived in the House, and outside by reformers, was one of information deficiency – of a representative body attempting to control and scrutinise the complexities of modern government. MPs were 'deficient', given their backgrounds and their parliamentary routines and modes of activity, both in the sense of lacking information and comprehension of the intricacies of policies and also of the requirements of specialist policy communities. If paucity of information was a problem, then part of the solution was to establish mechanisms whereby more information could not only be collected but also analysed by and for MPs and then disseminated within the House. In this process the House, through select committees, would serve as a conduit between specialised publics and the executive receiving, decoding and transmitting information in both directions. If select committees were simply designed to perform 'the work of informing the House .... that is, the finding out the facts of the case; the examining of witnesses; the sifting of evidence; the drawing up of reasoned conclusions' (Taylor 1979:124), then there would have been an internal, if limited, logic to the expansion of the select committee system in the past thirty years.

In practice, however, the logic of reformist arguments, and the motivations of many MPs in advancing the cause of select committees, was neither so simple nor so consistent as the 'information deficiency' thesis suggested. Instead of seeing information as a necessary commodity to perform the House's traditional roles of deliberation and scrutiny, reformers became seduced by the *transformatory* potential of greater access to, and utilisation of, information by MPs. The glib 1960s' phrase 'information is power' seemed to blind many advocates of internal procedural reform to the realities of power in an executive-centric and adversarial political system.

A characteristic feature of the reform movement throughout the 1960s, therefore, was both its desire for an increased parliamentary contribution to decision-making – through control of the executive – and also its political sensitivity, in recognising that such change could only be effected through the compliance of the executive. Yet, its political realism was not matched by a realistic appraisal of what investigatory committees in the British tradition could achieve in a partisan and executive dominated chamber. In this respect one of the most influential proponents of reform, Bernard Crick, was not alone. Indeed, for all his talk of *parliamentary* control of the executive, control in the literal sense of 'command, restraint and regulation' was not seen to rest with the House of Commons but with the *electorate* (Crick 1968:238). The Commons was to be revitalised not as a direct check on the government but as the 'centre of information, something that broadcasts ideas and facts relevant to political decisions' (1968:241). The true parliamentary function, therefore, was to inform each of the other's opinions. The power source in this model is information, hence the significance of investigatory committees designed to collect and disseminate information. Charged with this task, select committees had no need to question ministerial responsibility for policy initiatives, neither were their members required to adopt adversary stances, because as long as the committees were simply advisory bodies the requirement to decide upon matters of policy was beyond their remit. In turn as long as parliamentary control was defined, or more accurately redefined, to mean '*influence*, not direct power; *advice*, not command; *criticism*, not obstruction; *scrutiny*, not initiation; and *publicity*, not secrecy' then the essence of twentieth-century parliamentary government in Britain was not challenged. In so redefining the concept of control, and in endowing the electorate alone with the power to check the executive, Crick evaded the need to reconcile the contradictions inherent in a model of parliamentary control over a strong executive.

Similarly, the 1977/8 Procedure Committee failed to reconcile these contradictions. To a large degree it did so by wishing them away. The avowed aim of the committee was to strike a new balance in the relationship between the executive and the legislature and so to bring about the position in which 'the duty of the executive should be to assist the House in exercising surveillance over its work' (HC 588 1978:viii). Instead, it was hoped that the creation of new departmental committees, charged with the examination of all aspects of expenditure, administration and policy would tip the balance of advantage in favour of the legislature. However, in proposing a 'permanent committee system, tailored to the needs of the House rather than imported from other parliaments' (HC 588 1978:lxvi), the Committee focused primarily upon the limited questions of the technicalities of the supply and dissemination of information at the expense of the wider question of what the House could be expected to do with the information. But, as argued above, this was consistent with the earlier approaches adopted in the 1960s by the Procedure Committee and the most influential advocates of reform.

Evaluation of the Post-1979 Committees

The leader of the House of Commons when the committees were set up spoke boldly and perhaps rhetorically in terms of a radical constitutional innovation. He, and other advocates of the new system, saw it as a shift in the balance of power between government and Parliament, an episode in the Commons historic struggle to control the executive. But what has happened is rather different. (Giddings 1985:367)

Measuring the gap between objective and performance has become something of a growth industry in itself (see for example Davies 1980; Hill 1984; Drewry 1985; Johnson 1988). Yet relatively few studies establish what it is they are measuring or whether what they seek to measure (influence) can in fact be measured. Too often generalised conclusions stem from generalised statements about the objectives of committees.

Recently, however, more rigorous approaches to the evaluation of the performance of select committees have been adopted by Jaqi Nixon (1986) and Ian Marsh (1986). Nixon, for example, asks at the outset not only what are the objectives against which success is to be measured, but also what kind of evidence and what measures are to be used to assess the input of committees. In the light of these fundamental questions she discovers that the evaluation of performance is plagued by methodological and technical problems.

The first difficulty is the existence of multiple objectives ascribed to select committees. Manifestly, the improved scrutiny and control of the executive is the primary objective specified by reformers and Procedure Committees alike. Yet, subsumed within this is a second objective: the collection and transmission of information both inside and outside Westminster; from and to government; from and to interested groups and individuals. Although the dissemination of information is a prerequisite for increased scrutiny it is an objective in itself in that it deepens and extends the sources and quantity of information available to 'open up' the democratic process. A third, and largely independent, objective is the desire to involve select committees not simply in monitoring government policies but also in the making of policy itself.

Whereas most studies restrict themselves to an examination of the performance of committees in comparison with their original objectives; Nixon considers three other modes of evaluation: by performance; by outcome; and by 'response'. Evaluation by performance revolves around input-output measures of activity either in quantitative terms of members' attendance and participation, or the number of reports produced by committees; or in qualitative terms of an assessment of performance in terms of the posing of questions or the articulation of criticisms or ideas. Invariably such studies are concerned with process rather than outcomes.

The third type of evaluation – that by outcome – seeks to assess the impact of select committees upon their primary targets – most particularly the executive. Quantitative analyses of the acceptance or rejection of committee recommendations by the government provides one output measure. (In June 1986, for example, the prime minister, in answer to a PQ, listed over 150 select committee recommendations accepted by government between March 1985 and March 1986). Yet such simple quantitative measures fail to weigh the relative importance of recommendations or the magnitude of criticism entailed within each proposal. To overcome these difficulties Nixon (1986:421) has attempted to develop a qualitative analysis of department responses, but the problems of outcome evaluation still remain.

A fourth, and what Nixon calls 'an alternative perspective', is based upon a 'responsive' approach to evaluation. This approach examines the impact of select committee activity and reports upon relevant publics beyond Whitehall and Westminster. It emphasises the ability of select committees to affect the 'climate of opinion' and to influence the balance of debate, if not actually to tip the balance, by giving public voice to the opinions of organisations either normally privately expressed inside closed policy communities, or unheard by a process of exclusion from the normal consultative practices of departments. In so widening the focus of analysis, Nixon encounters the problem of 'selecting from an infinite range of potential perceptions and effects' (Pressman and Wildavsky 1984). Inevitably, as Nixon (1986:435) eventually concedes, 'the selection of viewpoints from [beyond the centre] has been limited with the possibility that an alternative choice would throw up different perspectives and lead to somewhat different conclusions'. Nonetheless, Nixon's consideration of different methods of evaluation is a significant advance in the academic assessment of the performance of select committees.

A different approach to the problem of evaluation has been adopted by Ian Marsh (1986). Like Nixon, however, he also is concerned with the internal and external dimensions of evaluation in his attempt to discover the ability of select committees both to permit 'parliamentary consideration of executive proposals and also in mobilising the consent of interest groups' (Marsh 1986:28). Much of his attention is devoted to an assessment of the contribution of committees to the budget cycle; current policy programmes; and strategic policy-making. This policy focus, though couched in terms of a concern with the deliberative contribution of committees to the process of policy-making, embroils Marsh in an assessment of policy-making itself. There is a tendency on his part to assess the potential of committees to 'act as independent agents in a more plural policy-making structure' or 'towards a developing role for committees in policy-making' (Marsh 1986:64). Yet, in concentrating upon policy-making Marsh diverts attention away from the stated objectives of the committees themselves i.e. advice and scrutiny; and uses criteria, of 'decision' and 'policy-making', unsuited to the modern British parliamentary system. Not surprisingly, he finds limited impact of committees upon the budget cycle; little movement towards, or coherence in, playing a role in current departmental policy-making (Marsh 1986:96); and he also finds committees lacking the ability to follow up findings in strategic policy reviews (1986:150). Ultimately, therefore, Marsh (1986:150) has to admit that 'habits and attitudes nourished by the two-party system work against further committee-initiated activity'.

If Marsh's policy focus is inappropriate in circumstances of British adversarial politics and parliamentary procedures, his study remains of value in its confirmation of select committees as both providers and enhancers of information, and also as channels through which interest groups may express their opinions on government policy and have those opinions publicly recorded.

In terms of the more limited concern with information, Marsh (1986:61-2) observes that in the budget cycle:

the volume of additional information these committees make available is evident not only on the public record but in the publicity that they have received. This information bears upon those determinants of the public interest that are now the private preserve of ministers and departments. This is the kind of information external interest groups require if they are to calculate general interests from their point of view or relate their judgements to those of the government.

The ability of committees and groups to provide each with new information is further demonstrated in Marsh's study (1986:98,149) in the cases of both current and strategic policy making.

Similarly, Marsh's study reveals the significant, if still essentially *ad hoc*, capacity of committees to link organised groups and departments of state more closely to the parliamentary system and of registering their respective concerns in a public forum. Whether the committees' own contribution to policy-making is enhanced in this process is indeed doubtful, with Marsh (1986:177) himself noting that whilst groups hold committees in high regard they also realise that they are 'impotent'. But the significance of Marsh's study, along with that of Nixon, is the emphasis placed upon the *informational* and *outreach* roles of committees.

Select Committee on Trade and Industry: Evaluation

The Negative Postulate. What Is Not Being Evaluated: Policy-making
The version of parliamentary government developed in Britain over the last 150 years, and the one certainly subscribed to by Mrs Thatcher's governments since 1979, is that parliament should have no pretensions in the field of policy-making. Indeed, one powerful explanation of why the new select committees have been successfully consolidated into this system is, according to Nevil Johnson (1988:166), because of:

> their members' realistic appreciation of [the] overarching political conditions. They have recognised the style of executive leadership which began to take shape after 1979. They have acknowledged that they should seek success by respecting the limits inherent in a more traditional view of the constitution than that which was becoming fashionable in the 1970s and which for a few more years still was to charm those with visions of 'breaking the mould' of British politics.

Precisely because departmental select committees were not established to contribute to policy-making directly 'it was not to be expected, for it was not sought, that such committees would impose wholesale changes on governmental policy' (Giddings 1985:373). Hence their impact upon policy should not provide the major criterion of assessment of their performance. In practice, the complexities of policy-making – the multiplicity of stimuli for executive action and the sheer number of contributors to the policy process – make it difficult, if not impossible, to assess the specific contribution of committees to this process. At best one is dealing with the problems of multi-correlliniality, at worst of spurious correlation.

Outcome:Influence upon Executive and Departmental Attitudes
A major objective of select committees has been to increase the transparency of the administrative process and to reinforce the accountability of the executive to parliament. The outcomes in terms of 'transparency' will be examined shortly; in the meantime it is worth stating why the response of the executive to committees is not evaluated here. The simple reason is that without detailed interviews with civil servants and ministers, interviews which penetrate the constitutional fictions of executive relations with parliament, then there is little possibility of judging exactly how executive members view the work of committees. One recent study that attempted such an assessment merely revealed that senior civil servants accepted the increased demands made upon their time by the new committees with 'commendable equanimity' (Flegmann 1986:35). Little else, beyond the conventional, was revealed about their attitudes to the committees.

More generally, the evidence adduced to evaluate the response of the civil service to committees is anecdotal or simply mere assertion. Such 'evidence' can lead either to the conclusion that this response 'was predictably positive, once it became clear that [the committees] are here to stay. There has been virtually no evidence of lack of cooperation' (Giddings 1985:378); or, more sanguinely, that 'awareness of [the committees'] weaknesses induces a kind of amused condescension in some officials: they cooperate cheerfully enough, but they neither fear the committees nor expect all that much of them' (Johnson 1988:178).

Equally ministers are seldom overtly troubled by committee investigations. Certainly they are exposed to more rigorous and protracted questioning in committee than on the floor of the House, and certainly committees have used their powers to call ministers before them both as a token of their ability to control, by sheer fact of enforcing ministerial attendance, and out of a recognition of the publicity value of direct interrogation of ministers. Correspondingly, ministers too may value the publicity and positively welcome appearances before committees in order to use them for their own partisan or departmental purposes. Thus, other than deference to the formal authority of committees, the extent of substantive accountability exercised through ministerial appearances before committees remains open to question (see Judge 1981:198-200; Johnson 1988:175).

Outcome: Impact upon the House

In 1982 the Liaison Committee (HC 92 1982:20) in its first report on the select committee system maintained that 'the connection between select committee work and the floor of the House is of cardinal importance. If committee work is isolated, it is stunted'. Yet, establishing the exact linkages between committee work and activity in the chamber is a daunting and almost impossible task. For example, it is widely acknowledged that a simple count of the number of committee reports debated in the House provides an imprecise estimate of the use of committee reports (see Giddings 1985:396-72; Lock 1985:345; Johnson 1988). Even by this count it has been estimated that in the 1979-83 parliament only 10 per cent of reports were debated in some form in the House (Lock 1985:345). Obviously, this does not include reference to committee reports by individual members in other debates. But here again the problem of quantifying such usage is huge. Often such references are oblique and limited, with the bulk of any specific report left unconsidered in debate. This is despite the fact that members are assisted in determining the relevance of committee reports by the practice of appending italicised reminders on the order paper, referred to as 'tags', to draw the attention of backbenchers to a report deemed to be pertinent to an item on the day's business (see HC 92 1982:20).

Towards Assessment of the Trade and Industry Committee

From the discussion above it is apparent that the logical criteria for the assessment of the work of committees are those which focus upon the inputting and outputting of information. Indeed, the one criterion common to all assessments is the processing of information itself. This process is important not only within Westminster but also outside as well through the collection and dissemination of information from and to Whitehall and interested publics. Indeed, ensuring the flows of factual information is, as the Liaison Committee (HC 92 1982:9) acknowledged, 'one of the principal services which an effective select committee system provides' for the House.

Not surprisingly, therefore, an evaluation of the performance of the Select Committee on Trade and Industry needs to be conducted in terms of the process of information management by the committee. The performance indicators of value in assessing this process are: the rates of membership participation; levels of membership expertise; interlocutory skills displayed by committee members; capacity to secure relevant information from departments and organised interests; and the ability to disseminate information. Each of these criteria will be examined in the following sections.

Membership Expertise

One of the central problems confronting representative institutions in the performance of their their functions is the management of complexity. One solution to this dilemma is 'specialisation' – both formal and informal – within such bodies. But, traditionally, within the House of Commons the development of specialisation has been restricted (see Judge 1981). A central objective of the new select committee system was, therefore, the facilitation of specialisation through a formal division of labour within the House. This, in turn, was to provide the context in which individual members could focus their attention upon specific subjects or policy areas. Throughout the discussion preceding the creation of the committees there was a tendency to confuse 'specialist knowledge' – in other words expertise – with the *process* of specialisation itself. This confusion still remains. Many select committee members may be specialised in the sense of concentrating their time and energy upon the affairs of the committee without necessarily being 'expert' in the sense of possessing or developing detailed knowledge about those policy areas covered by the committee. This point was forcefully made by an ex-chairman of a select committee in his statement that: 'not all MPs are up to the job [of committee scrutiny] .... they simply do not have time to master the complicated matters at issue ... only a limited number of MPs [have] proved equal to coping with the workload and sufficiently flexible for the wide range of subjects' (Price 1984:29).

For select committees to be effective as 'information processors' requires the process of specialisation to be matched by the development of expertise within the committee. One should be both cause and consequence of the other. In which case it helps if those MPs selected to serve on a particular committee have 'primary' – i.e. detailed and practical – knowledge of its subject area.

When the membership of the Select Committee on Trade and Industry (SCTI) between 1983-7 is analysed in terms of 'primary' knowledge of industry then it is apparent that collectively they constituted a considerable pool of expert knowledge on this subject. Of the 17 MPs who served on the SCTI between 1983-87 only one, Stradling Thomas, had no direct pre-entry experience of industry. Stradling Thomas, a farmer and former Minister of State for Wales, only briefly served as a stop-gap on the committee after the death of Martin Stevens in February 1986. All other members brought detailed knowledge of some aspects of industry with them to the committee.

Seven Labour members served on the committee at some stage during the 1983-87 parliament. Of these, six were sponsored by trade unions (2 AUE, 2 TGWU, 1 ASTMS, and 1 Steel and Metalworkers); and six represented industrial constituencies as defined in chapter 6. Richard Caborn (Sheffield Central), joined the committee in June 1986, and was a time-served engineer in a Sheffield steelworks. Lewis Carter-Jones (Eccles) had a more tangential career link with industry in that he had taught business and industrial studies in a technical college for fourteen years before entering Westminster. But he had developed a deep interest in advanced technology, especially avionics, stemming from service in the RAF and constituency interests. Bernard Conlan, was a member of the select committee between July 1984 and June 1986, and had over twenty years experience as an engineer as well as being sponsored by the AUE. Stan Crowther (Rotherham), whilst lacking direct industrial experience, nonetheless, had developed 'an automatic substantial interest in industrial development and the coal and steel industries' (interview with Crowther) as a journalist and local councillor in Rotherham. Crowther was also sponsored by the TGWU. Doug Hoyle (Warrington, North) had a career background in engineering and as vice-president of ASTMS. Michael Martin, equally, brought direct knowledge to the committee having worked as a sheet metal worker with Rolls Royce, and as a member sponsored by the National Union of Sheet Metal Workers, as well as representing a constituency, Glasgow Springburn, with a long history of locomotive engineering. The other Labour member, who served for less than two months on the committee before becoming Labour spokesman on trade and industry, was Geoffrey Robinson (Coventry North West). Indeed, Robinson had the distinction of attending only the first meeting of the committee on 15th December, which was held to choose the chairman, and even then did not vote on the issue. But Robinson's background is of some significance in that he was one of the few Labour members of the House with direct managerial experience gained as managing director and chief executive of Jaguar cars before entering the House in 1976.

Indeed, Robinson's career background was more congruent with that of Conservative members of the committee. With the exception of Stradling Thomas, mentioned above, and Barry Porter (South Wirrall) – a solicitor specialising in commercial law – all of the other Conservative members had managerial or executive experience in industry. Sir Peter Emery (Honiton), for instance, had been a director of Phillips petroleum and Tees Oil Company. In addition he had extensive personal business interests and had served as a front bench spokesman on trade in the 1964-66 parliament before holding junior ministerial office in the DTI in the early 1970s. Robert McCrindle, had pre-entry experience primarily in insurance but had a long standing interest in tourism and the travel industry. Moreover, he had served as the chairman of the all-party Aviation Group since 1980.

The connections between Conservative committee members and the aviation industry were further represented through Robin Maxwell-Hyslop and Kenneth Warren. Maxwell-Hyslop had been employed in the aero-engine division of Rolls-Royce before entering the House; whilst Warren had served as a research engineer with BOAC, and as an engineering apprentice with de Haviland, as well as holding a series of management posts in Smiths Aircraft Instruments Ltd, and an executive position with the military flights systems firm Elliot Automation Ltd. As an MP Warren had also developed consultancy positions and directorships with a range of aviation and computing companies.

The engineering connections of the committee were strengthened on the Conservative side by Charles Wardle (Bexhill), who was a director and chairman of an established engineering firm. Wardle's replacement in February 1984, was Michael Woodcock who had direct knowledge of running four businesses as well as being a management consultant. In addition Woodcock's Ellesmere Port constituency had significant energy industries within its boundaries.

Teddy Taylor, on the basis of his service as an industrial relations officer with Clyde Shipbuilders Association before entering the House, extended the experience of industrial relations amongst Conservative committee members. Taylor had also served as parliamentary adviser since entering the Commons to, amongst others, Northern Engineering Industries, the National Association of Shipbuilders and Repairers, and the Lawrence Construction Company.

Clearly then members of the SCTI brought substantial 'primary' knowledge of industry to the deliberations of the committee. Most committee members who were interviewed acknowledged that their own experience before entering parliament had indeed been a significant determinant of the choice of their committee, and that this experience had helped to secure their nomination for membership of the committee. (Of the seventeen members who served on the SCTI at some stage between 1983-87, seven were interviewed by the author –four Conservatives and three Labour members. In addition, four other committee members provided specific information in correspondence). Conservative members maintained that there had been strong competition on their side to secure a place on the SCTI. Similarly, one senior Labour MP provided figures showing that there were approximately twice as many Labour applicants as places on the committee. By half way through the 1983-87 parliament, however, one Labour committee member gained a seat on the committee simply by receiving a letter from the Chief Whip saying that he had been appointed, despite the fact that he had not applied for membership. In his own words he 'hadn't a clue' how he came to be nominated.

Despite claims to the contrary (see Silk 1987:227), in practice, the whips of both parties play a substantial role in the appointment of select committee members. Formally, the powers of selection rest with the Committee of Selection, but one Labour MP in interview was adamant that 'the whips pick everyone who gets on the committee', going so far as to suggest that whips in both parties enter into negotiations about which members should be given preference in appointment to particular committees. This view contrasts markedly with the formal position that it is the House acting upon the recommendation of the Selection Committee which appoints committee members.

Once MPs have been appointed to committees, however, they tend to operate largely independently of the whips (see Silk 1987:229). This was demonstrated on the SCTI in the choice of the committee's chairman in 1983 and again in 1987. In 1983, Sir Peter Emery was the whips' preferred choice, but as one Conservative member remarked 'we [the Conservative members on the committee] soon stopped them'. Kenneth Warren was the majority choice of both Conservatives and Labour members on that occasion. Similarly in 1987 the whips sought to advance the claims of Sir Anthony Grant against incumbent Warren (see *Times* 19 November 1987). Once again the committee exerted its right to choose its own chairman. The position of Warren in the new parliament was weakened, however, by the removal from the committee of his staunch ally, Michael Woodcock. One Conservative member of the committee was in no doubt that 'the heavy hand of the government whips was felt by the Selection Committee on this issue .... it was wrong [to remove Woodcock], it was bad for parliamentary democracy. But in part it reflects the growing concern of government with the significance of the committee'.

Development of Specialisation Through Committee Activity

Members of the SCTI were divided amongst themselves as to the degree to which membership expertise had been developed on the committee. One Conservative argued that 'even those who came from industry in the first place did so so long ago that industry now is a different ball game!'. Alternatively, a Labour member stated that there was indeed a 'substantial background knowledge brought to the committee especially by Conservative members. This knowledge is then reinforced by the work of the committee'. Another of his Labour colleagues supported this view by maintaining that the committee had become 'the focus of backbench expertise on this subject. Members have become pretty expert, I certainly have learned a great deal from our enquiries. As indeed I believe the rest of the committee has'. One of his junior colleagues questioned this view stating that, 'I suppose in a macro-sense the committee has developed a sense of the way industry is developing. But on day-to-day details and issues you can't really say the committee knows an awful lot'. A Conservative member concurred and went so far as to suggest that 'committee members aren't really experts. Basically the committee has tried to do too much. I don't think MPs should spend much more time on select committees. The big danger is that parliamentarians have a higher opinion of themselves than their ability justifies'.

If members are to maintain or develop their expertise through committee service then a prerequisite is regular attendance at committee sessions. In practice however the attendance record of SCTI members was extremely variable. One senior Conservative judged that 'out of eleven members, we had one really bad attender, two who tended to appear and disappear and the rest who really put some effort in'. Another Conservative committee member confessed that: 'Attendance occasionally has been a problem. There is always a problem of conflicting time interests admittedly, and the changing parliamentary schedule certainly doesn't help, but it is true to say that some of my colleagues just didn't bother'. These views were most forcefully expressed, however, by a Labour member who concluded that: 'In practice the committee doesn't work as a whole. Some members' attendance is quite deplorable. There is a friction under the surface about the different workloads and commitment to the committee'.

Table 7.1   Attendance at SCTI Sessions 1983-87

		1983/4 Meetings (total N 33)		1984/5 Meetings (total N 39)		1985/6 Meetings (total N 46)		1986/7 Meetings (total N 23)	
Member		n	% of N	n	% of N	n	% of N	n	% of N
Caborn	(add 8/86)	-	-	-	-	7	*	17	73.9
Conlan	(add 7/84, dis 6/86)	1	*	21	53.9	13	*	-	-
Crowther		32	96.7	32	82.1	43	93.8	19	82.6
Emery		27	81.8	21	53.9	30	65.2	11	47.8
Hampson	(add 3/87)	-	-	-	-	-	-	4	*
Hoyle	(add 2/84)	1	*	13	33.3	22	47.8	16	69.6
McCrindle	(dis 3/87)	16	48.5	24	61.5	22	47.8	1	*
Martin		12	36.4	11	28.2	18	39.1	8	34.8
Maxwell-Hyslop		29	87.9	36	92.3	44	95.7	22	95.7
Porter	(add 4/85)	-	-	13	*	30	65.2	17	73.9
Robinson	(dis 2/84)	1	*	-	-	-	-	-	-
Stevens	(died 1/86)	18	54.6	27	69.2	4	*	-	-.
Stradling Thomas	(add 2/86)	-	-	-	-	15	*	17	73.9
Taylor	(dis 4/85)	19	57.6	3	*	-	-	-	-
Wardle	(dis 2/84)	3	*	-	-	-	-	-	-
Warren		30	91.0	34	87.2	41	89.1	21	91.3
Woodcock	(add 2/84)	20	*	21	53.9	22	47.8	11	47.8
Average Attendance			69.4		61.5		65.7		69.1
(members serving full session)									

Table 7.2   Questioning Activity by Members of SCTI (1983/4 and 1984/5)

	Session 1983/4									Session 1984/5										Combined	
	HC 344	HC 461	HC 490	HC 640	HC 491	HC 577	HC 600	83/4 Total	83/4 %	HC 171	HC 172	HC 219	HC 441	HC 473	HC 509	HC 532	HC 569	84/5 Total	84/5 %	83-5 Total	83-5 %
Carter-Jones	23	-	-	-	-	-	-	23	1.0	-	-	-	-	-	-	-	-	-	-	23	0.4
Conlan	-	-	-	-	-	-	-	-	-	42	35	64	-	-	1	25	0	167	5.0	167	3.0
Crowther	190	72	29	116	24	67	22	520	22.3	184	80	10	97	26	55	15	28	495	14.9	1015	17.9
Emery	77	71	32	47	43	71	0	341	14.6	223	50	21	39	25	0	-	-	358	10.8	699	12.3
Hoyle	5	23	15	31	0	0	0	74	3.2	53	32	19	9	-	0	37	0	150	4.5	224	4.0
McCrindle	48	25	0	56	0	10	0	139	6.0	221	69	-	-	15	55	-	21	381	11.4	520	9.2
Martin	10	0	8	0	0	0	0	18	0.8	9	1	-	-	8	8	-	0	26	0.8	44	0.8
Maxwell-Hyslop	28	55	25	62	0	89	43	302	12.9	152	141	97	0	0	63	26	16	495	14.9	797	14.1
Porter	-	-	-	-	-	-	-	-	-	12	-	9	3	0	2	2	6	34	1.0	34	0.6
Stevens	19	15	0	16	0	3	0	53	2.3	80	27	7	-	7	44	2	-	167	5.0	220	3.9
Taylor	25	66	12	25	0	24	0	152	6.5	-	35	dis	dis	dis	dis	dis	dis	35	1.1	187	3.3
Wardle	4	-	-	-	-	-	-	4	0.2	-	-	-	-	-	-	-	-	-	-	4	0.1
Warren	145	85	10	144	39	89	21	533	22.8	351	141	30	88	39	131	-	28	808	24.3	1341	23.7
Woodcock	11	33	33	49	0	32	16	174	7.5	128	33	-	-	23	13	-	17	214	6.4	388	6.9
Total	585	445	164	546	106	385	102	2333	100.0	1455	644	257	236	143	372	107	116	3330	100.0	5663	100.0

Table 7.1 outlines the attendance record of SCTI members in the 1983-87 parliament. The average attendance in each session, calculated for those members who served on the committee throughout a particular session, was 66 per cent. Attendance levels were, as the comments above suggested, extremely variable. The poor attender is clearly identifiable as Michael Martin, who was present for only just over one-third of committee meetings. Doug Hoyle, Robert McCrindle and Mike Woodcock respectively attended around one-half of all meetings. Whereas the 'workhorses' of the committee were Stan Crowther, Robin Maxwell-Hyslop and Kenneth Warren who averaged a 90 per cent attendance record.

Attendance figures, however, provide only the most rudimentary of performance indicators for committee members. A more precise quantitative measure of activity is the number of questions asked by each member in evidences sessions (see Table 7.2). On this measure the three most regular attenders also turn out to be, perhaps not surprisingly, the most prolific questioners as well. Crowther, Maxwell-Hyslop and Warren together accounted for nearly 60 per cent of questions in the two parliamentary sessions under examination in this study. Emery, McCrindle and Woodcock were consistent if less active questioners in 1983/4 and 1984/5. Whilst in the same period, Hoyle, although having a similar attendance record as McCrindle and Woodcock, was less active in the questioning of witnesses.

Martin lagged way behind all other members, only averaging one per cent of questions in the two year period under scrutiny. Indeed, not only was his activity closely restricted but the substantive attention of his questions was also very narrowly focused. The bulk of his interventions were aimed, therefore, at raising constituency or regional industrial matters in committee, or at eliciting information of relevance for these interests. Thus, in the investigation in 1983/4 into British Steel's prospects, Martin's almost exclusive concern was with the threat of closure to the Ravenscraig steelworks near his constituency. This concern was apparent in his questioning of Robert Haslam, BSC's chairman:

> obviously you do understand the concern that the community at Ravenscraig has for this particular situation also, the people of Scotland because British Steel – Ravenscraig – is an important part of the Scottish economy. Could I then ask: how long will this uncertainty go on because there is nothing worse than people having this cloud hanging over them.(HC 344 1884:16 q58)

Similarly, in the 1985 examination of the financial position of Rolls Royce, Mr Martin's contributions were more delimited and more directly focused than most of those of his other committee colleagues:

at a parochial point of view I have a lot of constituents who come from Hillington and East Kilbride. Could I ask you [Sir Francis Tombs, Chairman of Rolls Royce] what the future of those plants are, and how they will be affected by privatisation? (HC 473 1985: 3 q19)

Yet, even beyond the limited horizons of Mr Martin there was a general organisational problem at the heart of the evidence sessions of the committee. One of the more active members pointed to this problem in his comment that, 'it isn't sufficient for members to be interested in the work of the committee – they have to turn up!'. The problem was in his opinion:

On several occasions members of the committee turned up late, so missing the quarter of an hour briefing session when the ordering of questions is agreed. They would arrive half an hour into the questioning and cut right across the agreed line of questioning. On more than one occasion this has led us into a dead-end with witnesses.

Whilst the excessive time demands upon backbenchers and the vagaries of parliamentary business exacerbated this problem, a more specific and deep-rooted organisational difficulty was the limited preparation time allocated by the committee to the structuring of evidence sessions and the formulation of tactics for these sessions. Several Conservative members raised this issue in interview, with one candidly admitting that:

The committee never addressed the procedural issues – it just got on with what it was doing, sending for evidence and questioning witnesses. The job itself became all important. There was no serious discussion of what it was we were trying to do; of how you went about monitoring trade and industry. There should have been a day set aside before the committee started its work to discuss what exactly it was about, about what was happening, about where we were going and why.

SCTI's Mode of Operation
Given the enormous potential remit of the SCTI the basic difficulty of the committee has been in deciding which issues *not* to investigate. The more overtly partisan subjects, those likely to cause splits along party lines, might have appeared to be candidates for non-selection. The attendant danger of this approach is that the committee might be confined to the side-lines of industrial matters in a period of radical and 'theological' (see Heald and Thomas 1986) restructuring of industrial policy. This dilemma had already been confronted in the 1979-83 parliament when the very first major inquiry, into Britain's import and export trade, revealed deep differences of opinion amongst

committee members and convinced them of the advisability of minimising the partisan content in the choice of its future inquiries (see Lee and Shell 1985:210).

In the 1983-87 parliament the committee maintained its essentially pragmatic approach to the choice of its investigations; an approach best summarised by a senior Conservative member who had served on the committee since its inception in 1980:

> If there is good reason that *ab initio* we are likely to get a split report then we steer clear of such an inquiry.

Whilst all interviewed committee members agreed that the committee worked harmoniously along bipartisan lines, not all agreed that the committee 'ducked' party sensitive issues. Indeed, the one member who voiced most concern at the 'depoliticisation' of the committee's choice of inquiries was a Conservative:

> The committee works harmoniously, certainly, but only by avoiding issues. It doesn't address contentious issues. If you take privatisation, it was assumed that the committee wouldn't comment on the *policy* of privatisation. If this is the case, then you have to recognise that it isn't going to address the real issues – the political ones. What you end up doing therefore is operating within the confines of government policy.

This member seemed to hanker after the adversarial conflict of the floor of the House. Yet, it was left to one of his Labour colleagues to note the obvious point that:

> Adversarial politics, is generally a good thing. It opens up options. *But* on the committee the very process itself is not adversarial. The committee tries hard to come to a consensus. In that respect there has been no great difficulties. Now within this consensus the committee is often critical of the government. Take for example the Phoenix development in the steel industry. We issued a highly critical report, not in any partisan way, but in an industrial development way, as a criticism of what was happening in the industry.

This political sensitivity, and realistic appraisal of the objectives of select committees, was echoed in another Labour member's comments on the subject of bipartisanship:

> It is not part of the duty of a select committee to argue about policy – that is the government's job. Yet, within the broad policy statements of

government there are all sorts of ways of analysing government performance. In this respect we don't argue whether privatisation is good or bad, but whether a particular privatisation is logical and to express warnings about the consequences of such policies.

If you look at our sessions you will find that bipartisanship has never led members not to raise an issue. Our investigation into Westland is a good example of this. Now there is of course an argument about whether we should have done that inquiry in the first place, and the committee certainly split on party lines on that occasion, but I think you'll find that we were still useful in detailing the long series of events on share dealings.

The standard mode for choosing topics of investigation, however, was that the committee collectively agreed its programme at the beginning of each parliamentary session. The practice has developed that the SCTI conducts in each session one or two major investigations with simultaneously several shorter 'monitoring' studies into the affairs of associated bodies of the DTI, primarily public corporations but also including such agencies as the Export Credits Guarantee Department.

'Monitoring'

These 'monitoring' exercises are seen to be an important part of the committee's work (see HC 92 1983:88; Lee and Shell 1985:211-3). Committee members themselves testified as to the value of these exercises:

Although we don't produce reports on monitoring exercises, the evidence itself has produced significant and detailed information on the activities of nationalised industries.

Of particular importance was the fact that the committee 'monitored' public corporations over a period of time, informing the House, and perhaps equally importantly trade unions and other interested groups in the industries themselves, of progress and management views upon the prospects of those industries. Thus in the 1983-7 parliament the committee issued a series of monitoring reports on BSC, BL, British Shipbuilders, the Post Office, and Rolls Royce.

British Steel was the subject of a substantial report in 1983/4 (HC 344 1984). This report itself was a follow-up to the Industry and Trade committee's report into the prospects of BSC produced in March 1983. The government's reply to this earlier report prompted the new Trade and Industry committee to reexamine the corporation's prospects in the light of the reply itself and the changes that had occurred in the industry since the initial report had been published. The committee emphasised the significant improvements in the operating efficiency of BSC plants and in the quality of steel produced. In view of these improvements and the existing levels of demand for steel products it recommended that BSC's proposal to close another strip mill was inappropriate at that time. Furthermore, the proposed merger of two engineering steel companies and the subsequent privatisation of the new company to form a major private sector monopoly (the so called Phoenix II scheme) was heavily criticised by the committee. Indeed, so great was the magnitude of change that the committee pledged to continue to monitor BSC's prospects and recommended that 'the government [should] report regularly to Parliament on [these] matters during the critical period until the end of 1985' (HC 344 1984:xix).

One year later, as part of its annual monitoring programme, the committee returned to the prospects of BSC to check on developments since its 1983/4 report. On the 18th and 20th June 1985 the committee took evidence from representatives of both management and trade unions in BSC and issued a report detailing both the general performance of the corporation and specific developments relating to the Phoenix II project and the closure of the Tinsley Park works in Sheffield. In the report the unions were able to place on public record their concern about the future of BSC Special Steels and the impact further plant closures would have upon the commercial viability of the company. Moreover, they were able to voice their frustration at the continuing lack of consultation and provision of information within the corporation (see HC 444 1985:20-1). In fact it was left to Kenneth Warren, the chairman of the committee, to inform the trade union representatives that BSC was currently preparing a corporate plan. This was greeted with some surprise by the union representatives as 'at no time [had the corporation's managers] discussed with the steel committee [of trade union representatives] a plan' (Assistant General Secretary, ISTC, HC 444 1985:21 q159).

Exactly a year earlier, in June 1984, this very issue of the availability and status of corporate plans of public companies had been a source of conflict between the committee and the chairman of British Shipbuilders (Graham Day). Mr Day was asked at a regular monitoring meeting whether his company had a corporate plan and whether the documentation submitted to the committee by British Shipbuilders constituted the plan referred to in the House by the Minister of State at the DTI a month earlier. In reply Mr Day stated:

Yes, there is a Plan. That Plan is submitted to the Committee. That Plan may not be the Plan which the Secretary of State may choose to approve, He may amend that – I'm not trying to be difficult. (HC 577 1984:3 q8)

It soon became apparent, however, that the plan submitted to the committee was not, at the time, the one under consideration by the Secretary of State. In addition it was revealed that Day had been requested by Norman Tebbit not to supply this document in its entirety. The committee reacted by laying an order before the House compelling Day to present it with 'the Corporate Plan as recommended by the Corporation to the Secretary of State for Trade and Industry, together with such other additional material which the Secretary of State has requested the Corporation to prepare and furnish him' (HC 657 1984:xiv). This order was dutifully complied with; and use was made of the plan by some committee members to question the adequacy of communications between the chairman of BS and Norman Tebbit over the exact details of the privatisation of BS's warship yards. It became apparent under questioning that Day was unaware of precisely which yards were to be sold off:

> The companies contemplated in the corporate plan and those which were publicly announced to the House yesterday and confirmed to us by the Secretary of State subsequently are in some general accordance, not necessarily in time but in subject. (HC 577 1984:43 q332)

In February 1985 Graham Day along with other executives from BS and directors of Morgan Grenfell, the company charged with conducting the sale of BS assets, were called before the committee to discuss the procedures concerning the privatisation of BS yards (HC 219 1985). Later that year, in July, the committee turned its attention to the progress of the sale of the warship yards. On this occasion, the specific decision to link the Cammell Laird and Vickers yards in a joint sale was queried by committee members.The general viability of BS after the privatisation of the warship yards gave Labour members particular cause for concern (HC 219 1985).

The two evidence sessions with the chairman and directors of Rolls Royce Ltd in June 1984 and 1985 (see HC 491 1984; HC 473 1985) recorded the company's enthusiasm to return to the private sector. The chairman, Sir William Duncan, was able to record on the first occasion his opposition to any piecemeal sale as he maintained that the three major business sections within Rolls Royce were highly inter-dependent. A year later his successor, Sir Francis Tombs, was equally adamant that 'there is no possibility of bits being sold off .... I do not think privatisation in parts arises *per se*' (HC 473 1985:6-7). But equally committee members took the opportunity of reiterating concerns expressed at the earlier session. Thus, for example, Kenneth Warren raised the issue of over-capacity within the aero-engine industry in 1984, and then queried the over-optimistic answer given a year later (see HC 473 1985:10 q85). Similarly, Warren, using information gained at the 1984 evidence session, asked for clarification of the export figures contained in the company's annual report (HC 473 1985: 11 q89).

British Leyland was the fourth major public sector company subject to regular review by the SCTI. In the 1979-83 parliament the committee held evidence sessions and issued reports on BL in three successive years, building in the process what it believed to be the 'most comprehensive public explanation of BL's current situation' (HC 194 1982:i). This process continued in 1983/4 with the committee taking evidence from a management team the day after Norman Tebbit announced BL's 1984 corporate plan. Included in this plan were proposals to close the commercial vehicle plant at Bathgate in Scotland, as well as to sell off Jaguar from the Cars Group. Again the committee used its earlier investigations to query current policy, this time citing the words spoken in 1982 by BL's then chairman, Sir Michael Edwardes:

> If we sell our profitable businesses, it will impact very unfavourably on our cash flow and we will need more funds from somewhere. (HC 194 1982: q63)

This opinion was in marked contrast to that of Mr Horrocks, Group Chief Executive of the BL Cars division, in 1984 (see HC 490 1984:9-10). The committee sided with Edwardes, and reinforced its criticism of the sale of Jaguar by reference to its report on the PhoenixII programme of BSC. In its view, the prospect of leaving only a 'rump' of loss-making industries in the public sector, after the piecemeal privatisation of the profitable parts of these companies, was as valid for BL as it was for BSC. The committee concluded in strong language that: 'the dangers inherent in this approach to privatisation do not appear to have been grasped by the Government' (HC 490 1984:vi).

Indeed, it is this 'comparative' approach to its monitoring role which is one particular strength of the SCTI. It is able to chronicle the effects of policy change and development over time, both within individual corporations and across the range of public corporations. Information gained in one year, or in one company, may be contrasted with information provided in subsequent years or in other companies. The consistency of decisions and management styles can thus be recorded. Indeed, the very existence of such decisions, in the form of corporate plans themselves, can be, and have been, brought to light through the committee's investigations. In this sense, the committee comes to serve the function of the 'collective memory' of the Commons: to remind the government and public sector managers of previous decisions and statements that they might wish to forget; to record the views of trade unions; and to provide a point of perspective from which criticism or praise of policy can be assessed. In this assessment it is the provision of raw material – of information – that is important. What happens subsequently to this information, what use is made of it elsewhere by the committee itself, or other parliamentarians or organised publics, is dependent upon other power relationships. In this sense information itself is not 'power', but it certainly is one resource necessary in the exercise of power. What the committee provides in its monitoring role, therefore, is access into the corporate affairs of public enterprises and, if nothing else, a vocal and continuing reminder to their managements of their public status and the formal requirement of 'openness' and public responsibility. Committee members themselves claim no more than this, arguing that 'monitoring produces much more detail on the activities of these industries than otherwise would be the case', or that 'the monitoring role is useful it sheds a little light on what the industries are up to – be this at the level of the services provided by sub-post offices, or multi-million pound write-offs, or investment programmes' (for evidence sessions on the Post Office see HC 600 1984; HC 532 1985).

Major Inquiries

For all that committee members are generally in agreement about both the necessity and usefulness of the monitoring role it constitutes only a relatively minor portion of their overall work. In the words of one Conservative member 'the monitoring role is useful, but it is only a small part of the process. I suppose it has to be because MPs aren't management consultants and shouldn't be expected therefore to play such a role'.

Of more significance for members of the committee and affected organised groups alike were the major inquiries. Approximately two major inquiries per session were undertaken. The prime purposes of these investigations were to air issues of contemporary concern, or those which members believed *should be* of concern; to collect information; and to process this information in such a manner as to reach a wider audience, through press and media reports, or a specific audience – most particularly the government or sections of industry. In assessing this process, Paul Silk's (1987:227) observation is undoubtedly correct: 'at the end of the day the committee's conclusions may not be as important as the simple fact that they conducted an inquiry'. But how did the committee choose the topics to be investigated?

Choice of Subject

The answer is simple: 'there is a good deal of argument about which subjects the committee looks at' (Labour committee member). The personal interests of members certainly affected the choice of topic. Several Conservative members were quick to point to the example of how Stan Crowther had pressed for the inquiry into BSC's prospects, and how he had also succeeded in interesting the committee in the waste disposal industry. One of his Conservative colleagues remarked piquantly: 'Stan doesn't shut up until he gets what he wants, and he dearly wanted us to look at waste'. Nobody suggested, however, that Crowther's position as parliamentary adviser to the British

Reclamation Industries Confederation was in any way improper. Indeed, Crowther openly declared his pecuniary interest throughout the course of the investigation (see HC 640 1984:9,50,83,141). Thus, as one of the more senior Conservatives on the committee concluded:

> We all knew about Stan Crowther and the waste disposal trade association. It was up to the committee as a whole to choose the subject, Stan couldn't have started the inquiry unless the rest of us believed that it was sufficiently important. I maintain that if interests are declared by members in the House and in committee then the work of parliament is enriched. If interests go undeclared, however, then it is an evil.

Other inquiries suggested themselves because of their intrinsic importance. Hence, the committee embarked upon its investigation into trade with China in view of that country's importance in the world economy and the opportunities provided by its 'open door policy' (HC 509 1985:vii). Similarly, the committee examined the trading deficit in manufactured goods with the EEC in the light of the, then, 1983 record overall trade deficit. Amongst the committee's ten recommendations in its subsequent report were two which directly challenged government policy. One called for 'urgent action to prevent the decline of the UK's manufacturing base', the other called for 'a simple and accessible mechanism of investment support for manufacturing industry' (HC 461 1984:xx;xxi). In a sense, the committee was issuing a warning about the future consequences of government policy. This warning was to be dramatically amplified by the House of Lords Committee in 1985/6; a fact upon which one SCTI member remarked ruefully:

> We were ahead of the game in pointing out the alarming trends in the trade of manufactured goods. We produced a very detailed study of the subject but, as we noted in our report, nobody seemed particularly interested at the time. [The report stated: 'The most surprising and depressing feature of our inquiry was the fact that so few people were interested in providing evidence to us on this important topic, and also at how few of those who did give evidence to us had any suggestions as to how the Common Market could be made to work more in our favour'. (HC 461 1984:xxi)].

Similarly, at least part of the reason for the choice of the vehicle components industry for investigation was the 'revolution under way in the motor industry and to make MPs aware of the significance of what is happening' (Labour committee member). Indeed, this inquiry was one of those which had been 'stacked up' on the committee's agenda waiting for time to become available to conduct the inquiry. In part also the committee became interested in this issue because it was close to the heart of the committee's adviser, Garel Rhys.

Still other issues, in the words of one of its members, 'fall into the lap of the committee' and are chosen both because of their topicality and importance. Hence, the Westland inquiry was embarked upon at short notice and in the light of the enormous publicity surrounding the whole episode at the time. Although the choice was determined along party lines, with the chairman using his casting vote to enable the investigation to proceed, the focus of the inquiry was essentially non-partisan concentrating upon the sponsoring role of the DTI and the share dealings of the company itself. Similarly, the report into the Tin Crisis (HC 305 1986) was precipitated by the suspension of trading on the London Metal Exchange (LME) market and the detrimental consequences of this suspension for the Cornish Tin industry.

Figure 7.1 Subject of SCTI Major Reports

Session 1983/4

HC 344	British Steel Corporation's Prospects.
HC 461	Growth in Trade Imbalance in Manufactured Goods between UK and Existing/Prospective EEC Member States.
HC 490	BL PLC
HC 640	The Wealth of Waste

Session 1984/5

HC 171	Operation of Export Credits Guarantee Department
HC 474	British Steel Corporation
HC 509	Trade with China

Session 1985/6

HC 106	Tourism in the UK.
HC 305	The Tin Crisis

Session 1986/7

HC 71	The Tin Crisis: Supplementary Report
HC 176	Westland plc
HC 407	UK Motor Component Industry

Obtaining Information

In 1982 the Liaison Committee observed that one of the principal services provided by the select committee system was ensuring the flow of factual information between government departments and the House (HC 92 1982:9). To this end the Liaison report concluded: 'All the committees have, to varying degrees, been able to establish a right to be kept informed by their departments' (HC 92 1982:9). In the case of the SCTI this has been a hard won right!

Civil Servants

The tactics adopted by some members in committee have been positively bruising in their efforts to prise information from civil servants. One ex-civil servant has commented that 'Mr Kenneth Warren's Trade and Industry Committee has a bit of a reputation .... for being a tough one' (McNeish 1987:95). In the opinion of those members interviewed for the present study this reputation was entirely deserved and stemmed from several battles between the committee and officials for the release of departmental information. Essentially, both Labour and Conservative members agreed with the assessment of a young Labour member that:

> Basically the civil servants need sorting out. They don't like us. In fact some of them hate us. They're secretive. In a world where knowledge is power, they intend to hold on to as much information as they can.

Equally, committee members were convinced that departmental civil servants took their appearances before the committee with 'the utmost seriousness'. In the words of one of the more aggressive members of the committee, 'civil servants in the DTI are fearful of the SCTI. They know that they will get a bloody nose if they don't prepare themselves properly'. He then proceeded to outline one tactic whereby: 'if you humble the Permanent Secretary then things begin to happen. Then you begin to get the relevant information'.

Robert Maxwell-Hyslop was undoubtedly the master tactician in these terms. The evidence sessions of the inquiry into the motor components industry provide a vivid example of the bruising tactics employed in the committee. At the first session, on 27 November 1985, it was apparent to committee members that the middle-ranking officials from the DTI appearing before them were inadequately prepared and incapable of providing detailed information upon the components industry. One exchange at the end of the examination typifies the problem:

Mr Maxwell-Hyslop

82. Is the reason why our witnesses (who incidently were chosen by the Department, not ourselves) cannot give the answer today the fact that they do not know?
(Mr Cochlin) I do not have the information with me.

83. It is not of such concern to you that it is something you carry with you?
(Mr Cochlin) Not the situation of an individual piece of componentry.
Mr Maxwell-Hyslop: Very illuminating!
Chairman: Do you have anything else?
Mr Maxwell-Hyslop: I think there is very little point in detaining the witnesses any longer.

So concerned was the committee about the performance of the departmental witnesses that a complaint was lodged with the Secretary of State. Furthermore, the Permanent Secretary (Sir Brian Hayes) was summoned before the committee to answer for the conduct of his junior officials. Again, Maxwell-Hyslop was at the forefront of the action. The overall direction of his attack is typified in the following questions:

Mr Maxwell-Hyslop

98. Sir Brian do you share the same complacency as that evinced by your Department's witnesses at the last hearing on this subject as to the performance and prospects of the British motor vehicle components industry? If you do not would you tell the Committee why they were unable to say in specific detail what causes you particular anxiety in the British motor vehicle components industry?

When Sir Brian replied that the reason why his officials had not provided specific information was because the details of shortcomings in the components industry had been provided in confidence by companies, he drew a fiery retort from Maxwell-Hyslop:

Sir Brian, are you telling us that the range of components not produced in this country is a matter so secret that your witnesses cannot share it with this committee in private session? Are you really inviting the Committee to believe that, that knowledge of whether there are automatic gearboxes produced in this country or gas filled shock absorbers or suspension units is a matter so unknown and so secret that although officials were aware of it – and they denied they were – they were prepared to defy the Committee and not give it in private session? Are you really inviting the Committee to believe that?

Eventually the DTI was forced to submit seven notes providing much of the detailed information which had been requested by the committee at its first evidence session.

Clearly, some members of the committee regularly used the tactic of discomfiting civil servant witnesses as a means of obtaining information (see also, for example, HC 640 1984 :21; HC 171 1985:17). This was held to be a legitimate tactic, even though several members acknowledged the strain this placed individual civil servants under. The example was frequently cited in interviews of a civil servant who suffered, what committee members believed to be, a nervous breakdown as a result of ferocious questioning. Little remorse was evident on their part, as typified by the sanguine comment of one senior committee member that what had happened on this occasion was that the civil servant had been 'knocked around the room'.

Ministers

Equally, SCTI members were not averse to 'roughing up' ministers when the necessity arose. Both Labour and Conservative members were willing to press ministers forcibly for information. Stan Crowther, for instance, left Norman Tebbit in no doubt that he found the Secretary of State's evidence on the imbalance of trade in manufactured goods 'alarmingly complacent' (HC 461 1984:28 q40), and reminded the minister that he was there to answer, not ask, questions (HC 461 1984:29 q45). Correspondingly, on the Conservative side, Mr Maxwell-Hyslop was unwilling to let his own ministerial colleagues avoid answering specific questions. During the Westland inquiry he threatened Paul Channon, then Secretary of State, with recall before the committee and accused him of flagrantly insulting the committee by not providing the information requested from him (HC 176 1987:151 q1138-41).

However, the roughest exchanges came on those occasions when ministers obstructed the release of information to the committee on the grounds of 'confidentiality'. DTI ministers willingly invoked commercial and constitutional confidentiality, sometimes at the same time, to deny the SCTI necessary information for its inquiries. Perhaps the two best examples of this process are to be found in the 1984 evidence sessions on British Shipbuilders (see HC 577 1984) and in the 1986 investigation into the Tin Crisis (see HC 305 1986).

The report on the Tin Crisis was judged 'not to be a satisfactory outcome' by several committee members in interview. The crisis was precipitated on 24th October 1985 when tin trading was suspended on the London Metal Exchange as a consequence of the announcement by the International Tin Council that its Buffer Stock Manager could not pay his debts. Part of the reason, therefore, for the 'unsatisfactory' nature of the committee's inquiry was the very complexity of the relationships between international agencies (ITC), national commercial organisations (LME), national financial institutions (the Bank of England and creditor banks), government departments (most particularly the DTI), and private industry (Cornish tin mining companies – Geevor, RTZ, Medway Tin Ltd etc). In inquiring into 'the causes of the crisis, the international repercussions and the effects in Cornwall, considering what solutions and Government action might be possible', the SCTI was setting itself a monumental task. This task was made more onerous by the constraints placed upon the committee by several of the organisations listed above. Some constraints were exclusive to this particular inquiry, but most, and certainly the major, constraints were endemic features of the constitutional context within which select committees have to work. Indeed, the report into the Tin Crisis (HC 305 1986) is worthy of attention for the three pages chronicling the various obstructions placed before the committee.

From the outset, the ITC refused to release any information, or even to give evidence to the committee. The committee was powerless to enforce attendance at its sessions because of the diplomatic immunity conferred by international treaties upon the ITC. In the absence of information from the ITC the committee turned to the DTI. However, the department also considered itself to be bound by the confidentiality provisions of the International Tin Agreement, under which the ITC itself operated. Moreover, DTI ministers and officials believed that they were unable to comment on certain matters as these were the subject of current legal proceedings. But, ultimately and symptomatically, the committee's investigation was frustrated by 'the normal constraints set out in the memorandum of guidance to officials' (HC 305 1986:v).

The constrictions placed by this memorandum upon the flow of information from Whitehall to Westminster are well documented (see Judge 1981,1982,1984b; Drewry 1985; Johnson 1988). In practice, the responsibility of ministers and their departments to parliament are avoided in the practical operation of those very constitutional conventions which claim to enforce this responsibility. On the basis of these conventions officials from the DTI refused to answer a series of detailed questions. Observance of the guidelines of the Osmotherly memorandum led to what the committee itself called a series of 'fatuous exchanges' (HC 305 1986:vi) wherein the permanent secretary, for example, refused to answer certain questions on the grounds that: 'We can never disclose the advice to ministers .... whether we gave advice or not is itself advice' (HC 305 1986:220 q786-7).

Not surprisingly the committee was deeply concerned about the failure of DTI officials to furnish it with the necessary information. It pointed out in its report that the secretary of state could have instructed his civil servants to have provided the information, but that he chose, instead, to hide behind the constitutional conventions himself.

The consequences following from this ministerial refusal were twofold. First, the SCTI had to base its conclusions on second hand sources. In fact, some of its evidence was from primary sources obtained from intermediary institutions. Thus, for example, some ITC documents were released in the USA under the provisions of the Freedom of Information Act. Yet, despite having possession of these documents, DTI officials still righteously refused to discuss their contents with members of the committee (HC 305 1986:210 q697). The second consequence, according to the committee itself, was 'the implications for the working of other Select Committees' (HC 305 1986:vii). The report went on to state:

> The Memorandum of Guidance is of course not new. In the vast majority of previous Select Committee inquiries no serious problem has arisen; when there have been potential difficulties they have been resolved by a

flexible interpretation of the memorandum. In our present inquiry no such solution has been possible. As a result, we have been effectively prevented from discovering all the facts about one of the principal facets of our inquiry: the role of the Government in the crisis. The House has a right to know about this, and it must be a cause of grave concern to all Members of the House that one of its Select Committees, appointed specifically for the task of finding out the facts on behalf of the House, has been thwarted. (HC 305 1986:vii)

The report and the government's reply were debated in the House in July 1986 (HC Debates 1986 vol 101:cols 72-118). But the reply itself gave further cause for concern. Two issues were raised by the response: first, the specific role of the Bank of England, of which the committee was unaware of in its initial investigation; second, what warnings were given by government, and to whom. Once more, however, the committee was to be blocked in its pursuit of crucial information by the government . This time the government restricted the papers and details of papers utilised by the Bank of England in its capacity as adviser to the DTI, with the government maintaining that a select committee did not have the right under its powers to 'send for persons, papers and records' to see internal papers of a department, nor those papers passing between departments and agencies acting as their professional advisers. On these latter grounds the government instructed the Governor of the Bank of England to provide a list of those ITC documents seen by the Bank but not to disclose the titles or content of those documents; nor was the Governor granted permission to disclose the advice given by the Bank to the DTI (HC 71 1986:48-9). In this manner the committee's quest for further information was frustrated.

The experience of the SCTI between 1983-87 confirms what is already known: that select committees are dependent upon the 'goodwill', however reluctant, of the executive for the release of departmental information. In this respect the executive has to demonstrate its willingness to sustain parliamentary scrutiny through inflicting upon itself – through the release of sensitive documents and internal ideas – public scrutiny and criticism. Perhaps not surprisingly in the adversarial context of Westminster, executives have not been prone to accept such self-inflicted wounds and have preferred instead effacement rather than embarrassment. This does not mean that the investigations and monitoring exercises of the committee are futile or fatally impaired. What it does mean is that the distribution of political resources needs to be taken into account in an assessment of their performance. To say that the committee does not receive all of the information that it wants or requests, is not to say that it is ineffective as an information gatherer in absolute terms: it merely points to the need for qualificatory clauses in such statements. Indeed, the examination of the SCTI reveals its ability to coax from departments and associated agencies information which they might have preferred, on pragmatic grounds, to have remained concealed within the closed circuit of Whitehall, but which they have no principled or political objections to its ultimate disclosure. The examples of the discovery of the existence of British Shipbuilder's corporate plan, and of the supplementary documents provided by DTI in the components inquiry support this conclusion. Offsetting, and qualifying, these 'successes' are of course the intransigence displayed by the government throughout the investigations into Westland and the Tin Crisis.

Outside Organisations

If departments are occasionally reluctant to disclose information, outside organisations – trade associations, industry representatives, trade unions etc. – are invariably only too pleased to provide evidence to the committee. This conforms with the general picture found by Michael Rush in a recent survey of the connections between groups and select committees: 'In effect, therefore, outside organisations provide the committees with a great deal of information and opinion and are a major source for committees of non-departmental information' (Rush 1990).

The importance of outside information for committees is partly reflected in the extensive circulation lists that all of them use to publicise their forthcoming inquiries and to call for evidence. In the case of the SCTI the list includes 103 organisations of which 19 are classified as pressure groups. On average such outside organisations provide around one-half of the committee's oral and written evidence (see Rush 1990). The range of organisations presenting evidence to the major inquiries in the 1983-87 parliament can be seen in Appendix C. However, what is more important than the sheer range and number of groups providing evidence to the committee is the quality of the information provided by these groups.

Individual Firms and Industrial Organisations

In the case of individual firms and industrial organisations the committee has endeavoured to provide conditions under which they can provide their evidence with full candour. It is recognised by committee members that firms may be reluctant to reveal information which they consider to be commercially sensitive. To this end the committee has demonstrated both its willingness to hold its sessions in private when sensitive information is being divulged, and also its willingness to treat such evidence confidentially in its reports. As Mr Maxwell-Hyslop reminded the secretary of state during the inquiry into the tin crisis:

May I say, for instance, when this Committee is taking detailed evidence about the new model programmes of motor manufacturers – a matter which is highly confidential and which could ruin the firms concerned if it were known to their competitors – the Committee has shown that it is well able to handle such matters with discretion .... The practice of Select Committees .... is that evidence is sidelined and offered to those giving it so that they can interdict publication of sidelined evidence. (HC 71 1986:7)

There was some concern in the committee that company managements occasionally invoked confidentiality, in the words of one of its members, 'to fob us off'. He continued by pointing out that 'industry often doesn't want the details of its operations published, which in many circumstances is understandable. However, some witnesses can be a little too sensitive. What I've noticed increasingly is that management has become more skilled in their attempts to keep us in the dark'. In part the 'skill' of witnesses from industry in dealing with the SCTI has increased as they have taken its activities more seriously. Several members noted the practice of some firms and representative organisations to send 'scouts' to the committee 'to see how the committee operates and to establish which members specialise in which areas'. Senior executives were then briefed accordingly before appearing before the committee.

In the main, individual firms and employers organisations were seen to be only too willing to get their views on the public record. 'They provide us with masses of information. We are seen to be useful to them', commented one Labour member. Another of his Labour colleagues proceeded to explain that this information was not provided merely on management's own terms:

Most of us on the committee have our own outside sources of information. We have close contacts with the trade unions on our side, and on the Conservative side they have significant contacts with business. This means that we know when we are being sold a pup. Naturally they [management] are not always forthcoming. They often think that I don't know the things that I do know, through my trade union contacts, so that I am able to confront them with the facts gained from other sources. This can really shake them up!

Where members felt that they had been of particular value to industry was in articulating the grievances felt by individual firms or entire manufacturing or trading sectors. Thus, for example the 48 Group of traders with China were able to express their public concern at the 'penny-wise/pound-foolish policy' of the government (HC 509 1985:57). Similarly, the Geevor Company was able to amplify, through its evidence to the committee, its desperate plea for government assistance to the Cornish tin industry (HC 305 1986:15).

Trade Unions
But it was the opinion of many members that 'the other side' of industry – the
trade unions – had benefited most from the investigations of the committee.
Labour and Conservative members alike maintained that the committee served
to maintain a channel whereby the arguments of trade unions could still be
filtered into Whitehall, even in an age when the corporatist channels of a
preceding collectivist age were being systematically blocked off by the
Thatcher government:

> Trade Unions particularly see the committee as a useful forum for putting
> their views on record and so indirectly pressing the government,and in
> some cases their own managements. (Labour)

> Trade Unions are delighted with the committee .... the main benefit is to
> put into the 'public domain' information that otherwise might not be
> available. (Labour)

> Our relationship with the trade unions is pretty good. In the steel industry I
> certainly got on well with Bill Sirs. When looking at BSC's prospects, for
> example, we visited three strip mills, with the trade unions taking us
> around Llanwern. It was a marvelous breakthrough, they were able to get
> their views across in a most compelling manner. In fact, if you look at
> their evidence it had the weight of 'hands-on' experience behind it.
> (Conservative)

> The trade unions get a fair shout at our meetings. Doug Hoyle is always
> keen to get the trade union voice heard in our inquiries, or Stan Crowther
> goes banging-on about something. (Conservative)

The sympathetic hearing offered to trade unions has led to accusations that the
SCTI, like its predecessor in the 1979-83 parliament, has been 'captured' by
the trade unions (see Marsh 1986:60). Undoubtedly, the committee has
pressed the trade union case on notable occasions against government policy,
for example on the closure of a strip mill by BSC and the Phoenix II initiative
(HC 344 1984; HC 474 1985), or over the piecemeal privatisations in the
shipbuilding and motor manufacturing industries (see HC 490 1984; HC 219
1985). But the committee can hardly be accused of being a captive of the trade
unions in light of the consensus of its members that it should operate within
the general policy framework set by the government. Criticism was couched,
therefore, essentially within these terms. But there was also a deeper rooted
and unspecified commitment to the interests of manufacturing interests in
general, to what one adviser called in conversation 'a hankering after some

coherent industrial policy by the committee – although its members probably wouldn't specify it in those terms'.

Dissemination of Information
Within the House
Kenneth Warren, as chairman of the SCTI, noted in his 1985 report to the Liaison Committee (HC 363 1985:lix) that: 'The reports we have produced have attracted a good deal of coverage, both in the House (although none has been formally debated) and in the media'. This impression was shared generally by other members of the committee. A typical assessment was provided by one of the Labour members:

> Information from the reports is frequently used in debates, even though the reports themselves might not be debated. But they do get referred to in other debates. The reports on Trade with China, and on Tourism are always being referred to.

Yet another Labour member argued that because:

> The research facilities for individual members in the House are basically crap, therefore, they need all the predigested information they can get. It is here that committee reports can be of some help; bringing together a range of expert views, and some not so expert, for easy consumption. Don't ask me to prove that our reports are valuable in this way. But they are!

Similar views are also held outside of the House. The CBI, for example, in *Working With Politicians* (1987) is in no doubt that; 'The Committees are able to draw attention to particular issues. Their reports undoubtedly influence the attitudes of MPs'.

The difficulty with these statements, however, is that no evidence is provided, nor cited, to substantiate such general claims. In this respect, the thirty-five interviews conducted for the present study provide more evidence than is normally offered. But, given the restricted number of interviews and the fact that these were not primarily focused upon the work of select committees, the results can only be suggestive as to the broader picture. Of the ten backbenchers (other than members of the SCTI) who expressed an opinion in interview on the reports of select committees, six (five Labour and one Conservative) believed them to be of significance in bringing information to the attention of backbenchers. All praised the reports of the SCTI claiming variously that they were 'absolutely marvelous' and a 'tremendous mechanism for finding out what is going on – particularly in what used to be the nationalised industries'. The Conservative backbencher argued that the SCTI reports 'do make a significant contribution to the exposure of policy in the

House'. On the other hand, three Conservatives and one Labour member harboured doubts about the value of SCTI reports. One senior Conservative backbencher was especially sceptical:

> They [the committee] end up asking questions suggested by outside experts. Reports are then completed by outside advisers and the clerk. The committee then rubber stamps the report. No wonder the reports aren't taken seriously.

Another younger, and more Thatcherite, MP remarked that:

> The committee is a stodgy committee. I can't think of a major policy area which has been dealt with adequately, by that I mean 'professionally', in its reports.

The Labour sceptic was similarly dismissive of the committee's reports, and its work generally, claiming that, along with the other select committees, it upheld 'a sloppy consensus, a sloppy compromise' and so tended to 'run away' from the main industrial issues.

Press coverage

A rough guide to the amount of press coverage of reports was gained by measuring the number of column inches devoted to the reports of the SCTI in the *Times* and *Guardian*. Only those articles dealing exclusively with the substance of reports were included in the analysis. Thus reports of intra-committee politics or clashes between the committee and the government or general references to the committee's work in other articles were excluded from this total.

In session 1983/4 the report on the prospects of BSC published in April 1984 attracted two articles in the *Times*, of some 35 column inches in total, from the paper's industrial correspondent Edward Townsend. Whilst in June 1984 Richard Evans, the *Times* lobby reporter, filed an article of 15 column inches on the report on the trading deficit with the EEC , and a further 6 column inches on the criticism of the sale of Jaguar in August. In total the *Times* devoted some 56 column inches to SCTI reports in this session.

In 1984/5 the report on BSC again attracted the attention of Townsend and Evans, with the former's comments running to 18 column inches and the latter's to 11 column inches. The same report was covered by the *Guardian*'s industrial editor, Michael Smith in 12 column inches. July 1985 saw the publication of the report on trade with China, and this was duly commented upon in 8 column inches in the Finance and Industry section of the *Times*. The Wealth of Waste report attracted attention in December 1984. Indeed, so great was the public interest in this report that it achieved the distinction of being the first SCTI report to be reprinted by HMSO (see HC 321 1985:vii).

In the following session, 1985/6, the report on the tin crisis produced coverage of 21 column inches in the *Guardian*, and the supplementary report in December resulted in a further 20 column inches in the *Times*. In comparison, the committee's inability to secure ITC documents from the Bank of England produced a total of 36 column inches in both papers.

In early 1987 the committee's report on Westland plc attracted coverage in both papers – 10 column inches in the *Guardian* and 16 in the *Times*. Significantly, these articles were written a month before the committee's report was published and were, therefore, based upon informed speculation as to what the final report would contain. In turn, the government's reply to the Westland report warranted eleven column inches by Michael Smith, the industrial editor of the *Guardian*, in April of the same year. Finally, the report on the components industry had the misfortune to be published just before the general election in 1987, so that press coverage was remarkably sparse at the time. Nonetheless, Martin Fletcher, the political reporter of the *Times* published a short piece of 7 column inches on this report in July.

Whilst no claims are made that these figures are an entirely accurate indication of the total coverage of SCTI reports in these quality papers, nonetheless, they point to the fact that although the major quality papers do comment regularly on the SCTI reports the space devoted to them is relatively small. Whether the former point – that they are covered at all – outweighs the latter – that they are not reported in detail – is a moot point. Some members of the committee maintain, however, that the coverage in the quality press is merely a welcome additional benefit in alerting a wider audience of the existence of the committee's reports. What matters more is the coverage of committee reports in the specialist press of the industries concerned. The experience of the SCTI between 1983-7 thus appears to reinforce Nevil Johnson's (1988:184) impressionistic observation that: 'in general select committees rate only a short notice on the inside page of the quality newspapers and rarely gain a headline'.

Conclusion

So what is the overall assessment of the SCTI as an information processor? As a conduit of information the committee has successfully tapped reservoirs of information both inside and beyond Whitehall. It has transmitted information within policy communities when those communities have been internally fractured – as in the case of the trade unions in British Steel and British Shipbuilders, and the case of Cornish tin companies during the tin crisis. It has extracted information from the DTI and other government agencies which the government has been reticent to reveal; but has been unable to retrieve information when the government has adamantly set its face against disclosure. On these occasions the committee has been quick to publicise the intransigence of government and to point out the constitutional implications of such action. More generally, the committee has served as one constant source of criticism of the government's industrial policy, returning periodically to the examination of the same issues and core industries over a protracted time span. The committee thus has operated as the collective memory of the House – never letting it forget what the issues are and how the government has responded to these issues.

At its simplest, therefore, the committee has placed on public record the thoughts and reasoning of departments, government agencies, private firms, representative organisations, and trade unions. In so doing it has amplified, and in some cases engendered, a dialogue between Whitehall and outside industrial interests. Departments and groups have been led to address the same questions and issues through the medium of the committee. At the very least, as the evidence in this chapter suggests, the participants in this 'dialogue' have become better informed of each other's positions. But defenders of the SCTI and the select committee system generally would argue that the benefits of committee activity are far more profound than the simple processing of information. Members of the SCTI implicitly believe that the committee is there to affect behaviour in the DTI. This is evident in its report published in 1988 on its monitoring of the DTI. The bulk of the report is concerned with recording what 'the department has *done* as a result of the recommendations of the committee' (HC 343 1988:v). On this criteria the record of achievement is decidedly mixed. On the tin crisis the recommendation that the government 'should begin negotiations with the industry on the possible types and amounts of aid and conclude them without delay' (HC 305 1986) was accepted by the government and led to assistance being offered to RTZ in August 1986. Equally, however, the government refused to assist the Geevor company against the recommendation of the committee. Similarly, the report on BSC's prospects led to the acceptance by the DTI and BSC that one of the three existing strip mills should not be be closed at present, though no long-term commitment was secured from the government, or from the company since privatisation, about the future of the threatened mills. At the same time the government was unwilling to accept the views of the committee on the commercial effects of piecemeal privatisation upon BSC. In other words, the government refused to be deflected from its overall policy objectives, and rejected those recommendations which impinged upon its strategic decisions.

Where the government was more amenable to pressure from the committee was when its recommendations supported action or advanced arguments which were compatible with the policy objectives of the DTI or were at the margins of its remit. In this respect, the report on the Wealth of Waste (HC 640 1984) illustrates the capacity of the committee to accelerate up the policy agenda an issue which is not currently at the forefront of departmental thinking but which has potential to become a significant item for the future. In these circumstances, with the committee identifying an area of *future* importance, and hence one upon which departmental attitudes have not fully emerged or hardened, then the committee can be influential in prompting the government to act. On these occasions the committee can help in the process of the initiation of policy, as demonstrated in the Wealth of Waste special report:

> We are very pleased to note that the government has given serious consideration to the recommendation we have made, and has gone some way towards developing a policy for recycling as a whole. (HC 321 1985:iii)

Admittedly these circumstances are rare in the extreme, but happen nonetheless.

More frequently the committee can keep the pressure on the government by revealing the depth of interest or support for its own recommendations. This it did to great effect in its special report on the government's observations on the Wealth of Waste report (HC 321 1985). There it reproduced comments on its original report submitted by three local authorities, the Glass Manufacturers Federation, and the Industry Committee for Packaging and the Environment (INCPEN). Each organisation praised the work of the committee and supported its major recommendations. Clearly, the SCTI's intention was to prompt further action from the government.

The use of special reports to inform the government and a wider public audience of reactions to its policies was also demonstrated in 1985 in the report on the Treasury's proposed legislation in respect of the nationalised industries (HC 334 1985). The committee believed that the significance of the proposals announced on 20th December in a written answer (indicating the government's clear intention of *not* securing widespread publicity for these proposals) deserved 'the widest possible circulation' (HC 334 1985:iii). To this end it invited comments from the chairmen of the nationalised industries. The replies were uniformly critical of the new proposals. Essentially the chairmen maintained that an already difficult and complicated relationship would simply be exacerbated by the proposed legislation. Moreover, the SCTI also invited further submissions from interested parties and threatened an inquiry into this issue 'in due course'.

What this example reveals, along with those cited above, is the capacity of the SCTI to interpose itself into the debate upon policy issues, to act as a channel through which information can be transmitted and routed through parliament. This is not the passive role that is often portrayed in the basic texts on parliament, rather it is an attempt to exercise influence through the processing of information, through delimiting the terms of discussion in the way that questions are posed, in soliciting for memoranda, and in the evidence sessions themselves. In this manner departments and organised interests are required to examine policies from the perspective defined by the committee. New information and novel attitudes can cause re-examination and reappraisal of their respective policy positions in this process. This is certainly the case for organised groups outside of the Westminster/Whitehall triangle (see Lea 1984:52-3; Marsh 1986:171-80), and there is sufficient evidence in the special report on monitoring to suggest that the government itself is receptive to fresh perspectives when these do not challenge its own ideological certainties.

All of this is a far cry from an influential policy role. But, as argued at the outset of this chapter, this is not the relevant criterion to be used in the context of British parliamentary committees. What has been demonstrated here is that the significance of the SCTI has been the ability to involve itself, often uninvited, into the dialogue between government and industry, to amplify certain themes which otherwise might not have been heard in public, and to record others for use in evidence for or against the government at some future date. The verdict upon the government rests with others. What the committee does is to ensure that, wherever possible, the evidence is available for such a verdict to be returned.

8 Informing and Influencing Members of Parliament

The Select Committee on Trade and Industry and the other select committees investigating industrial issues, primarily Energy, Employment and Transport, are not the only institutional channels linking backbenchers and industry. The House also has range of 'unofficial' committees which provide further points of access for outside organisations and lobbyists, both to feed information into Westminster and also to gauge the reactions of MPs to their respective causes. Indeed, so close has this linkage become, so numerous the points of entry, and so easy the access afforded to lobbyists that fears as to the system's probity have increasingly been voiced. So much so, that the inherent potential for exploitation has attracted the attention of two parliamentary investigations into the process of lobbying in recent years (see HC 408 1985; HC 518 1988). In practice, however, the relationship between outside organisations and backbench committees is essentially mutual and symbiotic rather than predatory or parasitic.

This chapter will examine first, the specific relationship between party and all-party committees and organised industrial interests, and second the general relationship between political consultants and backbench MPs. These relationships are founded upon the concept of influence: of the capacity to trade information and affect opinion. Whether the former actually has as its corollary the latter is open to question. What is certain, however, is that the sheer volume of transactions between lobbyists and MPs confers a quantitative significance, at the very least, upon this relationship. MPs and outside organisations alike are caught up in an escalating search for more, and 'better' information and contacts. Increasingly, the point of contact is through the institutional forms of 'unofficial' committees and the activities of consultants. These act as the parliamentary equivalents of 'market makers' who, in the language of the Stock Market, bring together suppliers and consumers, buyers and sellers of commodities. In the Commons, information is the commodity to be traded .

To discover the extent of contacts between backbench committees and outside groups interviews were conducted with officers of each of the major committees and parliamentary groups concerned with industry in the 1983-87 parliament. In total 34 officers, from 32 committees were questioned. In addition, interviews conducted with other backbenchers were used to discover opinions of, and contacts with, political consultants.

Party Committees

In 1985, at the end of the period of the detailed study for this book, there were some fifty party committees and regional party groups in existence at Westminster. The Conservative party had a more extensive range of committees than Labour with twenty-two subject committees and six regional groups, in comparison with fourteen Labour groups and eight regional groups. Each party had four committees covering the range of industrial matters as defined in chapter 4. In addition to a Trade and Industry committee in each party, industrial matters were also covered in committees on Employment, Energy and Transport. In turn, each Trade and Industry committee was subdivided into subcommittees: three in each party – shipping and shipbuilding, space, tourism in the Conservative party; and shipbuilding and ship-repairing, steel, and aviation in the Labour party.

Party committees are generally regarded to be of some significance in the life of parliamentary parties (see Judge 1981:124-40; Norton 1983:7-27; Jones 1990). In one of the more detailed examinations of activity in party committees it was discovered that nearly 90 per cent of backbenchers claimed to attend party subject committees/groups on a regular basis, and that attendance at these committees/groups was overwhelmingly a consequence of a member's prior interest in that subject (see Judge 1981:129-33). Given their specific combination of specialised knowledge and political judgement party committees have been identified as possessing the *potentiality* to exercise influence upon party policy. In acting as 'cue givers' to their party colleagues, committee members are in a position to influence, indirectly, party policy. As Philip Norton (1983:8) puts it:

> Party committees would thus appear to provide a structured means by which Members may seek to develop a degree of specialisation and forums through which Members may communicate with and seek to influence their party leaders, communication which may be more uninhibited and effective than on the floor of the House given the privacy and party exclusivity of committee meetings.

But an emphasis upon 'influence' is misleading in the assessment of party committees. Ultimately, the influence of party committees remains potential rather than actual in most cases. They provide but one strand in the complex web of influence at Westminster. And between the parties themselves there are notable organisational and factional differences which create differentials in the amount of influence wielded by the respective backbench committees. Whilst both party hierarchies monitor the proceedings of party subject committees, the Conservative committees are more finely attuned to the policy norms of the leadership than those in the Labour party. This is so on at least two counts. First, Conservative subject committees regularly have in attendance a representative from the whips office, unlike Labour party groups where whips do not normally attend. Labour whips do, nevertheless, receive copies of the agenda and minutes of each group. In addition, the policy orientation of Conservative committees is monitored through the attendance of research officers from the Conservative Research Department. Overall, therefore, committee meetings are treated by the Conservative whips as important sources of intelligence upon backbench opinion (see Norton 1983:16).

The second reason for the relatively greater policy effectiveness of Conservative subject committees is the greater concern to ensure ideological compatibility between the committee and party leaderships. Factions (a term no longer considered inappropriate for the Conservative party) seek to ensure the election of officers to the important subject committees. In recent years for instance 'Thatcherites' have been largely successful in securing the key posts on the most important financial and industrial committees. Being a chairman of one of the major subject committees confers considerable status within the party and beyond; providing ready access to the minister responsible for the relevant policy area; preference in catching the Speaker's eye in debate on that subject; and ready media attention and exposure.

Conservative Party Committees on Industry
The chairmanship of the Conservative Trade and Industry committee is one of the more prestigious backbench posts in the party and, along with other positions on the committee, is keenly contested. Throughout the 1983-87 parliament the committee was firmly in the hands of the 'right' of the party. Michael Grylls, as chairman, clearly identified himself with the 'privatisers' and declared himself to be against state intervention and in favour of the state providing merely the conditions within which private industry could prosper. Similarly, Neil Hamilton, as vice-chairman, was elected at the beginning of the parliament as a reflection of the strength of the right in the party. Significantly, the day before he was interviewed by the author he lost his position to Tim Smith; partly because the right did not mobilise for the election, and partly because by 1987 some 'Thatcherite' backbenchers had become a little complacent after the successes of the privatisation programme. As one of Hamilton's colleagues put it 'there isn't much industrial policy left'.

In the proceedings of the committee, however, ideological divisions were notably absent. In the words of one of the committee's officers: 'There isn't a great deal of discourse on ideological positions on the committee. Ideological debate just doesn't happen much'. Instead, greater emphasis is placed upon expertise within the committee. Hence, detailed understanding of, and attention to, the daily concerns of industry outstripped general ideological debate as the main preoccupation of regular committee members.

About one dozen backbenchers fell within the category of 'hard core' attenders of the party Trade and Industry committee. These members were described by one officer as 'the industry buffs, the genuine experts in the party', and they formed the nucleus of the membership which varied within a normal range of twelve to twenty-four members. Occasionally, an outside speaker on a matter of current controversy could attract significantly more members than the standard attendance. Indeed, the fact that Conservative committees are open to all members of the parliamentary party enables their meetings to serve as a barometer of backbench concern with specific issues. Norton (1983:16) makes the additional point that a large turn-out at a committee means, 'a minister cannot dismiss a hostile audience of ninety or a hundred Members as reflecting the opinion of a small out-of-touch clique'. Normally, however, 'the House is too chaotic. There are too many competing attractions to ensure regular and high attendance at committee meetings. Occasionally there is an embarrassingly low turn-out' (Trade and Industry officer).

The attendance figures for the other committees dealing with 'industrial' issues tended to be lower than those for the Trade and Industry committee itself. The Small Businesses committee in particular had a small membership. One of its officers estimated that if a minister was speaking on a new initiative then his committee was likely to attract between fifteen and twenty members. On the other hand, if the speaker was not well known, or was addressing the committee on a technical subject, attendance was likely to be confined to the five officers themselves. The regular memberships of the Energy, Employment and Transport committees were estimated to fall between the figures for the Small Businesses and the Trade and Industry committees.

In each of these committees, however, 'knowledge' was deemed to be the essential prerequisite of committee influence. This reinforces the findings of the survey of party committees conducted in the mid-1970s (see Judge 1981:136-7). Officers of the 'industrial' committees maintained that one of the main reasons why ministers were willing to listen to them was because they knew that the opinions expressed were 'authoritative' in the sense of being informed both in subject and political content.

For the nine Conservative officers interviewed, the party committees were of importance primarily as two-way channels between ministers and backbenchers. In one direction, ministers were able to inform, and occasionally warn, committee officers of ministerial statements in advance. In return, officers were able to tell ministers what backbenchers were thinking on the subject under consideration. And in this process committees had been able, in the opinion of one officer, 'on occasion to point ministers in certain directions'. Equally, committee officers had proved useful to ministers in the House by asking questions, seeking ministerial statements, or in contributing to debates in support of ministers.

But the flow of information is not confined to within the party. Not only do committees tell ministers what backbenchers think, but they also provide an additional channel through which the thoughts of industry can be transmitted. Thus the chairman of one of the major committees noted that he was 'actively sought out by industrial organisations and representatives of firms in order to present their case to ministers'. He went on to note that 'when industry has a problem it will come and see us', though often it did so 'too late. Often mistakes could have been stopped if industry had acted sooner, if it had contacted committee officials earlier'. But he, and other interviewed officers, were in no doubt that party committees provided a vital 'machinery of linkage' between industry and ministers. A link distinct from Whitehall departments and one which did not suffer, therefore, from civil service screening.

In this respect party committees provide another access point for outside interests into the process of decision-making. Most groups are under no illusions, however, that the committees actively and directly impact upon decisions. Hence, in many instances, recourse is to the committees *after* industry hits trouble. But what committees do provide is a further opportunity, supplementary in many instances, for the dissemination of information in an attempt to affect the climate of opinion within which ministers and departments have to reach decisions.

Labour Groups on Industry
The orthodox assessment of Labour party groups is that they are less effective than their Conservative counterparts. Their impact upon party policy is considered to be 'extremely limited' (Norton 1983:21) – given the extra-parliamentary sources of policy initiation in the Labour party and the factional differences within the PLP itself. The survey of group officers conducted in the mid-1970s itself underlined the marginal influence of Labour party groups at the time (see Judge 1981:140).

Whilst this conclusion might adequately reflect the collective impotence of PLP subject groups, it does not capture the relative importance ascribed to some of the groups. In particular, it does not capture the contribution of the industrial groups to the parliamentary activities of, what still remains in the 1980s, an industrially based party. In fact, all ten of the officers of Labour's industrial groups interviewed for this study – Trade and Industry, Energy,

Employment – believed that their respective groups contributed significantly to the development of party policy and strategy *within* parliament. All pointed to a close liaison between frontbench spokesmen and their groups and all were able to provide examples of how group activity had influenced either the content or the presentation of party policy in the House. Thus, one very senior officer of the Trade and Industry group pointed out:

> The group contributes to party policy-making. It draws up policy papers which then feed into the party decision-making structure. It conducts research. It's employed researchers to do the job. Frontbenchers see the group to be of great use.

In similar vein a subcommittee chairman noted how Labour frontbench spokesmen came to industry group meetings and how they 'take heed and assimilate the arguments'. He proceeded by describing how his subcommittee helped the appropriate frontbench spokesman to plan the tactics and 'run the debate' on the particular industry in the House. In this way the party group was held to play a direct part in the party's decision-making process. That it did so was largely a consequence of its expertise. Indeed, it was suggested that the Labour spokesmen on industry needed all the help they could get:

> These chaps [frontbench spokesmen] are bright. They're articulate certainly. But many of them haven't seen a pair of overalls, let alone worn a pair. Whereas my members [of the party subcommittee] have long experience of the industry, or direct contact through their constituencies, and often both.

The primary importance of expertise was acknowledged by all interviewed officers. It was specialist knowledge which provided group members with the opportunity to influence the actions and thoughts of the parliamentary leadership. As one group chairman put it:

> We deal with the facts of the case. We supply information. We bring the real world of industry into this place. We ensure that our frontbench team is briefed on what is happening in the various sectors. And because of all of that, frontbenchers see the group to be of great value and regularly attend our meetings.

Ideology, in the form of factional divisions, was not a major consideration in the working of Labour groups. Rather, ideological disputes tended to surface at PLP meetings, though even here 'industrial knowledge was normally given credence in debate' (Trade and Industry group officer). One subcommittee chairman summarised the position thus: 'ideology isn't the major thing. It doesn't apply to our group. The concerns of our industry are geographical rather than ideological'.

The geographical specificity of the steel, shipbuilding and coal industries effectively meant that the core of regular attenders at the respective group and subcommittee meetings were themselves from geographically limited areas. Thus the steel group had as its core in the mid-1980s Welsh members, Abse, Foot, Hughes, Morris, Coleman, Powell, Wardell; Sheffield-area MPs, Crowther, Flannery, Maynard; and two West of Scotland members, Lambie and Bray. Similarly, regular attenders at the shipbuilding subcommittee, Nick Brown, Clay, Dixon, Douglas, Field, Garrett, Godman, Ross, and Lambie, essentially came from the restricted areas of Merseyside, Tyneside and Clydeside.

One problem encountered by the industrial groups of the Labour party in the 1980s was the dramatic reduction in industrial plant and employment. Industrial closure reverberated through the work of the groups in many distinct ways. First, there was the paradoxical impact upon membership. On the one side, there was a diminishing band of MPs with a constituency interest in industrial matters. In the words of one member of the steel subcommittee:

the industry has been devastated. Given the reduced capacity, given the major cutbacks, many constituencies no longer have steel companies. Many Labour members are no longer interested directly in the industry. Our regular core of attenders has been reduced.

But this member then went on to observe that at the time of the major reductions in steel quotas there had been large attendances at the subcommittee's meetings. A similar picture was painted for attendance figures at the Energy committee, which retained a core of some 30 members, still largely drawn from NUM sponsored backbenchers, but one which was diminishing.

Not only was the internal composition of party groups affected by industrial closures, but their work between 1983-7 often revolved around combating closures. The Trade and Industry group and its subcommittees had regularly met trade unionists, and to a lesser extent management of threatened firms; and individual members of the group had organised mass lobbies, tabled Early Day Motions and sought to raise the issue of particular closures on the floor of the House.

However, the industry groups were not simply defensive in their policy-orientations. The aviation subcommittee, for example, was active in the early 1980s in the campaign to gain British government funding for the A320 European Airbus. Several members told of how the Labour subcommittee had organised a joint delegation of management and trade unionists to meet

Norman Tebbit at the DTI; and of how key members had informally discussed the issue with the Secretary of State. At one such meeting the minister had expressed his opinion that the government would be more inclined to support the A320 if it had Rolls Royce engines. Whereupon the chairman of the subcommittee was reported to have contacted Airbus Industrie, the European consortium, to ascertain that there were no technical problems to the incorporation of Rolls Royce engines in the design of the aircraft. Yet for another member the real success of the campaign over the A320 was not gaining the contract for Rolls Royce, but in securing the contract to build the wings of the aircraft:

> Our success [on Airbus] was in convincing people that building the wing section was crucial for technological advance, that the wing section is at the leading edge of high technology. We had the belief that there are still aspects of avionics and aerospace technology where Britain can make a major contribution. We never forgot that the aviation industry is important – it has over 250,000 people employed in it in one way or another.

What is also notable about the episode of the A320 is not simply that the campaign was successful in securing government assistance for the project, and Labour members seek no direct credit for this, but that there was a commonality of interest between the respective Labour and Conservative party subcommittees on this matter. In practice, as one Labour member pointed out, there was a *dual* parliamentary campaign, with both party committees pressing in the same direction:

> Both party delegations worked in parallel, not jointly. Conservatives would see Tebbit first then we'd go in. We were both pushing the same case. On our side we knew the line the Conservatives had been pushing as we had close liaison behind the scenes. We knew what each other was doing. This unity of view makes it very difficult for ministers *not* to listen.

For all that the Airbus example reveals the policy input of backbench committees, and for all that officers were able to provide examples of policy influence, the real value of Labour groups, as far as many of their members are concerned, is in the processing of information. Repeatedly in interview, the same comment was to be heard that groups were 'two-way channels' in the flow of information between Labour backbenchers and outside organisations, and, in turn, between backbenchers and frontbenchers. Thus, each group had a regular programme of meetings with outside speakers from both sides of industry and other industrial interests. The prime purpose of these sessions was educational: to inform members of current lines of thought within industry and to alert them to new developments.

As processors and transmitters of information the party groups play a similar role to that performed by select committees in the House as a whole. Indeed, two group officers drew attention to the linkages between party and House committees. One pointed to the 'cross pollination' between Labour members on the Select Committee on Trade and Industry and those on the party group, to the extent that the former kept the latter informed of what was happening on the select committee. But he went on to add that there was no attempt to conduct parallel investigations or to make formal links with the select committee. Similarly, the other officer noted that issues raised in the party committee often influenced his line of questioning in select committee sessions, and in return he kept group members informed of the select committee's findings. But generally there was no indication that party group members saw select committee service as an alternative to group membership, as suggested by Norton (1983:22). Rather membership of both types of committee was deemed to be compatible and in many ways desirable. This is a view supported by Barry Jones (1990) who points to the 'tangible benefits of increased information flows and greater expertise' to be derived from 'overlapping membership between cognate select and party committees'.

All-Party Committees

Unlike party committees and groups there is no *system* of all-party committees – in the sense of a structured division of labour. Indeed, the overall pattern of all-party groups is amoebic in form; with a core of relatively permanent committees surrounded by a host of *ad hoc* and temporary ones forming and reforming around issues and interests over time. At the end of the period under study in this book, 1985, there were 102 all-party committees, of which seventeen were concerned with individual industrial sectors. Interviews were secured with representatives from sixteen of these single industry groups.

The difficulties in assessing the connection between information and influence are encapsulated in the study of all-party committees. The common assumption amongst commentators and MPs is that possession of the former necessarily increases the exercise of the latter. But for influence to be exerted information has not merely to be collected but also needs to be 'organised' and 'applied' at the relevant juncture of the parliamentary process. All-party committees serve the purpose of providing and disseminating information to MPs, and through this process seek in some way, either directly or indirectly, to affect the context within which decisions are reached in the House.

All-party groups served initially as a forum in which MPs with a common subject interest could meet to enhance their understanding, to monitor parliamentary developments in the area, and to develop contacts with similarly interested organisations outside of the House. Indeed, the primary objective of the first all-party group – the Parliamentary and Scientific Committee (PASC) was the provision of authoritative information for MPs through access to outside sources of information (see Walkland 1964; Powell 1979; Morgan 1979). And, throughout the period of rapid expansion in the numbers of all-party groups in the 1970s, the PASC served as a role model for the new groups. Indeed, the increased numbers of such groups was seen as but one reflection of the increased desire of MPs to play a more professional and specialised role (Morgan 1979:64). Equally, and in some eyes more sinisterly, was the potentiality of these backbench committees to be 'hijacked' by outside organisations for the promotion of their partial interests within Westminster itself. Fears about the autonomy, or rather the lack of it, of some all-party groups has led, in part, to the recent investigations by the Select Committee on Members' Interests into the activities of all-party groups and their association with political lobbyists (HC 408 1985; HC 518 1988). This concern was evident in the 1985 committee's recommendation that:

> Commons officers of All-Party and Registered Groups be required to register the names of officers of the Group, the source and the extent of any benefits, financial or in kind from outside sources which they enjoy, together with any other gainful occupation of any staff which they may have. Where a public relations agency provides the assistance, the ultimate client should be named. (HC 408 1985:viii)

Clearly visible here is the misgiving that all-party groups are not simply neutral transmitters and amplifiers of information but that many of them have become lobbyists for specific sectional interests. The fear is that they have become 'pressure groups' inside the House on behalf of pressure groups outside. In many ways, this is a danger inherent within the very nature of all-party committees themselves. Even the PASC, the role model of other all-party committees, for all its invaluable informational aspects 'also manages to behave as an avenue through which science-based industries can influence parliamentary and government proceedings' (Alderman 1984:67). Indeed, from its inception the secretariat of the PASC was provided by Watney and Powell, a firm of political consultants. The enlarged firm of Charles Barker, Watney and Powell still serves in this administrative and organisational capacity. The complex linkages between functional interests, lobbyists, all-party committees, backbenchers and governmental policy outputs have thus been in place since the beginning of the system itself. What has prompted recent concern appears, therefore, to be the sheer scope and opaqueness, rather than the nature, of the 'lobbying' activities of these committees (see HC 408 1985:iii).

All-Party Industry Committees

The scope of all-party committee coverage of industry is extensive. Most major sectors of industry find representation from developing sectors such as high technology (PITCOM) and pharmaceuticals, through the chemical and motor industries, to the declining sectors of the footwear and leather, knitwear, and wool textiles industries.

Many single industry committees are closely associated with congruent trade associations or political consultants. Thus, for example, at the time of the interviews for the present study, the Chemical Industry committee had as its secretary Margaret Stewart of the Chemical Industries Association Ltd; the secretariat of the Engineering Development committee was provided by the Fellowship of Engineering; PITCOM and the Motor Industry group had their secretariats provided by the same firm of political consultants as PASC – Charles Barker. In turn, Charles Barker acted respectively on behalf of major electronic communication firms, and the Society of Motor Manufacturers. Whilst such close connections between committees and outside agencies was deemed to be entirely benign by interviewed parliamentary officers of the relevant groups, doubts remain about the outside 'sponsorship' of subject groups. Some of these doubts arose tangentially in interview, with one committee vice-chairman acknowledging that 'when you talk to the secretary of the committee you are also talking to the consultants at the same time'. The Treasurer of another recently-formed committee indicated his own dependence upon his outside 'sponsoring' agency by being unable to recall the stated objectives of his committee. Nonetheless, he reassured the author that the respective outside organisation would be able to provide a written statement of the committee's aims!

Even some political consultants themselves have reservations about the provision of all-party secretarial services by outside lobbyists. Public Policy Consultants – a firm of parliamentary lobbyists – in its evidence to the 1988 investigation into parliamentary lobbying, recorded its misgivings about the possibility of outside administrative assistants restricting access to MPs on the committees by other lobbyists, pressure groups or members of the public (HC 518 1988:87; see also evidence of Jenny Jeger of GJW Government Relations:97). Clearly, such restriction would be a danger if committee members did not possess alternative sources of information or if committees sought exclusively to influence policy. On both counts, however, interviewed officers maintained that committee members, as acknowledged subject specialists, had their own network of contacts beyond the committee. Moreover, in many cases the committees were not concerned with the consideration of specific policy issues but concentrated instead upon facilitating the exchange of information. However, before analysing the policy impact of all-party committees it is worth examining the more mundane question of membership. In discussing all-party committees it is very easy to forget that not all are vibrant or provide an active programme of meetings and discussions for their members.

Membership and Activities
The level of membership and mode of activity varies significantly amongst all-party groups concerned with industry. The general assumption is that size of membership and extent of activity is closely associated with the degree of involvement of outside organisations in committee affairs. In large part this is an accurate assumption, with those groups with the services of outside secretariats also tending to have the largest memberships. The PASC is at the top end of the membership scale with some 125 MP members (along with around 90 members of the House of Lords, 25 MEPs, representatives from some 90 companies and 40 higher education institutions). PITCOM similarly is highly organised with in excess of 80 MPs amongst its extensive membership (which also includes over 100 corporate members). The Minerals, Engineering, Textiles, and Chemical Industry committees all have nominal memberships of between forty and sixty MPs. At the other end of the scale Footwear and Leather, and Paper and Board have few more than a handful of members. Indeed, one officer of the Footwear committee commented that 'effectively the committee no longer exists. The whole thing is a nonsense'.

In practice, however, the 'official' membership lists of all-party groups reveal little as to the actual rates of participation by backbenchers. Thus, PITCOM with a large formal membership was estimated by one of its officers to have 'a typical attendance of only fifteen MPs. We get a better attendance from outside'. He explained the low average turn-out in terms of the general pressure of time upon MPs and the fact that many PITCOM members found the committee's subject matter 'a little bit complex'. Similarly, the Motor Industry group had a core of only ten MPs regularly in attendance, and these were largely members with a constituency interest in, or prior experience of, the industry. The rates of backbench participation at the Chemical Industry, Minerals, and Knitwear groups were somewhat higher with average attendances in the low twenties; whilst other groups, such as Paper and Board, and Footwear, were regarded by one member as 'merely mailing lists' with 'very few members meeting very infrequently'.

Indeed, it is not surprising to find that the industrial sectors amongst those hardest hit by the recession of the early 1980s – Wool Textiles, Footwear and Leather, and Paper and Board – were the least active in the second half of the 1980s. As one renowned maverick Labour member commented:

> On Paper and Board we used to have briefings, discussions, arguments. We used to 'have a go' at The Paper and Board Federation. What happens now? We have an annual dinner – and that's about it!

Another Conservative officer noted that the Wool Textiles group 'rarely meets' and that its activities were organised largely around visits.

Again, the PASC provides a stark contrast with those groups dealing with the declining industries. As a leading Conservative officer of the committee noted:

> PASC is not short of active members or of subjects for our consideration. The committee has a constant round of activities and conferences. It has developed international links – we invited the Chinese across recently and took a delegation to China. We do the rounds of most European centres. We were designed to increase the interface between industry, parliament and the educational world and that is what our considerable activities are aimed at.

In between, activities varied from the Knitwear group, with its twenty regular attenders – drawn mainly from the East Midlands – holding quarterly meetings, without calling upon many outside speakers, and organising the occasional conference with local councils in Nottinghamshire and Leicestershire; through Chemical Industries with six meetings a year, regular seminars and interchanges between parliamentarians and industrialists; to PITCOM with its own programme subcommittee arranging a series of eight or nine formal meetings addressed by outside experts each parliamentary session, as well as producing its own journal *Information Technology and Public Policy*.

Outcomes of All-Party Committee Activity

But what is the impact of such diverse patterns of activity upon the House and upon policy? The first part of the question is far easier to answer than the second, insofar as all-party groups absorb two of the scarcest resources at Westminster – time and accommodation. The problem of time many backbenchers resolve simply by not attending all-party meetings but continuing to receive group briefing material. Membership thus tends to distil into a hard core of active specialists. The second problem, that of accommodating the multitudinous meetings of all-party groups, was addressed by the Services Committee in 1984 and steps have since been taken to regulate their use of committee rooms in the House (HC 256 1984).

The second part of the question is much harder to answer. One way to attempt an answer may be to specify the potentiality of all-party committees to exert influence and then to contrast this potentiality with the actuality of the Commons in the 1980s. The foundations of any claim to the exercise of influence by all-party groups is that they serve as a channel of communication for specialised knowledge. In turn, this claim rests not so much upon the actual degree of expert or specialist knowledge possessed by MP committee members (though as seen above the committees do act as a focus for such members) but in the *linkage* and *filtration* of outside expertise into the House. In this sense, all-party committees serve to affect the broader context of deliberation within the House through increasing the information resources available to backbenchers. At this level all-party committees are simply additional access points into the parliamentary system.

But, if committees were merely concerned with increasing the quantity of information their existence would be counter-productive both for MPs and for groups outside of Westminster. What MPs require is not *more* information but information which is precise, concise and readily 'usable'. In other words, specific and targeted analysis of the merits or demerits of particular policies. Correspondingly, outside organisations are aware of the qualitative as well as quantitative dimensions of informational inputs into the House. The provision of more and untargeted information to MPs is often unwelcome; immobilising members under the sheer volume of material. Manifestly, the quality of a group's presentation and the ability to place information into the appropriate member's hands at the right time are far more important in the transmission of information into the House than mere quantity. All-party committees thus serve the useful purpose of linking functional groups with specialised members, and so of providing a two-way flow of information in the parliamentary system. In fact, where a relevant all-party group does not already exist outside organisations are likely to seek to establish one. Thus, for example, a Labour officer of the Motor group explained that the group had been 'set up in recognition of the fact that knowledge of the motor industry was thin on the ground in Westminster; so it was established to secure a nucleus of members with a knowledge of the industry'.

The value of the information-exchange role was affirmed by all interviewed officers, and two at least claimed that this was the *only* role of value:

> The emphasis of the committee is to raise understanding of [industry x]. Its importance is in raising contacts with industry in the House. It seeks no policy role, nor does it get embroiled in ideological discourse. (Conservative treasurer)

> There is no political pressure from the group [on industry y]. Its intention is to keep members informed .... basically it is a talking shop. (Labour vice-chairman)

The latter officer then proceeded to point out how the group did not 'press anything collectively', and how it was 'up to MPs in the respective parties to revert back to their party to press any particular policy-line'.

This ascribed policy-neutral, indeed *neutered*, role was not shared, however, by officers of other committees. Nor, indeed, is it a view shared by outside interests or, for that matter, by successive Select Committees on Members' Interests. The ultimate logic of outside organisations' involvement with all-party committees is that their particular interest can be advanced to the point of influencing policy. This might be through a process akin to osmosis, whereby information permeates the consciousness of backbenchers over a long period of time; or to cathexis, whereby information is injected into the parliamentary process at a time when the House is actively considering a particular issue. Once MPs have been provided with information they are clearly expected to do something with it!

In interview several officers revealed how their committees had been used to organise joint delegations to ministers to press for policy change. Examples of the 'success' of joint delegations were cited by officers of both the Chemical Industries and Wool Textile committees. In the first case a joint approach was deemed to have persuaded the British government to oppose the EC proposal that surplus wine should be turned into industrial alcohol. Recognition of the detrimental impact upon employment in the British chemical industry was believed to have been a major consideration in the government's decision. Similarly, the Wool Textiles' delegation to British ministers before the EC multifibre negotiations was believed by one of its officers at least to have had some influence upon the government's position. It should be noted, however, that this backbencher made no claim that the all-party group had been *the* decisive influence; merely that it had 'formed one point of pressure among different kinds of pressure'. Indeed, in the context of EC policy it should also be noted that several groups have developed contacts with the EC Commission in recognition of the importance of EC directives and regulations.

The expectation that all-party groups will actively seek to *promote* and not simply retail information within the House is apparent from ex-Labour MP Alf Dubs' (1989:192) observation that: 'Commercial lobbyists will seek to influence .... all-party groups'. Group members thus are often expected by outside organisations to use parliamentary devices, such as questions and Early Day Motions, to elicit information or to generate publicity. All-party committees may also serve as the forums within which support for a group's case can be organised, and potential support, or opposition beyond the group can be identified and addressed. In addition, as the Select Committee on Services (HC 256 1984:v) pointed out, although all-party groups have no official connection with the House they do draw upon and use the status of the House to promote their own objectives – some of which are non-parliamentary. In fact, as Jones (1990) maintains: 'ministers are reluctant to deny access to delegations promoted by all-party groups, and the media tend to look less critically on a press statement which carries an all-party parliamentary imprint upon it than one issued by an identifiable or self-proclaimed pressure group'. In other words all-party groups have tangible benefits to offer organised groups and lobbyists both as a point of entry into the House and as point of pressure therein. Even where direct benefit in the form of policy influence is not always apparent, all-party groups remain of some importance in their indirect consequences: in providing yet another point of access for outside groups; in facilitating contact with the *executive* through the intermediation of parliament; in conferring through the all-party 'tag' a quasi-official status to publicity material; in contributing to 'climate setting' through raising, maintaining, or even blocking, issues on the policy agenda.

Political Consultants

Thus far this chapter has been concerned with those backbench committees and groups within the House which are 'interested' in industry, either in informational or promotional terms, and, often, both at the same time. What now needs to be examined are those organisations which are active on an unofficial basis in Westminster and which seek to advance their own interests or those of a client or group of clients. The rest of this chapter will therefore examine the role of political consultants in linking parliament and industry.

Before examining this particular linkage, however, it should be remembered that there are several other types of lobbying organisations concerned with industrial policy. Many do not have parliament itself as their main focus of attention, but all acknowledge the necessity of some form of parliamentary activity. For instance, as noted earlier, local firms and trade unionists frequently maintain contacts with their constituency MP. Such informal contact was invariably used both to inform and to 'pressure' members, and, on the whole, was welcomed by the MPs concerned (see chapter 5). In fact, many backbenchers find these individual contacts to be amongst the most useful sources of information about the world of industry (see Ellis 1988:44). In addition, many large industrial firms now operate government relations departments, part of whose functions is to maintain the flow of information between the company and interested constituency MPs (see Grant 1987:92-116). Thus, ICI for example holds periodic receptions at its Millbank headquarters for MPs with ICI plants in their constituencies. IBM has a particularly impressive Government Affairs division, headed by Gerry Wade, which amongst its many functions produces a *Parliamentary Newsletter* for distribution to MPs.

Local contacts with individual firms is often supplemented and built upon by national representative organisations such as the CBI, IoD, ABCC and trade associations. However, their effectiveness as lobbyists is often questioned, not least by MPs themselves, given the representation of often diverse interests (see also Grant and Marsh 1977; Marsh 1983:25-8; Grant 1987:117-

38). In some sectors, however, trade associations are seen to be highly efficient and often effective promoters of their case. In interviews with members, the British Textile Confederation fell into this category, as did the Chemical Industries Association (for a discussion of the CIA see Grant 1983; Grant et al 1987).

Since 1977 the CBI has operated a parliamentary unit in its efforts to inform and influence parliamentary opinion. Although the regional activities of the CBI were commended by MPs many remained agnostic in their assessment of national CBI lobbying. In particular, the informational efforts of the CBI were uniformly criticised by Conservative and Labour interviewees alike. Only one interviewed MP admitted to reading the CBI's fortnightly bulletins on a regular basis. More typical comments were:

The CBI sends its regular bulletin. But I've seen it all before. It tends to deal with things in the past, matters of historical interest. (Conservative, West Midlands)

I don't pick up much [information] from the CBI. Trade Associations give me much of what I need, along with material from firms in my constituency. No, the CBI isn't much use to me. Its glossy magazine invariably goes straight in my bin. (Conservative, North West England)

Organised labour on the other hand, working through the trade union group and individual union groups, was held to be more effective in communicating issues of concern to interested members. Although the trade union group had declined from its former position as 'a major force within the party' (Muller 1977:89), nonetheless, it still continued to perform an informational role for sponsored MPs. As one of its officers stated: 'the group allows trade unions to bring to our attention matters of importance to them. These can be general or individual problems arising from single unions or regional problems'. But an increasing problem confronting the group, and one pointed out by another officer, was the 'simple fact that a lot of sponsored people now have no experience of industry'. This fact was believed to reduce the 'clout' of the trade union group within the party and in its meetings with visiting trade union leaders. In contrast, individual trade union groups, and most particularly that of the AEU, were singled out by several Labour interviewees as of importance 'in getting the union's message across in the right way' within the PLP. Often the message was that the AEU needed help in defending its members interests. And several examples were provided by its officers of how the group had mobilised support within the House with some success; these included pressuring the government to purchase British engineering products in the reconstruction of the war-torn Falklands islands, and also of highlighting the problems encountered by British engineering firms with British Rail's tendering policies. In both cases officers of the group believed that 'a good result' had been achieved.

Consultants and Backbenchers

It is perhaps ironic that, at a time of massive expansion of the business of parliamentary lobbying, MPs themselves still prefer to be approached directly by firms or industrial organisations. Consultants acting on behalf of the latter were far less likely to receive a sympathetic hearing than the principals themselves. Repeatedly in interview backbenchers concurred in general terms with one or other of the following statements:

> Consultants are a plague on this House. They invariably oversell their client's case. They constantly want to wine and dine you. What I want is a single sheet of paper outlining the case, or half an hour with the company concerned, not two hours over lunch. (Conservative, Midlands)

> Political consultants are a fact of political life. You have to recognise that they are pushing hard for their client's interests. Some do a very good job. If consultants limit their range they can be first class at it. Having said that, however, I prefer individual firms to contact me. (Labour, Lancashire)

Whether 'a plague' or 'first class', in both instances consultants were seen at heart to be superfluous to the representative process. One left-wing Merseyside MP went further and denounced consultants as a 'basic contradiction of parliamentary government. Inside Westminster it is the people's interest that should be promoted, not the interests of those who could afford to pay'. This comment typifies the critical perspective on consultants – that they are essentially distorters of the representative process. On the other hand, proponents argue that political consultants merely bring the 'suppliers' and 'consumers' of information together to their mutual advantage. Indeed, the very buoyancy of the consultancy 'market', estimated to be some £10 million in 1988 (HC 518 1988:85), is used as evidence of the demand for such 'facilitating services'.

Now the scope of consultancy is such that a recent survey of 180 large companies in the UK revealed that four out of ten engaged the services of political consultants (Grantham 1989:505). Those industries closely regulated by government – for example pharmaceuticals and airlines – were especially prone to hire consultants to monitor parliamentary activity. Even firms with their own in-house corporate parliamentary lobbying staff may also retain political consultants to facilitate access to MPs (See HC 518 1988:16). Indeed, several agencies are recognised for their sectoral specialisation – even though they do not seek themselves to confine their activities to specific industries. Grantham and Seymour-Ure (1990) note, for example, that Political Communications has a strong weighting in its list of clients towards the transport industry; Market Access International attracts several of its clients from the pharmaceutical sector; whilst Sallingbury Casey is retained by a large number of trade associations. Charles Barker, as noted earlier, act for a number of electronic communications firms and have clients involved in the extractive and motor industries. If anything this sectoral specialisation is likely to deepen given that two of the major methods bringing clients and consultants together are by 'word of mouth' recommendation from existing clients, and by 'targeting' potential clients by the agencies themselves.

But what can consultants offer to industrial firms and groups that could not be achieved through direct dealings with MPs? And of course the reverse question also needs to be addressed: what benefit can MPs derive from the work of political consultants? Not surprisingly, there are common elements to both answers. Consultants frequently justify their role in terms of 'briefing' and 'timing'. Briefing in both directions is vital: both to inform industry of pending and current legislation and policy deliberations; and in return to alert MPs to industry's opinions and requirements. Timing is equally essential. Thus, for example, amendments to bills may have to be drafted quickly at committee stage and tabled at the appropriate time to the appropriate person. This process often entails working to a strict timetable. Invariably, all but the largest industrial companies do not have the necessary resources or procedural expertise to operate within such tight time limits. In reverse, MPs – always short of time to conduct their own research – may appreciate being fed by consultants with accurate and concisely presented information at the 'right' time. Consultants provide, therefore, the parliamentary equivalent of the 'just-in-time' practices now employed by many modern industrial organisations.

As part of the briefing role most lobbying agencies offer their industrial clients a detailed monitoring service. This invariably includes daily surveillance of the order paper and official report of the House (and the Lords), government publications, as well as the meetings of official and backbench committees and the tabling of EDMs in the Commons. In reverse, agencies offer MPs information 'packs', as well as documents and publications outlining developments in the industry concerned. Such collection and dissemination of information is in itself an arduous task, unsuited respectively to the majority of firms and backbenchers.

Not only is the consultant's monitoring role of potential value to industrial client and backbench MP alike, but the 'counselling' role is also claimed to be of mutual benefit. 'Counselling' is best described by Grantham and Seymour-Ure (1990) as involving 'identifying those actors of relevance in the political domain and then facilitating contact with them.' David Wedgewood, a government relations consultant, similarly sees counselling in terms of 'keeping the client in the picture [as] he may want more feedback or to talk to a sympathetic MP' (Grant 1987:110). He then goes on to subdivide the 'facilitating' role into 'passive' and 'active' representation. Passive representation is simply arranging meetings between client and MP; active representation is 'where there is a specific objective in mind; getting something raised, launching a piece of legislation or trying to check or stop it' (Grant 1987:110).

Almost without exception the MPs interviewed for the present study believed that the best advocates of industry's case were those immediately involved in industry itself. MPs, therefore, were more likely to be sympathetic to a case made directly by a firm or sectoral organisation, rather than one made indirectly by political consultants. Consultants themselves are aware of this, preferring their clients to speak directly to MPs and simply advising them of the most effective way to communicate their case at such meetings (see Ellis 1988:86).

In terms of 'active' representation consultants like to adopt a long-term perspective and talk of 'climate setting' or 'consciousness-raising'. In essence, according to Peter Luff director of Good Relations Public Affairs, this means maintaining 'good communication .... over a long period of time to create an atmosphere of understanding for your case' (quoted in Ellis 1988:77). It also means identifying MPs policy positions, and either reinforcing support or weakening opposition through sustained provision of briefing materials. Although long-term campaigns are favoured by consultants, in practice much of their work is short-term 'fire-fighting'. Individual firms in crisis, or whole sectors adversely affected by government policies, are invariably 'innocents abroad' in the world of Westminster and Whitehall. With little time to master the complexities of parliamentary procedures and practices they frequently turn to consultants for assistance. Often, it must be said, too late for consultants to have any positive effect upon the outcome.

The balance of success and failure of consultants' parliamentary lobbying is difficult to establish precisely. By its very nature 'influence' is often intangible with many interlocking strands culminating in the making of a single decision. Thus, to examine but one of these strands is invariably misleading. Nonetheless, lobbying agencies for their own publicity purposes are willing to claim the credit for many changes of decisions. Grantham and Seymour-Ure (1990) provide a table of twenty recent successes claimed by consultancy firms. Similarly, Nigel Ellis (1988:77-101), a director of a large public relations consultancy, provides examples of notably successful consultancy campaigns. Ellis does acknowledge, however, that agencies don't always boast too readily of their successes for fear of 'revenge at some later date' (1988:77). Equally, agencies are not renowned for publicising their failures.

What is not in dispute, however, is that political consultants have *some* impact upon decision-making within parliament. What is in dispute is the actual extent of lobbyists' influence (see Grantham 1989).

The fact that lobbying 'works', and can be seen to work in many instances, gives rise to concern about *how* it works. This concern has been articulated most recently in investigations by the Select Committee on Members' Interests and in attempts to regulate consultants through backbench legislation (see HC Debates 1988 vol 125:col 291). What gives rise to most worry is the fact that much of the lobbying process is conducted in private; so that exactly who is talking to whom and on behalf of whom is often difficult to piece together. Hence, much of the discussion about the role of political consultants revolves around 'openness' – of opening-up the lobbying process to public scrutiny. 'For parliament', as Colin Seymour-Ure noted in his evidence to the Select Committee on Members' Interests (HC 518 1988:29), 'the problems all echo the last line of Sammy Finer's classic essay of the 1960s on pressure groups – "Light! More Light"'. Demands for the registration of political consultants have to be seen in this context – as a desire to bring greater transparency to the dealings of consultants; to know who their clients are and the sources of their expenditure. Indeed, the principle of registration is not in dispute. The overwhelming majority of consultants themselves acknowledge the need for registration, if only to allay public fears about their activities. What divides opinion is the effectiveness of registration (see HC 518). To base the case for registration on 'we want to know whence [information] cometh and who's behind it' (Dale Campbell-Savours on BBC Radio 4 10 May 1988) tells one little about the information itself. It also assumes that MPs are influenced by the mere act of lobbying, rather than by the nature and quality of the case itself. It views MPs as receivers of information in a political void wherein the simple receipt of information is sufficient to 'influence' their decision. In other words, it ignores the countervailing pressures upon MPs – of ideology, party, constituency, competing groups and lobbyists, and other specialist sources of information. Far from being infinitely capable of absorbing consultants' representations, MPs appear to be 'growing increasingly impervious to glossy brochures and endless invitations to drinks parties' (Grantham 1989:517). Formal regulation of access to and usage (and abusage) of the facilities of the House, as well as official registration of political lobbyists, is within the capacity of the House itself. However, the fundamental issues are of self-regulation and the exercise of political judgement by MPs; and most members have shown themselves to be quite capable of resisting outside pressure, and of assessing the merits of any particular case in the light of the variety of other 'cues' available to them.

Indeed, it is clear from the investigations of the Members' Interests Committee that parliamentarians are often more concerned about protecting the clients of consultants than they are about protecting themselves. Ironically what gives rise to so much concern is the 'over-selling' of parliament itself. Ian Greer has noted the 'naivety of many national and international companies in their understanding of .... the democratic process' (HC 518 1988:102). The fear is that this lack of understanding can be exploited by unscrupulous agencies to their own pecuniary advantage. They exaggerate the complexities of lobbying and mislead clients into believing that MPs are more influential in the process of decision-making than they actually are (HC 518 1988:89). Perhaps just as worrying is the view expressed by Charles Miller, a well-known practitioner and author on the subject of commercial lobbying, that 'most lobbyists do not fully understand the role of Members of Parliament in government related decisions' (HC 518 1988:89). Another public relations director maintained:

> it is because of the mystique of this place [the Commons] and Members of Parliament that so much time is spent with Members of Parliament rather than dealing with a technical boring subject by directing themselves [consultants] perhaps towards government departments. (HC 518 1988:17)

Conclusion

This chapter has revealed a series of paradoxes concerning the linkages and levels of communication between backbenchers and industry. The particular focus of analysis has been the points of access afforded to industrial interests through party and all-party committees and through political consultancies. The wider paradoxes of the role of parliament in industrial policy making will be returned to in the next chapter. What will be examined here are the paradoxes apparent in the operation of these committees and agencies.

The first seeming contradiction is that all of the committees and agencies analysed above have as their primary purpose the transmission of specialist information into and within the House. That more information now flows into the Commons is indisputable. Indeed, the common complaint amongst backbenchers is that the place is now awash with briefing documents and glossy brochures of all kinds. One consequence of the information technology revolution has been that the ready availability of word-processors and desk-top publishing has increased the quantity of unsolicited material landing on backbenchers' desks (at least momentarily before being consigned to the waste-basket). Fred Silvester (ex-MP for Manchester, Withington) has estimated that each MP receives, and leaves unopened, a ten foot high pile of lobbying mail every year (HC 518 1988:44). 'More' information in itself may be counter-productive if 75 per cent of it is summarily discarded (another statistic provided by Silvester). What backbenchers require are filters, or, in the language of systems theory, 'gatekeepers', to allow only relevant information through to them. Clearly, this raises the problem of who determines what is of relevance. Manifestly, any individual member is incapable of sifting all information flooding into and around Westminster; hence the necessity of institutional and organisational mechanisms of selection. All three of the organisations examined in this chapter serve this vital sifting and selecting process.

Dealing only with the process of information transmission for the moment, party and all-party committees and political consultants all provide in their various ways points of connection between the institutional world of Westminster and the industrial world beyond. They are two-way channels of communication between subject specialists and would-be specialists inside the House and industrial experts outside. All three are mechanisms of information-exchange; and are valuable insofar as they identify and bring into contact the relevant actors both inside and outside of the House.

That industry has been more active in developing contacts with MPs in recent years has already been noted in earlier chapters, and was testified to by several witnesses appearing before the Select Committee on Members' Interests (HC 518 1988:57; 95-6; 102). In part, this was a reflection of the continued activism of government in the sphere of industry. Activity to 'roll back the state', to reduce the levels of regulation and intervention, and to restructure the relationship between government and industry requires in itself significant legislative and administrative activity. In part also increased attention to parliament was a reflection of manufacturing industry's general belief that its sectoral voices no longer carried the same resonance in Whitehall and a concomitant desire to develop supplementary channels through which these voices could be amplified. The paradox is that the very conditions which directed industrial interests increasingly towards Westminster were the same ones which mitigated parliamentary influence upon the executive. The grand issues – of the pursuit of the free market, of monetarist policy, of privatisation, and the reduction of bureaucratic encumbrances upon industry – were the ones least amenable to parliamentary influence. The ideological hegemony of 'Thatcherism' meant that attempts to influence policy, to be successful, had to accept the basic premises of the New Right ideology – yet these were the very premises which large sections of domestically-based manufacturing industry sought to challenge in the first place. This argument is of significance in that the House of Commons in the 1980s became, at one and the same time, both more and less capable of influencing industrial policy. At the micro-level when backbenchers have accepted the general frame of policy they have been successful on many occasions in amending the details of policy and in redirecting the focus of ministers. They have been notably unsuccessful, however, in diverting the government from its macro-policy objectives.

One important independent variable in assessing the potential influence of unofficial backbench committees and political consultants is, therefore, their relative position along the ideological continuum. Those clearly located near the government's own position – the Conservative Trade and Industry committee under Michael Grylls' chairmanship, or those consciously eschewing any such position and espousing the neutrality of expertise – PASC, PITCOM for example – are more likely to be seen to be 'influential' than those groups clearly anti-pathetic to the current ideological thrust of industrial policy. In this latter category falls the Labour party's industrial groups (though these have the potential to influence *party* policy), and those all-party groups and lobbyists challenging the very essence of the government's industrial strategy. This point was brought home by one of the officers of the all-party Footwear group in his observation:

> In the past, before Mrs Thatcher's government, the group was a significant lobby pressing the case for the control of imports, and generally questioning free market positions. But, as the present government extended its free market principles, so the door was practically closed on effective lobbying. Meetings became a sham.

Other groups studiously avoid ideologically-sensitive areas. Even so, as several officers noted, whilst their groups might willingly accept, for example, the general principle of free trade and minimal state intervention, when it comes down to their specific industry being affected by 'dumping' or discriminatory trade practices overseas then the general preference is subverted by specific calls for government action and controls. Thus, Labour members on the Motor Industries committee recounted with some glee how 'many Conservative members with constituencies to nurse have been out there advocating intervention and assistance to the industry'. However an officer of the group then noted that 'in the run up to an election government members become more wary about what they say and what they will do on the group. They aren't going to say things which can be used by others for propaganda purposes'. Generally, therefore, all-party groups are sensitive to the political context within which they operate and which affords them 'space' – on non-adversarial territory in an adversarial setting – to exert influence.

Ultimately, the point of pressure of party committees, all-party groups, and consultants and their clients alike is the executive. Direct contact and communication with ministers is achieved, obviously, by Conservative party committees. Direct access is also afforded to joint delegations organised by all-party groups and, as noted above, ministers are reluctant to deny access to such delegations. But indirect communication is also a powerful objective of unofficial groups and parliamentary lobbyists. Throughout, this chapter has noted the emphasis upon 'climate-setting', 'consciousness-raising' and 'agenda-setting' as the underlying rationale of much of the activity described. The climate and the agenda to be influenced in the long-term are those within which the executive itself has to operate. The provision of information is crucial to such an exercise – but in qualitative rather than simply quantitative terms. We are back to where we started! Who provides the information and under what conditions is certainly a matter of concern, but, ultimately, of greater concern would be a parliament denied information on important industrial issues. To conclude with the words of Sir Michael McNair-Wilson:

I think the weakness all Members of Parliament suffer from .... is a lack of precise information. If I am interested in a subject and somebody offers me information on it , I am grateful for it. I have my own critical faculties to decide whether or not to accept what is given, but I cannot see anything inherently wrong in being supplied with that information.
(HC 518 1988:32)

Party committees, all-party groups and political consultants are all in the business of supplying information. What use is made of that information is another matter and one for consideration in the next chapter.

9 Conclusions

The pervasive sense – one shared by many academics, politicians and those engaged directly in industry itself – that 'something is wrong' with the relationship between the industrial and political systems has surfaced at various points throughout this book. Too often in the past, however, the causes of this malaise have been examined at a disaggregated level – with blame variously attached to specific economic institutions and policies, or specific political institutions and their outputs (see Judge and Dickson 1987:1). Whilst monocausal analyses have the advantage of simplicity they do not significantly enhance the understanding of the complex causes and often paradoxical dimensions of Britain's relative industrial decline. One of the maxims of this book, therefore, has been that only through aggregate analysis of the inter-connections of industry, industrial society and representative democracy can an adequate understanding be gained of British industrial and political development. Just such macro-considerations guided, in the opening chapters of this book, the historical and theoretical discussion of the state form of parliamentarism and the socio-economic form of British industrialism. And, in turn, these wider considerations were tempered by a detailed micro-analysis of activity within the Commons on industrial issues. An exercise some critics would undoubtedly see as moving from the sublime to the ridiculous!

From The Sublime to the Ridiculous?

Yet the connections between macro- and micro-analysis have to be made and derive ultimately from the paradoxes inherent within parliamentarism itself. Successive attempts to deal with the 'problem of industry' have confronted these paradoxes – often in the negative sense that a failure to recognise that there is, indeed, a paradox renders the solution to the initial problem inoperable. It is essential, therefore, to expose the paradoxes of parliamentarism at both the systemic and institutional levels if reasoned conclusions about the linkages between parliament and industry are to be drawn. Whilst the approach is schizoid it certainly should not slide aimlessly from elevated theory to mundane description. Theory and practice are inextricably interlinked – or should be. Unfortunately, too often in the analysis of the British parliament they are not.

Paradoxes of Parliament

The first, and perhaps most profound, paradox is that parliament is simultaneously both of vital importance and routinely impotent in the making of industrial policy. Historically, industrial development in Britain was incubated within the supportive shell of a constitutional settlement which focused political demands and political aspirations upon Westminster. In taking upon itself a proactive role the legislature established the statutory framework within which liberal capitalism could flourish. But this very legislative activism in the first half of the nineteenth century served to accrue increased regulatory responsibilities to the executive; and to engender a host of extra-parliamentary representative associations which came to constitute a parallel system of functional representation. By the end of that century, therefore, the British state was moulded into its recognisably modern form – an executive-centric pluralist system. A form moreover which was sufficiently malleable to accommodate changing economic and social relationships in the subsequent century.

The important point is that for most of this period the practice and theory of representative government in Britain has constantly been at odds. Critics have pointed persistently to this disjunction as cause for concern. The fact that constitutional theory has traditionally reflected an idealised view of parliament's contribution to policy-making has only heightened the sense of contemporary malaise at any particular time over the past century and a half. In this specific sense, almost by definition, there has always been 'something wrong' with parliament simply because the theory was 'wrong' in the first instance. Thus to claim that parliament ill-serves industry – a consistent refrain – is essentially to misdirect criticism. The parliamentary system, as demonstrated earlier in this book, served industry well at its incipient stage, and has continued to provide the over-arching language of legitimacy – of representative government – which alone authorises legislative outputs of specific benefit to industry. Again as seen earlier, no other system of representation, whether pluralist or corporatist, has such endemic and enduring authority.

Thus, at the macro-level of analysis, parliament, or rather the parliamentary system, has provided the *necessary* frame of legitimation within which specific industrial policies can be formulated and implemented. Yet, as Pross (1986:256) observes 'the language of parliament .... is not the language of policy formulation'. To proceed then to argue that specific legislative outputs have been unsuited to the requirements of industry – whether because of their myopic nature, ideological content, or adversarial origins – is to change the focus of criticism away from parliament itself (unless Diceyean constitutional fictions of parliamentary sovereignty are invoked) towards the wider political and economic systems within which policy is framed. If policy failure, in terms of inadequate or inappropriate conception or implementation, is the perceived problem then explanation has to be sought at the interstices of the political and economic systems themselves. The fact that in the post-war period industrial policy in Britain has been unstable, incoherent and basically reactive reflects the complex configuration of economic forces influencing state policy. At the centre of this pattern is the preeminence of financial capital and its ability to appropriate the definition of the 'national interest' – in terms of free trade and internationalism – as its own. Industrial capital has proved either unwilling or incapable of countering economic orthodoxy thus defined. Equally industrial capital has been confronted with the peculiar nature of the British labour movement and its profound economic and political ramifications for industrial development. Any discussion of present British industrial performance thus has to take cognisance of these major socio-economic variables and their interconnection with the political form of the British state. Consideration of either political form or socio-economic forces in isolation only simplifies analysis at the expense of comprehension. The pattern of industrial development, and of decline and 'deindustrialisation', is inherently convoluted. Simple explanations and solutions consequently are frustrated by this very complexity. And arguments which target specific institutions or individual independent variables inevitably produce false panaceas. If there were indeed simple solutions to Britain's manufacturing malaise they would have already been tried.

With these preliminary words of caution in mind it is intended to review here some of the recurrent schemes aimed at reinvigorating the linkages between industry and parliament; to deal in other words with matters of political arrangements and political personnel.

Quality of Parliamentarians

The Commons is very low on industrial experience .... the lack of industrial experience lessens the understanding of what it takes to get the workforce to produce and how to coordinate such an exercise. (Lewis Stevens MP, quoted in *Chief Executive* 1986:18)

With considerable justification, those in industry often complain that Parliament and government do not understand the nature or the problems of industry. (David Knox MP 1986:26)

These quotations reflect the widespread impression outside of the House that there are relatively few members with practical experience of industry. But, as pointed out in chapter 4, rarely is it stated explicitly what would constitute an adequate representation of industry in the House. Calls for a 'better balance of occupational experience amongst members' (Ross 1948:196), however, invariably entail notions of microcosmic representation. In this respect productive industry is clearly under-represented in the composition of the House if pre-entry occupation is defined in 'primary' terms. However, if categorisation is extended to include those MPs who have worked in the productive industries at any stage of their pre-parliamentary career, then the data in chapter 4 reveals that the composition of the 1983 House was not as deficient as many outside appeared to believe. Moreover, the House also appeared capable of reflecting, admittedly in an unstructured manner, the changing pattern of industrial employment. Indeed, as manufacturing employment continued to decline throughout the 1980s the composition of the House became more representative of the profile of the wider workforce, in part, simply through the diminution of the industrial workforce itself.

Yet chapter 4 also revealed the limited collective experience of significant sectors of industry at Westminster. Those sectors that had substantial representation, particularly coal mining and mechanical engineering, did so largely as a result of the sponsorship policies of the relevant trade unions. Over a decade ago Muller (1977:xix) suggested that 'sponsored MPs have helped to make the British House of Commons more typical or representative of the British population'. Traditionally, trade union sponsorship facilitated entry into the House of working class representatives generally and sectoral industrial interests specifically. On both counts, however, there has been a dilution of 'industrial' representation in recent years. First, whilst, there is still a substantial working class base amongst sponsored MPs, nonetheless, they are 'becoming more like the rest of the Labour MPs' (Park et al 1986:312). Second, and linked to this, is the fact that several industrial unions now place greater emphasis upon 'parliamentarist' criteria in the selection of their sponsored members; in so doing the possession of parliamentary skills and ambitions are stressed rather than direct knowledge of, or prior involvement in, the industry concerned. Not surprisingly this has had a corrosive effect upon the link between industrial experience and parliamentary activity.

Whether this link can be, or indeed should be, reforged is an open question. MPs sponsored by unions still committed to 'actual representation' of sectoral industrial interests ardently believe that practical experience should remain the bedrock of parliamentary representation. Other Labour MPs maintain that the case of industry can be pressed just as effectively, if not more so, by eloquent and incisive arguments presented by articulate and well-briefed members from the 'talking classes'. What is not in dispute, particularly since the reassessment of the role of sponsored members in the wake of the 1984 Trade Union Act, is the value of MPs directly representing the interests of organised labour in a 'House of Commons dominated by business interests' (Taylor

1989:77; see also *Labour Research* 1986:10-12; *Labour Research* 1988:8-10).

There is, indeed, a long tradition of MPs, primarily Conservative backbenchers, being associated with industrial firms through directorships and other extra-parliamentary remunerated posts in companies. Indeed, Jordan and Richardson (1987b:266) maintain that this kind of association is 'so long established that it is, generally, not controversial'. Whilst, the underpinning assumption is that occupational involvement with firms outside Westminster has an impact upon activity in the House, in practice there does not appear to be such a close or direct relationship. Perhaps it is not overly cynical to suggest, therefore, that money – as much as a substantive interest in industrial issues – is often the prime determinant of the choice of outside occupation by some members (Radice et al 1987:113). In which case, pre-entry experience may be more influential in shaping the profile of parliamentary activity. Overall, however, as shown in chapter 6, industrially experienced backbenchers were not significantly more active in the formal procedures in the Commons, though they tended to 'specialise' more in industrial policy matters than other MPs. But, repeatedly in interview and in parliamentary debates, members who had formerly been employed in industry stressed the importance of that experience for their work in the House. They believed that the possession of 'first-hand information' and 'hands-on' experience brought a critical edge to their consideration of industrial policy.

Recruiting Industrially Experienced Members
The belief that pre-entry experience of industry enhances the consideration of industrial policy matters in the legislature has guided repeated calls for the recruitment of increased numbers of suitably 'experienced' members. Ultimately such calls founder upon the simple fact that 'those with prestige in industry no longer find it desirable or possible to pursue a parliamentary career' (Coombes 1982:47). The reasons why will be examined presently, but in the meantime it is appropriate to consider some recent proposals as to how the numbers of industrially experienced MPs might be increased.

One obvious scheme would be to extend the sponsorship policies of the AEU and NUM to other industrial unions – in other words to ensure that sponsored MPs had an extensive background in the appropriate industry. The plea by one northern AEU MP in interview for more 'representation from the shopfloor; from people who have mastered a trade and worked their way through the ranks of the trade union movement' was typical of such sentiments. But this MP then went on to list the predominantly white collar composition of his own constituency; a constituency, moreover, with one of the highest proportions of working class electors in the whole country. Two related phenomena thus serve to limit the capacity of trade unions to promote 'actual representation'. One is the changing economic composition of several safe Labour seats as a consequence of the decimation of manufacturing employment in these areas – this has particularly affected the NUM in recent years. The other is the changing nature of the selection process within the Labour party itself. Whereas in the past there was a certainty in the selection of trade union sponsored candidates, given the dominance of trade union delegates on the GMC in certain industrial constituencies, by the end of the 1980s this dominance was under challenge. In 1984 Neil Kinnock, as leader of the Labour party, advocated the introduction of a 'one member one vote' system of candidate selection, but the system actually introduced in 1987 enshrined the union's block vote at constituency level by guaranteeing 40 per cent of the vote in the selection process. Paradoxically therefore the position of the unions was strengthened in the local selection process. However, this enhanced position prompted a review of the selection process with proposals placed before the 1990 party conference for the introduction of 'one member one vote'. In these circumstances it is unlikely that the wish expressed by an NUM backbencher in interview will be fulfilled:

> Trade unions should play a larger role in the selection of candidates. They should make sure they have a proper industrial voice in the party. The PLP is full of those without any experience of industry. Let's make it an industrial party once again!

On the other side of the House, on the Conservative backbenches, and, indeed, on the other side of industry, the recruitment of industrial managers and executives is even more of a serendipitous process. As noted in chapters 4 and 6 the newly elected Conservative cohort in 1983 had proportionately more industrial experience than the new Labour entry. This was largely the fortuitous result of unexpected Conservative gains in marginal industrial constituencies. As one backbencher with considerable experience of the motor industry remarked it was the remote possibility of electoral victory that dissuaded the 'normal Conservative aspirants – lawyers and city-types' from seeking the nomination and enabled him ultimately to enter parliament. Moreover, electoral uncertainty in itself may reinforce such a member's desire to retain contact with industry – both to advance the interests of his constituents but also, more pragmatically, to enhance his own personal prospects of reemployment should his electoral majority be overturned. This point is reinforced in the statement of Radice et al (1987:113)

> It is clear that there will always be MPs who realise that their political careers are insecure and that it would be naive and premature of them to sever their professional connections. Many of the Conservatives we talked to put themselves in this category, several agreeing that they did not expect

to get into the House and that they might need their old job back if the
government has a smaller majority at the next election.

Obviously, proponents of increased representation of industrial management
would like to see some of the more random features of the selection process
removed. Yet, of the industrially experienced Conservative MPs interviewed
for the present study, who themselves had benefited from the vagaries of the
selection and electoral process, they all believed that it would be impractical,
or, indeed, in the opinion of one member 'dangerous', for Conservative local
associations to discriminate in favour of industrialists. Instead, the way to
increase the numbers of MPs with industrial experience was believed to be
through increasing their number amongst party activists and amongst those
seeking parliamentary candidacies.

CBI: Helping Employees Into Parliament
In 1977 the CBI established a working party 'to consider what guidance, if
any, the CBI should give to member companies on the question of release of
employees to enable them to become Members of the House of Commons'
(CBI 1978:5). The guiding premise of the working party was that there was a
scarcity of first-hand industrial experience amongst MPs which could only be
rectified with the recruitment of more representatives with business
experience. Irrespective of the political party concerned the working party
believed that industry would benefit, along with parliament and the country,
from the election of people with practical knowledge of industry on both sides
of the Commons.

The CBI inquiry made a number of recommendations, not the least of which
was that, 'welcoming Parliamentary candidature would .... be a significant
advance in itself .... It means, quite simply, companies making it known to
their employees that they accept that Parliamentary ambitions are a good thing
and not a bad thing'. The report stated that more tangible assistance could be
provided by employers allowing prospective parliamentary candidates 18 days
time off per year to undertake the necessary political work of nursing a
constituency and for attending party meetings and conferences. In addition, a
further three weeks should be granted at the time of an election to enable
candidates to devote themselves to full-time campaigning. Clearly these
provisions were offered as guidelines for enlightened employers.

Similarly, in terms of the post-election relationship between employer and
(former) employee, the most difficult but equally the most important provision
was for a guarantee of reemployment. Such a guarantee, within a suggested
period of the duration of two parliaments, was obviously easier for large
companies to make, but in a survey of CBI members nearly 45 per cent of
respondent firms with fewer than 1,000 employees were prepared to consider

such a guarantee (CBI 1978:15). The likelihood that this would apply 'in isolated cases at infrequent intervals' (CBI 1978:16) undoubtedly contributed to such a degree of consideration on the part of small business respondents.

Beyond reengagement policies, however, the working party found the issues involved in maintaining a relationship between employer and ex-employee to be more thorny. Some CBI members raised the question of CBI sponsorship of its own MPs, but this was firmly rejected by the working party: 'We .... have no doubt in recommending against sponsorship of candidates either by the CBI or any of its members' (CBI 1978:17). The main ground for rejection was that the CBI wished to remain an 'independent body' with no formal links with party politics. However, the CBI saw no objection to its member companies retaining a former employee on a part-time basis to act as a parliamentary adviser or consultant in the House. Part-time reemployment would also have the added benefit of maintaining the industrial expertise of MPs.

Company Policies

In the CBI's survey 48 per cent of the 508 respondents believed that companies should have a positive policy towards encouraging employees to stand for parliament. In practice, however, relatively few companies (15 per cent) operated such a policy. And as the *Chief Executive* (1986:17) magazine discovered this position remained relatively unchanged by the mid-1980s. Perhaps not surprisingly large British trans-national companies conform most closely with the guidelines suggested by the CBI. BP and ICI are particularly enlightened employers in this respect. BP allows employee candidates with at least five years service up to three weeks leave on full salary prior to polling day. If elected the 'employee' will then be considered to be on unpaid leave for up to ten years after the date of first election. During this time the company guarantees reemployment of the 'employee' at the same job-level as held at the time of election, with salary and pension adjusted in accordance with general company settlements. However, to safeguard the 'independence' of the 'employee' MP, BP requires any outstanding loans from the company to be repaid, any company car to be returned or purchased from the company, and withdrawal from company medical insurance schemes.

ICI has operated, since the mid-1970s, a scheme designed to encourage more of its employees to serve in parliament. To this end leave is granted to parliamentary candidates from the dissolution of parliament up to the election itself; successful candidates are guaranteed reemployment at the same level within the company for ten years after first election; and for pension purposes parliamentary service is treated as the equivalent of company service. The attractiveness of this scheme can be gauged from the simple fact that in the 1983 parliament some nine former ICI employees were members of the Commons.

Unfortunately, behind the formality of these enlightened company policies there still remains the informal pressures restricting managerial involvement in constituency party politics. Time off during the course of an election campaign is only a fraction of the time commitment required to nurse a candidacy in a constituency. With senior executives in industry reputed to work in excess of sixty hours per week there is little spare time to engage actively in party politics. Further disincentives for industrial managers contemplating a career switch into parliament include the relatively poor salary, working conditions and reactive role of a backbencher, in addition to the self-inflicted hiatus in an established and highly competitive industrial career hierarchy. On both counts – the unattractive aspects of an MPs job description (see Cmnd 8881 1983: 146-67) and the uncertain prospects of reinstatement and career advancement after a spell in the Commons – managers in industry are likely to remain reluctant to engage in a parliamentary career.

Industry and Parliament Trust

There are of course ways of increasing the understanding of industry's problems and requirements other than by direct representation. Indeed, the practical value of prior industrial experience is likely to depreciate in the Commons as daily contact with industrial concerns and issues recedes under the welter of other immediate problems jostling for the attention of a backbencher. As one experienced Conservative member pointed out in interview:

> For all that an MP might bring knowledge of industry into the House when he is first elected such knowledge is, if you like, 'date stamped' – it can become stale, even outdated as technology advances or as the competitive environment changes. In which case we need to be kept up-to-date on what's happening in the field.

In addition, there is a residual scepticism whether MPs previously employed in industry necessarily bring into the House *appropriate* experience of industrial decision-making. The CBI (1987:9), for instance, asked rhetorically: 'How much does a long-standing trade unionist translated into an MP understand the boardroom worries over finance?' Similarly, even former managers may lack the breadth of experience and vision required to appreciate the gamut of industrial policy. In the words of Jim Craigen MP (1987:19): 'Big firms can be like airports where things are going on all the time and are somehow expected to inter-relate. The shop assistant in the duty free is no more involved in the work of the control tower than the airline pilot is with the ticket sales clerk'. Thus, simply to recruit more members with an industrial background is not in itself a guarantee of informed consideration of all aspects of industrial policy within the Commons.

One other obvious strategy to improve parliament's collective understanding of industry, therefore, is through some form of informative and educative linkage between the two. But MPs traditionally have been suspicious of such links given their propagandistic and lobbying potential. Hence, it is to the credit of the Industry and Parliament Trust over the past decade that it has developed a highly successful scheme designed to link parliamentarians with industrial companies to mutual educative advantage .

Structure and Objectives of the Industry and Parliament Trust
In 1977, at the invitation of Sir Leslie Smith of BOC International, senior executives from eleven industrial companies came together to discuss how the informational gap between industry and parliament could be bridged. 'They were united in the belief that if industry was misunderstood it had only itself to blame, and that something ought to be done' (Industry and Parliament Trust 1986:2). As a result, a strictly non-partisan educational charity was established, which was advised and scrutinised by Trustees from each of the main parties, along with a representative of the trade union movement and a churchman who had considerable knowledge of industry (Michael Mann, the Dean of Windsor). Since then the Trust has maintained a board of nine or ten Trustees.

The Trustees have the sole responsibility for electing fellows of the Trust and meet with the Council to determine policy and regulate the Trust's activities. In practice the Council and its Management Committee are the main decision makers, developing a rolling strategy of expansion and supervising the election of prospective member companies. Indeed, as one officer of the Trust noted, member companies are largely recruited by word of mouth, with companies effectively electing each other. On at least one occasion, however, 'it [has been] made plain to a prospective member company that the Trust wasn't the place for them'. One early major policy decision taken by the Council with regard to membership was to admit banks to the Trust, with Barclays, Lloyds and the Royal Bank of Scotland taking up membership; and more recently the Council has decided to include representation of small businesses in its composition, along with one of their representatives on the Management Committee. On the other side – fellowships and industrial study programmes – the Council has variously decided to admit officers of the Commons to the scheme; to decline an approach from the Cabinet Office to run short courses for civil servants; to develop attachments for industrialists to MPs; and to extend the attachment scheme to ministers.

In terms of structure the Trust had by 1989 expanded from the initial membership of eleven firms to fifty companies with a collective turnover in excess of £147,400m and a combined total of over 2,375,000 employees. In that year each major company paid an annual subscription of £4,425 to finance the various activities of the Trust. Throughout, the Trust's finances have been geared to maintaining a small secretariat (of five members headed by the full-time director, Frederick Hyde-Chambers), to reimbursing members for necessary out-of-pocket expenses incurred in the course of their fellowships, and to meeting the administrative costs entailed in organising seminars and conferences run by the Trust. Indeed, the organisational and financial structure of the Trust is a tangible manifestation of the fact that it is *not* a lobbying organisation and does not wish itself to be mistaken for one. Thus, as one of its full-time officials commented: 'We are a very trusting and open organisation. Frankness is the key to our success. We are careful to ensure that neither MPs nor companies are embarrassed by our activities'.

Fellowship Study Courses
This sensitivity is most pronounced in the operation of the fellowship scheme. As the Trust (Industry and Parliament Trust 1989:9) states: 'The scheme is not another Parliamentary lobby. Its purpose must be to inform and *not* indoctrinate'. Moreover, the intention of the fellowship programme is to provide a realistic picture of company life –'warts and all' as one company puts it – for participating MPs. Indeed, the key points of the programme as listed by one of the original member companies (Industry and Parliament Trust 1983:7) are as follows:

- To provide a bird's eye view of our business objectives, our strategies for achieving them and institutional framework for implementing them.
- To give an appreciation of the scope of operations from grass roots to management and functional supporting structures.
- To show how a professionally managed group tackles planning, budgeting, investment appraisal, overseas expansion and other decision-making activities. To involve the MP in the practical processes involved so that they can see at first hand how decisions are reached and their quality and scope.
- To have dialogue with them on problems of industrial relations and employee participation and give them the opportunity to see some union consultation/employee participation in action.
- To improve their understanding of the extent to which Government strategies and legislation affect our business.

In other words to inform MPs of the daily routine and policy concerns of industry. But equally the scheme is intended to stimulate a two-way exchange whereby participating companies can also gain a better understanding of parliament, and parliamentarians. However, staying with the MP fellowships for now, the objectives of the scheme are met through individual study programmes of between 20 to 25 days.

Each parliamentarian (the scheme also includes members of the European parliament and peers) interested in participating in the scheme applies to the Trustees for election. Once accepted by the Trust its secretariat then approaches one of the member companies to see if it would provide a study course for the fellow-elect. Companies are not involved with the initial appointment of parliamentarians to the scheme, but, thereafter, individual companies are directly involved in drafting and finalising the content of specific courses in discussion with the fellow-elect. These preliminary discussions are usually conducted between the company liaison officer and MP with the Trust secretariat assisting at this stage. In planning a fellowship every effort is made to accommodate within the programme an MP's special interests. In this sense each study programme is unique, with members designing a programme both in duration and scope suited to their own particular needs. Obviously, however, there are common elements in most programmes, for example MPs will invariably start with a few days at the company's head office to be briefed on company organisation and management policy. Thereafter, members will be invited to attend board meetings, policy and planning committees, sales conferences, and union/management strategy meetings where appropriate. The result is that within the normal study period of between twelve to eighteen months:

> Fellows-elect have been able to see for themselves how businesses deal with such matters as health and safety at work, conditions of employment, productivity, research and development, quality control, investment and exports. They have had face-to-face meetings with chairmen, managers, shop-floor workers and their official representatives. The subjects they have discussed have included of course, the effects of legislation by UK and overseas governments and of EEC regulations. (Industry and Parliament Trust 1986:5)

In the case of small businesses, study courses normally last around four to five days rather than the lengthier period expected of large companies. Given the exacting demands upon management time, small firms have proved difficult to incorporate into the scheme. Indeed, by 1989 the Trust only had five small business members. Similarly, hard-pressed medium sized manufacturing companies are also weakly represented amongst the Trust's membership. In both cases the Trust has actively sought the recruitment of suitable organisations.

In the selection of MPs for fellowships the Trust is careful to choose those members who are likely to be able to fulfill the commitment to the study programme as well as those who, in the words of a Trust officer, 'have no axes to grind'. The preferences of the member are taken into account in the choice of company. Invariably the geographical location of the company will be of importance to the member, but traditionally MPs have avoided placements within their own constituencies for fear of becoming embroiled in industrial relations disputes or conflicts over closures and redundancies. Equally the Trust's secretariat informally monitor the internal changes within major companies to ensure that MPs are not embarrassed by major organisational or board-room upheavals.

During the course of a fellowship the relationship between MP and host company is monitored to ensure that there is indeed a linkage between the project and the member's interests. And at the end of the placement there is an extensive debriefing of both the fellow and the respective company chief executive, as well as an informal debriefing between the two. Any comments of wider significance for other fellowships are then be relayed to other Trust companies. In this way there is a cross-fertilisation of experience amongst the various study programmes. Indeed, this cross-fertilisation is formalised through regular Liaison Officer conferences, where those responsible for the operation of the fellowship scheme within companies meet to discuss developments within the programme along with more general aspects of parliamentary and industrial life.

Upon completion of the fellowship a member is presented with a framed certificate from the Trust, but the link with the host company invariably does not stop there. In recent years the Trust has arranged a series of briefings, whereby a fellow is able to retain contact with his company of attachment and meet other parliamentarians who have undertaken a study programme with the same company. Initially the Trust's secretariat arranges the briefing in Westminster, but thereafter briefing sessions are usually held at the company's head office on a six-monthly or annual basis. The value of this continuing relationship is highlighted by the Trust itself (Industry and Parliament Trust 1989:18):

> The frankness and openess of the original Fellowship attachment is maintained as all involved are operating on the same framework of the Trust philosophy of providing the means for 'practitioner' to speak to 'practitioner', to exchange information free of any promotion or political partisanship or industrial lobbying.

In addition to briefing sessions, short 'refresher' courses for fellows are also available. These enable members to monitor developments within the company of first attachment and to see the outcome of decisions taken during their placement period. Moreover, six-day 'post-graduate' courses are on offer to fellows to enable them to appreciate the workings of small businesses.

Assessment of the Fellowship Scheme
Not surprisingly the Industry and Parliament Trust proclaims its own success in its publicity material. The 'feedback' from parliamentarians recorded therein is fulsome in its praise. To take but two examples:

> The work has significantly broadened my view of a number of aspects of industrial policy and the impact of Government policies on the efficient working of British industry.
> The experience I have gained will help me carry out my duties as a Member of Parliament more effectively and will make a significant contribution to the way in which I am able to represent my constituents. (John Cunningham, Labour frontbench spokesman, quoted in Industry and Parliament Trust 1986:14)

> If I had stereotypes beforehand, I think they have been dissipated by a personal experience which is real and valuable and which I believe will serve me well for the future. (Michael Meacher, Labour frontbench spokesman, quoted in Industry and Parliament Trust 1986:14)

In numerical terms the Trust had overseen by the end of the 1980s the completion of 140 study programmes, with a further 67 fellows-elect still on attachment. The distribution of the award of fellowships between the major parties was 109 to Conservative MPs and 62 to Labour (including fellowships which had lapsed or were temporarily suspended). Moreover, the Trust points with some pride to the number of fellows or fellows-elect who in 1989 held opposition frontbench positions, some twenty-six, or junior positions in government, some twenty-one.

However, the praise of the Trust's endeavours extends well beyond its own publicity brochures and the assessments of its fellows (see Knox 1986; Craigen 1987). The report of the Hansard Society's (1979:58) investigation into the relations between government and industry concluded that: 'it is to be hoped that the work of the Industry and Parliament Trust will develop and that further initiatives along similar lines may take place in the near future'. Similarly, *Chief Executive* (1986:20) commended the Trust for stimulating interest in industry amongst MPs: 'One barometer of this [interest] is the Industry and Parliament Trust. .... For a busy MP to spend this amount of time [25 days] away from other duties shows a real interest in the subject'. Less dispassionately perhaps, Nigel Ellis as a political lobbyist, paid 'tribute to those who had the vision and foresight to form the Industry and Parliament Trust' as a means of providing 'balanced information' for parliamentarians. More academic analyses (see for instance Grant 1987:256) point to the degree to which 'organisations like the Industry and Parliament Trust can help to educate politicians in the priorities of business, but also business persons in the ways of politicians'. Indeed, it is hard to find criticism of the Trust's activities in print.

Equally, criticism of the Trust's activities was notable by its absence in the interviews conducted for the present study. In the general comments on the relationship between parliament and industry made by the 35 key backbenchers questioned, over half of them (sixteen in total, ten Conservatives and six Labour) mentioned, without prompting, the positive role of the Trust. A further six saw some merits in the principle but were agnostic on the practice; and only one Labour MP, a member of the Campaign Group and noted radical in the party, after some coaxing, made a tangential criticism of the Trust in his wider comments upon his 'class instincts':

> I'm a working class MP, I represent my class not the interests of industry. I don't like sloppy consensus. Many people in the PLP espouse consensus and compromise. I don't. I practice my beliefs. I don't just state them. For this reason I don't engage in all-party groups. Most of them are Anglo-this and Anglo-that .... and all of them are part of the gravy train. Similarly, I wouldn't 'get into bed' with industrialists [including, when asked, the Industry and Parliament Trust] .... the interests of workers, not bosses, are my concern.

Other Labour MPs were less dogmatic in their approach to the work of the Trust. Of the nine backbenchers who saw some value in either the principle or the practice of the fellowship scheme the level of enthusiasm ranged from 'it has a use but I don't set any great store by it'; to '[it] has to be seen as a very valuable experience'. This latter MP then went on to suggest that trade unions should introduce a similar scheme. In turn this suggestion was echoed in a Welsh member's comment that: 'Whereas this outfit [the Trust] increases the knowledge of business and is useful in that respect, it would help if the trade unions ran a similar programme. It would certainly help many Conservative members to appreciate more directly the concerns and opinions of the labour movement'.

Whether the scheme was of more value to members with or without pre-entry experience of industry produced an even split in the comments of Labour backbenchers, but there was unanimous agreement that the time commitment of the fellowship programme deterred many members from participating. And this was identified as a particularly acute problem on the Labour backbenches:

> Conservatives can take on that kind of thing [a Trust fellowship]. But for us it's a question of finding the time. Our lads have enough on their plate running around manning committees, dealing with their constituencies,

watching their backs on reselection. The sheer pressure of parliamentary work, of being in opposition, stops us from getting involved.

However, the problem of time was far from the exclusive concern of Labour members. Six Conservatives in interview saw the time commitment required of fellows to be a major limitation upon the scheme and its future expansion. One member proclaimed:

> You're talking to a fan of the Trust. I've been with a nationalised industry under two different chairmen. On the basis of my experience I am in no doubt that the scheme should be extended. Too few MPs have practical experience of industry therefore it is essential to cultivate this link between parliament and industry. We have to recognise the importance of manufacturing .... having said all that, however, finding 25 days in a year is almost impossible!

Unlike Labour interviewees, who were evenly divided upon the question of whether the fellowship scheme was of more value to those MPs already possessing industrial experience or to those who did not, the majority of Conservative members in interview (n 9) saw the benefits of the scheme accruing most to those backbenchers without prior experience. One MP with a career background in small business stated the case thus:

> It [the fellowship] scheme is undoubtedly a good thing. Its main role is for members without industrial experience. It is invaluable in developing an understanding of the wider industrial ethos. But essentially the Trust is a philanthropic exercise by large industry. You have to appreciate that the direct gains or benefits to any firm is entirely marginal.

Another, Thatcherite, member, whilst sympathetic to the objectives of the scheme, was more sanguine in his assessment of its results:

> Generally I would support the proposition that industry should get closer to parliament and vice versa. But there are two specific qualifications to my support. The first is that there is no coherent theme emerging from industry given the divisions within manufacturing between domestically and internationally oriented firms and between large and small firms. Not surprisingly, therefore, the Trust cannot articulate a common theme. And, secondly, although most of my colleagues who have been members of the scheme have thoroughly enjoyed it .... I am not convinced that they get a rounded picture of what's going on. I often get the impression that they have been on the equivalent of twenty or so 'state visits' to the attached company.

Indeed, the Trust itself is aware of such opinions, and, as seen above, seeks to ensure, through its monitoring and debriefing sessions, both the coherence and continuity of each study programme. But ultimately the main problem remains time. Having overcome the initial suspicions of Labour members (see Craigen 1987:19) about the independence of the Trust – in part through securing the support of Labour whips and in large part through sufficient successful completions to spread the virtues of the Trust by word of mouth on the Labour benches – time constraints are the ultimate deterrent to any significant expansion of the scheme. Thus, in the words of one of the Trust's secretariat: 'We work hard for success. Members put in great commitment if they feel that it is worthwhile, and they do, but the greatest problem is time!'

A Two-Way Process

But it is not one-way traffic. Part of the arrangement is for MPs to try to inform company executives on the way Parliament works, and the considerations that an MP has to take into account. (*Chief Executive* 1986:20)

The Trust has always been concerned that the flow of information should be in both directions between parliament and industry. Initially a series of seminars were organised specifically for senior executives to introduce them to the workings of Westminster, Whitehall and local government, as well as European institutions in Strasbourg and Brussels. On the basis of these seminars the Trust, in conjunction with the publishers Longman, produced a series of handbooks about the structure and operation of government. Given the success of the initial seminars, an annual seminar on 'understanding parliament' has been organised over the past nine years for senior industrialists; and in 1990 an additional seminar on this topic was included for industrialists in Scotland.

A major innovation came in 1986 with the introduction of the parliamentary study programme for industrialists (PSPI). The PSPI is designed to provide, over a period of nine days, intensive practical study of the work of Westminster (and Whitehall). An industrialist is attached to an MP and 'shadows' his designated member's activity in the House and in the constituency. The intention of the programme is for 'practitioners' in Westminster to explain all aspects of parliamentary life to industrialists. At the end of the programme participating MPs, industrialists and appropriate civil servants then meet together to assess its operation and also to discuss general issues raised in the course of the scheme. Interestingly, this is one of the few occasions when parliamentarians meet directly with civil servants. Indeed, at the review session in 1988 all the industrialists 'referred to the recurring comment, by those in Whitehall, on the impact of parliamentary scrutiny and the recurring comment, by parliamentarians, on how little impact they made on Whitehall' (Industry and Parliament Trust 1989:12). In addition to the debriefing session at the end of each programme the Trust has also monitored the long-term effects of the scheme by bringing together, periodically, successive cohorts of participants in PSPI.

1986 also saw the introduction of fellows' company seminars. The purpose of these seminars is to consolidate the relationship between a company and its fellows and also to develop greater understanding on the part of company managers of the working environment of an MP. To this end, mid-way through a parliamentarian's study-period, fifteen senior managers of the company concerned are brought to Westminster for a one-day seminar chaired by the current fellow-elect. An additional benefit, as described by several parliamentarian participants at these seminars, is 'the opportunity of talking with 15 senior managers, usually drawn from all parts of the country, in the neutral forum of the Trust' (Industry and Parliament Trust 1989:14). By the end of 1989 some 535 senior industrialists had participated in the fellows' company seminar programme.

A further indication of the Trust's desire to enhance and expand the links between Westminster and industry is the series of informal dinners recently organised to bring together ten fellows and industrialists at a time to discuss matters of mutual concern within the 'neutral, non-partisan, non-lobbying' ethos of the Trust. More significantly, perhaps, a pilot programme of ministerial attachments was undertaken in 1989 as an extension of the PSPI. Nine senior executives, from a range of companies in the banking, energy, engineering, electronic and food sectors, were provided with practical insights into the daily routine of junior ministers in the Northern Ireland Office, the Welsh Office, the Department of Health, as well as the DTI itself. 'The industrialists have been unanimous in the value they have found in the attachments, and from preliminary results it appears the ministers have found them useful' (Industry and Parliament Trust 1989:13).

That the Trust achieves with some distinction its stated objectives – of, on the one hand, widening the experience and increasing the knowledge of MPs of industry, and on the other, of improving the understanding of managers and industrial personnel about parliament – has been demonstrated above. But, as Nigel Ellis (1988:52) speculates, 'possibly the most striking evidence that the idea [of the Trust] was worthwhile is the fact that similar schemes have been set up in .... countries in Europe and the Commonwealth'. In fact, the Trust now organises international conferences where representatives of sister organisations, and for the first time in 1989 parliamentarians, discuss issues of mutual concern. Indeed, at the 1989 conference, the unanimous praise of participants from other companies acknowledged the success of the Trust's work in Britain in setting both the direction and pace of linkage programmes. Simply, the Trust was seen as setting the standard for 'best practice'. The kernel of this practice, followed by other international industry-parliament groups, remains a non-lobbying informative role.

CBI Linkman Scheme

Another practical scheme designed to improve MPs understanding of industrial issues is the Linkman scheme operated by the CBI. Unlike the work of the Industry and Parliament trust however the Linkman project is overtly a lobbying exercise. Under this scheme the CBI organises some 900 of its members to maintain individual contact with their local MP so as to 'keep them in touch with CBI policies and concerns' (CBI 1987:51). The CBI believes that such contact is in itself 'a good thing' for industry' but also has the more immediate benefit of bringing approved CBI policy briefings to the attention of constituency MPs. When the 'linkmen' bring these attitudes to the attention of backbenchers 'in any number [then] there is little doubt that MPs are made aware of the strong feeling of business throughout the country on whatever particular issue is in question' (CBI 1987:52). In turn this awareness 'can – and often does – lead to important changes in policies affecting business in more than merely a peripheral sense' (CBI 1987:52). Clearly, the CBI believes in the importance of backbench opinion in 'deflecting' government policy – even in an era of ideologically committed government (CBI 1987:52). And this belief reflects the general findings of chapter 5 where backbenchers believed both that individual companies and representative associations such as the CBI were paying more attention to briefing them, and also that activity in parliament was capable of influencing industrial policy. In the words of one Midlands Conservative backbencher:

> There is an increased movement for industry to approach parliament. If their case is right then MPs with knowledge of industry and [who are] properly briefed can present that case as a 'prosecuting counsel' in the chamber .... It means, quite simply, that ministers cannot avoid industry's own questions. Whereas civil servants may seek to hide from these questions in the anonymity of Whitehall, they can be forced to address them through their ministers in Westminster.

A House of Industry Revisited

> It is almost certainly easier to improve the quality of our system of government than to improve the quality of our politicians. (Gilmour 1983:187)

Not that Gilmour believes that the quality of British politicians has declined in recent years, in fact the reverse, but that explanations of industrial malaise have to look beyond inadequate politicians to the inadequacies of the political system itself. Constitutional reform for him is thus to be contemplated not simply for its democratic dividends but also as a means of rejuvenating the relationship between industry and government. The central objective remains that identified in chapter 2 – of securing industrial efficiency whilst reconciling sectional industrial objectives to wider consensual public purposes. This objective is to be achieved through melding the diverse principles of representation – of function and territory – into a new political relationship. A relationship, moreover, which would more accurately reflect the contemporary distribution of political power in Britain whilst simultaneously serving to redress the imbalance of power between the executive and the legislature (Gilmour 1977:245-6).

The specific proposal Gilmour advances to effect this redistribution is the creation of a 'public industrial forum' (1977:247). Its precise form could vary in degrees of radicalism from a reformed House of Lords, through a 'completely new institution' – a House of Industry, to an enlarged and enhanced NEDC (Gilmour 1983:205-14). Each institution would be based upon functional representation and so articulate directly the interests of industrial producers and consumers within the centre of government. In bringing together these interests several 'truths' would be made clear to each group: first, that they would have to argue their respective cases to each other and not unilaterally to government; second, that they would have to advance their case on its merits and not in accordance with their traditional 'ideological uniforms' (Gilmour 1983:209); third, and concomitantly, that they would have to accommodate their own interests to wider consensual interests; and, finally, that the limitations of governmental action would be revealed and so expectations of such action would be diminished.

In proposing a new House of Industry Gilmour aligns himself firmly with the modern Conservative tradition of Churchill, Macmillan and Amery, and even invokes Disraeli in defence of this innovation (Gilmour 1977:245; 1983:192). Equally, he draws directly upon academic analyses (Bogdanor 1977; Mackintosh 1982) which canvass incorporation of greater functional representation in a supplementary and advisory assembly alongside the Commons, and he echoes the thoughts of other academics making much the same case (see Coombes 1982:189). The unifying theme of these writers was that a new functionally-based institution would be a deliberative, consultative and representative body designed to work alongside the House of Commons and not to be a substitute for it.

Given this wide and persistent advocacy of new functional institutions then why no practical action? Part of the answer has already been outlined in chapter 2. At the level of theory there are manifest contradictions in reconciling functional representation with prevailing individualistic conceptions of representation in Britain. Ultimately, the arguments used to demonstrate the need for supplementing 'miscellaneous' representation in the

Commons with functional expertise in a House of Industry simultaneously, and effectively, undermine the claims to continued sovereignty on the part of the legislature.

At a practical level, again as revealed in chapter 2, the advocacy of new functional institutions has tended to correspond to periods of heightened concern about Britain's industrial and economic performance. Yet these periods have engendered state policy responses – in the form of orthodox financial policy, free market and free trade emphases – which question the utility of existing corporatist strategies let alone advance the practical case for greater institutionalisation of functional or tripartite representation. Certainly, the most dramatic illustration of this has been provided since 1979. The neo-liberal economic strategy of Thatcherism has been promoted on the back of the precepts of liberal government – of individualistic representation and parliamentary sovereignty. The indivisible legitimacy of the parliamentary system, derived from the electoral process itself, has been used to great effect to counter the claims of legitimacy on the part of 'divisive' sectional interests.

That it is the form rather than the substance of parliamentary government that has been invoked by the Thatcher governments has already been noted. Mrs Thatcher has proved in many fundamental ways to have been deeply conservative on constitutional matters, maintaining both executive ascendancy alongside the essence of pragmatic pluralistic structures of functional representation centred upon Whitehall. She has simply 'played the game for real .... [using] the power of Parliament .... to force through fundamental reforms' (Hirst 1989:48). Indeed, it is Mrs Thatcher's very orthodoxy in the interpretation of the rules of the constitutional game that has brought those rules into question, as will be seen shortly. More immediately, in these circumstances, proposals for a House of Industry conflict with both the constitutional and economic orthodoxies of Thatcherism. On both counts industry is to be awarded no higher priority than any other interest in state policy and its making.

Yet opposition to the concept of a 'public industrial forum' is shared even by those who seek to accord manufacturing industry just such priority. Significantly, of those backbenchers interviewed for the present study – that is many of the most active MPs on industrial matters in the House of Commons – the proposal for a House of Industry was greeted with less than derision by only two out of 35 MPs. The exceptions were both Conservatives and both came from entrepreneurial backgrounds. One, an experienced Yorkshire MP, stated that he had been very keen on the idea in the early 1960s and that the concept of a House of Industry had been much discussed when the NEDC was created. Over twenty five years later, however, he conceded that:

I'm not convinced that the concept is now so attractive. In part the NEDC, has played a somewhat limited deliberative role; and in part select committee proceedings have provided a forum for industry's views to be fed into the system. These weren't in operation [in the earlier period].

The other backbencher, who had entered the House in 1983, stated:

It's an intriguing prospect. I'm against reforming the House of Lords anyway, but I wouldn't see it operating as a functional assembly. If anything needs reforming it's the Commons. In this respect an advisory body might be useful, once you appreciate that the NEDC doesn't play much of a role at the moment. There's too much fragmentation of industry's views on it. But there again this would be a problem with any advisory body.

All other interviewed Conservative backbenchers expressed negative opinions about the idea. Typically the responses were brief and pithy: 'an absolute waste of time'; 'I'm totally against'; 'what a load of nonsense'; 'the idea is ridiculous. It obviously smacks of corporatism, and as we know that is ridiculous'; 'such an institution would be a glorious talking shop. No thank you!'; and 'let's not waste time talking about that nonsense'. These sentiments were echoed almost verbatim by the eighteen Labour members interviewed: 'Basically I'd say no to a special chamber. At root industrial issues should be discussed here [in the Commons]; 'such a House [of Industry] wouldn't work'; 'it's a nonsense, particularly as the present government only regards industry as some necessary evil anyway'; ' what a [expletive deleted] silly idea'. In more reflective mood a South Yorkshire MP argued that:

I have to say a new institution on the lines of an industrial parliament is clearly a nonsense, but there might be some merit in reforming the Lords – to extend its membership to include a wider spectrum. It could play an enhanced advisory role but only if its legislative powers were dispensed with. One of the things a revised second chamber might be able to do is to bring home the extent and consequences of the decline of manufacturing industry.

If these views are representative of wider parliamentary opinion, and in a sense they should be in the van of backbench thinking on this issue given the respondents' interest in industrial matters, then the practical antipathy to the introduction of a functionally-based advisory sub-parliament, combined with the logical inconsistencies of such a scheme, should continue to conspire to exclude it from the agenda of constitutional reform. More importantly, as noted above, Mrs Thatcher has set her face against constitutional innovation. The Thatcher government has exercised constitutional probity if not conventional propriety to advance its economic and social 'revolution'. The last thing Mrs Thatcher would countenance, let alone actively promote, is consensual inhibition of her industrial policies by an advisory House of Industry.

Labour's Policy Review

Should Mrs Thatcher's, or a 'Thatcherite', Conservative government be reelected at the next general election then the interpretation of the rules of the constitutional game probably would continue to support centralised executive power. Undoubtedly, the prime minister would still proclaim that 'parliamentary sovereignty is safe with us' (to misquote an earlier electoral pledge on the NHS). However, in pressing the conception of sovereignty to its limit since 1979, one consequence has been that 'all of the opposition parties, without exception now favour constitutional change of one sort or another, so that the constitution, as it now exists, depends for its survival upon the continuation of Conservative government' (Bogdanor 1989:139-40).

The Labour party, as the most likely successor should the Conservatives fail to survive in government, has been so shaken by the experience of the past decade and 'the present government's arbitrary use of power' that it has already pledged itself 'to introduce constitutional reforms to protect Britain against any future elective dictatorship' (Labour Party 1990:42). Yet, in reality, 'for a radical party Labour has displayed a marked lack of radical imagination as far as the constitution is concerned' (Wright 1989:202). Indeed, in the early stages of the party's policy review, in 1987 and 1988, constitutional issues were accorded a very low priority. Only with the public prompting of Charter 88 and the debate in the Scottish Constitutional Convention did the national party leadership begin to address some of the more radical ideas emerging from within the party. The result, documented in *Looking to the Future* (Labour Party 1990), lacked sufficient detail to provide anything other than an ambiguous pointer to future reform, but just enough to attract criticism from both the left of the party (see *Guardian* 31 May 1990) and from right-wing commentators (see Ronald Butt in the *Times* 28 May 1990).

Without going into detail here, the constitutional provisions of *Looking to the Future* still uphold the sovereignty of parliament. Indeed, there are non-specific proposals to 'improve the procedures and facilities of the House of Commons to make it more effective as a legislative chamber' and to 'ensure all actions of government are subject to parliamentary scrutiny' (Labour Party 1990:42). But the commitment to redress the imbalance between the legislature and the executive is qualified, implicitly at least, in the statement that: 'Labour is opposed to changing the electoral system for the House of

Commons' (Labour Party 1990:43). The major attraction held by the present electoral system for the Labour leadership has to be its capacity to secure majority government and to enable governments to govern. In fact this was made explicit in the final report of the party's policy review, *Meet the Challenge: Make the Change* (Labour Party 1989). There it was clearly stated that:

> The Labour Party intends to form the next government with a majority of seats in the House of Commons. We will present our manifesto to the British people, and, when elected will carry out the mandate we have been given. That is the most honest, the most efficient and the most effective form of government for this country. (Labour Party 1989)

Oppositions have traditionally lamented executive control of the Commons, as indeed did Mrs Thatcher before 1979, but when confronted with the exigencies of government these considerations tend to evaporate in the heat of office. Whether a future Labour government would be less immune to the 'hothouse' atmosphere of Whitehall remains to be seen.

It is within the framework of the implicit commitment to the principle of parliamentary sovereignty (but not to its modern corollary of 'elective dictatorship') that the review document's proposals for industrial policy need to be located. In stating that 'Labour believes decisions should be taken by democratic bodies at levels as close as possible to the people they affect' (Labour Party 1990:42); and in proposing a Scottish parliament, an all-Wales assembly, and elected regional assemblies in England, it is presumed that these decisions will be made within the enabling powers delegated by the sovereign legislature at Westminster. The significance of this for industrial policy is that it is the regional assemblies which are to have a 'strategic and coordinating role' in this area. Power is to be devolved from Whitehall to the regions. A series of Regional Development Agencies are to be created, based upon the experience of the Scottish and Welsh Development Agencies (ironically the SDA will have been replaced by Scottish Enterprise before the next election). Substantial devolution and decentralisation of policy-making is clearly envisaged, therefore, yet quite how this fits with the commitment to 'restore the Department of Trade and Industry to its proper place as a key department of state – and give it the enhanced status enjoyed in other countries' (Labour 1990:18) is not specified. Gordon Brown, as Labour's industry spokesman, envisages that: 'Because the objective is to be at the service of industry where it is located, powers will be taken from Whitehall and services removed to the regions where they should be' (*Guardian* 23 May 1990). There, partnerships between the public agencies and the private sector would be encouraged to promote long-term industrial investment.

Clearly, regional DTIs are expected to play an important 'enabling' role. Yet for them to operate effectively would require a substantial degree of independence from the 'enhanced' DTI in Whitehall.

Whether this independence would, or could, be granted in practice depends upon the willingness of the national parliament and the majority government therein to delegate the necessary powers. Past experience of Labour government does not bode well in this respect. Present doubts are also evident in leftist writings. Thus Hirst (1989:222), for example, points to the ingrained support within the Labour party for the 'Westminster model' of government:

> The Labour left has lived in hope of "another 1945", and decisive reform through legislation and government action. Roy Hattersley denies the need for PR because it would prevent majority governments able to use governmental power to implement exclusively party policies.

But without a renunciation of the privileges and prejudices of the 'Westminster model' the scope for effective locally-based industrial strategies to be established and flourish is in doubt.

In making the case for locally- and regionally-based industrial reconstruction Labour has followed the logic of its argument to the extent that decentralisation of policy-making is recognised as one of the prerequisites for success. At the moment, however, the party cannot bring itself to accept the necessary conditions of a legally entrenched decentralisation – of some sort of federalism and attendant judicial review. Nowhere in *Looking to the Future* are such ideas to be found. The leadership remains enamoured by a centralised parliamentary system and simultaneously attracted to a decentralised industrial strategy. Consequently, there is a mismatch of political and economic principles, which, if past practice is anything to go by, is likely to be resolved in favour of the 'political' and centralism.

Electoral Reform
Despite its stated opposition to any change in the system for electing the House of Commons, the leadership of the Labour party is willing to consider the introduction of other systems for other elected bodies:

> in view of the wider considerations which relate to the Scottish Parliament, the assemblies for Wales and the English regions, the new Second Chamber and elections to the European Parliament, the National Executive Committee will propose to the 1990 Labour Party Conference that a working party be established by the NEC to consider what electoral system is appropriate for these bodies. The working party will be asked to make recommendations for each institution separately. (Labour Party 1990:43)

The exclusion of a review of the electoral system for Westminster has been called 'bizarre' even by Labour supporters of the policy review process itself (see *Guardian* 31 May 1990), and is taken as a further evidence of the party leadership's continuing belief in strong party government.

But, accepting for the moment, the exclusion of Westminster elections from the review process, the consideration of electoral reform opens up the question of what specific benefits are to be derived for industry from such change. Clearly advocates of electoral reform within the Labour party, and the other opposition parties for that matter, do not propose reform primarily on grounds of assisting industry. Principles of equity and democracy, rather than practical concern with engendering a political climate within which industry can prosper, are the main propulsion behind calls for reform. Nonetheless, within industry some mitigation of the worst excesses of the present adversarial system through electoral reform would be welcomed in the nurturing of consensual centrist government and policies (see chapter 3; see also Hansard Society 1979:60; Heller 1987:127).

This is not the place, however, to consider the variety of electoral systems on offer, nor, indeed, their parliamentary consequences. It is sufficient merely to note that there is profound scepticism as to the likely efficacy of electoral reform in itself to redress the imbalance within British government (see Judge 1983b:182-6; Norton 1985:148-9). Instead, a more restricted focus is adopted here, and one which circles back to the problem of how to increase the representation of industry within representative bodies.

The most effective system for ensuring the election of industrially experienced members to representative assemblies is the party list system (for details see Lakeman 1974:92-110). This system encompasses the total electorate within a single constituency and then allocates seats to political parties in accordance with their proportion of the total vote. Effectively therefore the actual choice of individual representatives rests with the party rather than the electorate. Should the party so decide to include representatives from industry, or any other sectional interest, then their election would be guaranteed in accordance with the number of seats secured in the election. Perhaps not surprisingly this system has never been seriously canvassed as an alternative in Britain. A viable variant, one that combines the first-past-the-post system with a regional party list system, and one that is already in operation in West Germany, has, however, attracted considerable support in Britain (see Roberts 1975:219-22; Hansard Society 1976). The attraction of this system for those seeking to increase the collective knowledge of industry within the representative assembly is that:

> [it] allows parties to bring into the parliament, through a high position on the list, representatives of interest groups and experts with specialised

knowledge who would for various reasons .... have a difficult time winning a grass roots campaign. (Conran 1986:123, see also Loewenberg 1966; Judge 1981:57-9)

This system might hold some attraction for the NEC working party considering the electoral system for a reformed second chamber. It would have the possible advantage of combining both a regional spatial dimension and the prospect for increased functional representation within the second chamber.

Conclusion

But the introduction of new elements to the British constitution – whether some system of proportional representation, elected regional assemblies, or a revised second chamber – and cross-national comparison with other countries, is no guarantee that 'transplanted' ideas and institutions would function in the same way or with the same effect as in the comparator countries. The argument here is that the political system has to be viewed as a whole, and the ramifications of constitutional reform for industrial representation have to be seen within this whole. Thus, to argue for instance that the West German electoral system allows for enhanced functional representation within the legislature requires the qualificatory statement that this needs to be set within the context of the wider political culture and the social bases of the established political parties in West Germany (see Loewenberg 1966; Conran 1986:104-6,123-5; Padgett 1989:136-9). Equally, to countenance regional devolution as part of a strategy to establish a 'partnership economy' incorporating government and both sides of industry at its heart (Labour Party 1990:11), and then to point as an exemplar to the West German model with its 'strong regional dimension' (Labour Party 1990:11), also requires some acknowledgement that devolution in itself does not explain the apparent strength of this model. For as Smith (1989:39) notes:

> Little of this devolution and self-regulation .... takes place just because of custom and accepted practice or through the invoking of such formulae as 'social partnership' to bring together the disparate interests. Behind .... stands the close regulation provided by the legal framework and the courts. The 'legal ethos' that suffuses german politics is one aspect of the characteristic that underlies public and political culture.

Indeed, it is salutary to end with Smith's (1989:39) conclusion about the German political system: '[It] is static because it works'. In Britain calls for constitutional change are invariably driven by the sense that the system does not work. In particular it does not work to sustain a vibrant industrial economy. This sentiment is apparent in the Hansard Society's (1979:60) conclusion that: 'no formula aimed at improving the present unhappy effect of Government policy on industr[y] .... will be more than a palliative unless it includes or at least allows for measures of Parliamentary reform'.

To place the blame for Britain's relative industrial malaise upon parliament and to seek industrial regeneration through constitutional reform is to oversimplify and misunderstand the directionality of the immensely complex causal connections between political and economic forces. If nothing else this book should have revealed the intricate interweaving of these forces. Whereas there has been an identifiable historical pattern within this weave, with industry locked within a state framework which has simultaneously sustained but undernurtured it, this pattern may yet be frayed by the centrifugal forces apparent within modern British politics. The policy review of the Labour party acknowledges the strength of these forces in its plans for subnational and regional devolution on the one hand and in its recognition on the other of the increasing significance of decision-making at the level of the European Community. Devolution of decision-making in either direction, and most logically in both at the same time, would have significant repercussions both for parliament and industry. If returned to power in the mid-1990s, the Conservative party may be forced, no matter how reluctantly, to acknowledge the strength of these centrifugal forces; as indeed it did in the late-1980s in the incremental reformulation of its position on European political union as a result of the pursuit of free market objectives through the Single European Act.

If, in the uncertainity of the 1990s, 'the future is not the same as it used to be', one thing is perhaps predictable and that is that the past – in the shape of the concept of parliamentary sovereignty, and the organisational logic of the parliamentary state – will provide potent symbols and powerful practical obstructions to radical constitutional change. Moreover, the very nature and magnitude of Britain's industrial problems may conspire to sideline constitutional change as governments grapple with pressing economic problems – problems magnified by the decimation of manufacturing industry over the past decade. Continued industrial decline in Britain may yet constitute 'a grave threat to the standard of living and to the economic and political stability of the nation' (HL 238 1985:83). Optimists may hope that this decline can be reversed through asserting that 'industry matters' and reinforcing this with constitutional change. What this book has pointed to, however, are the paradoxes that would have to be resolved before such hopes could be realised. The daunting prospect is that Britain's future might yet be the same as it used to be!

Appendices

Appendix A1

Industrial Matters

Oral and Written Questions
Data for oral and written questions on industrial matters were derived from the Parliamentary On-Line Information System (POLIS) database of the House of Commons. The POLIS search was conducted by Scicon Ltd on a UNIVAC 1100 at the company's premises in Milton Keynes. The search terms used were industrial, industry, industries, and trade. The most important narrower search terms encompassed by these terms are listed on page 253 (for the precise details of all the latest search terms covered see House of Commons Library Thesaurus 1989).

Debate
Data for debates was derived from a content analysis of the text of Hansard. Initially a POLIS search was conducted using the broad search terms listed above. Unlike activity in questions, where POLIS provides a highly accurate listing of industrial questions, activity in debate was subject to significant vagaries of classification and indexing. Examination of the initial print-out of the POLIS search, when cross-checked with the recorded proceedings of the House, revealed significant ommissions of the discussion of industrial matters. A laborious analysis of debates in Hansard thus had to be undertaken. To reduce the time-costs involved in this exercise a decision was taken, on the basis of earlier experience (see Judge 1981), to record substantive contributions to debate, but not minor interjections. Contributions to debate were recorded in units of 0.5 columns. Whilst not presenting a totally accurate measure of activity in debate, this measure gives a more realistic indication of backbench contributions to debate than any measure based upon a POLIS search, or derived from the sessional index of Hansard.

Appendix A1 continued

Industrial	*Industries/industry*	*Trade*
accidents	aerospace	agreements
arbitration	brewing	associations
building allowances	building	balance
chemicals	building materials	barriers
democracy	bus	competitiveness
design	ceramic	descriptions
development	chemical	documentation
development assocs	coal mining	EC internal trade
development certificates	computer	fairs
disablement	clothing	formalities
diseases	craft	marks
disputes	defence	promotion
energy conservation	electricity supply	*trade unions*
energy consumption	electronics	elections
energy prices	engineering	finances
estates	extractive	membership
EC policy	film	officials
finance	food	political funds
health and safety	footwear	recognition
injuries	furniture	
injuries scheme	gas supply	
injuries tribunals	heavy	
injury benefit	information technology	
investment	leather	
loans	machine tools	
noise	manufacturing	
production	metal	
relations	motor	
relations law	microelectronics	
research	nationalised	
safety	oil	
strategy	packaging	
training	paper	
training boards	pharmaceutical	
training schemes	printing	
waste	power	
	railway	
	road haulage	
	rubber	
	shipbuilding	
	telecommunications	
	textile	
	toy	
	water supply	

Appendix A2

Interval levels: Level of Industrial 'Specialisation' (Tables 5.6; 6.12)

Although mathematical formulas have been given that may serve as guides to the number of intervals to use, such formulas often give the impression of exactness where the best decision is usually that based on common sense and a knowledge of the use to which the frequency distribution will be put. (Blalock 1979:44)

In determing the interval widths for level of industrial specialisation in Tables 5.6 and 6.12 the different 'costs of participation' exacted by each of the procedures –oral questions, written questions and debate – and recognition of the fact that scores are skewed towards low values finds reflection in the unequal interval widths for those procedures.

Oral Questions:
Low   1.79 – 6.9
Medium   7.00 – 12.9
High   13.0 +

Written Questions:
Low   0.12 – 2.99
Medium   3.00 – 5.99
High   6.00 +

Debates:
Low   0.83 – 9.99
Medium   10.0 – 24.9
High   25.0 +

Interval levels: Index of Specialisation (Tables 6.4; 6.8)
The measure of specialisation used here is the aggregate average proportion of activity expended on industrial matters. This measure was computed by summing the percentage of total activity expended on industrial matters in each procedure and then dividing by six (i.e. three procedures in both sesions 1983/4 and 1985/6). Scores ranged from 0.25 to 42.61. On this basis the interval levels were set at:

Low: 0.25 – 4.43
Medium   4.44 – 9.99
High   10.0 +

Appendix B1   **Sector by Party: Oral Questions (1983/4 and 1984/5)**

| Sector | | | | | | | Party | | | | | |
| | | Conservative | | | Labour | | | Other | | | Total | |
	n	%	s%	n	%	s%	n	%	s%	n	%	s%
Coal	109	24.1	(43.3)	137	34.0	(54.3)	6	14.0	(2.4)	252	28.0	(100.0)
Coke	1	0.2	(100.0)	0	0.0	(0.0)	0	0.0	(0.0)	1	0.1	(100.0)
Oil Extract	3	0.7	(75.0)	1	0.2	(25.0)	0	0.0	(0.0)	4	0.4	(100.0
Petrol	2	0.4	(50.0)	2	0.5	(50.0)	0	0.0	(0.0)	4	0.4	(100.0)
Nuclear	2	0.4	(50.0)	1	0.2	(25.0)	1	2.3	(25.0)	4	0.4	(100.0)
Elect/Gas	28	6.2	(60.9)	16	4.0	(34.8)	2	4.7	(4.3)	46	5.1	(100.0)
Water	0	0.0	(0.0)	0	0.0	(0.0)	0	0.0	(0.0)	0	0.0	(0.0)
Metal Ext	0	0.0	(0.0)	1	0.2	(100.0)	0	0.0	(0.0)	1	0.1	(100.0)
Metal Man	28	6.2	(58.3)	19	4.7	(39.6)	1	2.3	(2.1)	48	5.3	(100.0)
Min Ext	2	0.4	(50.0)	2	0.5	(50.0)	0	0.0	(0.0)	4	0.4	(100.0)
Min Prod	0	0.0	(0.0)	0	0.0	(0.0)	0	0.0	(0.0)	0	0.0	(0.0)
Chemicals	2	0.4	(22.2)	7	1.7	(77.8)	0	0.0	(0.0)	9	1.0	(100.0)
Man-Made	0	0.0	(0.0)	0	0.0	(0.0)	1	2.3	(100.0)	1	0.1	(100.0)
Met Goods	0	0.0	(0.0)	2	0.0	(100.0)	0	0.0	(0.0)	2	0.2	(100.0)
Mech Eng	5	1.1	(55.6)	4	1.0	(44.4)	0	0.0	(0.0)	9	1.0	(100.0)
Data	8	1.8	(57.1)	4	1.0	(28.6)	2	4.7	(14.3)	14	1.6	(100.0)
Elect Eng	3	0.7	(30.0)	4	1.0	(40.0)	3	7.0	(30.0)	11	1.1	(100.0)
Motor Man	16	3.5	(53.3)	14	3.5	(46.7)	0	0.0	(0.0)	30	3.3	(100.0)
Trans Eq	10	2.2	(34.5)	14	3.5	(48.3)	5	11.6	(17.2)	29	3.2	(100.0)
Instr Eng	0	0.0	(0.0)	0	0.0	(0.0)	0	0.0	(0.0)	0	0.0	(0.0)
Food/Drink	0	0.0	(0.0)	1	0.2	(33.3)	2	4.7	(66.7)	3	0.3	(100.0)
Textiles	9	2.0	(47.4)	9	2.2	(47.4)	1	2.3	(5.3)	19	2.1	(100.0)
Leath/Foot	6	1.3	(54.3)	4	1.0	(36.4)	1	2.3	(9.1)	11	1.2	(100.0)
Furniture	0	0.0	(0.0)	1	0.2	(100.0)	0	0.0	(0.0)	1	1.6	(100.0)
Paper	7	1.5	(63.6)	3	0.7	(27.3)	1	2.3	(9.1)	11	1.2	(100.0)
Rubber	0	0.0	(0.0)	0	0.0	(0.0)	0	0.0	(0.0)	0	0.0	(0.0)
Miscell	0	0.0	(0.0)	0	0.0	(0.0)	0	0.0	(0.0)	0	0.0	(0.0)
Construct	21	4.6	(44.6)	24	6.0	(51.1)	2	4.7	(4.3)	47	5.2	(100.0)
Rail Trans	1	0.2	(33.3)	2	0.5	(66.7)	0	0.0	(0.0)	3	0.3	(100.0)
Road Trans	4	0.9	(80.0)	1	0.2	(20.0)	0	0.0	(0.0)	5	0.6	(100.0)
Sea Trans	2	0.4	(100.0)	0	0.0	(0.0)	0	0.0	(0.0)	2	0.2	(100.0)
Air Trans	0	0.0	(0.0)	1	0.2	(100.0)	0	0.0	(0.0)	1	0.1	(100.0)
Telecom	2	0.4	(100.0)	0	0.0	(0.0)	0	0.0	(0.0)	2	0.2	(100.0)
General	182	40.2	(55.8)	129	32.0	(39.6)	15	34.9	(4.6)	326	36.2	(100.0)
Total	453	100.0	(50.4)	403	100.0	(44.8)	43	100.0	(4.8)	899	100.0	(100.0)

Appendix B2   Sector by Party: Written Questions (1983/4 and 1984/5)

Sector												
						Party						
		Conservative			*Labour*			*Other*			*Total*	
	n	%	s%	n	%	s%	n	%	s%	n	%	s%
Coal	68	6.2	(28.8)	158	10.7	(66.9)	10	6.8	(4.2)	236	8.7	(100.0)
Coke	0	0.0	(0.0)	0	0.0	(0.0)	0	0.0	(0.0)	0	0.0	(0.0)
Oil Extract	3	0.3	(50.0)	3	0.2	(50.0)	0	0.0	(0.0)	6	0.2	(100.0)
Petrol	8	0.7	(42.1)	10	0.7	(52.6)	1	0.7	(5.3)	19	0.7	(100.0)
Nuclear	5	0.5	(25.0)	13	0.9	(65.0)	2	1.4	(10.0)	20	0.7	(100.0)
Elect/Gas	40	3.7	(54.1)	23	1.6	(31.1)	11	7.4	(14.9)	74	2.7	(100.0)
Water	5	0.5	(41.7)	7	0.5	(58.3)	0	0.0	(0.0)	12	0.4	(100.0)
Metal Extr	1	0.1	(50.0)	1	0.1	(50.0)	0	0.0	(0.0)	2	0.1	(100.0)
Metal Man	18	1.6	(40.0)	27	1.8	(60.0)	0	0.0	(0.0)	45	1.7	(100.0)
Min Extr	3	0.3	(37.5)	5	0.3	(62.5)	0	0.0	(0.0)	8	0.3	(100.0)
Min Prod	5	0.5	(55.6)	4	0.3	(44.4)	0	0.0	(0.0)	9	0.3	(100.0)
Chemicals	61	5.6	(55.0)	39	2.6	(35.1)	11	7.4	(9.9)	111	4.1	(100.0)
Man-Made	0	0.0	(0.0)	0	0.0	(0.0)	0	0.0	(0.0)	0	0.0	(0.0)
Met Goods	1	0.1	(100.0)	0	0.0	(0.0)	0	0.0	(0.0)	1	0.0	(100.0)
Mech Eng	11	1.0	(25.6)	31	2.1	(72.1)	1	0.7	(2.3)	32	1.0	(100.0)
Data	22	2.0	(51.2)	31	1.4	(46.5)	1	0.7	(2.3)	43	1.6	(100.0)
Elect Eng	7	0.6	(24.1)	22	1.5	(75.9)	0	0.0	(0.0)	29	1.1	(100.0)
Motor Man	21	1.9	(44.7)	25	1.7	(53.2)	1	0.7	(2.1)	47	1.7	(100.0)
Trans Eq	24	2.2	(29.3)	48	3.3	(58.5)	10	6.8	(12.2)	82	3.0	(100.0)
Instr Eng	1	0.1	(33.3)	2	0.1	(66.7)	0	0.0	(0.0)	3	0.1	(100.0)
Food	24	2.2	(30.4)	50	3.4	(63.3)	5	3.4	(6.3)	79	2.9	(100.0)
Textiles	52	4.8	(52.0)	44	3.0	(44.0)	4	2.7	(4.0)	100	3.7	(100.0)
Leath/Foot	11	1.0	(84.6)	2	0.1	(15.4)	0	0.0	(0.0)	13	0.5	(0.0)
Furniture	0	0.0	(0.0)	3	0.2	(100.0)	0	0.0	(0.0)	3	0.1	(100.0)
Paper	9	0.8	(40.9)	11	0.7	(50.0)	2	1.4	(9.1)	22	0.8	(100.0)
Rubber	0	0.0	(0.0)	2	0.1	(100.0)	0	0.0	(0.0)	2	0.1	(100.0)
Miscell	7	0.6	(43.8)	9	0.6	(56.3)	0	0.0	(0.0)	16	0.6	(100.0)
Construct	85	7.8	(41.5)	110	7.5	(53.7)	10	6.8	(4.9)	205	7.5	(100.0)
Rail Trans	4	0.4	(40.0)	6	0.4	(60.0)	0	0.0	(0.0)	10	0.4	(100.0)
Road Trans	11	1.0	(50.0)	8	0.5	(36.4)	3	2.0	(13.6)	22	0.8	(100.0)
Sea Trans	15	1.4	(55.6)	12	0.8	(44.4)	0	0.0	(0.0)	27	1.0	(100.0)
Air Trans	6	0.5	(50.0)	6	0.4	(50.0)	0	0.0	(0.0)	12	0.4	(100.0)
Telecom	9	0.8	(75.0)	3	0.2	(25.0)	0	0.0	(0.0)	12	0.4	(100.0)
General	557	50.9	(39.7)	770	52.2	(54.9)	76	51.4	(5.5)	1403	51.7	(100.0)
Total	1094	100.0	(40.3)	1474	100.0	(54.3)	148	100.0	(5.4)	2716	100.0	(100.0)

Appendix B3　　Sector by Party: Debates (columns) (1983/4 and 1984/5)

Sector		Conservative			Labour			Other			Total	
	n	%	s%	n	%	s%	n	%	s%	n	%	s%
Coal	323	13.5	(32.8)	652	22.4	(66.3)	9	0.9	(3.4)	984	17.7	(100.0)
Coke	0	0.0	(0.0)	5	0.2	(100.0)	0	0.0	(0.0)	5	0.1	(100.0)
Oil Extr	126	5.3	(66.0)	62	2.1	(32.5)	3	1.1	(1.6)	191	3.4	(100.0)
Petrol	40	1.7	(88.3)	6	0.2	(12.5)	2	0.8	(4.2)	48	0.9	(100.0)
Nuclear	47	2.0	(56.6)	29	1.0	(34.9)	7	2.7	(8.4)	83	1.5	(100.0)
Elect/Gas	30	1.3	(24.2)	69	2.4	(55.6)	25	9.5	(20.2)	124	2.2	(100.0)
Water	42	1.8	(58.4)	24	0.8	(33.3)	6	2.3	(8.3)	72	1.3	(100.0)
Metal Ext	0	0.0	(0.0)	0	0.0	(0.0)	0	0.0	(0.0)	0	0.0	(0.0)
Metal Man	36	1.5	(24.2)	107	3.7	(71.8)	6	2.3	(4.0)	149	2.7	(100.0)
Min Ext	5	0.2	(100.0)	0	0.0	(0.0)	0	0.0	(0.0)	5	0.1	(100.0)
Min Prod	4	0.2	(80.0)	1	0.1	(20.0)	0	0.0	(0.0)	5	0.1	(100.0)
Chemicals	20	0.8	(47.6)	19	0.7	(45.2)	3	1.1	(7.1)	42	0.8	(100.0)
Man-Made	0	0.0	(0.0)	0	0.0	(0.0)	0	0.0	(0.0)	0	0.0	(0.0)
Met Goods	0	0.0	(0.0)	0	0.0	(0.0)	0	0.0	(0.0)	0	0.0	(0.0)
Mech Eng	16	0.7	(30.8)	32	1.1	(61.5)	4	1.5	(7.7)	52	0.9	(100.0)
Data	113	4.7	(47.9)	86	3.0	(36.4)	37	14.1	(15.7)	236	4.2	(100.0)
Elect Eng	0	0.0	(0.0)	0	0.0	(0.0)	0	0.0	(0.0)	0	0.0	(0.0)
Mot Man	126	5.3	(59.4)	82	2.8	(38.7)	4	1.5	(1.9)	212	3.8	(100.0)
Trans Eq	177	7.4	(32.7)	338	11.6	(62.5)	26	9.9	(4.8)	541	9.7	(100.0)
Instr Eng	0	0.0	(0.0)	0	0.0	(0.0)	0	0.0	(0.0)	0	0.0	(0.0)
Food	12	0.5	(36.4)	21	0.7	(63.6)	0	0.0	(0.0)	33	0.6	(100.0)
Textiles	78	3.3	(65.0)	34	1.2	(28.3)	8	3.1	(6.7)	120	2.2	(100.0)
Leath/Foot	6	0.3	(100.0)	0	0.0	(0.0)	0	0.0	(0.0)	6	0.1	(100.0)
Furniture	0	0.0	(0.0)	0	0.0	(0.0)	0	0.0	(0.0)	0	0.0	(0.0)
Paper	46	1.9	(55.4)	37	1.3	(44.6)	0	0.0	(0.0)	83	1.5	(100.0)
Rubber	0	0.0	(0.0)	6	0.2	(100.0)	0	0.0	(0.0)	6	0.1	100.0)
Miscell	54	2.3	(50.3)	44	1.5	(41.1)	9	3.4	(8.4)	107	1.9	(100.0)
Construct	46	1.9	(34.8)	83	2.9	(62.9)	3	1.1	(2.3)	132	2.4	(100.0)
Rail Trans	33	1.4	(55.9)	24	0.8	(40.7)	2	0.8	(3.4)	59	1.1	(100.0)
Road Trans	108	4.5	(44.6)	128	4.4	(52.9)	6	2.3	(2.5)	242	4.3	(100.0)
Sea Trans	49	2.0	(50.5)	42	1.4	(43.3)	6	2.3	(6.2)	97	1.7	(100.0)
Air Trans	5	0.2	(55.6)	4	0.1	(44.4)	0	0.0	(0.0)	9	0.2	(100.0)
Telecom	145	6.1	(42.5)	169	5.8	(49.6)	27	7.9	(10.3)	341	6.1	(100.0)
General	706	29.5	(44.6)	808	27.7	(51.0)	69	26.3	(4.4)	1583	28.4	(100.0)
Total	2393	100.0	(43.0)	2912	100.0	(52.3)	262	100.0	(4.7)	5567	100.0	(100.0)

Appendix B4   Specific   Focus   of   Industrial   Activity: Oral Questions   (1983/4   and   1984/5)

Subject												
						Party						
		Conservative			Labour			Other			Total	
	n	%	s%	n	%	s%	n	%	s%	n	%	s%
Constit	16	3.5	(29.6)	35	8.7	(64.8)	3	7.0	(5.6)	54	6.0	(100.0)
EEC	25	5.5	(50.0)	23	5.7	(46.0)	2	4.7	(4.0)	50	5.6	(100.0)
Econ Pol	40	8.8	(57.1)	25	6.2	(35.7)	5	11.6	(7.1)	70	7.8	(100.0)
Employ	10	2.2	(31.3)	21	5.2	(65.6)	1	2.3	(3.1)	32	3.6	(100.0)
Govt. Ass.	28	6.2	(46.7)	27	6.7	(45.0)	5	11.6	(8.3)	60	6.7	(100.0)
Govt Reg	15	3.3	(55.6)	11	2.7	(40.7)	1	2.3	(3.7)	27	3.0	(100.0)
Ind Envir	3	0.7	(75.0)	1	0.2	(25.0)	0	0.0	(0.0)	4	0.2	(100.0)
Ind Injury	0	0.0	(0.0)	2	0.5	(100.0))	0	0.0	(0.0)	2	0.2	(100.0)
Ind Invest	17	3.8	(50.0)	17	4.2	(50.0)	0	0.0	(0.0)	34	3.8	(100.0)
Ind Output	28	6.2	(73.7)	9	2.2	(23.7)	1	2.3	(2.6)	38	4.2	(100.0)
Ind Regul	5	1.1	(55.6)	2	0.5	(22.2)	2	4.7	(22.2)	9	1.0	(100.0)
Ind Rels	70	15.5	(44.9)	84	20.8	(53.8)	2	4.7	(1.3)	156	17.4	(100.0)
Ind Safety	1	0.2	(100.0)	0	0.0	(0.0)	0	0.0	(0.0)	1	0.1	(100.0)
Ind Train	16	3.5	(64.0)	9	2.2	(36.0)	0	0.0	(0.0)	25	2.8	(100.0)
Local Auths	3	0.7	(23.1)	9	2.2	(69.2)	1	2.3	(7.7)	13	1.4	(100.0)
MNCs	2	0.4	(40.0)	3	0.7	(0.0)	0	0.0	(0.0)	5	0.6	(100.0)
Nat Inds	13	2.9	(50.0)	10	2.5	(38.5)	3	7.0	(11.5)	26	2.9	(100.0)
New Tech	1	0.2	(100.0)	0	0.0	(0.0)	0	0.0	(0.0)	1	0.1	(100.0)
Privatis	14	3.1	(50.0)	13	3.2	(46.4)	1	2.3	(3.6)	28	3.1	(100.0)
Prod gen	3	0.7	(60.0)	1	0.2	(20.0)	1	2.3	(0.0)	5	0.6	(100.0)
R&D	3	0.7	(75.0)	1	0.2	(25.0)	0	0.0	(0.0)	4	0.4	(100.0)
Reg Aid	13	2.9	(68.4)	4	1.0	(21.1)	2	4.7	(10.5)	19	2.1	(100.0)
Regional	23	5.1	(44.2)	25	6.2	(48.1)	4	9.3	(7.7)	52	5.8	(100.0)
TUs	37	8.2	(58.7)	24	6.0	(38.1)	2	4.7	(3.2)	63	7.0	(100.0)
Trd agree	51	11.3	(63.0)	26	6.5	(32.1)	4	9.3	(4.9)	81	9.0	(100.0)
Trd vol	16	3.5	(40.0)	21	5.2	(52.5)	3	7.0	(7.5)	40	4.4	(100.0)
Total	453	100.0	(50.4)	403	100.0	(4.8)	43	100.0	(4.8)	899	100.0	(100.0)

Appendix B5 **Specific Focus of Industrial Activity: Written Questions (1983/4 and 1984/5)**

Subject												
						Party						
		Conservative			*Labour*			*Other*			*Total*	
	n	*%*	*s%*	*n*	*%*	*s%*	*n*	*%*	*s%*	*n*	*%*	*s%*
Constit	38	3.5	(23.6)	113	7.7	(70.2)	10	6.8	(6.2)	161	5.9	(100.0)
EEC	109	10.0	(54.5)	88	6.0	(44.0)	3	2.0	(1.5)	200	7.4	(100.0)
Econ Pol	89	8.1	(49.2)	85	5.8	(47.0)	7	4.7	(3.9)	181	6.7	(100.0)
Employ	60	5.5	(24.6)	169	11.5	(69.3)	15	10.1	(6.1)	244	9.0	(100.0)
Govt Ass	60	5.5	(50.0)	53	3.6	(44.2)	7	4.7	(5.8)	120	4.4	(100.0)
Govt Reg	48	4.4	(47.5)	44	3.0	(43.6)	9	6.1	(8.9)	101	3.7	(100.0)
Ind Environ	13	1.2	(50.0)	11	0.7	(42.3)	2	1.4	(7.7)	26	1.0	(100.0)
Ind Injury	15	1.4	(20.3)	57	3.9	(77.0)	2	1.4	(2.7)	74	2.7	(100.0)
Ind Invest	28	2.6	(41.8)	34	2.3	(50.7)	5	3.4	(7.5)	67	2.5	(100.0)
Ind Output	70	6.4	(44.6)	76	5.2	(48.4)	11	7.4	(7.0)	157	5.8	(100.0)
Ind Regul	63	5.8	(54.8)	44	3.0	(38.3)	8	5.4	(7.0)	115	4.2	(100.0)
Ind Rels	62	5.7	(35.0)	102	6.9	(57.6)	13	8.8	(7.3)	177	6.5	(100.0)
Ind Safety	16	1.5	(28.1)	38	2.6	(66.7)	3	2.0	(5.3)	57	2.1	(100.0)
Ind Train	58	5.3	(35.8)	98	6.6	(60.5)	6	4.1	(3.7)	162	6.0	(100.0)
Local Auths	16	1.6	(30.2)	33	2.2	(62.3)	4	2.7	(7.5)	53	2.0	(100.0)
MNCs	1	0.1	(33.3)	2	0.1	(66.7)	0	0.0	(0.0)	3	0.1	(100.0)
Nat Inds	25	2.3	(51.0)	24	1.6	(49.0)	0	0.0	(0.0)	49	1.8	(100.0)
New Tech	1	0.1	(20.0)	4	0.3	(80.0)	0	0.0	(0.0)	5	0.2	(100.0)
Privatis	16	1.5	(37.2)	27	1.9	(62.8)	0	0.0	(0.0)	43	1.6	(100.0)
Prod gen	4	0.4	(57.1)	2	0.1	(28.6)	1	0.7	(14.3)	7	0.3	(100.0)
R&D	10	0.9	(52.6)	8	0.5	(42.1)	1	0.7	(5.3)	19	0.7	(100.0)
Reg Aid	24	2.2	(31.2)	42	2.8	(54.5)	11	7.4	(14.3)	77	2.8	(100.0)
Regional	20	1.8	(29.9)	40	2.7	(59.7)	7	4.7	(10.4)	67	2.5	(100.0)
TUs	56	5.1	(58.9)	35	2.4	(36.8)	4	2.7	(4.2)	95	3.5	(100.0)
Trd agree	159	14.5	(49.2)	148	10.0	(45.8)	16	10.8	(5.0)	323	11.9	(100.0)
Trd vol	33	3.0	(24.8)	97	6.6	(72.9)	3	2.0	(2.3)	133	4.9	(100.0)
Total	1094	100.0	(40.3)	1474	100.0	(54.3)	148	100.0	(5.4)	2716	100.0	(100.0)

Appendix B6 **Specific Focus of Industrial Activity: Debate (Columns) (1983/4 and 1984/5)**

Subject					Party								
		Conservative			*Labour*			*Other*			*Total*		
	n	%	s%	*n*	%	s%	*n*	%	s%	*n*	%	s%
Constit	248	10.4	(35.8)	419	14.4	(60.5)	25	9.5	(3.6)	692	12.4	(100.0)
EEC	34	1.4	(32.7)	54	1.9	(51.9)	16	6.1	(15.4)	104	1.9	(100.0)
Econ Pol	337	14.1	(52.5)	275	9.4	(42.8)	30	11.5	(4.7)	642	11.5	(100.0)
Employ	71	3.0	(48.0)	69	2.4	(46.6)	8	3.1	(5.4)	148	2.7	(100.0)
Govt Ass	296	12.4	(40.2)	422	14.5	(57.3)	19	7.3	(2.6)	737	13.2	(100.0)
Govt Reg	20	0.8	(55.6)	16	0.5	(44.4)	0	0.0	(0.0)	36	0.6	(100.0)
Ind Envir	34	1.4	(72.3)	11	0.4	(23.4)	2	0.8	(4.3)	47	0.8	(100.0)
Ind Injury	2	0.1	(15.4)	11	0.4	(84.6)	0	0.0	(0.0)	13	0.2	(100.0)
Ind Invest	42	1.8	(89.4)	3	0.1	(6.4)	2	0.8	(4.3)	47	0.8	(100.0)
Ind Output	48	2.0	(62.3)	27	0.9	(35.1)	2	0.8	(2.6)	77	1.4	(100.0)
Ind Regul	39	1.6	(43.8)	46	1.6	(51.7)	4	1.5	(4.5)	89	1.6	(100.0)
Ind Rels	222	9.3	(36.8)	369	12.7	(61.2)	12	4.6	(2.0)	603	10.8	(100.0)
Ind Safety	57	2.4	(40.4)	79	2.7	(56.0)	5	1.9	(3.5)	141	2.6	(100.0)
Ind Train	37	1.5	(38.9)	53	1.8	(55.8)	5	1.9	(5.3)	95	1.7	(100.0)
Local Auths	0	0.0	(0.0)	2	0.1	(100.0)	0	0.0	(0.0)	2	0.0	(100.0)
MNCs	0	0.0	(0.0)	0	0.0	(0.0)	0	0.0	(0.0)	0	0.0	(100.0)
Nat Inds	6	0.3	(54.4)	5	0.2	(45.5)	0	0.0	(0.0)	11	0.2	(100.0)
New Tech	57	2.4	(78.1)	12	0.4	(16.4)	4	1.5	(5.5)	73	1.3	(100.0)
Privatis	323	13.5	(40.1)	437	15.0	(54.3)	45	17.2	(5.6)	805	14.4	(100.0)
Prod gen	0	0.0	(0.0)	0	0.0	(0.0)	0	0.0	(0.0)	0	0.0	(100.0)
R&D	7	0.3	(22.6)	19	0.7	(61.3)	5	1.9	(16.1)	31	0.6	(100.0)
Reg Aid	181	7.6	(48.3)	173	5.9	(46.1)	21	8.0	(5.6)	375	6.7	(100.0)
Regional	29	1.2	(35.4)	49	1.7	(59.8)	4	1.5	(4.9)	82	1.5	(100.0)
TUs	205	8.6	(39.0)	298	10.2	(56.8)	22	8.4	(4.2)	525	9.4	(100.0)
Trd agree	96	4.0	(50.8)	62	2.1	(32.8)	31	11.8	(16.4)	189	3.4	(100.0)
Trd vol	2	0.1	(50.0)	2	0.1	(50.0)	0	0.0	(0.0)	3	0.1	(100.0)
Total	2393	100.0	(43.0)	2912	100.0	(52.3)	262	100.0	(4.7)	5567	100.0	(100.0)

Appendix C

Evidence from Outside Organisations to the Select Committee on Trade and Industry

Session 1983/4

HC 344 British Steel Corporation's Prospects.
Oral
BSC; TUC Steel Committee; National Association of Steel Stockholders; Austin Rover Group Ltd.
Written
BSC; Iron and Steel Trades Confederation; TUC Steel Committee; Manchester Steel Ltd; British Iron and Steel Consumer's Council; Llanwern Trade Union Committee; Joint Branches Union Committee, Ravenscraig.

HC 461 Growth in Trade Imbalance in Manufactured Goods between UK and Existing/Prospective EEC Member States.
Oral
Confederation of British Industry; British Paper and Board Industry Federation; Economic Research Council; Association of Scientific and Technical and Managerial Staffs
Written
British Paper and Board Industry Federation; Economic Research Council; Association of Scientific and Technical and Managerial Staffs; Cocoa, Chocolate and Confectionery Alliance and the Cake and Biscuit Alliance; ICI plc; British Leyland Cars Group; Land Rover-Leyland; National Association of Steel Stockholders; Federation of British Electro-technical and Allied Manufacturers Association; British Textile Confederation; British Clothing Industry Association Ltd; Society of Motor Manufacturers; Ford Motor Company; TUC; British Chicken Association; Confederation of British Industry.

HC 490 BL PLC
Oral
BL

HC 640 The Wealth of Waste
Oral
Glass Manufacturers' Federation; British Scrap Federation; Reclamation Association; British Independent Steel Producers Association; British

Nuclear Fuels; British Waste Paper Association; Leeds City Council; Greater London Council.
Written
Glass Manufacturers' Federation; British Scrap Federation; Reclamation Association; British Independent Steel Producers Association; British Waste Paper Association; Leeds City Council; Greater London Council; Process Plant Association; Institute of Wastes Management; British Reclamation Industries' Confederation; INCPEN; Metal Packaging Manufactures Association; British Plastics Federation; CBI; Associated Heat Services PLC; Warmer Campaign; Lead Development Association; UK Reclamation Council

Session 1984/5

HC 171 Operation of Export Credits Guarantee Department
Oral
Committee of London Clearing Bankers; Citibank; Export Credit Insurance Group; Credit Insurance Association; Society of British Aerospace Companies Ltd; London Chamber of Commerce and Industry; CBI.
Written
Committee of London Clearing Bankers; Citibank; Export Credit Insurance Group; Society of British Aerospace Companies Ltd; London Chamber of Commerce and Industry; CBI.

HC 474 British Steel Corporation
Oral
BSC; TUC Steel Committee.

HC 509 Trade with China
Oral
Sino-British Trade Council; The 48 Group.
Written
Gambica; British Textile Confederation; Chemical Industries Association.

Session 1985/6

HC 106 Tourism in the UK
Oral
British Incoming Tour Operators' Association; British Tourist Authority;

British Railways Board; British Waterways Board; Wales Tourist Board; Scottish Tourist Board; English Tourist Board; National Bus Company; British Hotels, Restaurants and Caterers Association; Northern Ireland Tourist Board; HM Customs and Excise; Association of British Travel Agents; London Visitor and Convention Bureau.

Written

British Incoming Tour Operators' Association; British Tourist Authority; British Railways Board; British Waterways Board; Wales Tourist Board; Scottish Tourist Board; English Tourist Board; National Bus Company; British Hotels, Restaurants and Caterers Association; Northern Ireland Tourist Board; HM Customs and Excise; Association of British Travel Agents; London Visitor and Convention Bureau; Kent County Council; Cumbria Tourist Board; Heart of England Tourist Board; West Country Tourist Board; Thames and Chilterns Tourist Board; Yorkshire and Humberside Tourist Board; East Midlands Tourist Board; South East Tourist Board; Southern Tourist Board; East Anglia Tourist Board; Northumbria Tourist Board; North West England Tourist Board; Southampton Tourist Group; Isle of Wight Tourist Board; Manpower Services Commission; Bus and Coach Council; Hotel Catering and Institutional Management Association; CBI; British Caledonian; British Airports Authority; Settle-Carlisle Joint Action Committee; Dan-Air; Horizon Travel; Ramblers Association; National Trust; Historic Houses Association; Association of Guide-Booking Agency Services; European Travelhouse and BITOA; Countryside Commission; Brewers Society; Automobile Association; CAA; Owl Sales Management Ltd; Association of Tourist Officers; Association of District Councils; British Association of Conference Towns; British Exhibition Venues Association; Birmingham Convention and Visitor Bureau; British Resorts Association; South Wight Borough Council; Travel Association Consultative Council; Caravan Club; Forestry Commission; Hertfordshire Society; European Ferries; National Association of Holiday Centres; American Express; DAvid Powell & Associates; Licenced Victuallers and Brewers Society; Scottish Museum Council; Yorkshire and Humberside County Councils Association; Sports Council; Salmon Conservancy.

HC 305 Tin Crisis

Oral

Geevor Tin Mines PLC; Penwith District Council; Camborne School Of Mines; Group of 16 Creditors; London Metal Exchange; Tin Crisis Joint Action Group; TGWU; Ring Dealing Members of the London Metal Exchange; Rio Tinto-Zinc Corporation plc; Medway Tin Ltd.

Written

Geevor Tin Mines PLC; Camborne School Of Mines; London Metal

Exchange; Penwith District Council; Cornwall County Council; TGWU; Ring Dealing Members of the London Metal Exchange; Rio Tinto-Zinc Corporation plc; F. Murphy Metal Ltd; Kerrier District Council; Cornish Mining Development Association; Marine Mining Cornwall Consortium; Southwest Minerals Ltd; Concord Tin Mines Ltd; Cornish Tin and Engineering Ltd; Metal Packaging Manufacturers Association; Cornish Tin and Engineering Ltd; Carrick District Council; International Wrought Copper Council; Grain And Feed Trade Association; Amalgamated Metals Corporation plc.

Session   1986/7

HC 71 Tin Crisis: Supplementary Report
Oral
Bank of England; Tinco Realisations.
Written
London Metal Exchange; Bank of England; Tinco Realisations; Creditor Banks; Amalgamated Metal Corporation; TGWU; Medway Tin Ltd; Rio Tinto-Zinc.

HC 407 UK Motor Components Industry
Oral
GKN plc; TASS; ASTMS; TGWU; Leyland Trucks; ERF(Holdings) plc; Austin Rover Group; Land Rover Group; A.B. Electronic Products Group plc; Lucas Industries plc; BTR plc; Turner & Newall plc; Armstrong Equipment Ltd; TRW Cam Gears Ltd; TI Automotives; Avon Rubber Company; British Steel Corporation; United Engineering Steels Ltd; BBA Group plc; Pilkington Glass Ltd; British Automotive Parts Promotion Council.
Written
Ford Motor Company Limited Group; Jaguar plc; TASS; ASTMS; AEU; TGWU; ERF(Holdings) plc; Land Rover-Leyland Limited; AB Electronic Products Group plc; Lucas Industries plc; BTR plc; Turner & Newall plc; TRW Cam Gears Ltd; TI Automotives; Avon Industrial Polymers Ltd; British Steel Corporation; United Engineering Steels Ltd; Mintex Division BBA Group plc; Pilkington Glass Ltd; Peugeot Talbot Motor Company; Electronics Components Industry Federation; Matthey Catalytic Systems Division; Industrial Copyright Reform Association; Society of Motor Manufacturers and Traders Ltd; British Automotive parts Promotion Council; Motorola Ltd; Robert Bosch Ltd; European Automotive Industry; Strategy Audit Consultants Ltd; Chloride Exide; Borough of Luton; Britax; BAPPC.

HC 176 Westland plc
Oral
British Aerospace plc; Lloyds Merchant Bank Ltd; Stock Exchange Council; Westland plc.
Written
Aerospace Committee of the Confederation of Shipbuilding and Engineering Unions; Slaughter & May; Stock Exchange Council.

References

ABCC 1985, *British Manufacturing Decline 1975-84*, Association of British Chambers of Commerce, London.

Abromeit, H. 1987, 'The UK's Privatisation Programme: A View from Europe', PSA Conference, Aberdeen.

Alderman, G. 1984, *Pressure Groups and Government in Great Britain*, Longman, London.

Alt, J. E. and Chrystal, K. A. 1983, *Political Economics*, Wheatsheaf, Brighton.

Anderson, P. 1964, 'Origins of the Present Crisis', *New Left Review*, 23, pp.26-53.

Anderson, P. 1987, 'The Figures of Descent', *New Left Review*, 161, pp.20-77.

Appleby, C. and Bessant, J. 1987, 'Adapting to Decline: Organisational Structures and Government Policy in the UK and West German Foundry Sectors', in S. Wilks and M. Wright (eds.), *Comparative Government-Industry Relations*, Clarendon, Oxford.

Barratt Brown, M. 1988, 'Away With All The Great Arches', *New Left Review*, 167, pp.22-51.

Beasley, M. and Littlechild, S. 1986, 'Privatisation: Principles, Problems and Priorities' in J. Kay, C. Mayer and D. Thomson 1986, *Privatisation and Regulation: The UK Experience*, Clarendon, Oxford.

Beer, S. H. 1969, *Modern British Politics* (2nd edn.), Faber, London.

Beer, S. H. 1971, 'The British Legislature and the Problem of Mobilising Consent' in G. C. Byrne and K. S. Pederson, *Politics in Western European Democracies*, John Wiley, New York.

Beer, S. H. 1975, 'Introduction' to S. Webb and B. Webb, *A Constitution for a Socialist Commonwealth of Great Britain*, LSE/ CUP, Cambridge.

Beer, S. H. 1982, *Britain Against Itself*, Faber & Faber, London.

Bentham, J. 1843, *Collected Works*, William Tait, Edinburgh.

Berrington, H. B. 1968, 'Partisanship and Dissidence in the Nineteenth Century House of Commons', *Parliamentary Affairs*, 21, pp.338-373.

Beynon, H. 1985, *Digging Deeper: Issues in the Miners' Strike*, Verso, London.

Birch, A. H. 1964, *Representative and Responsible Government*, Unwin, London.

Birch, A. H. 1971, *Representation*, Macmillan, London.

Blalock, H.M. 1979, *Social Statistics* (2nd edn.), McGraw-Hill, Tokyo.

Bogdanor, V. 1977, 'A House of Industry', in T. Raison (ed.) *The Corporate State – Myth or Reality?*, London.

Bogdanor, V. 1989, 'The Constitution', in D. Kavanagh and A. Seldon (eds.), *The Thatcher Effect*, Clarendon, Oxford.

Booth, A. 1982, 'Corporatism, Capitalism and Depression in Twentieth-Century Britain', *British Journal of Sociology*, 33, 2, pp.200-23.

Brittan, S. 1977, *The Economic Consequences of Democracy*, Temple Smith, London.

Brittan, S. 1983, *The Role and Limits of Government*, Temple Smith, Middlesex.

Bruce-Gardyne, J. 1984, *Mrs Thatcher's First Administration*, Macmillan, London.

Butler, D. and Kavangh, D. 1984, *The British General Election of 1983*, Macmillan, London.

Butt, R. 1969, *The Power of Parliament*, Constable, London.

Cannon, J. 1972, *Parliamentary Reform 1640-1832*, CUP, Cambridge.

Carpenter, L. P. 1976, 'Corporatism in Britain 1930-45', *Journal of Contemporary History*, 11, 1, pp. 3-25.

Cawson, A. 1978, 'Pluralism, Corporatism and the Role of the State', *Government and Opposition*, 13, 2 , pp. 178-98.

Cawson, A. 1982, *Corporatism and Welfare*, Heinemann, London.

Cawson, A. 1985, 'Varieties of Corporatism: The Importance of the Meso-Level of Interest Intermediation' in A. Cawson (ed.), *Organised Interests and the State*, Sage, London.

Cawson, A. 1986, *Corporatism and Political Theory*, Blackwell, Oxford.

Cawson, A. 1988, 'In Defence of the Old Testament: A Reply to Andrew Cox', *Political Studies*, 36, 2, pp.309-15.

Cawson, A. 1989, 'Is There a Corporatist Theory of the State', in G. Duncan (ed.), *Democracy and the Capitalist State*, CUP, Cambridge.

CBI 1987, *Working with Politicians*, CBI, London.

Chandler, G. 1984, 'The Political Process and the Decline of Industry', *Three Banks Review*, 141, March, pp.3-17.

Chief Executive 1986, 'MPs and Industry', *Chief Executive*, December, pp.16-20.

Churchill, W. 1930, *Parliamentary Government and the Economic Problem*, OUP, Oxford.

Clark, J. C. D. 1980, 'A General Theory of Party, Opposition and Government 1688-1832', *The Historical Journal*, 23, pp.295-325.

Clarke, T. 1977, 'The Raison D'Etre of Trade Unionism' in T. Clarke and L. Clements (eds.), *Trade Unions Under Capitalism*, Fontana, Glasgow.

Close, D. H. 1977, 'The Collapse of Resistance to Democracy', *The Historical Journal*, 20, pp.893-918.

Cm 278 1988, *DTI: The Department of Enterprise*, HMSO, London.

Cmnd 8881 1983, *Review of Parliamentary Pay and Allowances*, Review Body on Top Salaries, HMSO, London.

Cmnd 9111, 1983, *Regional Industrial Development*, HMSO, London.

Coates, D. 1975, *The Labour Party and the Struggle for Socialism*, CUP, Cambridge.

Coates, D. 1980, *Labour in Power?*, Longman, London.

Coates, D. 1983, 'The Character and Origins of Britain's Economic Decline', in D. Coates and G. Johnston (eds.), *Socialist Strategies*, Martin Robertson, Oxford.

Coates, K. and Topham, T. 1986, *Trade Unions and Politics*, Blackwell, Oxford.

Cole, G. D. H. 1920a, *Social Theory*, Methuen, London.

Cole, G. D. H. 1920b, *Guild Socialism Restated*, Parsons, London.

Conran, D. P. 1986, *The German Polity*, Longman, London.

Conservative Manifesto 1979, Conservative Central Office, London

Conservative Manifesto 1983, Conservative Central Office, London.

Conservative Party 1983, *Conservative Parliamentary Candidates*, Conservative Central Office, London.

Coombes, D. 1982, *Representative Government and Economic Power*, Heinemann, London.

Coombes, D. and Walkland, S.A.W. 1980, *Parliaments and Economic Affairs*, Heinemann, London.

Cox, A. 1980, 'Corporatism as Reductionism', *Government and Opposition*, 16, 1, pp.78-95.

Cox, A. 1984, *Adversary Politics and Land*, CUP, Cambridge.

Cox, A. 1988, 'The Old and New Testaments of Corporatism: Is it a Political Form or a Method of Policy-Making?', *Political Studies*, 36, 2, pp.294-308.

Craigen, J. 1987, 'Ten Years of the Industry and Parliament Trust', *The House Magazine*, 12, 361, pp.19-20.

Crewe, I. 1983, 'The Electorate: Partisan Dealignment Ten Years On', *Western European Politics*, 6, 4, pp.183-215.

Crewe, I. 1990, 'The Policy Agenda: A New Thatcherite Consensus?', *Contemporary Record*, 3, 3, pp.2-7.

Crick, B. 1968, *The Reform of Parliament* (2nd edn.), Weidenfeld and Nicolson, London.

Crick, B. 1989, 'Republicanism, Liberalism and Capitalism: a Defence of Parliamentarianism', in G. Duncan (ed.), *Democracy and The Capitalist State*, CUP, Cambridge.

Criddle, B. 1984, 'The Election Locally' in D. Butler and D. Kavanagh, *The British General Election of 1983*, Macmillan, London.

Crouch, C. 1977, *Class Conflict and the Industrial Relations Crisis*, Heinemann, London.

Crouch, C. 1979, 'The State, Capital and Liberal Democracy', in C. Crouch (ed.), *State and Economy in Contemporary Capitalism,* Croom Helm, London.

Crouch, C. 1983, 'Pluralism and the New Corporatism: A Rejoinder', *Political Studies*, 31, 3, pp. 452-60.

Crouch, C. 1985, 'Corporatism in Industrial Relations: A Formal Model' in W. Grant (ed.), *The Political Economy of Corporatism*, Macmillan, London.

Dahl, R. A. 1956, *A Preface to Democartic Theory*, University of Chicago Press, Chicago.

Davies, A. 1980, *Reformed Select Committees: The First Year*, Outer Circle Policy Unit, London.

Davies, P. 1988, 'Nationalised Industries Under Thatcher: How Much Has Changed, *Politics*, 8, 2, pp.16-21.

Dearlove, J. and Saunders, P. 1984, *Introduction to British Politics*, Polity, Cambridge.

Dicey, A. V. 1885, *An Introduction to the Study of the Law of the Constitution* (10th edn. 1959), Macmillan, London.

Dod 1983, *Dod's Parliamentary Companion 1983*, Dod's Parliamentary Companion Ltd, London.

Drewry, G. (ed.) 1985, *The New Select Committees*,Clarendon, Oxford.

Drewry, G. and Butcher, T. 1988, *The Civil Service Today*, Blackwell, Oxford.

Dubs, A. 1989, *Lobbying: An Insider's Guide to the Parliamentary Process*, Pluto Press, London.

Duncan, G. 1989, 'Introduction' in G. Duncan (ed.), *Democracy and The Capitalist State*, CUP, Cambridge.

Dunleavy, P. and O'Leary, B. 1987, *Theories of the State*, Macmillan, London.

Dyson, K. 1983, 'The Cultural, Ideological and Structural Context' in K. Dyson and S. Wilks (eds.), *Industrial Crisis*, Blackwell, Oxford.

Easton, D. 1966, *A Systems Analysis of Political Life*, Wiley, New York.

Eccleshall, R. 1986, *British Liberalism*, Longman, London

Ellis, J. and Johnson, R. W. 1974, *Members From The Unions*, Fabian Society, London.

Ellis, N. 1988, *Parliamentary Lobbying: Putting the Business Case to Government*, Heinemann, London.

Englefield, D. 1984, *Today's Civil Service*, Longman, London.

Eulau, H. and Wahlke, J. C. 1978, *The Politics of Representation*, Sage, Beverly Hills.

Eulau, H.; Wahlke, J. C.; Buchanan, W.; Ferguson, L. C. 1959, 'The Role of the Representative: Some Empirical Observations on the Theory of Edmund Burke', *American Political Science Review*, 53, 3,pp.742-56.

Fatchett, D. 1987, *Trade Unions and Politics in the 1980s*, London, Croom Helm.

Fine, B. and Harris, L. 1985, *The Peculiarities of the British Economy*, Lawrence and Wishart, London.

Fine, B. and Millar, R. 1985, *Policing the Miners' Strike*, Lawrence and Wishart, London.

Finer, H. 1923, *Representative Government and a Parliament of Industry*, Fabian Society/Allen and Unwin, London.

Finer, S. E. (ed) 1975, *Adversary Politics and Electoral Reform*, Anthony Wigram, London.

Finer, S. E. 1980, *The Changing Party System 1945-79*, AEI, Washington.

Flegmann, W. 1986, *Public Expenditure and the Select Committees of the Commons*, Gower, Aldershot.

Florence, P. S. 1957, *Industry and the State*, Hutchinson, London.

Fraser, P. 1960, 'The Growth of Ministerial Control in the Nineteenth Century House of Commons' , *English Historical Review*, 75, pp.444-63.

Freeman, J. L. 1955, *The Political Process*, Randon House.

Fry, G. K. 1969, *Statesmen in Disguise*, Macmillan, London.

Gamble, A. 1985, *Britain in Decline* (2nd edn.), Macmillan, London.

Gamble, A. 1988, *The Free Economy and the Strong State*, Macmillan, London.

Gamble, A. 1989, 'The Politics of Thatcherism', *Parliamentary Affairs*, 42, 3, pp.350-61.

Gamble, A. and Walkland, S. A. W. 1984, *The British Party System and Economic Policy 1945-83*, Clarendon, Oxford.

Gennard, J. 1984, 'Implications of the Messenger Group Dispute', *Industrial Relations Journal*, 15, 3, pp.7-20.

Giddings, P. 1985, 'What Has Been Achieved?', in G. Drewry (ed.), *The New Select Committees*, Clarendon, Oxford.

Gilmour, I. 1977, *Inside Right*, Hutchinson, London.

Gilmour, I. 1983, *Britain Can Work*, Martin Robertson, Oxford.

Grant, W. 1982, *The Political Economy of Industrial Policy*, Butterworths, London.

Grant, W. 1983, *The Organisation of Business Interests in the UK Chemical Industry*, Wissenschaftszentrum, Berlin.

Grant, W. 1985, 'Introduction', in W. Grant (ed.), *The Political Economy of Corporatism*, Macmillan, London.

Grant, W. 1987, *Business and Politics in Britain*, Macmillan, London.

Grant, W. 1989a, *Pressure Groups, Politics and Democracy in Britain*, Philip Allen, London.

Grant, W. 1989b, *Government and Industry*, Edward Elgar, Aldershot.

Grant, W. and Marsh, D. 1977, *The CBI*, Hodder and Stoughton, London.

Grant, W., Patterson, W., and Whitson, C. 1987, 'Government-Industry Relations in the Chemical Industry: an Anglo-German Comparison', in S. Wilks and M. Wright (eds.), *Comparative Government-Industry Relations*, OUP, Oxford.

Grant, W., Paterson, W. and Whitston, C. 1988, *Government and the Chemical Industry*, Clarendon, Oxford.

Grant, W. and Streek, W. 1985, 'Large Firms and the Representation of Business Interests in the UK and West German Construction Industry', in A. Cawson (ed.), *Organised Interests and the State*, Sage, London.

Grantham, C. 1989, 'Parliament and Political Consultants', *Parliamentary Affairs*, 42, 4, pp.503-518.

Grantham, C. and Seymour-Ure, C. 1990, 'Parliament and Political Consultants' in M. Rush (ed.), *Parliament and Pressure Groups*, OUP, Oxford.

Griffith, E. S. 1939, *The Impasse of Democracy,* Harrison-Hilton, New York.

Griffith, J. A. G. 1982, 'The Constitution and the Commons', in RIPA *Parliament and the Executive,* RIPA, London.

Grove, J. W. 1962, *Government and Industry in Britain*, Longmans, London.

Hall, S. 1984, 'The State in Question' in G. McLennan, D. Held, and S. Hall (eds.), *The Idea of the Modern State*, Open University Press, Milton Keynes.

Hailsham, Lord 1978, *The Dilemma of Democracy*, Collins, Glasgow.

Hansard Society 1976, *Report of the Hansard Society Commission on Electoral Reform*, Hansard Society, London.

Hansard Society 1979, *Politics and Industry – The Great Mismatch*, Hansard Society, London.

Harden, I. 1988, 'Corporatism Without Labour: The British Version', in C. Graham and T. Prosser (eds.), *Waiving The Rules*, Open University Press, Milton Keynes.

Hayward, J. 1986, *The State and the Market Economy*, Wheatsheaf, Brighton.

HC 161 1931, *Procedure on Public Business*, Special Report from theSelect Committee on Procedure, Session 1930/1.

HC 269 1965, *Third Report from the Committeee of Privileges*, Session 1964/5.

HC 588 1978, *First Report from the Select Committee on Procedure*, Session 1977/8.

HC 367 1980, *Minutes of Evidence*, Industry and Trade Committee, HMSO, London.

HC 92 1982, *The Select Committee System*, First Report from the Liaison Committee, Session 1982/3.

HC 181 1983, *British Steel Corporation's Prospects*, Observations by the Government, First Special Report from the TIC, Session 1983/4.

HC 256 1984, *All-Party and Parliamentary Groups*, Select Committee on House of Commons (Services), Session 1983/4

HC 344 1984, *British Steel Corporation's Prospects*, First Report from the TIC, Session 1983/4.

HC 461 1984, *The Growth in the Imbalance of Trade in Manufactured Goods Between the UK and Existing and Prospective Members of the EEC*, Second Report from the Trade and Industry Committee, Session 1983/4.

HC 490 1984, *BL plc*, Third Report from the TIC, Session 1983/4.

HC 491 1984, *Rolls Royce Ltd*, Minutes of Evidence, Session 1983/4.

HC 540 1984, *British Steel Corporation's Prospects*, Obsevations by the Government, Third Special Report from the TIC, Session 1983/4.

HC 577 1984, *British Shipbuilders*, Minutes of Evidence, Session 1983/4.

HC 600 1984, *The Post Office*, Minutes of Evidence, Session 1983/4.

HC 607 1984, *BL plc*, Observations by the Government, Fourth Special Report from the TIC, Session 1983/4.

HC 640 1984, *The Wealth of Waste*, Fourth Report of the TIC, Session 1983/4.

HC 657 1984, *Minutes of Proceedings*, TIC, Session 1983/4.

HC 171 1985, *The Operation of the Export Credits Guarantee Department*, First Report from the TIC, Session 1984/5.

HC 219 1985, *British Shipbuilders*, Minutes of Evidence, Session 1984/5.

HC 321 1985, *The Wealth of Waste*, Government Observations, Second Special Report of the TIC, Session 1984/5.

HC 334 1985, *HM Treasury's Consultation Proposals for Legislation in Respect of the Nationalised Industries*, Third Special Report from the TIC, Session 1984/5.

HC 363 1985, *The Select Committee System*, First Report from the Liaison Committee, Session 1984/5.

HC 408 1985, *Select Committee on Members' Interests*, First Report, Session 1984/5.

HC 413 1985, *The Operations of the Export Credits Guarantee Department*;

Observations by the Government, Fourth Special Report from the Trade and Industry Committee, Session 1984/5.

HC 444 1985, *British Steel Corporation*, Minutes of Evidence, TIC, Session 1984/5.

HC 473 1985, *Rolls-Royce Ltd*, Minutes of Evidence, TIC, Session 1984/5.

HC 474 1985, *The British Steel Corporation*, Second Report from the TIC, Session 1984/5.

HC 509 1985, *Trade With China*, Third Report from the TIC, Session 1984/5.

HC 532 1985, *The Post Office*, Minutes of Evidence, Session 1984/5.

HC 617 1985, *Minutes of Proceedings*, TIC, Session 1984/5.

HC 106 1985, *Tourism in the UK*, First Report from the TIC, Session 1985/6.

HC 71 1986, *The Tin Crisis: Supplementary Report*, First Report from the TIC, Session 1986/7.

HC 305 1986, *The Tin Crisis*, Second Report from the TIC, Session 1985/6.

HC 472 1986, *British Shipbuilders*, Minutes of Evidence, TIC, Session 1985/6.

HC 628 1986, *Minutes of Proceedings*, TIC, Session 1985/6.

HC 176 1987, *Westland plc*, Second Report from the TIC, Session 1986/7.

HC 407 1987, *UK Motor Component Industry*, Third Report from the TIC, Session 1986/7.

HC 518 1988, *Select Committee on Members' Interests*, Session 1987/8.

HL 238 1985, *Report from Select Committee on Overseas Trade*, Session 1985/6

Heald, D. 1983, *Public Expenditure*, Martin Robertson, Oxford.

Heald, D. and Steel, D. 1984, 'Privatising Public Enterprise: An Analysis of the Government's Case', *Political Quarterly*, 55, 3, pp.333-49.

Heald, D. and Thomas, D. 1986, 'Privatisation as Theology', *Public Administration and Policy*, 1, 2, pp.49-66.

Heffer, E. 1986, *Labour's Future*, Verso, London.

Held, D. 1989, *Political Theory and the Modern State*, Polity, Oxford.

Heller, R. 1987, *The State of Industry*, Sphere, London.

Hill, D. M. (ed.) 1984, *Parliamentary Select Committees in Action*, Strathclyde Papers on Government and Politics, 24, University of Strathclyde, Glasgow.

Hinton, J. 1983, *Labour and Socialism*, Wheatsheaf, Brighton.

Hirst, P. 1989, *After Thatcher*, Collins, London.

Hobsbawn, E. J. 1969, *Industry and Empire*, Pelican, Harmondsworth.

Hobson, S. G. 1931, *The House of Industry*, King & Son, London.

Holmes, M. 1985, *The First Thatcher Government 1979-83*, Wheatsheaf, Brighton.

Hoover, K. and Plant, R. 1989, *Conservative Capitalism in Britain and the United States*, Routledge, London.

House of Commons All Party Reform Group 1985, *Findings of MPs' Attitudes to Reform and the Role of the MP,* mimeo, London..

Hughes, C. and Wintour, P. 1990, *Labour Rebuilt : The New Model Party*, Fourth Estate, London.

Hyman, R. 1986, 'British Industrial Relations: The Limits of Corporatism', in O. Jacobi, B. Jessop, H. Kastendiek, M. Regini, *Economic Crisis, Trade Unions and the State,* Croom Helm, London.

Hyman, R. 1987, 'Trade Unions and the Law: Papering Over the Cracks', *Capital and Class*, 31, 2, pp.93-111.

Industry and Parliament Trust 1983, *Industry and Parliament Trust*, Industry and Parliament Trust Ltd, London.

Industry and Parliament Trust 1986, *Industry and Parliament Trust*, Industry and Parliament Trust Ltd, London.

Industry and Parliament Trust 1989, *Industry and Parliament Trust: Annual Report and Accounts*, Industry and Parliament Trust Ltd, London.

Ingham, G. 1984, *Capitalism Divided?*, Macmillan, London.

Ingle, S. 1987, *The British Party System*, Blackwell, Oxford.

Ionescu, G. 1975, *Centripetal Politics*, Hart-Davis, London.

Jessop, B. 1978, 'Capitalism and Democracy: The Best Possible Political Shell?, in G. Littlejohn, B. Smart, J. Wakeford and N. Yuval-Davis (eds.), *Power and the State*, Croom Helm, London.

Jessop, B. 1979, 'Corporatism, Parliamentarism and Social Democracy', in P. C. Schmitter and G. Lehmbruch (eds.), *Trends Towards Corporatist Intermediation*, Sage, London.

Jessop, B. 1980, 'The Transformation of the State in Post-war Britain', in R. Scase (ed.) *The State in Western Europe*, Croom Helm, London.

Jessop, B. 1986, 'The Prospects for the Corporatisation of Monetarism in Britain' in O. Jacobi, B. Jessop, H. Kastendiek, M. Regini (eds.), *Economic Crisis, Trade Unions and the State,* Croom Helm, London.

Jessop, B.; Bonnett, K.; Bromley, S. and Ling, T. 1988, *Thatcherism*, Polity, Oxford.

Johnson, N. 1977, *In Search of the Constitution*, Pergamon, Oxford.

Jones, J. B. 1990, 'Party Committees and All-Party Groups', in M.Rush (ed.), *Parliament and Pressure Groups*, OUP, Oxford.

Jordan, A. G. 1984, 'Pluralistic Corporatisms and Corporate Pluralism', *Scandinavian Political Studies*, 7, 3, pp.137-52.

Jordan, A. G. 1989, 'Insider Lobbying: The British Version', *Political Studies*, 37, 1, pp.107-113.

Jordan, A. G. 1990, 'Networks: How Much Space Between the Threads?', *Journal of Theoretical Politics*, 2, (forthcoming).

Jordan, A. G. and Richardson, J. J. 1982, 'The British Policy Style or The

Logic of Negotiation?' in J. J. Richardson (ed.), *Policy Styles in Western Europe*, Allen & Unwin, London.

Jordan, A. G. and Richardson, J. J. 1987a, *British Politics and the Policy Process*, Allen & Unwin, London.

Jordan, A. G. and Richardson J. J. 1987b, *Government and Pressure Groups in Britain*, Clarendon, Oxford.

Judge, D. 1979, *Backbench Specialisation in the House of Commons: A Study of Oganisation and Representative Theories*, Ph.D. Thesis, University of Sheffield, Sheffield.

Judge, D. 1981, *Backbench Specialisation in the House of Commons*, Heinemann, London.

Judge, D. 1982, 'Ministerial Responsibility and Select Committees', *The House Magazine*, 219, 8, pp.4-20.

Judge, D. 1983a, 'Why Reform? Parliamentary Reform Since 1832' in D. Judge (ed.), *The Politics of Parliamentary Reform*, Heinemann, London.

Judge, D. 1983b, 'Considerations on Reform' in D. Judge (ed.), *The Politics of Parliamentary Reform*, Heinemann, London.

Judge, D. 1984a, 'The Politics of MPs Pay', *Parliamentary Affairs*, 37, 1, pp.59-75.

Judge, D. 1984b, *Ministerial Responsibility: Life in the Strawman Yet?*, Strathclyde Papers on Government and Politics, 37, University of Strathclyde, Glasgow.

Judge, D. 1987, 'Incomplete Sovereignty: The British House of Commons and the Completion of the EC Internal Market', paper delivered to American Political Science Association, Chicago.

Judge, D. 1990, 'Parliament and Interest Representation', in M. Rush (cd) *Parliament and Pressure Politics*, Clarendon, Oxford.

Judge, D. 1992, *The Parliamentary State*, (forthcoming) Sage, London.

Judge, D. and Dickson, T. 1987, 'The British State, Governments and Manufacturing Decline', in T. Dickson and D. Judge (eds.), *The Politics of Industrial Closure*, Macmillan, London.

Johnson, N. 1988, 'Departmental Select Committees', in M. Ryle and P. G. Richards (eds.), *The Commons Under Scrutiny*, Routledge, London.

Kateb, G. 1981, 'The Moral Distinctiveness of Representative Democracy', *Ethics*, 91, 2, pp.357-374.

Kavanagh, D. 1986, *British Politics: Continuities and Change*, OUP, Oxford,

Keir, D. L. 1966, *The Constitutional History of Modern Britain* (8th edn.), Adam & Black, London.

Kilpatrick, A. and Lawson, T. 1980, 'On the Nature of Industrial Decline in the UK', *Cambridge Journal of Economics*, 4, pp.85-102.

King, D. 1987, *The New Right*, Macmillan, London.

Kingsley, J. D. 1944, *Representative Bureaucracy*, Antioch Press, London.

Knox, D. 1986, 'The Industry and Parliament Trust: A Concrete Connection', *The Parliamentarian*, 1, 67, pp.26-7.

Labour Party, 1983, *General Election Candidate Directory*, Labour Party, London.

Labour Party, 1989, *Meet The Challenge: Make The Change*, Labour Party, London.

Labour Party, 1990, *Looking To The Future*, Labour Party, London.

Labour Research 1986, 'MPs Register – Not Just a Commons Interest', *Labour Research*, April, pp.8-12.

Labour Research 1988, 'Conservative MPs Get on With Their Business', *Labour Research*, May, pp.8-10.

Laski, H. J. 1938, *Parliamentary Government in England*, Allen & Unwin, London.

Lea, D. 1984, 'A Trade Unionist's View' in D. Englefield (ed.), *Commons Select Committees*, Longman, London.

Lee, J. M. and Shell, D. 1985, 'The Industry and Trade Committee', in G. Drewry (ed.), *The New Select Committees*, Clarendon, Oxford.

Leys, C. 1983, *Politics in Britain*, Heinemann, London.

Lock, G. 1985, 'Resources and Operations of Select Committees', in G. Drewry (ed.), *The New Select Committees*, Clarendon, Oxford.

Loewenberg, G. 1966, *Parliament in the German Political System*, Cornell University Press, New York.

Longstreth, F. 1979, 'The City, Industry and the State' in C. Crouch (ed.) *State and Economy in Contemporary Capitalism*, Croom Helm, London.

Longstreth, F. H. 1988, 'From Corporatism To Dualism?' *Political Studies*, 36, 3, pp.413-432.

MacInnes, J. 1987, *Thatcherism at Work*, Open University Press, Milton Keynes.

Mackintosh, J.P. 1982, 'Taming the Barons' reproduced in D.Marquand (ed.), *J.P. Mackintosh on Parliament and Social Democracy*, Longman, London.

Macmillan, H. 1933, *Reconstruction: A Plea For National Unity*, Macmillan, London.

Macmillan, K. and Turner, I. 1987, 'The Cost-Containment Issue: A Study of Government-Industry Relations in the Pharmaceutical Sectors of the United Kingdom and West Germany' in S. Wilks and M. Wright (eds.), *Comparative Government-Industry Relations*, Clarendon, Oxford.

Macpherson, C. B. 1973, *Democratic Theory: Essays in Retrieval*, Clarendon Press, Oxford.

Macpherson, C. B. 1977, *The Life and Times of Liberal Democracy*, OUP, Oxford.

McCord, N. 1967, 'Some Difficulties of Parliamentary Reform', *The Historical Journal*, 4, pp.376-90.

McIlroy, J. 1985, 'Police and Pickets: The Law Against the Miners', in J. Beynon (ed.), *Digging Deeper*, Verso, London.

McNeish, T. 1987, 'Select Committees at the House of Commons', *Contemporary Review*, February, pp.89-95.

Maitland, F. W. 1962, *The Constitutional History of England*, CUP, Cambridge.

Marquand, D. 1988, *The Unprincipled Society*, Fontana, London.

Marsh, D. and Locksley, G. 1983, 'Capital: the Neglected Face of Power', in D. Marsh (ed.), *Pressure Politics*, Junction Books, London.

Marsh, I. 1986, *Policy Making in a Three Party System*, Methuen, London.

Marshall, G. 1984, *Constitutional Conventions*, Clarendon, Oxford.

Martin, R. M. 1983a, 'Pluralism and New Corporatism', *Political Studies*, 31, 1, pp.86-102.

Martin, R. M. 1983b, 'Pluralism and New Corporatism: A Reply', *Political Studies*, 31, 3, pp.461-3.

Marx, K. 1980, *Collected Works*, vol 14, Lawrence and Wishart, London.

Mellors, C. 1978, *The British MP*, Saxon House, Farnborough.

Metcalf, L. and McQuillan, W. 1979, 'Corporatism or Industrial Democracy?', *Political Studies*, 27, 2, pp.266-82.

Middlemas, K. 1979, *Politics in Industrial Society*, André Deutsch, London.

Miliband, R. 1972, *Parliamentary Socialism* (2nd edn.), Merlin, London.

Miliband, R. 1982, *Capitalist Democracy in Britain*, OUP, Oxford.

Mill, J. S. 1861, *Representative Government* (1910 edn.), Everyman, London.

Miller, C. 1987, *Lobbying Government*, Basil Blackwell, Oxford.

Moran, M. 1984, *The Politics of Banking*, Macmillan, London.

Morgan, G. 1979, 'All-Party Committees in the House of Commons', *Parliamentary Affairs*, 32, 1, pp.56-65.

Muller, W. D. 1977, *The Kept Men*, Harvester, Sussex.

Muller, W. D. 1986, 'The Kept Men Revisted, 1975-86', paper delivered to American Political Science Association, Washington, D.C.

Murie, A. 1989, 'Housing and the Environment', in D. Kavanagh and A. Seldon (eds), *The Thatcher Effect*, Clarendon, Oxford.

Nairn, T. 1982, *The Break Up of Britain* (2nd edn.), NLB, London.

Nixon, J, 1986, 'Evaluating Select Committees and Proposals for an Alternative Perspective', *Policy and Politics*, 14, 4, pp.415-38.

Norton, P. 1978, *Conservative Dissidents*, Temple Smith, London.

Norton, P. 1981, *The Commons in Perspective*, Martin Robertson, Oxford.

Norton, P. 1982, *The Constitution in Flux*, Martin Robertson, Oxford.

Norton, P. 1983, 'Party Committees in the House of Commons', *Parliamentary Affairs*, 36, 1, pp.7-27.

Norton, P. 1985, *Parliament in the 1980s*, Blackwell, Oxford.

Norton, P. 1990, 'Mrs Thatcher and Conservative MPs', *Parliamentary Affairs*, 43, 1, pp.41-58.

Oakley, J. and Harris, L. 1982, 'Industry, the City and Foreign Exchanges: Theory and Evidence' *British Review of Economic Issues*, 4, pp.15-36.

Padgett, S. 1989, 'The Party System', in G. Smith, W. E. Patterson and P. H. Merkl (eds.), *Developments in West German Politics*, Macmillan, London.

Pahl, R. and Winkler, J. 1974, 'The Coming Corporatism', *New Society*, October 10.

Panitch, L. 1979, 'The Development of Corporatism in Liberal Democracies' in P. C. Schmitter and G. Lehmbruch (eds.), *Trends Towards Corporatist Intermediation*, Sage, London.

Panitch, L. 1980, 'Recent Theorisations of Corporatism: Reflections on a Growth Industry', *British Journal of Sociology*, 31, 2, pp.159-87.

Panitch, L. 1981, 'Trade Unions and the Capitalist State', *New Left Review*, 125, pp.21-44.

Park, T.; Lewis, M. and Lewis, P. 1986, 'Trade Unions and the Labour Party: Changes in the Group of Trade Union Sponsored MPs', *Political Studies*, 34, 2, pp. 296-305.

Parker, P. 1977, *The New Industrial Polity,*Stamp Memorial Lecture, London.

Parris, H. 1969, *Constitutional Bureaucracy*, Allen & Unwin, London.

Parris, H.; Pestieau, P. and Saynor, P. 1987, *Public Enterprise in Western Europe*, Croom Helm, London.

Peele, G. 1990, 'British Political Parties in the 1980s', in A. Seldon (ed.), *UK Political Parties since 1945*, Philip Allan, London.

Pelling, H. 1987, *A History of British Trade Unionism* (4th edn.), Penguin, Harmondsworth.

Percy, E. 1931, *Democracy on Trial: A Preface to an Industrial Policy*, Eyre, London.

Pitkin, H. 1967, *The Concept of Representation*, University of California Press, Berkeley.

Poggi, G. 1978, *The Development of the Modern State*, Hutchinson, London.

Pollard, S. 1983, *The Development of the British Economy,* (3rd edn.), Edward Arnold, London.

Pollard, S. 1984, *The Wasting of the British Economy*, (2nd edn.), Croom Helm, London.

Poulantzas, N. 1975, *The Crisis of Dictatorships* (1976 edn.), New Left Books, London.

Powell, C. 1979, *The Parliamentary and Scientific Committee: The First Forty Years*, Croom Helm, London.

Pressman, J. and Wildavsky, A. 1984, *Implementation* (3rd edn.), University of California Press, California.

Price, C. 1984, 'Making a Select Committee Work', *Public Money*, March, pp.29-33.

Pross, A. P. 1986, *Group Politics and Public Policy*, OUP, Toronto.

Pugh, M. 1982, *The Making of Modern British Politics*, Blackwell, Oxford.

Radice L.; Vallance E. and Willis, V. 1987, *Member of Parliament*, Macmillan, London.

Redlich, J. 1908, *The Procedure of the House of Commons: A Study of its History and Present Form*, Constable, London.

Rhodes, R. A. W. 1988, *Beyond Westminster and Whitehall,* Unwin Hyman, London

Richardson, J. J. and Jordan. A. G. 1979, *Governing Under Pressure*, Martin Robertson, Oxford.

Richardson, J. J. 1990, Government and Groups in Britain: Changing Styles, *Strathclyde Papers on Government and Politics*, 69, University of Strathclyde, Glasgow.

The Right Approach: A Statement of Conservative Aims, 1976, Conservative Central Office, London.

Ripley, R. B. and Franklin, G. A. 1976, *Congress, the Bureaucracy and Public Policy*, Dorsey, Homewood.

Roberts, G.K. 1975, 'The Federal Republic of Germany', in S. E. Finer (ed.), *Adversary Politics and Electoral Reform*, Anthony Wigram, London.

Rose, R. 1982, *The Territorial Dimension in Government: Understanding the United Kigdom*, Longman, London.

Rose, R. 1984, *Do Parties Make a Difference?* (2nd edn.), Macmillan, London.

Rose, R. 1989, *Politics in England* (5th edn.), Faber, London.

Roseveare, H. 1969, *The Treasury*, Allen Lane, London.

Ross, J. F. S. 1948, *Parliamentary Representation*, Eyre and Spottiswoode, London.

Ross, J. F. S. 1955, *Elections and Electors: Studies in Democratic Representation*, Eyre and Spottiswoode, London.

Roth, A. 1984, *Parliamentary Profiles*, Parliamentary Profile Services, London.

Rubery, J. 1986, 'Trade Unions in the 1980s: The Case of the United Kingdom', in R. Edwards, P. Garonna and F. Toedtling (eds.), *Unions in Crisis and Beyond,* Auburn House, Dover, Mass.

Rush, M. 1981, 'The Members of Parliament', in S. A. Walkland and M. Ryle (eds.), *The Commons Today*, Fontana, Glasgow.

Rush, M. 1990, 'Pressure Groups and Select Committees', in M. Rush (ed.), *Parliament and Pressure Group Politics*, Clarendon, Oxford.

Sanders, D.; Ward, H. and Marsh, D. 1987, 'Government Popularity and the Falklands War: A Reassessment', *British Journal of Political Science*, 17, 3, pp. 281-314.

Sartori, G. 1968, 'Representational Systems', in D. L. Sills (ed.), *International Encyclopedia of the Social Sciences*, Macmillan/Free Press, New York, pp. 465-74.

Saville, J. 1986, 'An Open Conspiracy: Conservative Politics and the Miners' Strike 1984-5', *Socialist Register*, Merlin, London.

Searing, D. D. 1982, 'Rules of the Game in Britain: Can Politicians be Trusted', *American Political Science Review*, 76, 2, pp.239-58.

Searing, D. D. 1985, 'The Role of the Good Constituency Member and the Practice of Representation in Great Britain', *Journal of Politics*, 47, 2, pp. 348-81.

Schmitter, P. C. 1974, 'Still The Century of Corporatism?', *Review of Politics*, 36, 1, pp.85-131

Schmitter, P. C. 1979, 'Modes of Interest Mediation and Models of Societal Change in Western Europe', in P. C. Schmitter and G. Lehmbruch (eds.), *Trends Towards Corporatist Intermediation*, Sage, London.

Schmitter, P. C. 1982, 'Reflections on Where the Theory of Neo-Corporatism Has Gone and Where the Praxis of Neo-Corporatism May Be Going', in P. C. Schmitter and G. Lehmbruch (eds.), *Patterns of Corporatist Policy-Making*, Sage, London.

Schmitter, P. C. 1985, 'Neo-corporatism and the State', in W. Grant (ed.), *The Political Economy of Corporatism*, Macmillan, London.

Self, P. 1976, *Administrative Theories and Politics*, Allen & Unwin, London.

SIC 1980, *Standard Industrial Classification*, HMSO, London.

Silk, P. 1987, *How Parliament Works*, Longman, London.

Sissons, C. H. 1966, *The Spirit of British Administration* (2nd edn.), Faber, London.

Smith, D. 1987, *The Rise and Fall of Monetarism*, Penguin, Harmondsworth.

Smith, G. 1989, 'Structures of Government', in G. Smith, W. E. Patterson and P. H. Merkl (eds.), *Developments in West German Politics*, Macmillan, London.

Smith, T. 1979, *The Politics of the Corporate Economy*, Martin Robertson, Oxford.

Streek, W. and Schmitter, P. C. 1985, *Private Interest Government: Beyond Market and State*, Sage, London.

Strinati, D. 1979, 'Capitalism, the State and Industrial Relations', in C. Crouch (ed.), *The State and Economy in Contemporary Capitalism*, Croom Helm, London.

Taylor, A. 1984, *The Politics of the Yorkshire Miners*, Croom Helm, London.

Taylor, A. 1987, *Trade Unions and the Labour Party*, Croom Helm, London.

Taylor, A. 1989, *Trade Unions and Politics: A Comparative Introduction*, Macmillan, London.

Taylor, E. 1979, *The House of Commons at Work* (9th edn.), London, Macmillan.

Therborn, G. 1977, 'The Role of Capital and the Rise of Democracy', *New Left Review*, 103, pp.3-41.

Tholfsen, T. R. 1973, 'The Transition to Democracy in Victorian England', in P. Stansky (ed.), *The Victorian Revolution: Government and Society in Victorian Britain*, New Viewpoints, New York.

Thomas, D. 1984, 'The New Tories', *New Society*, February, pp.159-161.

Thomas, J. A. 1939, *The House of Commons 1832-1901*, University of Wales Press, Cardiff.

Thomas, J. A. 1958, *The House of Commons 1906-11*, University of Wales Press, Cardiff.

Thompson, E. P. 1968, *The Making of the English Working Class*, Penguin, Harmondsworth.

Times Guide 1983, *The Times Guide to the House of Commons 1983*, Times Newspapers, London.

Truman, D. B. 1951 (1971), *The Governmental Process* (2nd edn.), Knopf, New York.

Wahlke, J. C. 1971, 'Policy Demands and System Support: the Role of the Representative', *British Journal of Political Science*, 1, 2, pp.217-90.

Walkland, S. A. 1964, 'Science and Parliament: The Origins and Influence of the Parliamentary and Scientific Committee', *Parliamentary Affairs*, 17, 4, pp.389-402.

Walkland, S. A. 1968, *The Legislative Process in Britain*, Allen &Unwin, London.

Walkland, S. A. 1979, *The House of Commons in the Twentieth Century*, Clarendon, Oxford.

Walkland, S. A. 1983, 'Parliamentary Reform, Party Realignment and Electoral Reform', in D. Judge (ed.), *The Politics of Parliamentary Reform*, Heinemann, London.

Warwick, P. 1985, 'Did Britain Change? An Enquiry into the Causes of National Decline', *Journal of Contemporary History*, 20, pp.99-133.

Webb, S. and Webb, B. 1920, *A Constitution for a Socialist Commonwealth of Great Britain*, CUP, Cambridge.

Westergaard, J. 1977, 'Class, Inequality and Corporatism', in A. Hunt (ed.) *Class and Class Structure,* Lawrence and Wishart, London.

Wiener, M. 1981, *English Culture and the Decline of the Industrial Spirit*, CUP, Cambridge.

Williamson, P. J. 1989, *Corporatism in Perspective*, Sage, London.

Wilks, S. 1984, *Industrial Policy And The Motor Industry*, Manchester University Press, Manchester.

Wilks, S. 1986, 'Reversing the Industrial Ratchet?', PAC Annual Conference, York University.

Wilks, S. and Wright, M. 1987, 'Conclusion: Comparing Government-Industry Relations: States, Sectors, and Networks', in S. Wilks and M. Wright (eds.), *Comparative Government-Industry Relations*, Clarendon, Oxford.

Winkler, J. T. 1976, 'Corporatism', *European Journal of Sociology*, 18, 1, pp.100-36.

Winkler, J. T. 1977, 'The Corporatist Economy: Theory and Administration' in R. Scase (ed.), *Industrial Society: Class, Claevage and Control*, Allen & Unwin, London.

Wood, D. 1987, 'The Conservative Member of Parliament as Lobbyist for Constituency Economic Interests', *Political Studies*, 35, 3, pp. 393-409.

Woodward, S. N. 1986, 'Performance Indicators and Management Performance in Nationalised Industries', *Public Administration*, 64, 3, pp.303-17.

Wright, A. 1989, 'The Constitution', in L. Tivey and A. Wright (eds.), *Party Ideology in Britain*, Routledge, London.

Wright, M. 1988, 'Policy Community, Policy Network and Comparative Industrial Policies', *Political Studies*, 37, 4, pp.593-612.

Young, S. 1986, 'The Nature of Privatisation in Britain, 1979-85', *West European Politics*, 9, 2, pp.235-52.

Index